# MELBOURNE

WILLIAM LAMB afterwards 2nd Viscount Melbourne

# DAVID CECIL

# MELBOURNE

*The Young Melbourne* and *Lord M*
in one volume

THE REPRINT SOCIETY · LONDON

*The Young Melbourne* FIRST PUBLISHED 1939
*Lord M* FIRST PUBLISHED 1954
THIS COMBINED EDITION PUBLISHED BY THE REPRINT SOCIETY LTD.
BY ARRANGEMENT WITH CONSTABLE & CO. LTD. 1955

PRINTED IN GREAT BRITAIN BY RICHARD CLAY AND COMPANY, LTD.,
BUNGAY, SUFFOLK

# Special Preface
## to this Combined Edition

A WELL EXECUTED design should need no explaining, but the nature of my subject has involved me in certain peculiarities of treatment which perhaps need explanation. My book tells the story of William Lamb, Lord Melbourne. His was a complex nature slow to develop; it was not until middle age that it reached full maturity. My book is therefore divided into three sections. The first, extending from childhood into middle life, describes the formation of his character; the second gives an analysis, illustrated by references both to his earlier and subsequent history, of this character when set into middle life; the third tells how this character exhibited itself in action during his later years.

I must add some words of gratitude: to Her Majesty the Queen for graciously permitting me to consult the archives at Windsor Castle and to reproduce pictures from the collection there; to the late Lady Desborough, the Dowager Lady Hambleden, the late Lord Crewe, Lord Spencer, the late Lord Leconfield, Sir John Murray, Lord Brocket, L. U. Grace, Esq., and the Trustees of the National Portrait Galleries of England and Scotland for allowing me to reproduce other pictures; to the Countess Mountbatten, the late Lady Desborough, the Duke of Devonshire, the Marquess of Lansdowne, the Earl of Ilchester, the Earl of Besborough, Earl Grey and Lord Hatherton, for allowing me to make use of their private papers; and to Sir John Murray for permitting me to quote from the correspondence of Lord Granville Leveson-Gower.

# Contents

## The Young Melbourne

## Lord M

# Illustrations

ix

# Chief Events

# THE YOUNG MELBOURNE

*And the Story of his Marriage
with Caroline Lamb*

*To*
*Rachel Cecil*

# *Prologue*

## THE WORLD

THE GREAT Whig country houses of the eighteenth and early nineteenth centuries are among the most conspicuous monuments of English history. Ornate and massive, with their pedimented porticoes, their spreading balustraded wings, they dominate the landscape round them with a magnificent self-assurance. Nor are their interiors less imposing. Their colonnaded entrance halls, whence the Adam staircase sweeps up beneath a fluted dome; their cream and gilt libraries piled with sumptuous editions of the classics; their orangeries peopled with casts from the antique; their saloons hung with yellow silk, and with ceiling and doorways painted in delicate arabesque by Angelica Kauffmann, all combine to produce an extraordinary impression of culture and elegance and established power.

Yet, they are not palaces. There is something easy-going and unofficial about them. Between library and saloon one comes on little rooms, full of sporting prints and comfortable untidiness; the bedrooms upstairs are friendly with chintz and flowered wallpaper. Even the great rooms themselves, with their roomy writing-tables, their arm-chairs, their tables piled with albums and commonplace books, seem designed less for state occasions than for private life: for leisure and lounging, for intimate talk and desultory reading. And the portraits that glow down from the walls exhibit a similar character. The gentlemen lean back in their hunting coats, the ladies stroll in their parks with spaniels snapping at the ribbons that dangle from the garden hats, slung on their arms. In big and in detail these houses convey an effect of splendid naturalness. In this they are typical of the society which was their creator.

The Whig aristocracy was a unique product of English civilization. It was before all things a governing class. At a time when economic power was concentrated in the landed interest, the Whigs were among the biggest landowners: their Party was in

1

office for the greater part of the eighteenth century; during this period they possessed a large proportion of the seats in the House of Commons; they produced more ambassadors and officers of state than the rest of England put together. And they lived on a scale appropriate to their power. "A man," said one of their latest representatives, "can jog along on £40,000 a year." And jog very well they did. They possessed, most of them, a mansion in London and two or three in the country; they moved through the world attended by a vast retinue of servants, of secretaries and chaplains, of companions, librarians and general hangers-on; they never travelled but in their own carriages; they kept open house to a continuous stream of guests, whom they entertained in the baroque and lavish style approved by their contemporaries.

For the elaboration of their life was increased by the period they lived in. The eighteenth century, that accomplished age, did not believe in the artless and the austere. In its view the good man or, as they would have phrased it, "the man of sense and taste", was he whose every activity was regulated in the light of a trained judgment and the experience of the wise in his own and former ages. From his earliest years the Whig nobleman was subjected to a careful education. He was grounded in the classics first by a tutor, then at Eton, then at the university. After this he went abroad for two years' grand tour to learn French and good manners in the best society of the Continent. His sisters learnt French and manners equally thoroughly at home; and their demeanour was further improved by a course of deportment. The Whigs' taste was in harmony with the ideal that guided their education. They learnt to admire the grand style in painting, the "correct" in letters, the Latin tradition in oratory. And in everything they paid strict attention to form. Since life to them was so secure and so pleasant, the Whig aristocrats tended to take its fundamental values very much for granted; they concentrated rather on how to live. And here again, their ideal was not an artless one. Their customs, their mode of speech, their taste in decoration, their stylish stiff clothes, are alike marked by a character at once polished and precise, disciplined and florid. If one of them writes a note it is rounded with a graceful phrase, their most extempore speeches are turned with a flourish of rotund rhetoric.

Yet—and here it is that it differs from those of similar societies on the Continent—theirs was not an unreal life; no Watteau-like paradise of exquisite trifling and fastidious idleness. For one thing it had its roots in the earth. Founded as their position was on landed property, the Whig aristocracy were never urban. They passed at least half the year in their country seats; and there they occupied themselves in the ordinary avocations of country life. The ladies interested themselves in their children, and visited the poor; the gentlemen looked after their estates, rode to hounds and administered from the local bench justice to poachers and pilferers. Their days went by, active, out-of-door, unceremonious; they wore riding-boots as often as silk stockings. Moreover, they were always in touch with the central and serious current of contemporary life. The fact that they were a governing class meant that they had to govern. The Whig lord was as often as not a minister, his eldest son an M.P., his second attached to a foreign embassy. So that their houses were alive with the effort and hurry of politics. Red Foreign Office boxes strewed the library tables; at any time of day or night a courier might come galloping up with critical news, and the minister must post off to London to attend a Cabinet meeting. He had his work in the country too. He was a landlord and magistrate, often a lord lieutenant. While every few years would come a general election—when his sons, if not himself, might have to sally forth to stand on the hustings and be pelted with eggs and dead cats by the free and independent electors of the neighbouring borough. Indeed his was not a protected existence. The eighteenth century was the age of clubs; and Whig society itself was a sort of club, exclusive, but in which those who managed to achieve membership lived on equal terms; a rowdy, rough-and-tumble club, full of conflict and plain speaking, where people were expected to stand up for themselves and take and give hard knocks. At Eton the little dukes and earls cuffed and bullied each other like street urchins. As mature persons in their country homes, or in the pillared rooms of Brooks's Club, their intercourse continued more politely, yet with equal familiarity, while their House of Commons life passed in a robust atmosphere of combat and crisis and defeat. The Whigs despised the royal family; and there was certainly none of the hush and punctilio of Court

existence about them. Within the narrow limits of their world they
were equalitarians.

Their life, in fact, was essentially a normal life, compounded of
the same elements as those of general humanity, astir with the
same clamour and clash and aspiration and competition as filled
the streets round their august dwellings. Only, it was normal life
played out on a colossal stage and with magnificent scenery and
costumes. Their houses were homes, but homes with sixty bedrooms, set in grounds five miles round; they fought to keep their
jobs, but the jobs were embassies and prime ministerships; their
sons went to the same universities as humbler students, but were
distinguished from them there by a nobleman's gold-tasselled
mortarboard. When the Duke of Devonshire took up botany, he
sent out a special expedition to the East Indies to search for rare
plants; Lord Egremont liked pictures, so he filled a gallery with
Claudes and Correggios; young Lord Palmerston was offered the
Chancellorship of the Exchequer a year or two after entering
Parliament.

This curiously-blended life produced a curiously-blended type
of character. With so many opportunities for action, its interests
were predominantly active. Most of the men were engaged in
politics. And the women—for they lived to please the men—
were political too. They listened, they sympathized, they advised;
through them two statesmen might make overtures to each other,
or effect a reconciliation. But politics then were not the life sentence to hard labour that in our iron age they have become. Parliament only sat for a few months in the year; and even during the
session, debates did not start till the late afternoon. The Whigs
had the rest of their time to devote to other things. If they were
sporting they raced and hunted; if interested in agriculture they
farmed on an ambitious scale; if artistic they collected marbles
and medals; if intellectual they read history and philosophy; if
literary they composed compliments in verse and sonorous, plati-
tudinous orations. But the chief of their spare time was given up
to social life. They gave balls, they founded clubs, they played
cards, they got up private theatricals: they cultivated friendship,
and every variety, platonic and less platonic, of the art of love.
Their ideal was the Renaissance ideal of the whole man, whose

aspiration it is to make the most of every advantage, intellectual and sensual, that life has to offer.

In practice, of course, this ideal was not so broad as it sounds. The Whigs could not escape the limitations imposed by the splendour of their circumstances. Like all aristocrats they tended to be amateurs. When life is so free and so pleasant, a man is not likely to endure the drudgery necessary to make himself really expert in any one thing. Even in those affairs of state which took up most of the Whigs' time, they troubled little with the dry details of economic theory or administrative practice. Politics to them meant first of all personalities, and secondly general principles. And general principles to them were an occasion for expression rather than thought. They did not dream of questioning the fundamental canons of Whig orthodoxy. All believed in ordered liberty, low taxation, and the enclosure of land; all disbelieved in despotism and democracy. Their only concern was to restate these indisputable truths in a fresh and effective fashion.

Again, their taste was a little philistine. Aristocratic taste nearly always is. Those whose ordinary course of life is splendid and satisfying, find it hard to recognize the deeper value of the exercises of the solitary imagination; art to them is not the fulfilment of the soul, but an ornamental appendage to existence. Moreover, the English nobility were too much occupied with practical affairs to achieve the fullest intellectual life. They admired what was elegant, sumptuous and easy to understand; portraits that were good likenesses and pleasing decorations; architecture which appropriately housed a stately life. In books, they appreciated acute, wittily phrased observation of human nature, or noble sentiments expressed in flowing periods; Cicero, Pope, Horace, Burke. The strange and the harsh they dismissed immediately. Among contemporary authors they appreciated Jane Austen; condemned Crabbe, for the most part, as sordid and low; and neglected Blake almost entirely. If they had read him, they would not have liked him. For—it is another of their limitations—they were not spiritual. Their education did not encourage them to be; and, anyway, they found this world too absorbing to concern themselves much with the next. The bolder spirits among them were atheists. The average person accepted Christianity, but in a straightforward spirit, innocent alike of mysticism and theological exactitude.

Further, their circumstances did not encourage the virtues of self-control. Good living gave them zest; wealth gave them opportunity; and they threw themselves into their pleasures with an animal recklessness at once terrifying and exhilarating to a modern reader. The most respectable people often drank themselves under the table without shocking anyone. "Colonel Napier came in to-night as drunk as an owl," remarks Lady Sarah Napier, of the staid middle-aged gentleman who was her husband. And their drinking was nothing to their gambling. Night after night they played loo and faro from early evening till the candles guttered pale in the light of the risen sun. Lord Stavordale lamented he had not been playing higher, on a night when he won £11,000 in a single hand at hazard. Georgiana, Duchess of Devonshire, cost her husband nearly £1,000,000 in card debts. Rich as they were, they often ruined themselves. The letters of the time are loud with lamentations about the duns coming in and the furniture going out. Nor was their sexual life of a kind to commend them to an austere morality. "I was afraid I was going to have the gout the other day," writes Lord Carlisle to a friend, "I believe I live too chaste: it is not a common fault with me." It was not a common fault with any of them. In fact an unmarried man was thought unpleasantly queer if he did not keep under his protection some sprightly full-bosomed Kitty Clive or Mrs. Bellamy, whose embraces he repaid with a house in Montpelier Square, a box at the opera and a smart cabriolet in which to drive her down to Brighthelmstone for a week's amorous relaxation. Nor did he confine himself to professional ladies of pleasure. Even unmarried girls like Lady Hester Stanhope were suspected of having lovers; among married women the practice was too common to stir comment. The historian grows quite giddy as he tries to disentangle the complications of heredity consequent on the free and easy habits of the English aristocracy. The Harley family, children of the Countess of Oxford, were known as the Harleian Miscellany on account of the variety of fathers alleged to be responsible for their existence. The Duke of Devonshire had three children by the Duchess and two by Lady Elizabeth Foster, the

Duchess one by Lord Grey; and most of them were brought up together in Devonshire House, each set of children with a surname of its own. "Emily, does it never strike you," writes Miss Pamela Fitzgerald in 1816, "the vices are wonderfully prolific among Whigs? There are such countless illegitimates, such a tribe of children of the mist." It is noteworthy that the author of this lively comment was a carefully brought up young lady of the highest breeding. The free habits of these days encouraged free speech. "Comfortable girls," remarks a middle-aged lady of her growing nieces, "who like a dirty joke." And the men, as can be imagined, were a great deal freer than the women. For all their polish the Whigs were not refined people in the Victorian sense of the word.

It appears in other aspects of their lives. They could be extremely arrogant; treating their inferiors with a patrician insolence which seems to us the reverse of good breeding. Lady Catherine de Bourgh was not the caricature that an ignorant person might suppose. Fashionable young men of refined upbringing amused themselves by watching fights where the Game Chicken battered the Tutbury Pet into unconsciousness with bare and bloodstained fists. And the pamphlets, the squibs, the appalling political cartoons that lay open in the most elegant drawing-rooms show that the ladies of the day were not squeamish either.

Still, unseemly as some of its manifestations were, one must admit that there is something extremely attractive in this earthy exuberance. And, as a matter of fact, it was the inevitable corollary of their virtues. English society had the merits of its defects. Its wide scope, its strong root in the earth, gave it an astounding, an irresistible vitality. For all their dissipation there was nothing decadent about these eighteenth-century aristocrats. Their excesses came from too much life, not too little. And it was the same vitality that gave them their predominance in public life. They took on the task of directing England's destinies with the same self-confident vigour that they drank and diced. It was this vigour that made Pitt Prime Minister at twenty-four years old,[1] that enabled the Foxites to keep the flag of liberty flying against the united public opinion of a panic-stricken nation. Nor did they let

[1] Pitt diverged from the Whigs in later life: but he was brought up among them; and is, so far, representative of the Whig tradition.

their pleasures interfere with these more serious activities. After eighteen hours of uninterrupted gambling, Charles Fox would arrive at the House of Commons to electrify his fellow members by a brilliant discourse on American taxation. Rakes and ladies of fashion intersperse their narratives of intrigue with discussions on politics, on literature, even on morals. For they were not unmoral. Their lapses came from passion not from principle; and they are liable at any time to break out in contrite acknowledgments of guilt, and artless resolutions for future improvement. Indeed it was one of the paradoxes created by their mixed composition that, though they were worldly, they were not sophisticated. Their elaborate manners masked simple reactions. Like their mode of life their characters were essentially natural; spontaneous, unintrospective, brimming over with normal feelings, love of home and family, loyalty, conviviality, desire for fame, hero-worship, patriotism. And they showed their feelings too. Happy creatures! They lived before the days of the stiff upper lip and the inhibited public school Englishman. A manly tear stood in their eye at the story of an heroic deed: they declared their loves in a strain of flowery hyperbole. They were the more expressive from their very unselfconsciousness. It never struck them that they needed to be inarticulate to appear sincere. They were equally frank about their less elevated sentiments. Eighteenth-century rationalism combined with rural common sense to make them robustly ready to face unedifying facts. And they declared their impressions with a brusque honesty, outstandingly characteristic of them. From Sir Robert Walpole who encouraged coarse conversation on the ground that it was the only form of talk which everyone enjoyed, down to the Duke of Wellington who described the army of his triumphs as composed of "the scum of the earth, enlisted for drink," the Augustan aristocracy, Whig and Tory alike, said what they thought with a superb disregard for public opinion. For if they were not original they were independent-minded. The conventions which bounded their lives were conventions of form only. Since they had been kings of their world from birth they were free from the tiresome inhibitions that are induced by a sense of inferiority. Within the locked garden of their society, individuality flowered riotous and rampant. Their typical figures show up beside the muted introverts of to-day as clear cut and idiosyncratic as characters in Dickens. They took for granted that you spoke your mind and followed your impulses. If these were odd they were amused but not disapproving. They enjoyed eccentrics; George Selwyn who never missed an execution, Beau Brummell who took three hours to tie his cravat. The firm English soil in which they were rooted, the spacious freedom afforded by their place in the world, allowed personality to flourish in as many bold and fantastic shapes as it pleased.

But it was always a garden plant, a civilized growth. Whatever their eccentricities, the Whig nobles were never provincial and never uncouth. They had that effortless knowledge of the world that comes only to those who from childhood have been accustomed to move in a complex society; that delightful unassertive confidence possible only to people who have never had cause to doubt their social position. And they carried to the finest degree of cultivation those social arts which engaged so much of their time. Here we come to their outstanding distinction. They were the most agreeable society England has ever known. The character of their agreeability was of a piece with the rest of them; mundane, straightforward, a trifle philistine, largely concerned with gossip, not given to subtle analyses or flights of fancy. But it had all their vitality and all their sense of style. It was incomparably racy and spontaneous and accomplished; based solidly on a wide culture and experience, yet free to express itself in bursts of high spirits, in impulses of appreciation, in delicate movements of sentiment, in graceful compliments. For it had its grace; a virile classical grace like that of the Chippendale furniture which adorned its rooms, lending a glittering finish to its shrewd humour, its sharp-eyed observation, its vigorous disquisitions on men and things. Educated without pedantry, informal but not slipshod, polished but not precious, brilliant without fatigue, it combined in an easy perfection the charms of civilization and nature. Indeed the whole social life of the period shines down the perspective of history like some masterpiece of natural art; a prize bloom, nurtured in shelter and sunshine and the richest soil, the result of generations of breeding and blending, that spreads itself to the open sky in strength and beauty.

It was at its most characteristic in the middle of the century, it was at its most dazzling towards its close. By 1780 a new spirit was rising in the world. Ossian had taught people to admire ruins and ravines, Rousseau to examine the processes of the heart; with unpowdered heads and the ladies in simple muslin dresses, they paced the woods meditating, in Cowper-like mood, on the tender influences of nature. Though they kept the style and good sense of their fathers, their sympathies were wider. At the same time their feelings grew more refined. The hardness, which had marred the previous age, dwindled. Gainsborough, not Hogarth, mirrored the taste of the time; sensibility became a fashionable word. For a fleeting moment Whig society had a foot in two worlds and made the best of both of them. The lucid outline of eighteenth-century civilization was softened by the glow of the romantic dawn.

Dawn—but for them it was sunset. The same spirit that tinged them with their culminating glory was also an omen of their dissolution. For the days of aristocratic supremacy were numbered. By the iron laws which condition the social structure of man's existence, it could last only as long as it maintained an economic predominance. With the coming of the Industrial Revolution this predominance began to pass from the landlords to other ranks of the community. Already by the close of the century, go-ahead manufacturers in the north were talking of Parliamentary reform; already, in the upper rooms of obscure London alleys, working men met together to clamour for liberty, equality, and fraternity. Within forty years of its zenith, the Whig world was completely swept away. Only a few survivors lingered on to illustrate to an uncomprehending generation the charm of the past. Of these the most distinguished was William Lamb, second Viscount Melbourne.

## Part One

## CHAPTER I

# THE LAMB FAMILY

O**DDLY ENOUGH**, he did not come from an aristocratic family. By the stringent standards of the age the Lambs were parvenus. Their fortunes had been founded three generations before, by Peniston Lamb, an attorney of humble origin in Nottinghamshire, who died leaving a fortune of £100,000. His heir, a nephew called Matthew, was even more successful. With the help of his legacy he married an heiress, bought a country place, entered the House of Commons and eventually acquired a baronetcy. Here the family progress seemed likely to stop: his son, Sir Peniston Lamb, was a less effective personality. He makes his first appearance on the stage of history as a young man of fashion writing to his mistress, the notorious Mrs. Sophia Baddeley. "I send you a million kissis, remember I love you Satterday, Sunday, every day . . . I hope you will get the horsis, but I beg you will not be so ventersum, as there are bad horsis, but will get one quite quiett . . . pray destroy all letters lest anyone should find them by axcedent." Mrs. Baddeley found the author of these artless communications child's play. She deceived him often and flagrantly; but he always believed her protestations of innocence, and seldom visited her without bringing a £200 bill in his pocket as a present. Indeed his only noticeable characteristic seems to have been a capacity for getting rid of money. Handsome, festive and foolish, his main occupation was to squander the guineas laboriously accumulated for him by his forefathers. His money raised him to the peerage of Ireland as first Baron Melbourne, and procured him a seat in Parliament. But during the forty years he spent there, he only opened his mouth once. Such energy as he possessed was fully employed in drinking port, following the hounds and playing faro at Almack's Club.

However, any deficiencies on his part were more than made up for by his wife. Elizabeth Milbanke, Lady Melbourne, was one of the most remarkable women of her age. Not that she was original. On the contrary, she was a typical eighteenth-century woman of the world: but with all the qualities of her type intensified to the highest degree. She was very beautiful in the style approved by her contemporaries; "a fine woman", with a clear-cut mouth, challenging dark eyes and a figure moulded in the shapely contours which stirred the full-blooded desires of the gentlemen of Brooks's Club. Nor did they find her a disappointment on closer acquaintance. Her temperament was as full-blooded as their own; and she was even more satisfactory as a companion than she was as a lover. It was not exactly that she had charm: there was nothing appealing about her, nothing intoxicating, nothing mysterious. The cool, astringent atmosphere exhaled by her personality suggested prose rather than poetry. But it was singularly agreeable prose, at once soothing and stimulating. She could be amusing in a direct, caustic way; and she understood the art of getting on with men completely. Level-tempered and rational, she found scenes and caprices as tiresome as they did. After the unaccountable moods of stormier sirens, it was infinitely delightful to find oneself "laughing away an hour" on the sofa of her sitting-room in Melbourne House, with Lady Melbourne—Lady Melbourne, who could be depended upon never to be touchy, or exacting, or shocked, or low-spirited, who did not expect men to be monogamous, and who never asked an awkward question. She seemed to combine the social merits of both sexes, to possess, at the same time, male robustness and feminine tact, a woman's voluptuousness and a man's judgment. Moreover, she had an unusual power of entering into a man's interests. She disliked talking about herself: "no man is safe with another's secrets, no woman with her own," she once remarked. But she threw herself whole-heartedly into other people's problems; was always ready to listen sympathetically to a man's complaints about wives and political leaders, to advise him about how to manage a mistress, or an estate agent. And excellent advice it was too: Lady Melbourne's masculine point of view was the product of a masculine intelligence. By choice it showed itself in practical affairs; her friends noted with irritation that she was the only woman who made her garden a paying concern. But if she did turn her attention to other matters—to politics, for instance—her opinion was always shrewd and judicious. In a positive, plain-sailing way she was a very able woman. And, within the limits of her experience, she had an uncommon knowledge of life. No one had a clearer understanding of the social machine; no one could give a man a more accurate idea of the forces to be reckoned with in planning a career; no one could tell one better how to satisfy one's desires without offending convention. Deliberately to defy it was, in her eyes, as silly as deliberately to defy the law of gravity. "Anyone who braves the opinion of the world," she used to say, "sooner or later feels the consequences of it."

Her character was in keeping with the rest of her. She had the virtues of her common sense and her full-bloodedness. Though pleasure-loving she was not shallow. Her vigour of spirit showed itself also in her feelings. She cared for few people; but these she loved with a strong, unegotistic affection that could be absolutely depended upon. No effort was too great that might advance their interests. Yet, her feelings were always controlled by her judg-ment. In the most vertiginous complications of intrigue and dissipation, Lady Melbourne could be relied on to remain digni-fied and collected. And reasonable; her philosophy taught her that the world must be kept going. And to ensure its smooth working she was always prepared to make sacrifices. She had strong dislikes, but could suppress them in the cause of common peace: even though a woman might have lovers, it was no excuse, in her view, for her neglecting her duty to her family, or acting in such a way as to outrage social standards.

All the same it is impossible to approve of Lady Melbourne. Her outlook was both low and limited. To her the great world of rank and fashion was the only world; and she saw it as a battle ground in which most people fought for their own ends. Nor was hers an amiable cynicism. She was good-tempered, not good-natured; suave, but not soft. Her laughter was satirical and un-feeling, she could not resist a wounding thrust. And, on the rare occasions she judged it wise to lose her temper, she was both re-lentless and brutal. Indeed, in spite of her polish, there was something essentially coarse-fibred about her. She cared little what others did so long as they kept up appearances. And herself, if she found it convenient, would plot and make use of people without compunction.

But all her qualities, good and bad, were subordinated to one presiding motive, ambition. Since to her this world was the only one, its prizes seemed to her the only objects worth having. And her whole life was given up to getting them for herself and for her family. To this end she dedicated her beauty, her brains and her energy: it was for this she learned to be sagacious and smiling, tactful and dignified, ruthless and cunning. A single purpose united every element in her personality. Here we come to the secret of her eminence. It was not that she was more gifted than many of her rivals, but that her gifts were more concentrated. Amid a humanity frustrated by conflicting aspirations and divided desires, Lady Melbourne stood out all of a piece; her character, her talents, moved steadily and together, towards the same goal. One might suspect her, but one could not withstand her will. And so smoothly did life move under her sway, her judgment evinced so rational a grasp of reality, that in the end she generally brought one round to her view.

From the first she was successful. Her birth was higher than her husband's; Sir Ralph Milbanke, her father, was the head of an old Yorkshire county family. But it was early clear that his daughter was marked for a more brilliant destiny than could be achieved in provincial Yorkshire. Before she was seventeen she had married Lord Melbourne and his fortune, had established herself in his splendid family mansion in Piccadilly—it occupied the site where the Albany stands now—had re-decorated it in white and gold, and had begun her siege of London. Her chief weapon, naturally enough, was her power over men. She could not, indeed, make much of Lord Melbourne. "I am tired to death," he writes to Mrs. Baddeley, "with prancing about with my Betsy a-shopping." And shopping was about all he was good for. When he had bought her some diamonds and paid for the gold paint, he had done all that a reasonable woman could expect of him. However there were other men in the world; and Lady Melbourne lost no time in making their acquaintance. Characteristically she contrived that those she selected for peculiar favours should be both agreeable and useful. During the course

of her career her name was to be coupled with the fashionable
Lord Coleraine and the powerful Duke of Bedford. But the most
important man in her life was Lord Egremont. He was a worthy
counterpart to her. Except that he did not care for politics,
George Wyndham, third Baron Egremont, was the pattern grand
seigneur of his time. At once distinguished and unceremonious,
rustic and scholarly, he spent most of his time at his palace of Petworth in a life of magnificent hedonism, breeding horses, collect-
ing works of art and keeping open house for a crowd of friends and
dependants. He had the eccentricities of his type. Too restless to
remain in any one place for more than five minutes, he would
suddenly appear in the room where his guests were sitting, smiling
benevolently and with his hat on; would make a few genial remarks often revealing considerable erudition, and then go away;
an hour or two later he would reappear, continue the conversation
just where he had left it off, and after another few minutes, vanish
again. He had a number of children by various mistresses; but he
never married, largely, it was thought, owing to the influence of
Lady Melbourne. How their connection arose is not known.
Scandal had it that he bought her from Lord Coleraine for £13,000,
of which she took a share. It is an unlikely story; he was attractive
enough to win her on his own merits and she seems to have been
genuinely devoted to him. All we know for certain is that by 1779
Lord Egremont was established as her most trusted adviser and
chief lover. What Lord Melbourne thought of his Betsy's
amorous activities is also obscure. People noticed that he did not
seem to like his wife's friends. But he was not the man to make an
effective protest; moreover, Lady Melbourne always took particular care never to put him in an awkward position.

However, she did not look exclusively to men for her advancement. It is the measure of her perspicacity that she realized that
the security of a woman's social position depends on the support
given her by her own sex. And she set her wits to get it. So successfully, that within a few years of coming to London she had become a close friend of the most famous fashionable leader of the
day, the ravishing Duchess of Devonshire. It was an unnatural
intimacy. For one thing Lady Melbourne was essentially a man's
woman; it was only with men that she felt sufficiently sure of her

ground to be her robust self; with women she was at best no more than smooth and pleasant. Further, the Duchess was her opposite in every respect, refined, imprudent and emotional. But affinity of the spirit is not so necessary for friendship in the rush of fashionable life, as in soberer circles. It is enough to be agreeable and to enjoy the same pleasures. Lady Melbourne passed both these tests easily: besides, her discretion combined with her interest in other people's doings to make her the perfect confidante of the poor Duchess's tangled romances. When the outraged Duke banished her for some months to France, it was Lady Melbourne whom she chose to keep her in touch with her disconsolate lover, Mr. Grey.

What with the Duchess and Lord Egremont, Lady Melbourne's path was now easy. From the records of the day we catch glimpses of her during her dazzling progress: driving surrounded by gentlemen on horseback amid the shelving glades of her country home at Brocket; piquant in the costume of a macaroni at a masquerade at the Pantheon; adjusting her feathers before the glass while she discusses stocks and shares with Horace Walpole; dancing, "to his great delight, though in rather a cow-like style", with the Prince of Wales. For in 1784 she made her most distinguished conquest; she captured the affections of the future George IV. It was not for long—it never was with him. But Lady Melbourne saw to it that, even when all was over, they remained firm friends. In the meantime she took the opportunity to get Lord Melbourne made a Lord of the Bedchamber. Already in 1781 he had, by her efforts, been raised to a Viscounty. Even in the flush of her triumphs, she never forgot to use them for the acquisition of more lasting benefits. By 1785 she was securely fixed in that social position for which she had worked so hard.

It was not, it was never going to be, the best sort of social position. There was always a section of the *beau monde* who looked askance at Lady Melbourne as an upstart, and a shady upstart at that. Gentlemen still joked about Lord Coleraine and his £13,000; rival beauties alleged that Lady Melbourne could not see a happy marriage without wanting to break it up. But eighteenth-century society accepted people, whatever their sins, as long as they kept its rules of decorum. Lady Melbourne was an expert at these rules.

Audacious but completely in control, she knew just how close she could sail to the wind without disaster. And if she was not the most respected woman in society, she was among the very smartest. Melbourne House was recognized as one of the liveliest social centres in London. Day after day the great doors opened and shut to admit the cleverest men and the most fascinating women in the town; untidy delightful Fox; Sheridan sparkling and a little drunk; the dark Adonis of diplomacy, Lord Granville Leveson-Gower; the Duchess of Devonshire and her sister Lady Bessborough; the witty Mr. Hare; the artistic Mrs. Damer. While every few weeks at one in the morning the tables were spread and the candles lit for a supper party to the Prince of Wales.

Nor was Melbourne House merely a modish meeting-place. Social life there was a creation, with its own particular charm, its own particular flavour. It was the flavour of its mistress's personality; virile, easy-going, astringent. Manners were casual; elaborate banquets, huge rooms frescoed by Bartolozzi went along with unpunctualness and informality. "That great ocean," says the orderly Lady Granville in a moment of exasperation, "where a person is forced to shift for himself without clue; they wander about all day and sleep about all the evening; no meal is at a given hour, but drops upon them as an unexpected pleasure". And the mental atmosphere, too, was not fastidious. The spirit of Melbourne House offered no welcome to the new romanticism. It was plain-spoken, it laughed uproariously at fancifulness and fine feelings, it enjoyed bold opinions calculated to shock the prudish and the over-sensitive, it loved derisively to strip a character of its ideal pretensions. From mischief though, rather than from bitterness; an unflagging good humour was one of its two distinguishing attractions. The other was its intellectual vigour. The inhabitants of Melbourne House were always ready for an argument; about Whig policy or the character of the royal family or Miss Burney's new novel or Mr. Godwin's curious theories; shrewd, hard-hitting arguments full of assertion and contradiction, but kept light by the flash of wit and the accomplishment of men of the world.

The creator of such a circle might well feel justified in sitting back to rest on her laurels. Not so Lady Melbourne; her vitality only matured with years. Though a little fatter than she had been, she was still able to attract men and still willing to do so. But she was far too sensible to let herself lapse into the deplorable role of a fading siren. From the age of thirty-five or so the energy of her ambition centred itself on her children. In this, it followed natural inclination. The instincts of her normal dominating nature made her strongly maternal; it was on her children that she expended the major force of her narrow and powerful affections. Lord Melbourne took the same secondary part in their lives as he did elsewhere. As a matter of fact he was only doubtfully related to them. They were six in number: Peniston, born 1770; William, born 1779; Frederick, born 1782; George, born 1784; Emily, born 1787, and another daughter, Harriet, who died before she grew up. Of these, William was universally supposed to be Lord Egremont's son, George, the Prince of Wales's, while Emily's birth was shrouded in mystery. Nor had Lord Melbourne the character to achieve by force of personality that authority with which he had not been endowed by nature. On two occasions only is he recorded to have expressed his will with regard to his children. He rebuked William when he first grew up for following the new-fangled fashion of short hair: and he was very much annoyed with Harriette Wilson for refusing to become Frederick's mistress. "Not have my son, indeed," he said, "six foot high and a fine strong handsome able young fellow. I wonder what she would have." And meeting Miss Wilson, taking a morning walk on the Steyne at Brighton, he told her what he thought of her.[1] Such efforts were not of a kind to win him any exaggerated respect from his children. They regarded him with kindly contempt, varied by moments of irritation. "Although Papa only drinks a glass of negus," writes his daughter Emily some years later, "somehow or other he contrives to be *drunkish*," and again, "By some fatality Papa is always wrong and I pass my life in trying to set him right."

They viewed Lady Melbourne with different feelings. Indeed, she was a better mother than many more estimable persons. To the task of her children's education she brought all her intelligence

[1] This, like all Harriette Wilson's stories, must be taken as only doubtfully authoritative.

and all her knowledge of life. In the first place she saw to it that they had a good time. For the most part they lived at Brocket—Brocket, that perfect example of the smaller country house of the period, with its rosy, grey-pilastered façade, its urbane sunny sitting-rooms, its charming park like a landscape by Wilson, where, backed by woods, the turf sweeps down to a stream spanned by a graceful bridge of cut stone. Here the little Lambs played, and rode, and had reading lessons from their Jersey *bonne*. They were to be met at Melbourne House, too, running round the courtyard, or off to Sir Joshua Reynolds's or Mr. Hoppner's studio to sit for their portraits. And all round them, now loud, now muffled by nursery doors, but so continuous that it seemed like the rumour of life itself, sounded ever the huge confused hum of the great world. Often they caught an actual glimpse of it. Playing on the stairs, a child's eye would be arrested by the shapely silken legs of the Prince of Wales as he walked, "fit to leap out of his skin" with spirits, from Lady Melbourne's sitting-room. "Have you had your dinner yet?" he would ask, for he was fond of children and took notice of them. Sometimes they would be taken down for a visit to Petworth to gaze on the troops of Arab horses and the queer looking people, artists and antiquaries, with which Lord Egremont filled his house. Time passed; the elder boys went to school, first with a clergyman near Brocket, and then at nine years old to Eton, each of them with ten guineas in his pocket, and five shillings a week more to be supplied by a servant at the local inn. Eton was an easy-going place then: unhampered by the virtuous discipline of organized games, the boys spent their leisure rabbit-snaring, attending dog fights, stuffing at the pastry-cooks when they were small, and getting tipsy on beer when they were bigger; while after Peniston had left he would come down and take one of his brothers over to Ascot for a week's racing. In between whiles came holidays; riding and shooting and theatricals, and now and again a visit to the professional playhouse. It was a very pleasant life. But Lady Melbourne did more than just amuse her children. In the most hectic whirl of her social engagements, she found time to exert a persistent and purposeful influence on them. Her great carriage was always carrying her down to Eton: where, with characteristic efficiency, she combined her visit with a

B

dinner to the Prince of Wales, if he happened to be at Windsor. Sedulously she studied her children's characters, promoted their tastes, encouraged their ambitions. She read with them, wrote to them, she talked things over with them with a light and artful frankness that kept them always at their ease. Her diligence met with its reward. They had a profound respect for her judgment, and they were devoted to her. Further, they were devoted to each other. By the time they were grown up Lady Melbourne had contrived to weld them together into that strongest of social units, a compact family group; with its own standards, its own idiom of thought and speech, its own jokes, confronting the world with the cheerful confidence that, where it differed from others, it was right and the others were wrong.

This corporate personality was the appropriate product of its parentage and environment. Strikingly handsome, with their tall, well-made figures, firmly-cut countenances and dark eyes brilliant with animation, the Lambs were alike vital, sensual, clever, positive and unidealistic. People did not always take to them. They complained that they were hard and mocking, unappreciative of delicacy and romance; they were scandalized by the freedom alike of their morals and their conversation; and they disliked their manners. The boys, especially, ate greedily and were liable suddenly to go to sleep and snore; they asserted their opinions with arrogance, interlarded their speech with oaths and laughed very loud. Yet they attracted more than they repelled. It was difficult to dislike people with such a splendid talent for living. Love, sport, wine, food, they entered with zest into every pleasure. And their minds were equally responsive; alert to note and assess character and event with quick perspicacity. Born and bred citizens of the world, they knew their way about it by a sort of infallible instinct. And they had an instinctive mastery of its social arts. Their negligence was never boorish; it arose from the fact that they felt so much at home in life that they were careless of its conventions. Superficial brusqueness masked an unfailing adroitness in the management of situations: their talk was as dexterous as it was unaffected; its bluntness was made delightful by their peculiar brand of jovial incisive humour. For they possessed—it was their chief charm—in the highest degree, the high spirits of their home. A lazy sunshine of good humour shone round them, softening the edge of their sharpest sayings. Though they thought poorly of the world, they enjoyed every moment of it: not to do so seemed to them the last confession of failure. "What stuff people are made of," said one of them, "who find life and society tiresome when they are in good health and have neither liver nor spleen affected; and have spirits enough to enjoy, instead of being vexed by, the ordinary little tracasseries of life." This sentence might have stood for the family motto.

Within the frame of this common character, individual differences revealed themselves. Beautiful Peniston, the eldest, was the only one with a touch of Lord Melbourne: he had brains but used them mainly on the turf. Frederick, on the other hand, was a finished man of the world; combining lively intellectual interests and a life of many loves by means of a tact that was later to make him a distinguished diplomat. Did he not read Shakespeare to his mistress: and, what was more, persuade her to enjoy it? George's character, riotous, hasty-tempered, and a trifle vulgar, gave colour to the report that he was the son of the Prince of Wales. An excellent comedian, he spent his spare time scribbling farces and hobnobbing with the actors in the green-room of Drury Lane. Emily was a milder edition of her mother, with the same social gifts, the same amorous propensities; but softer, more easy-going, not so clever. The second son, William, was less typical.

He did not appear so on first acquaintance. With his manly, black-browed handsomeness, his scornful smile, his lounging manners, his careless perfection of dress—"no one," it was said, "ever *happened* to have coats that fitted better"—he looked the Lamb spirit incarnate. No less than his brothers he was genial and sensible, guzzled, swore, and went to sleep, in argument he was the most arrogantly assertive of the lot. Yet, talking to him for any length of time, one became aware of a strain that did not harmonize with the Lamb atmosphere. When a subject arose peculiarly interesting to him, suddenly his smile would give place to an expression of ardent excitement; a pathetic tale brought the tears starting to his eyes; at other moments he would lapse unaccountably into a musing melancholy: then in a twinkling his old smiling nonchalance would reappear, as surprisingly as it had

vanished. Indeed—it was to be the dominating factor in his subsequent history—there was a discord in the fundamental elements
of his composition. Much of him was pure Lamb or rather pure
Milbanke. He had the family zest for life, their common sense,
their animal temperament. But some chance of heredity—it may
well have been Egremont blood—had infused into this another
strain, finer and more unaccountable. His mind showed it. It
was not just that he was cleverer than his brothers and sisters:
but his intelligence worked on different lines, imaginative, disinterested, questioning. It enjoyed thought for its own sake, it was
given to curious speculations, that had no reference to practical
results. He could absorb himself in points of pure scholarship, sit
up for hours studying history and poetry. Along with this cast of
mind went a vein of acute sensibility. Affection was necessary to
him, he loathed to give pain, he responded with swift sympathy to
the appeal of the noble and the delicate. At his first school, he
would sit gazing out of the window at the labourers at work in the
placid Hertfordshire landscape, and long to be one of them. And
though this came no doubt mainly from a normal dislike of lessons,
it was in keeping with an inborn appreciation of the charm of
innocence and the pleasures of contemplation. Across the substantial, clear-coloured fabric of the man of the world, were dis-
cernible incongruous streaks of the philosopher and the romantic.

So strangely-blended a disposition portended a complex and
dissonant character. At odds with himself, he was bound also to
be at odds with any world with which he came into contact. Certainly there was a great deal in him out of harmony with the earthy
spirit of Melbourne House. Obscurely conscious of this perhaps,
he was as a little boy stormier and more self-willed than his
brothers and sisters. However, very soon any such outward signs
of conflict passed away. The growing William appeared uncon-
cerned by the discrepancy between his nature and his environment—if, indeed, he was aware that it existed. His very desire to
please made him adaptable. And circumstances encouraged his
adaptability. Children brought up in gay and patrician surroundings seldom react against them with the violence common in more
circumscribed lives. If their tastes differ from those of the people
round them, they have the leisure and money to follow them up in

some degree: and anyway their ordinary mode of living is too
agreeable for them to conceive any strong aversion to it. Further,
the Milbanke half of William's nature was perfectly suited by his
home. He loved the parties and the sport and the gossip, he felt
at home in the great world. Nor was his other side starved at
Melbourne House. He had all the books he liked, he could listen
enthralled to the clever men cleverly disputing, while his native
tenderness bloomed in the steady sunshine of the family affection.
His brothers and sisters were as fond of him as of each other. And,
in the half-laughing, unsentimental way approved by Lamb standards, they showed their feelings. He returned them. His
brothers were always his closest men friends, his favourite boon
companions. What could be better fun than acting with George,
arguing with Frederick, racing with Peniston? He was equally
attached to his sisters, especially "that little devil Emily". Like
many persons of a philosophical turn, he enjoyed giving instruction; would spend hours of his holidays superintending his sisters'
pleasures, hearing them their lessons: when they were at Brocket
and he in London, he wrote them long letters about the plays he
had seen. But as might have been expected, his most important
relationship was with his mother. He was the type of character
that is always most susceptible to feminine influence. Men were
excellent companions for a riotous evening or a rational talk. But
it was only with women that he could get that intensely personal
contact, that concentrated and intimate sympathy, of which his
sensibility was in need. As a matter of fact, Lady Melbourne
would have attracted him apart from her femininity. Her realism
roused an answering chord in his own, her single-minded certainty was reassuring to his divided spirit. He pleased her as much
as she pleased him. Was he not like Lord Egremont? Besides,
her practised eye soon discerned that he was the cleverest of her
children; and therefore the one most likely to realize her ambitions. William's happiness, William's success, became the chief
interest of his later life. To mould his character and win his heart,
she brought out every tested and glittering weapon in her armoury.
She studied his disposition, fostered his talents, applauded his
triumphs, kept up with his interests: read books with him; with
him discussed the characters of his friends—all in the free and easy

terms, the amused unshockable tone she employed with her mature men friends. This sometimes led to awkward consequences. Once when he was ten he told her of a school fellow called Irby, the son of a family acquaintance. "Every Irby is a fool," remarked Lady Melbourne trenchantly. William thought it very true of this particular Irby: when he went back to Eton he told him so. He in his turn repeated it to his family; and a row ensued which must have needed all Lady Melbourne's celebrated tact to smooth over. But the incident had taught William his first lesson in discretion. And he never forgot it. Under her purposeful hands his character began to take form; a form in which his Milbanke side was uppermost. By twelve years old he was already equable, controlled, and possessed of a precocious capacity for adjusting himself to facts. His stormy temper was suppressed; as for any deeper sources of discontent with his environment, life was too full and amusing to worry about them.

In these circumstances it is not surprising that his childhood was happy. He loved Brocket; he did not mind his first school, though he preferred it when his parents were in London and he was not tantalized by the thought of the pleasures of home only a few miles away: Eton he enjoyed enormously. It was a little unnerving at first for one who, up till then, had not moved a step unattended by nurses or tutors, to find himself at nine years old alone in a crowd of seven hundred boys, all rampaging in the uproarious barbarity of the unreformed public school. But William was himself sufficiently uproarious soon to feel at home there: while his perspicacity, improved by Lady Melbourne's training, showed him how to adapt himself to school life in such a way as to suffer as little as possible from its inevitable drawbacks. He managed never to become a regular fag, and to be flogged very seldom. If he was, he did not repine, but forgot it as quickly as he could. The bloody duels of fisticuffs which were at that time the approved method of settling schoolboy quarrels, presented a greater problem. William did not like fighting. However, here too he found a way to make it as little disagreeable as possible. Soon after he went to Eton he had to fight a boy bigger than himself. "He pummelled me amazingly," he related, "and I saw I should never beat him; I stood and reflected a little and *thought* to myself and then gave it up. I thought it one of the most prudent acts, but it was reckoned very dastardly." However, he remained blandly impervious to criticism so obviously inconsistent with common sense: from this time forward, he made it his sensible rule never to fight with anyone likely to beat him. "After the first round if I found I could not lick the fellow, I said, 'come this won't do, I will go away; it is no use standing here to be knocked to pieces'." So early did he evince that capacity for compromising genially with circumstances, which was to distinguish his later career.

For the rest he enjoyed everything: the drinking, the rabbit-hunting, the jam tarts, the weeks with Peniston at Ascot, the Festival of Montem, when, gaudy in cavalier plumes and Hussar uniforms, the boys stood about in the streets dunning distinguished visitors for guineas. Naturally gregarious, he also got pleasure out of his school fellows. They were sometimes a little ridiculous: Brummell, for instance, with his drawling speech and dandified appearance, especially preposterous to William whose locks were always in a tangle. But ridiculous people added to the amusement of life; besides Brummell was an entertaining fellow, if you set yourself to get the best out of him. Nor was school life without more glorious sources of satisfaction. William did not work hard, at least after his first two years; but early grounding and a natural gift for scholarship kept him in a high place. By the time he left, he was one of the acknowledged kings of the school. Even the holidays seemed a little flat, back at Brocket with no fag to run clattering at his call, no clusters of sycophants to gaze admiringly at him and his co-monarchs as, in careless lordliness, they strolled the Eton streets. There was no doubt that Eton, indolent, high-spirited, undisciplined Eton, was the school for him. During the rest of his life it was to linger in his memory, tinged with a golden sentiment; so that, forty years later, as a grey-headed statesman disillusioned by a lifetime of glory and agitation, he could never hear a clock like the Eton clock without a lift of happiness at his heart.

# THE BEAU MONDE

FOR CAMBRIDGE, where he went at seventeen, he could never feel the same affection. He was even less industrious there than at Eton. Rich young men always find it hard to work at a university, especially if they have the Lamb gift for pleasure. It is only the poor-spirited or the morbidly conscientious who can go on doing lessons, in the flush of their first appearance in the world as mature young men, able to do whatever they please. William did not even trouble to follow the regular course; along with the rest of the gilded youth at Cambridge, he spent the next four years revelling, talking, and making friends; sauntering the streets by day, and sitting up over the port at night. However, he was too active-minded to live without any intellectual occupation. He read a good deal in a desultory kind of way. And it is likely that he profited more by so doing than if he had kept himself to the narrow path of academic study. His strong young brain, rejoicing in its own activity, ranged over an enormous variety of subjects. Mathematics, indeed, he never cared for. They were too inhuman a science. But he read widely in the classics, ancient and modern, he devoured history books, he delved into the mysterious problems of ethical philosophy. With this intellectual development came a growing interest in public affairs. His realism had not yet learnt to apply itself to subjects outside his own experience; like other clever young men he was attracted to the idealistic, the daring, and the impractical; sentiments that roused a glow in the generous breast; opinions calculated to send a shiver down the spine of the timid and the conventional. His hero was Fox, his party the extreme Whigs. With a gloomy satisfaction he prophesied the ruin of his country under the sway of the contemptible Tories. "We have been for a long time the first nation in Europe," he remarked to his mother; "we have now lost our sovereignty and shall shortly be the last." As far as he could see the best thing for England would be to be defeated by the

French under the enlightened Buonaparte. How dreadful it was to think that our arms might drive him out of Egypt. "I was in despair at hearing of the intentions of the French to evacuate Egypt. I was in hopes they would have been able to maintain themselves there in spite of Canning's wit and Sir Sidney's valour." Canning, now at the height of his polemical brilliance, was castigating his opponents in the *Anti-Jacobin*. But William could not think much of his intelligence. He supported the Tories, he must be a fool.

The more theoretical aspect of William's political ideas found expression in an oration he composed in competition for the university declamation prize. The subject was the progressive improvement of mankind. William treated it in a lofty vein. "Crime is a curse," so runs his peroration, "only to the period in which it is successful; but virtue, whether fortunate or otherwise, blesses not only its own age but remotest posterity." These edifying reflections met with a most gratifying reception. Not only did William win the prize, but the great Fox himself selected the passage in question to quote in the House of Commons. Nor was this William's only public success. He wrote poetry as well as reading it; translations from the classics, and occasional verses, in the orthodox Augustan manner, full of classical allusion and noble commonplaces. In 1798 he blossomed forth in print as a satirist, crossing swords with Canning in a reply to some verses in the *Anti-Jacobin*. His poem was passed round the clubs and drawing-rooms of the Metropolis, to the general approbation. It was not very good. But, then as now, London society was disposed to look kindly on the literary efforts of handsome young men of good family.

In addition to applauding his writing, they asked him out to dinner. His intellectual debut coincided with his social: in the vacations he made his first entry into the *beau monde* as a grown-up man. No one could have done it in more advantageous circumstances. Born in the centre of its most entertaining circle, he found himself, without any effort on his part, elected to its best clubs, invited to its most brilliant parties. And he had the talents to make the most of his advantages. It was true that he did not always make a good first impression. He had some of the conceit of his time of life, and more of its shyness. Even Lady Melbourne's training had not been able to free him from that self-consciousness which afflicts clever young men at nineteen years old: the thought of making a fool of himself in public haunted him. To escape it, he assumed an exaggeration of the family manner, adopted a contemptuous pose, as of one who disdained to compete in a world which he despised. Introduced to someone with whom he felt himself likely to be out of sympathy, an Anti-Jacobin, for instance, he turned away; now and again he would try and overcome his nervousness by asserting, unnecessarily loudly, some outrageous paradox. But all this was superficial. A few minutes' talk revealed that he was in reality unassuming, appreciative, and as agreeable as Lady Melbourne herself. Within a short time he was one of the most fashionable young men in London.

Indeed, Whig society was his spiritual home; its order of life, at once leisurely and lively, suited him down to the ground. He rose late in the morning, breakfasted largely, strolled up St. James's Street, to loiter for an hour or two in the window of his Club, hearing the news, surveying the world. Later might come a ride in the park or an afternoon call; the evening was the time for dinner parties followed by the opera, the theatre, or a ball; then back to the Club for some supper till four or five o'clock struck, and it was time to go to bed. William enjoyed it all. Music and dancing in themselves did not please him; they were not the fashion among smart young men of the day. But he was happy at any sort of social gathering. And dinner parties he found perfectly delightful: succulent sumptuous feasts twelve courses long, then the pleasant hour with the gentlemen over the wine, whence they emerged to join the ladies about midnight. Several of the men, he noticed, were always drunk; but this did not displease him. "It tended to increase the gaiety of society," he said, "it produced diversity." After the session came the social life of the country; week-long visits to Petworth or Bowood, where the mornings were spent reading, while the ladies sketched or played the harp; followed by sporting afternoons, and evenings when, after another enormous meal, the party sat up till three in the morning, playing cards, writing verses, organizing theatricals. The theatricals were a trial to William's self-consciousness. At Inverary he consented to take the part of Leander in a farce, but could not bring himself to appear publicly in the wreath of roses and bunches of cherry-coloured ribbon which the producer thought the correct costume for his role. Into the other amusements he entered with unalloyed enthusiasm. We find him editing a comic paper during a visit, contributing stanzas to Brummell's album; and he was ready to talk to anyone. With such accomplishments to recommend him he soon got on friendly terms with the most agreeable conversationalists of the day: Fox, Sheridan, Canning—whom he found very pleasant on closer acquaintance—Rogers, Monk Lewis, Tom Moore.

Mainly his social life centred round four houses: Carlton House, Holland House, Devonshire House, and his own home. It was not the Piccadilly home of his childhood. In 1789 the Duke of York had taken a fancy to that: and Lady Melbourne, always ready to oblige influential persons, had agreed to exchange it for the Duke's own residence in Whitehall, that grey spreading pile of rusticated stone which is now the Scottish Office. However, re-decorated by its new mistress, the second Melbourne House was just as splendid as the first; and life there was equally brilliant, disorderly, and in the thick of things. Daily the gentlemen dropped in on their way to and from the House of Commons; nightly the court-yard re-echoed with the coach wheels that brought to dinner the Duchess of Devonshire, or the Prince of Wales. For a year or two there had been a coldness between the Prince and the Melbournes. He expected his friends to take his part in every chop and change of his endless quarrels. And when, after Mrs. Fitzherbert fell from favour, he discovered that Lady Melbourne continued to visit her he broke with her entirely. But now in 1798 Mrs. Fitzherbert was forgiven and the Prince back at Melbourne House, in wilder spirits than ever, and eating on a scale which even William, accustomed though he was to the appetites of the day, found amazing. The Prince took a fancy to him, that was why William went so much to Carlton House. Few weeks passed that he did not walk across the Mall to dine within its meretricious walls; where he sat, an observant young man, listening to his royal host as, hour by hour, he poured forth the kaleidoscopic effusions of his preposterous egotism; now abusing his parents, now

bragging of his amorous conquests, now courting the applause of
the company by his vivid mimicry of Mr. Pitt or Lord North, now
soliciting their sympathy by sentimental laments on the unexampled misery of his lot. It was very entertaining; it was also
instructive. At Carlton House William got his first lesson in an
art that was to be the instrument of his greatest success in later life,
the art of getting on with royal personages. Lady Melbourne carried this instruction a step farther; she showed him how to manage them for their good. One evening, when the Prince was dining
at Melbourne House, news was brought that an attack had been
made on the life of George III, while he was watching a play at
Drury Lane. The Prince, to whom the misfortunes of his parents
were agreeable rather than otherwise, was preparing to go calmly
on with his dinner. But Lady Melbourne perceived at once that
he ought to go and enquire. It would make him popular, it would
do him good with the King; it was, in any case, the correct thing
to do. He resisted, she coaxed and ordered the carriage. At last
sulkily he went off. But before midnight he had come back to
thank her for her advice. Certainly for William, to stay at home
was to see the world: and to get an education in public life thrown
in.

Holland House and Devonshire House were educative too; and
in a more delightful wisdom. They represented, in their different
ways, the apex of Whig civilization. In them all that made it
memorable found its fullest expression. Holland House showed
its masculine and intellectual side. Lady Holland was a divorced
woman: she had eloped with Lord Holland from her first husband,
Sir Godfrey Webster. With the consequence that, though the
easy-going circle of Lady Melbourne and the Duchess of Devonshire were on terms with her, she was never received by the more
rigid ladies; and the society that visited her was predominantly
male. Every night of the week gentlemen used to drive down
through the green fields of Kensington to dine and sleep at Holland House. Staying there had its drawbacks. It could be
agonizingly cold for one thing; and the dinner table was always
overcrowded, so that people ate as best they could, with arms
glued to their sides. Moreover, Lady Holland herself was in many
respects a tiresome woman, capricious, domineering and extremely

egotistic; given to a hundred deliberately cultivated fads, with which she expected everyone to fall in. She shifted her guests' places in the middle of a meal, she turned people out of the room for using scent, she interrupted, she had hysterics at a clap of thunder, suddenly she would summon an embarrassed stranger to her sitting-room in order that he might entertain her with conversation, while her page, Edgar, kneeling before her and with hands thrust beneath her skirts, rubbed her legs to alleviate rheumatism. Yet she was a good hostess; talked cleverly in a charmless combative style, and had the dominating vitality that keeps a party alive. It was Lord Holland, though, who attracted people to the house. With the bushy black brows, the clumsy figure of his uncle, Charles Fox—"in a white waistcoat," said a contemporary, "Lord Holland looks like a turbot standing on its tail"—he possessed also his culture, his bonhomie, his exquisite amenity of address. Perhaps he was a little detached—one needed to be, to live with Lady Holland—but this only seemed still further to emphasize the unvarying infectious good humour which spread like sunshine over every gathering of which he was host. Certainly life at Holland House had an extraordinary charm; there was nothing like it in Europe, people said. It was partly Lord Holland, partly the setting, the stately, red-brick, Jacobean mansion, with its carven painted rooms, mellow with historical memories; it was chiefly the conversation. Lady Holland complained that only men visited her; she complained of most things. But in fact it was this circumstance which gave the talk at her house its unique quality. It imbued it with that mental vigour found as a rule only in exclusively male society. The tone was free and sceptical, the subject-matter rational and cultivated. There of an evening in the long library, soft in winter with candle shine, in summer fresh with the garden air blowing in through the open windows, would flow forth, concentrated and easy as it could never be in the rush of London life, the strength, the urbanity and the amplitude of Whig culture; passing from politics to history, from history to literature, Madame de Sévigné's letters, the controversies of the early Church, the character of Buonaparte; and then Lord Holland would set everyone laughing with an imitation of Lord Chatham—he was an even better mimic than the Prince of Wales—and then someone would raise a point of scholarship, and taking a folio from the shelves would verify a reference. The company was always intellectually distinguished. There were a few habitués: Mr. Allen, the librarian, erudite and positive, his eyes always bright behind his spectacles, to argue on behalf of atheism; Sydney Smith, most humane of clergymen, crackling away like a genial bonfire of jokes and good sense and uproarious laughter; the sardonic Rogers; the epigrammatic Luttrell. But most of the remarkable men of the age came there at one time or another, statesmen, writers, artists, distinguished foreigners. Lord and Lady Holland were always on the look out for new talent; and William's reputation soon got him an invitation. "William Lamb, a rising young genius, dines here for the first time to-day," notes Lady Holland in her diary, 1799. He made his usual impression; "pleasant though supercilious"; and later, "clever and agreeable and will improve when he gets over his love of singularity". He, for his part, appreciated them. In Holland House he discovered an intellectual life deeper than could be found at home. From this time on, whenever he came to London, he found time to pay it a visit. In the course of years he became a regular habitué whose association was only to be ended by death.

All the same it is to be doubted if he did not enjoy Devonshire House more. Here flowered the feminine aspect of Whiggism. The Duke, a stiff, shy man, preferred to follow his own way, aloof from others; and the social life of his home revolved round the Duchess, her sister Lady Bessborough, and her friend Lady Elizabeth Foster. Each, in her way, was conspicuously charming; the Duchess in particular, lovely, exuberant, her whole personality flushed with a glowing sweetness which no heart could resist, seemed born to get and to give pleasure. From the time she was eighteen, the great house gazing across its courtyard at Green Park was the scene of all that was gayest and most brilliant in London society. Life there had none of the ordered rationality of Holland House. It passed in a dazzling, haphazard confusion of routs, balls, card parties, hurried letter-writings, fitful hours of talk and reading. But in its own way it was also unique. Rare indeed it is to find a real palace inhabited by a real princess, a position of romantic wealth and splendour, filled by figures as full

of glamour as itself. Moreover, in Devonshire House the graces
were cultivated in the highest perfection. Here, in the flesh, was
the exquisite eighteenth century of Gainsborough, all flowing elegance, and melting glances, and shifting silken colour. Its atmosphere was before all things personal. The characteristic conversation of the Devonshire House ladies was *tête-à-tête*, in a
secluded boudoir, or murmured in the corner of a sofa amid the
movement of a party; it was delightful for its charming gaiety, its
intimate sympathy, its quick perception of nuance. Their culture
—for they too were cultivated—was of a piece with the rest of
them, an affair of enthusiasm and sensibility. They read and wrote
poems, they listened to music, they appreciated subtle analyses of
emotion and character, *La Nouvelle Héloise, Les Liaisons Dan-
gereuses*. In politics they were all for the ideal, for honour and
liberty and enlightenment. Above everything they prized warmth
and delicacy of feeling, abhorred cynicism, vulgarity, and harshness. People spoke gently in Devonshire House, smiled rather
than laughed, expressed disapproval, if they had to, by a hint or an
intonation. Their less sensitive acquaintances criticized them as
sentimental and insincere; laughed at the gushing terms, interspersed at every turn with French phrases, in which they expressed
themselves, their cooing ecstatic voices, "the Devonshire House
drawl". But the Duchess and her sister, at any rate, were in
reality the very reverse of artificial. They seemed affected because
they were unselfconscious; their privileged position had always
allowed them to express their naturally refined and warm-blooded
temperaments with uninhibited freedom. Impulsive, spontaneous,
uncontrolled, they followed in everything the mood of the moment, the call of the heart. They danced till dawn, they gambled
wildly, they mourned and rejoiced with equal lack of restraint. In
them the affections, for friends, for relations, swelled to fever
pitch; while into love they flung themselves with a reckless abandon. Love was indeed their vocation, the centre and mainspring
of their lives. From earliest youth to the threshold of old age, the
ladies of Devonshire House had always an affair of the heart on
hand; ranging from light flirtation to the most agonizing drama
of passion. For privilege did not save them from suffering. How
should it, blown about as they were by every gust of desire, and

without the slightest vestige of self-control? The life of feeling does not make for happiness in this rough world. The very basis of Devonshire House life was complicated by it. Lady Elizabeth Foster, a penniless grass widow, living by her wits and of a more designing character than her friends, had, in addition to being the Duchess's friend, contrived also to become the Duke's mistress. And though a vigilant tact enabled them all to get along together without open explosions, they lived at an unceasing tension, rendered still sharper by the vicissitudes of the Duchess's own hectic amours. At once gorgeous and dishevelled, frivolous and tragic, life at Devonshire House was a continual strain on the spirit; beneath its shining surface seethed always a turmoil of yearning and jealousy, crisis and intrigue, gnawing hope and unavailing despair. All the same the source of its unrest was also the chief secret of its attraction. For it meant that it was quickened by that delicious emotional stir only found in societies whose chief concern is love. It was love that breathed warmth into the social arts in which its inhabitants were so accomplished: love suffused the atmosphere, in which they moved, with a soft enticing shimmer of romantic sentiment and voluptuous grace.

William responded to it at once. His animal nature and his taste for women's society united to make him amorous: and natural tendency had been encouraged by the tradition of his home. Already, we gather, he had sown some wild oats. Like the other young men of his circle, he thought chastity a dangerous state: and he seems early to have taken practical steps to avoid incurring the risks attendant on it. But he never became a regular habitué of the Regency *demi-monde* as his brothers did. He was at once too sensitive and too sophisticated to get much satisfaction from its boisterous revellings, the showy seductions of its sirens. This was all the more reason he should like Devonshire House. And he did. Beside its civilized femininity even that of Lady Melbourne looked crude: all the poetic and fastidious elements in him sprang to it, as to something he had always been seeking. It was not the Duchess herself so much who attracted him. By the time he was grown up, the wear and tear of her existence had begun to tell on her; she was only the wreck of what she had been, melancholy, abstracted and with her figure gone. William found her kindly but inattentive. Nor did he succumb to the insinuating allurements of Lady Elizabeth Foster. But he was immediately drawn to Lady Bessborough. It is not to be wondered at. For though her attraction was not so immediately compelling as that of the Duchess in her prime, it was of a rarer and more lasting quality. Alike her enthralling letters and her portrait—with its slanting glance, its amused, pensive mouth, its air of indescribable distinction—proclaim her to have been one of the most enchanting creatures that have ever lived; combining her sister's overflowing generosity of spirit, and a refinement of feeling, that years of dissipation failed to tarnish, with a vivid, responsive intelligence and an instinctive subtlety of the heart that enabled her to penetrate a friend's every mood and thought. Alas, no more to her than to the Duchess did her gifts bring happiness. She lacked those colder qualities which carry the Lady Melbournes of this world securely to prosperity. Too soft-hearted, too ungoverned, she could not take a firm line with herself or anyone else. With the result that her existence passed in a series of shattering emotional entanglements, and that she died with her reputation gone, and the dearest wish of her heart unsatisfied. "I must put down what I dare tell nobody," she noted in later years. "I should be ashamed were it not so ridiculous . . . in my fifty-first year I am courted, followed, flattered and made love to . . . thirty-six years, a pretty long life, I have heard and spoken that language, for seventeen years of it loved almost to idolatry the man who has probably loved me least of all of those that professed to do so—though once I thought otherwise." Lord Granville, to whom she devoted her life, whose career she had furthered against her own political opinions, and of whose very infidelities she had forced herself to become the sympathetic confidante, had never prized her at her true worth; and in the end had forsaken her to marry her niece. However, this was many years ahead yet; when William got to know her, Lady Bessborough was still light-hearted enough. He was never seriously in love with her: but he paid her marked attention. And London soon recognized him as one of her established train of beaux. He was always supping at her house in Cavendish Square with Sheridan and Lord Holland and the rest of her admirers, or staying at her country villa at Roehampton, where they spent delightful days walking, talking, and reading aloud. One day at Brocket he met another member of the family. A flock of child visitors were playing about the house: the young Devonshires, and among them a skimpy, elf-like little figure with a curly blonde head, Lady Bessborough's daughter, Caroline. She was an extraordinary child: at one moment a wild tomboy, galloping bareback round the field, the next conversing on poetry and politics like a woman of forty, her whole being vibrant with an electric vitality which dominated any room she entered. Precociously susceptible to the influence of her environment, she was much concerned with love. William's black eyes and his celebrated oration on progress seemed to make him a worthy object of her choice; she conceived a violent fancy for him. In his turn he found her very engaging. She appealed to his particular taste both for little girls and for entertaining characters. At times, as he lounged back in his chair listening to the flow of her odd, impudent, charming chatter, a more sentimental interest began to tinge his amusement. In four or five years what a paragon she seemed likely to become; more irresistible, because more original even than her mother. A captivating vision of the future fleeted before his musing eyes. "Of all the Devonshire House girls," he remarked half laughingly to a friend, "that is the one for me."

Meanwhile he was twenty-one and she fourteen, and he had to finish his schooling. In 1799 his four years at Cambridge came to an end: but Lady Melbourne still felt that something remained to be done. The Whig aristocracy had a high standard of education. Commonly they sent their children on the grand tour, after they had finished the ordinary academic course. But during the Napoleonic Wars this was impracticable: so it became the fashion for those young noblemen whose minds seemed susceptible of further development to be sent to one of the northern universities, famous at that time as leaders of all that was newest in philosophical and scientific thought. In the winter of 1799, therefore, William and Frederick proceeded for two winters to Glasgow: where they lodged with a distinguished philosopher, Professor Millar. It was an extraordinary contrast to the luxurious sophistication of the world they had left. Earnest, industrious and provincial, the raw-boned inhabitants of Professor Millar's house passed their time in an ordered round of plain living and hard thinking. However, the Lambs threw themselves into their new surroundings with their customary sardonic zest.

"There is nothing heard of in this house but study," writes Frederick to his mother, "though there is much idleness, drunkenness, etc., out of it as in most universities. We breakfast at half past nine, but I am roused by a stupid, silly, lumbering mathematician, who tumbles me out of bed at eight. During the whole of the day we are seldom out of the house or the lecture rooms for more than an hour, and after supper, which finishes a little after eleven, the reading generally continues till near two. Saturday and Sunday are holidays, on Mondays we have examinations in Millar's lectures. Millar himself is a little jolly dog, and the sharpest fellow I ever saw. All the ladies here are contaminated with an itch for philosophy, and learning, and such a set of fools it never was my lot to see. William quotes poetry to them all day, but I do not think he has made any impression yet."

Neither did they, nor the place they lived in, make any formidable impression on him. "The town is a damnable one and the dirtiest I ever saw," he said, "and as for the company and manners I do not see much different in them from the company and manners of any country town." Still he set himself to make the most of such compensations as he could find in his new surroundings. He dined out with the merchants of the town, where he thoroughly enjoyed the local custom of serving brandy with dinner; he gave rein to his passion for argument in a debating club where he became noted for his "caustic brilliance in reply"; and he absorbed himself in Professor Millar's philosophical ideas. So much so, that when he came to London in vacation he could talk of little else. This was not altogether approved of by his old friends. Lady Holland was critical; while Lord Egremont, whose interest in his career was noticeably paternal, became worried. It would be dreadful, he thought, if William turned into a doctrinaire prig. Lady Melbourne communicated these fears to William, who brushed them aside. Indeed, no one was less disposed to be a doctrinaire. Further, enriched as he was by the practical experience of mankind to be learnt in Melbourne House, he was not, except on purely intellectual subjects, impressed by the naïve and self-assured dogmatizings of the middle-class intelligentsia with whom he associated. Life had taught him—this is the advantage of living in the thick of things—always to relate thought to experience, to estimate theory in terms of its practical working. He might be a little wild in his political ideas; but he knew that statesmen were human beings, not embodied institutions. In consequence, he listened to his companions good-humouredly, but with an inner amusement that must have disconcerted them, had they realized it.

"No place can be perfect," he told Lady Melbourne, "and the truth is, that the Scotch universities are very much calculated to make a man vain, important, and pedantic. This is naturally the case where there is a great deal of reading. . . . We have two fellows in the house with us, who think themselves, each of them, as wise as Plato and Aristotle put together, and asked, with a supercilious sort of doubt, whether Pitt is really a good orator, or Fox has much political knowledge. This will all wear off in time; though, to be sure, one of them is three and twenty and has been in France since the revolution . . . the other is an Irishman, about my age, who knew nothing before he came here last year, and who therefore thinks that nobody knows anything anywhere else. . . . You cannot have both the advantages of study and of the world together. The way is to let neither of them get too fast a hold of you, and this is done by nothing so well as by frequent changes of place, of persons and of companions."

These words show a remarkably mature judgment for twenty-one. And William was old for his age. Lady Melbourne, watching him arrive in London, at last to take up that active role on the stage of the world for which she had prepared him so assiduously, could feel her work was thoroughly done. She had reason to be satisfied with it. He was, on the whole, all she thought a young man ought to be: handsome, agreeable, self-confident. Perhaps a shade too self-confident: William had not altogether outgrown his youthful intransigence; he still proclaimed his contempt for stupidity too openly. And his manners were not all she could have wished. "Although I have the highest opinion of your skill," she writes to Lady Holland about her sons, "yet I believe even you would find bringing them to what is called polish a very arduous undertaking." However, Lady Melbourne sympathized with his contempt; and manners to her were of small importance compared with the point of view that they expressed. William's point of view she found quite satisfactory. It would have been odd if she had not: for it was largely the same as her own. His ductile mind had been unable to resist the influence of a philosophy, exerted so continuously and so persuasively. Further, such experience of life as he had known had gone to confirm it. William early noticed that, if he differed from his mother about a character or a course of action, he generally turned out to be wrong. "My mother was the most sagacious woman I ever knew," he used to say in later years, "as long as she lived, she kept me straight." Her cynicism did not put him off. Clever young men like cynicism if it is agreeably presented. It makes them feel both bold and wise, imbues them with a sense of daring superiority to the timid gullible herd of common mankind. Like Lady Melbourne's, William's outlook was realistic and rational, thinking highly of the world's pleasures and poorly of its inhabitants; sensibly determined to adjust itself to life so as to be as comfortable as possible; cheerfully convinced that idealists—excepting always the Foxite Whigs—were fools or hypocrites. In the exuberance of his youth he expressed these opinions more explicitly than she did herself. "I do not like the dissenters," he remarked to her, "they are more zealous and consequently more intolerant than the established church. Their only object is power. If we are to have a prevailing religion let us have one that is cool and indifferent . . . toleration is the only good and just principle, and toleration for every opinion that could possibly be formed." It was not Lady Melbourne's habit to generalize in this fashion: she showed her religious views simply—by never going to church. But she would have agreed with every word William said.

All the same, she was not completely satisfied with him. His opinions, his demeanour, were all they should be; but there were elements in his character which she found baffling; what in her rare moments of irritation she called "his laziness and his selfish-ness". These were not quite the right words, but they meant something. Hidden beneath his exterior pliability lay a force impervious to her will. It arose from that other conflicting strain in his personality. Education had driven it underground; but had not been able to expel it. The romantic and the philosopher still stirred restlessly in the depths of his subconsciousness, colouring his reactions, disturbing his equilibrium. Now and again they rose to the surface, revealing themselves, as people noticed, in his conversation, with its sudden tears, its fitful moments of enthusiasm. They appeared more significantly in sporadic movements of antagonism towards his home. These were to be expected. In spite of its charms, life at Melbourne House had an ugly side. Its hard animalism, its rapacious worldliness, were bound to jar on a person of sensibility. Nor in that plain-spoken age were they concealed. "Your mother is a whore," shouted a Cambridge friend to George Lamb in the heat of an undergraduate quarrel. George knocked him down; but he cannot have failed to know that there was truth in the insult. William must have learned this truth early too. And though in theory he did not set much value on chastity, yet such a discovery about his own mother is generally upsetting to a sensitive boy; especially if, like William, he is temperamentally susceptible to the charm of innocence. Again—and here he had his brothers with him—he was irritated by the violence of Lady Melbourne's ambition for her children: loudly they protested that they wished she would sometimes let their careers alone. Still less did William like the hardness of her mockery; with the candour of his family he told her so.

"Everybody has foibles from which no quarantine can purify them," he writes to her. "No resource remains but to make up your mind to put up with them . . . as to Lewis' way of laughing people out of them—which by the way you are sometimes a little inclined to adopt—it only confirms them—and makes the person ridiculed hate you into the bargain."

The tone of this reproof is good-natured enough. And indeed none of these sources of irritation counted for much in themselves. But they accumulated in William to create a secret uneasiness which is the most striking evidence of his inner maladjustment. His prevailing state of mind when he first grew up was unusual for a man of his age. Except in politics he was all for caution, inactivity and putting up with things. Though happy, he was not hopeful. Beneath the smooth surface of his equanimity, had sown themselves the seeds of a precocious disillusionment.

His first acquaintance with the world encouraged their growth. Whig society was an entertaining place: but it did not foster sentimental illusions. Even Devonshire House life had its seamy side; at Carlton House and in the *demi-monde* the seamy side was uppermost. William entered them with some shreds of the ingenuous idealism of youth still hanging round him. He soon lost them; and he felt it. Once seizing a pen he poured forth his feelings in some verses to a friend.

> A year has pass'd—a year of grief and joy—
> Since first we threw aside the name of boy,
> That name which in some future hour of gloom,
> We shall with sighs regret we can't resume.
> Unknown this life, unknown Fate's numerous shares
> We launched into this world, and all its cares;
> Those cares whose pangs, before a year was past,
> I felt and feel, they will not be the last.
> But then we hailed fair freedom's brightening morn,
> And threw aside the yoke we long had borne;
> Exulted in the raptures thought can give,
> And said alone, we then began to live;
> With wanton fancy, painted pleasure's charms,
> Wine's liberal powers, and beauty's folding arms,
> Expected joys would spring beneath our feet,
> And never thought of griefs we were to meet.
> Ah! Soon, too soon is all the truth displayed,
> Too soon appears this scene of light and shade!
> We find that those who every transport know,
> In full proportion taste of every woe;
> That every moment new misfortune rears;
> That, somewhere, every hour's an hour of tears.
> The work of wretchedness is never done,
> And misery's sigh extends with every sun.
> Well is it if, when dawning manhood smiled
> We did not quite forget the simple child;

If, when we lost that name, we did not part
From some more glowing virtue of the heart;
From kind benevolence, from faithful truth,
The generous candour of believing youth,
From that soft spirit which men weakness call,
That lists to every tale, and trusts them all.
To the warm fire of these how poor and dead
Are all the cold endowments of the head.

Such moods seldom got the upper hand in him. And no one who met him seems to have noticed them. But they had their effect; his uneasiness persisted, was confirmed.

Indeed he had cause to be uneasy. Education, though it had muffled their clash, had done nothing to reconcile the opposing tendencies in his nature. One half of him still went out to the ideal, the romantic; the other told him that, in actual fact, self-interest and material satisfactions were the controlling motive forces in the world. As he grew older the struggle was further complicated by the fact that his personal and his ideal sympathies became engaged against each other. The people he was fondest of all took the anti-ideal side. Yet he continued to respond to the call of his imagination as strongly as before. He was in an impasse.

It did not worry him very much. Life was pleasant, he was adaptable. Moreover, gradually and insensibly, he had evolved a mode of thought and action, by which he could evade the more distressing implications of his situation. He did not suppress his real instincts; there was an obstinate integrity in his disposition which made him incapable of denying anything he genuinely felt. But still less did he throw over his realism, to follow the call of his heart. He would have thought it silly, for one thing: his reason told him that his family's point of view was right. Besides, to quarrel with it would have entailed a row; and he hated rows. No more now than as an Eton boy did he see the sense of standing up to be knocked to pieces. As at Eton, therefore, he compromised; adopted a neutral, detached position, which enabled him to enjoy the world he lived in, while avoiding those of its activities which most violently outraged his natural feelings. He refused to be ambitious, to join in the sordid scuffle for place and power; he conducted his own personal relationships by a rigid standard of delicacy and honour; and he always said what he thought, regardless of public opinion. On the other hand he taught himself to tolerate other people's opinions; he lived the life that was expected of him; and he concentrated his heart and interests chiefly on those pleasures which his home did provide. Social life, public affairs, occupied a growing share of his attention: while his emotions attached themselves primarily to his personal affections. In them, indeed, both sides of his nature did, in some sort, find fulfilment. Love for a living individual was both real and romantic. It became the strongest motive power in his life. For the rest, though he indulged his taste for philosophizing, he was doubtful if it had any value. He was a sceptic in thought, in practice a hedonist. Shelving deeper problems, he enjoyed the passing moment wholeheartedly, and took his own character as little seriously as he could.

Such an attitude worked very well for the time being. It was easy to be a successful hedonist in the Whig society of 1800, if one was as popular and as cheerful as William. His faculty for self-adaptation worked as well as it had at school: he continued to be happy. All the same he paid a heavy price for his happiness. His condition of mind was not a healthy one. Resting as it did on an unresolved discord, its basic foundation was insecure. This insecurity was increased by the bias given to his outlook by upbringing. In spite of all her wisdom and all her affection, it was a pity that Lady Melbourne was his mother. His view of life, if it was to be a stable affair, must be built, in part at least, on his ideal sentiments. Lady Melbourne's opinions, and still more her example, tended to make him distrust these. In her smooth efficient way she had managed to discredit his best feelings in his own eyes. And even if he was unaware of the cause, it made him feel uneasy all the time.

Nor was the philosophy he had adopted to meet the difficulties of his situation, good for him. It is unnatural to be a materialist when one is twenty-three years old and throbbing with idealistic feelings. And the efforts William was forced to make to maintain himself in his scepticism, against the pull of his nature, produced a sort of frustration in his character. He grew far too self-preservative, for one thing. Insecurely perched in his little patch of tranquil neutrality, he became dominated by the desire to preserve it from invasion. His hatred of trouble grew stronger and stronger, till he would make practically any sacrifice to avoid an unpleasant scene, to put off a difficult decision. It modified even his attitude to those personal relationships by which he set such store. Though he was unfailingly considerate and unselfish in little things, he never dreamt of letting his feeling for someone he loved divert him from the course of life he had marked out for himself: still less would he take the responsibility of guiding their lives. An enlightened policy of live and let live was his method of running a relationship.

But beyond this, his upbringing had a more formidable, a more disastrous effect upon him. It crippled the development of his most valuable faculties. These were intellectual. Nature had meant him for that rare phenomenon, a philosophical observer of mankind. His detachment and his curiosity, his honesty and his perceptiveness, his sense of reality and his power of generalization, all these mingled together to make his mind of the same type, if not of the same high quality, as that of Montaigne or Sir Thomas Browne: the mind of the botanist in the tangled jungle of men and their thoughts, exploring, observing, classifying. But to be a thinker, one must believe in the value of disinterested thought. William's education had destroyed his belief in this, along with all other absolute beliefs; and in so doing, removed the motive force necessary to set his creative energy working. The spark that should have kindled his fire was unlit: with the result that he never felt moved to make the effort needed to discipline his intellectual processes, to organize his sporadic reflections into a coherent system of thought. He had studied a great many subjects, but none thoroughly; his ideas were original, but they were fragmentary, scattered, unmatured. This lack of system meant further that he never overhauled his mind to set its contents in order in the light of a considered standard of value. So that the precious and the worthless jostled each other in its confused recesses: side by side with fresh and vivid thoughts lurked contradictions, commonplaces and relics of the conventional prejudices of his rank and station. Even his scepticism was not consistent; though he doubted the value of virtue, he never doubted the value of being a gentleman. Like so many aristocratic persons, he was an amateur.

His amateurishness was increased by his hedonism. For it led him to pursue his thought only in so far as the process was pleasant. He shirked intellectual drudgery. Besides, the life he lived was all too full of distracting delights. If he felt bored reading and cogitating, there was always a party for him to go to, where he could be perfectly happy, without having to make an effort. Such temptations were particularly hard to resist for a man brought up in the easy-going, disorderly atmosphere of Melbourne House; where no one was ever forced to be methodical or conscientious, and where there was always something entertaining going on. If virtue was hard to acquire there, pleasure came all too easily. Merely to look on kept one contented.

Indeed that was the danger. At twenty-one William was already an onlooker; an active-minded, lively onlooker, ready to respond to every thrill, every joke in the drama: but standing a little aloof, without any compelling desire to take part himself. He had made his peace with the world, and on favourable terms: but none the less the world had, in this first round of the fight, defeated him. Endowed by birth with one of the most distinguished minds of his generation, there was a risk that he might end as nothing more than another charming ineffective Whig man of fashion.

A risk but not a certainty: William's character had taken shape but it was not yet set into its final mould. And the rebellious elements within it still surged, seeking an outlet. At moments, as we have seen, they burst out in his talk: his Foxite idealism still sounded, a discordant trumpet note, in the minor harmony of his scepticism: even his intellectual arrogance was the sign of a spirit not yet resigned to accept life just as he found it. A change of circumstance, the pressure of a new influence, and there was a chance he might yet, in some later engagement, turn the tables on the world; that his creative energy, gathering its forces together, might break through the inhibitions induced by upbringing, and gush forth to fulfilment. There was still a chance.

## Part Two

### CHAPTER III

### LOVE

FOR A year or two his career marked time. There was a little uncertainty at first as to what profession he should adopt. He had been destined for the Bar; but now Lady Melbourne suddenly suggested he should become a clergyman. It was a curious idea, considering that he doubted Christian doctrines and disapproved of Christian morals. But the Whig aristocracy did not regard faith as an essential qualification for holy orders. To them the Church was primarily a good profession for younger sons. William's scholarly tastes and relatively discreet private character seemed to make him especially fitted for it; with any reasonable luck he should be a bishop before he died. However, he did not show any enthusiasm for the proposal; and Lord Egremont was flat against it. Turning therefore to the secular world, Lady Melbourne sat down and wrote to the Prince of Wales asking him for a job for William in connection with the Office of the Stannaries. The Prince replied with a refusal, in which the fulsome effusiveness of his language was only equalled by the obvious strength of his determination to do nothing at all. In the end it was settled that, after all, William should become a lawyer. He was quite willing. Going on circuit was a new experience; he found himself, as usual, pleasantly popular with his fellow barristers; it gave him a thrill of delighted pride to be offered his first brief. Still, law did not rouse his interest sufficiently to divert him from his chosen career of leisure and pleasure. He continued to write verses and prologues to private theatricals; he went to Carlton House and Roehampton more than ever; and he often found time to go down to the country for "a bath of quiet", reading and day-dreaming. In any case, after a few years, an event took place that made his indolence of little account. In January, 1805, Peniston Lamb died of consumption. For the moment all was forgotten in sorrow. On so devoted a family the blow fell with extraordinary force; Lady Melbourne herself was so

overcome by emotion as even to forget her usual worldly preoccupations. Openly disregarding public opinion she had invited
Peniston's mistress, the pretty Mrs. Dick Musters, to stay at Melbourne House that she might soothe his last moments; when he
died Lady Melbourne was desolated. For William the event was
momentous. His prospects were entirely reversed; he was now
the heir to a peerage and a large fortune. It was not in reality anything to be thankful for. He was now, even more inextricably than
before, entangled in the web of that worldly life which, since he
was a child, had hampered him in following the best course for
his talents. As a younger son there was no practical reason—if he
had ever felt the inclination—why he should not break away from
conventional existence and devote himself to that life of thought
and writing in which he could most fully have expressed himself.
But future peers in that day were not free. They were integral and
active parts of the great machine of aristocratic government and
social life; to them, almost as much as to a royal prince, was
allotted a ready-made role, function, responsibilities. For them,
to take up a life of contemplation was to act in opposition to the
whole pressure and tradition of the society of which they were
members. It was made all the more difficult by the fact that the
position imposed on them was such an attractive one. With some
of the duties of royalty they had all its pleasures and privileges.
They walked through life envied by men and courted by women,
recognized and acclaimed monarchs of a magnificent realm. Certainly William seems to have felt no qualm on accepting his new
position. No more at this juncture than in earlier days, did he
show the slightest conscious realization that the life to which he
was called diverted him from his true bent. He took it for granted,
for instance, that like other eldest sons, he must now go into the
House of Commons. The only problem that worried him was
what seat he should stand for. Should it be Leominster or Hertford? He went down to Hertford and delighted his supporters
with an excellent speech. But for some reason he preferred Leominster. In January, 1806, he was elected member. But before
this he had taken a more irrevocable step. He had married.

Ever since 1802 he had wanted to. In that year Caroline Ponsonby, now a grown-up young lady of seventeen, was launched on

the world. She had matured into all and more than all that William could have hoped for. Indeed she was the most dynamic personality that had appeared in London society for a generation. Outwardly she had hardly changed since he first met her. Slight, agile, and ethereal, with a wide-eyed wilful little face, and curly short hair, she still looked a child; like something less substantial even,—"the Sprite", people called her, "the Fairy Queen, Ariel". Her fresh lisping voice, too, trained though it was to linger cooingly on the syllables in the approved Devonshire House manner, was a child's voice; "Lady Caroline," said an irritated rival, "baas like a little sheep." Nor did her exterior belie what lay within. As much as at fourteen she still loved to gallop bareback, to dress up in trousers, to lose herself in day-dreams; when the fit took her she screamed and tore her clothes in ungovernable rage. No one could have been less like the conventional idea of a young lady. On fire for the dramatic, the picturesque, the ideal, openly at war with the tame and the trivial, at every turn she flouted convention; would rush into the street dressed anyhow, spoke her mind with *enfant terrible* candour, plunged straight into the subjects which interested her, regardless of the formalities of polite conversation. As for orthodox feminine employments, gossip, embroidery, they filled her with ineffable contempt. More normal girls like her cousin Harriet Cavendish, not unnaturally resented this. In fact, many people thought her tiresome; even her friends admitted she was difficult. Yet they forgave her everything. The Fairy Queen cast a spell, which, for those on whom it worked, was not to be resisted. It came partly from the sheer spontaneous intensity of her temperament. In each changing mood, her gusts of irresponsible gaiety, the trembling sensibility which responded like a violin string to poetry, music, eloquence, she seemed more alive than other people; and heightened their sense of life by her presence. She was very clever too, in a fitful, darting way. Too impatient to follow a logical process, and generally in the clouds, she could yet on occasion pierce to the heart of a subject with a lightning insight that dazzled her hearers. And she expressed herself with a direct vividness of phrase which made her every word memorable. But beyond all this, beyond her gifts and her vitality, there was in her a touch of something stranger and more precious

—was it genius?—a creative individuality, whimsical, extravagant, enchanting, which scrawled its signature in a thousand fanciful flourishes on everything she said or did. Sometimes it blossomed forth in an Elizabethan fantasy of humour, "my most sanative elixir of julep, my most precious cordial confection", so she begins a letter to a cousin thanking him for a medical prescription; the same quality flitted in zig-zag butterfly flights across her most sombre confessions of melancholy. "I am like a vestal who thought of other concerns than the poor flame she hoped Heaven would keep burning. Do not condemn me to be burnt alive; wait a little, I shall return to dust without any unusual assistance": or "I go off . . . and you will probably see among the dead in some newspaper—died on her voyage, Lady Caroline Lamb, of the disease called death; her time being come and she being a pre-destinarian"; she cannot recommend a governess without it break-ing out: "Miss X. is sensible, handsome, young, good, unsophisti-cated, independent, true, ladylike, above any deceit or meanness, romantic, very punctual about money; but she has a cold and a cough and is in love. I cannot help it, can you?" This spirit thrusts its irrepressible head into the very datings of her letters: "Brocket Hall, heaven knows what day," thus she heads a formal congratulation to a prospective sister-in-law she has not yet met. Here we come to the secret of her peculiar spell. Lady Melbourne might be more brilliant, the Duchess of Devonshire more winning, Lady Bessborough more intimately lovable; but where in them is to be found this bewitching unexpectedness, this elusive gleam lit at the very torch of will-o'-the-wisp?

William was born to be her victim. His sceptical, sophisticated spirit was at once entertained and invigorated by her naturalness and her certainty: his repressed idealism glowed, even against his better judgment, in response to the confidence of hers; and he appreciated her unique flavour, with the discriminating relish of the connoisseur in human nature that he was. If he were to live a hundred years, he knew, he would find no one else like this. All the force of his virile, tender nature went out to her; he fell irretrievably in love. For the time being it had to be a hopeless love. The social conventions of the day made it unthinkable that Lord Bessborough's only daughter should throw herself away on a younger son of small fortune. William was too unselfish and too sensible to involve Caroline in the fruitless unhappiness that must ensue from an attempt to combat universal custom. Though he could not altogether conceal his feelings, he never declared himself formally; and made some ineffective efforts to fall in love with other people. Caroline returned his passion, but oddly enough for one of her character, she also submitted to convention. Anyway, she told him, it would be a bad thing for them to marry; she was too much of a fury. Could not she, as an alternative, she suggested, accompany him on circuit disguised as a clerk? Meanwhile other young men, her cousins, Lord Althorp and Lord Hartington, were paying court to her; it seemed probable she would end by marrying one of them. For a year or two her relations with William remained, outwardly at least, no more than a fashionable flirtation.

Peniston's death put the situation on a new footing. Even now William was a less brilliant match than she might have anticipated; at least till his father died. For on his eldest son's death Lord Melbourne had, for the only recorded time in his history, cut up rough. The accumulated mortifications of thirty years boiled over; he refused point blank to allow William the £5,000 a year he had bestowed on the indisputably legitimate Peniston. So strongly did he express himself on the subject that Lady Melbourne actually lost her nerve. Too scared to approach him herself, she was reduced to asking a friend to persuade him to reconsider his decision. In vain; Lord Melbourne was adamant, and William had to make do with £2,000 a year. Still £2,000 a year, with the Melbourne fortune in prospect, was good enough. In May, when the first months of mourning were over, William wrote a letter to Caroline in which he poured forth his pent-up emotions.

"I have loved you for four years, loved you deeply, dearly, faithfully—so faithfully that my love has withstood my firm determination to conquer it when honour forbade my declaring myself—it has withstood all that absence, variety of objects, my own endeavours to seek and like others, or to occupy my mind with fixed attention to my profession, could do to shake it."

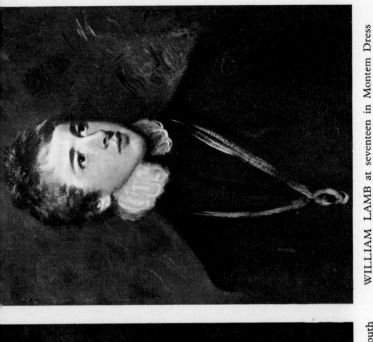

ELIZABETH MILBANKE Viscountess Melbourne in youth

WILLIAM LAMB at seventeen in Montem Dress

LADY CAROLINE LAMB

TWO DRAWINGS OF WILLIAM LAMB
and one of the 1st Viscount Melbourne

There was little doubt as to what Caroline's answer would be. But her family's attitude was not yet quite certain. It was not the marriage Lady Bessborough would have chosen. The Lamb spirit had always been unsympathetic to her; she was peculiarly repelled by cynicism, coarseness and off-hand manners; even in William, she was jarred by his "creed or rather no creed" as she put it. As for Lady Melbourne, though she had known her for years, she had never been able to feel easy in her company. Far too acute not to see through her suave exterior, she yet shrank too much from friction to be able to stand up to her. Beside Lady Melbourne's finished poise she felt herself continually at a disadvantage; she called her the Thorn. On the other hand, she liked William personally very much; she knew Caroline to be passionately in love with him. And she was anxious to get her off her hands as soon as she could. Caroline was altogether too temperamental for family life: and was sometimes so disagreeable in her manner that Lady Bessborough had come to the conclusion that only the settling influence of marriage would ever cool her down. Anyway she was not the woman to stand in the path of true love. Sighing, she left the matter to Caroline's decision. A day or two later William was asked to come to the play with the Bessboroughs in order to receive his final answer:

"We met him at Dy. Lane," Lady Bessborough tells Lord Granville, "I never saw anything so warm and animated as his manner towards her, and of course he soon succeeded in obtaining every promise he wished. I had not seen him to speak to, and he follow'd me into the passage (behind the D. Lane box). I was very nervous, and on telling him I knew Lord B. join'd with me in leaving everything to Caro's decision, he answered: 'And that decision is in my favour, thank heaven!' and so saying, threw his arms round me and kiss'd me. At that very moment I look'd up and saw the Pope [1] and Mr. Hammond before me in the utmost astonishment. W. frighten'd at their appearance, started back and ran downstairs. No words can paint to you my confusion, but, unable to bear the Pope's mortifying conjectures even till all was declar'd, I flew after him and calling

[1] A nickname for Canning.

C

him out, told him the cause of what he saw, and you can have no conception of his kindness; he was delighted, quieted all my fears, assur'd me my objections were Idle—prais'd William extremely, and did me more good than any one thing I had heard before. He touch'd me to that degree with his kindness that I could not resist pressing his hand to my lips (I hope it was not wrong?)"

The experience of the next few weeks confirmed the Pope's praises. William, now received as a son into the intimacy of the home circle, revealed to the full his genius for affection; Caroline, too, grew surprisingly more serene, once she was engaged. A delicious relationship established itself between the three of them, rosy with tenderness, sparkling with graceful gaiety.

"Your letter made me cry," Lady Bessborough writes to Caroline, "and then laugh at myself for crying. The truth is we are two simpletons, and unlike what mother and daughter ought to be—William may pride himself on his good conduct; for to nothing one atom less kind and delightful than he is, could I have yielded you. I should have forbid the banns at last, with anybody else; but as I told you the other day, he really appears to me like my *natural son*—I shall hasten to do your commission; for I know your happiness cannot be compleat without Rollin's ancient History, that dear beautiful light amusing book. What a pity that it should be in twenty-four volumes and in quarto, that you cannot carry it always about you—could not you contrive a little rolling bookcase, you might draw after you, containing these precious volumes? I do not despair of your being soon able to repeat the whole, heads of chapters and all; how lulling it will be for William when he is a little drowsy. The book on education seems to me rather premature: but I will get it. What Prince do you intend to marry your future daughter to? Some of the Buonaparte family perhaps, that I may have the pleasure of being Grandmother to an Empress."

All the same the wedding did not pass off without its storms. Lord Hartington, when the Bessboroughs came round to Devonshire House with the news, was seized with such paroxysms of agitation at the loss of his love, that a doctor had to be summoned. Then, the Thorn proved as thorny as Lady Bessborough could have feared. The antipathy between the two mothers-in-law was mutual. To Lady Melbourne, Lady Bessborough's virtues and faults were alike distasteful; sensitive, enthusiastic, imprudent persons were the type she had always found most tiresome; and she thought the gushing manner with which Lady Bessborough sought to conceal the nervousness she felt in her presence, both silly and insincere. To these original sources of irritation was now added jealousy. Though she approved his marriage from the worldly point of view, Lady Melbourne could not bear to see her adored William so obviously absorbed in two other women. In the exhausting rush of wedding preparations her exasperation betrayed itself:

"Yesterday, after various very unpleasant *cuts*," says Lady Bessborough, "she told me she hoped the Daughter would turn out better than the Mother, or William might have to repent of his choice; and would not (like many Husbands) be made to repent impunément. This was said half joke, half earnest; but there are subjects too sore to bear a joke. . . . I felt hurt and possibly could have retorted, but check'd myself, however; and only said I hoped and believ'd she would prove much better—'especially (I added) with the help of your advice' (I would not say example)."

Unluckily, too, as the ceremony approached Caroline became herself again. The strain of buying a trousseau and her alarm at the thought of leaving her family for the first time, united to disperse her unwonted calm. She was attacked with moods of tearful melancholy, which on the actual wedding-day rose to hysteria. They were married at eight o'clock in the evening in Cavendish Square. Towards the end of the service Caroline, seized by an unaccountable fit of rage with the officiating bishop, tore her gown and was carried fainting from the room. An hour later, as she drove off through the summer dusk for her honeymoon at Brocket under the gaze of a huge crowd, she was still in a violent nerve storm. However, she was in good hands. William had been stirred by this, the first powerful emotional experience of his life-

time, to break free from his customary attitude of amiable detachment. During the ceremony his manner was remarked on as
"beautiful, so tender and considerate"; once married, he took
complete charge of her. On his own responsibility he opened her
letters, only allowing her to see them if they contained nothing to
distress her; he asked Lady Bessborough not to visit her till she
had got over her home-sickness; and himself superintended her
day with vigilant care. Indeed his marriage released his nature in
more ways than one. The new atmosphere of delicate demonstrative emotion in which he found himself, thawed the Lamb reserve. Shyly, tentatively, and with a stiffness still far removed
from Devonshire House rhapsodizings, he tried to be demonstrative too.

"I am very bad at making professions," he writes to his
grandmother-in-law, Lady Spencer, "and have besides an
invincible aversion to them, but believe me I shall be very happy
to come to Holywell, the moment Caroline says she wishes it,
and to stay there, as long as you will allow us; and this not only
now, when I may be supposed to act so for the sake of appearance, but at any time and at all times in future—notwithstand-
ing what I have said above about professions I cannot help
acknowledging that I feel the greatest and sincere satisfaction
in my dear Caroline's love and respect for you."

And later we find him beginning a letter to her: "My dearest
Love, since you do not like the other opening." What the other
opening was is unknown; but clearly it was insufficiently demonstrative. However, during the honeymoon he showed affection
enough for his immediate purpose. His mingled tenderness and
good sense made him the ideal person to soothe disordered nerves.
In the mornings, with Caroline clinging to his arm, they walked
the glades of Brocket park, drowsy in the June sunshine: later in
the day she sketched, while he read aloud. Within a few weeks
Caroline was sufficiently recovered to throw herself into the delights of fulfilled love with all the intensity of her nature.

## CHAPTER IV

# MARRIAGE

FOR THE next three years they lived in a state of idyllic happiness. Not that they secluded themselves from the world. On the contrary they were one of the smartest young couples in London. Their home was in the heart of its whirling centre: Lady Melbourne, in the Continental fashion, had allotted to them the first floor of the family mansion in Whitehall. Here, attended by a retinue of pages in liveries of scarlet and sepia designed by Caroline, they kept open house; received morning and afternoon visitors, gave dinner parties lasting till one in the morning, after which the guests would sometimes descend to Lady Melbourne's apartments on the ground floor for supper. Two years after marriage a son was born, Augustus.

"Caroline was brought to bed about an hour ago of a very large boy for so small a woman," wrote William to Lady Holland with paternal jocoseness. Caroline's own emotions were of so lyrical a kind as to require verse for their expression.

> "His little eyes like William's shine—
> How then is great my joy,
> For while I call this darling mine,
> I see 'tis William's boy."

To celebrate the christening, Lady Melbourne gave a magnificent party. Melbourne House was illuminated outside and in; and a huge concourse of guests, headed by the Prince of Wales, entertained themselves with eating and drinking and composing rhymes. The young Lambs spent as much time out as at home. They were to be seen everywhere: at the opera, at Drury Lane, at Almack's; staying with the Duke of Gloucester at Cowes, taking part in theatricals at Lord Abercorn's country house—William, who appeared in the role of Captain Absolute, was remarked on as "rather too vehement but very gentleman-like and nothing bad"— and very often at Devonshire House, where scandal had it that

Caroline was once carried in concealed under a silver dish-cover, from which she emerged on the dinner table, stark naked, to the consternation of the company. We have glimpses of William alone, too; at Brooks's Club, to which he had been introduced by Fox himself, and staying at Brocket in order to take part in the exercises of the local yeomanry. At such times Caroline, left to herself, drew, danced, and improved her mind by serious reading. In her enthusiasm she summoned others to assist her.

> "My dear Mama," she writes in July, 1809, "if you are quite well, I should take it as a great favour if you would just write me the principal dates and events, wars, risings from Romulus till the time of Constantine the Great—if you are unwell do not do it."

Poor Lady Bessborough! she must have needed to be healthy indeed to perform such a task at the height of the London season. Caroline was equally interested in contemporary history; she and William had the Whig taste for public affairs. Every important event of that dramatic epoch stirred them; the Battle of Copenhagen, the Peninsular Campaign, the death of Pitt. This last, one might have expected to leave William unmoved, considering the unfavourable opinion he had always entertained of that statesman's policy. But the passing of so historic a figure kindled his inflammable imagination; all Pitt's faults were forgotten in the flow of generous emotion that welled up within him; moving him in fact to an uncharacteristic and slightly comical sententiousness.

> "When W. Lamb came in and told me," related Lady Bessborough, "the tears were in his eyes too: and as I had drawn my veil over my face, he said, 'Do not be ashamed of crying: that heart must be callous indeed that could hear of the extinction of such a man unmoved. He may have erred but his transcendent talents were an honour to England and will live in posterity.'"

As for the way that people began canvassing as to who should get Pitt's seat at Cambridge, before he was cold in his grave, William thought it absolutely disgusting. "Damn him," he exclaimed vehemently, on receiving a note from one of the Whig leaders asking for his vote, "can no feeling but party enter his cold heart?": and he crumpled the note in his hand. It was a sad year altogether. Fox died soon after Pitt; and a few months earlier, after a protracted and agonizing illness, the Duchess of Devonshire. To her immediate circle it was an irreparable loss. With her went the centre round which their whole social life had revolved for thirty years; Caroline was plunged into an agony of tears, while Lady Bessborough's spirits received a shock from which they were never to recover.

However, neither private nor public calamities had the power to shake the inner citadel of the young Lambs' happiness. Love breathed round them a rosy cloud in which they moved, entrancedly insulated from the world. "They flirt all day," said an observer. And they talked as much as they flirted. William had always liked to teach, Caroline to be taught. Entertaining, unpedantic, his mind a storehouse of varied information, he was a perfect teacher; her quickness, her responsive enthusiasm, made her the ideal pupil. Every day of their crowded lives they contrived somehow to find time to read together; history, poetry, theology. Even in the turmoil of the Abercorn theatricals, she would write:

> "Wm. and I get up about ten or half after or later (if late at night)—have our breakfast—talk a little—read Newton on the Prophecies with the Bible, having finished Sherlock—then I hear him his part, he goes to eat and walk—I finish dressing and take a drive or a little walk—then come upstairs where Wm. meets me and we read Hume with Shakespeare till the dressing bell."

When he was away he would send her translations from the classics he had made to pass the time, and ask her opinion of them: meanwhile she read the books he recommended that she might ply him with questions when he came back. And when they grew weary of serious subjects they would relax, she to enjoy his shrewd, subtle agreeability, he to savour her ever changing moods, the leaps and somersaults of her harlequin fancy. Whether serious or frivolous or sentimental, each was a continual delight to the other.

But it was not to last; their happiness was as short-lived as it was ecstatic. Before four years were over, a rift had begun to show itself in their relationship which was to bring down their married life in irreparable ruin. It was predominantly Caroline's fault. In spite of all her charms and all her talents, her character was of a kind to make her an unsatisfactory wife for any man. Not that it was a bad one. On the contrary, nature had made her generous, tender-hearted, fearless, and unworldly. She aspired far more genuinely than most people to live a noble life; if her heart was touched, no kindness was too much trouble for her. But with a glint of the unique fire of genius, she possessed in the highest degree its characteristic defect. A devouring egotism vitiated every element in her character. In her eyes she was the unquestioned centre of the universe. She did not acknowledge, she was not even aware of any authority beyond her own inclinations. What she liked was right; what she disliked was wrong. This made her abnormally selfish, abnormally uncontrolled and abnormally unreliable. One moment she would offer you her whole fortune, the next fly at you with nails and fists. In either mood she thought she was justified, and other people had to think so too. In addition, they had to admire her. Life was a drama in which she was cast as heroine; and both her fellow actors and her audience were expected to applaud her every movement. Capricious in all else, in one thing she was consistent, her determination to hold the centre of the stage. It was for this she dressed and behaved unlike other people; this was the reason of her faintings and sobbings and unconventional interruptions. Even her generous actions were partly a method of showing off. She liked to dazzle others by the spectacle of her munificence. For—it was the most dangerous effect of her egotism—her ambitions were never completely sincere. It would be inaccurate to call her deceitful. Her very lack of control made her incapable of conscious pretence; indeed she thought quite sincerely that, compared with herself, most people were shocking hypocrites. But self-absorption tainted the essential quality of her reactions. Her feelings were one part genuine, two parts self-indulgent pleasure in emotion for its own sake, and three parts a means of self-glorification. Her intensest affections, her most exalted enthusiasms, were largely make-believe.

False feelings lead to a false vision of the world. "Truth," she said, "is what one believes at the moment." What she believed was always something creditable to herself. Since it was essential for her to see herself in the sympathetic light appropriate to a heroine, she learnt to blind herself to all facts that went against her, and to invent such others as were needed to set her conduct in a favourable perspective. Her history, as it appears in the records left to us, is an ironical comedy of appearance and reality. Side by side run always two stories, what happened to Caroline and what she pretended had happened. Living wholly in a wish-fulfilment world of her own creation, she insisted it was the real one. Nor was she content simply to contemplate its perfections. In order to feel completely satisfied, she had to impose the false world on the real. Disgusted with life as she found it, she was yet confident it could be made what she wished, and spent all her energies seeking out occasions and creating situations in which her dreams could be realized. Of course they proved a disappointment, but undefeated she always tried again. Her career was a series of theatrical performances designed to exhibit the brilliance of her personality to herself and the world. The agility of her imagination made her repertory of parts a large one. Comedy and tragedy came equally easy to her: sometimes she appeared as an unconventional child of nature, sometimes as an experienced woman of the world, sometimes as a devoted wife and mother; she was also ready to take the boards as a queen of fashion, or an heroic idealist. And it must be owned that in all these parts she gave a brilliant performance. Here was where her touch of genius came in. However commonplace the character she was impersonating, it was transfigured into something unique by her wit, her eloquence, the flicker of her fascinating fancy. We of posterity, watching her from the comfortable distance of a hundred years, feel inclined to applaud such masterpieces of the histrionic art with unqualified admiration. But it was very different for the people who had to live with her. For they had to behave as if she were not acting; they were required to respect and sympathize with sentiments they knew were mostly imaginary. Moreover, Caroline made use of them to fill the supporting roles in her productions; to their bewilderment, unasked and unrehearsed, they found themselves being treated as heroes and villains in dramas, of whose very plots they were ignorant. Sometimes, exasperated by some particularly flagrant example of her insincerity, they told her the truth about herself. Then for a moment the mask did fall; appearances were forgotten in a spitfire explosion of wounded vanity. But it was not for long. Within a short time the old machinery of self-deception began to work: she would re-enter as some new character designed to meet her new situation; it might be a pathetic penitent or a generous nature quick to recognize its faults; complete in either case with such plausible misrepresentation of the facts as was needed to give verisimilitude to the part she had chosen.

The extraordinary thing is that she should have been able to keep herself so blissfully blind to reality during nineteen years' existence on this disillusioning planet. But circumstances had been favourable to her. Her upbringing for one thing; Lady Bessborough, for all that she was so affectionate, was a bad mother. Unable to say no, and distracted by the complications of her own private life, she did nothing to check the extravagance of her daughter's temperament. Besides, her own reputation was so tarnished that it was thought better that Caroline should spend most of her childhood away from her; partly with her grandmother, Lady Spencer, and partly at Devonshire House. Neither did her much good. Lady Spencer found her at ten years old already such an unmanageable bundle of nerves that she sent for a doctor. He, anticipating Madame Montessori, opined that discipline was likely to injure so sensitive a child; she must be allowed to do whatever she liked. This régime produced the results any sensible person might have predicted. Caroline grew worse than ever. Nor was Devonshire House the environment to put her right. There the children were alternately spoiled and neglected. Now and again they were sent for to the drawing-room to be petted and made to show off; but for most of the time they roamed about the great house unruled and uncared for, eating only off silver plate, but lucky if they got their meals at all. Their existence was utterly out of touch with that of ordinary humanity. Caroline relates that she grew up thinking bread and butter grew on trees and that the population of the world was composed half of dukes and half of beggars; and though like everything she said this was an exaggeration, yet it did contain a truth. Aristocratic Devonshire House was not the place to acquire a sense of reality.

Finally, the philosophy to be learnt there encouraged her in all her failings. It set no value on reason or self-restraint; on the contrary, it insisted that passion and sensibility were the only virtues, that man should be guided in everything by the instinctive movements of his heart. Caroline embraced with enthusiasm a creed so consonant with her predilections. Indeed it was the determining factor in her development, for it decided the principal form her day-dreams were to take. Of her many roles, the one she assumed oftenest and with most satisfaction to herself was that of the romantic heroine; reckless and imprudent, the creature of her emotions, but sensitive, imaginative and nobly superior to the conventions that ruled pettier lives; living always in an intoxicating whirl of tragedy, ecstasy, passion and renown. The object of her whole life was to achieve an existence in which this conception of herself could be realized.

Such a character was bound to make a bad wife. Marriage demands precisely the qualities in which she was most deficient: dependability, forbearance, above all a sense of reality. It is impossible for two people to live on such intimate terms without discovering the truth about each other's character: and unless they are ready to accept that truth, they will never get on. Caroline, unable to understand William and furious if he understood her, inevitably quarrelled with him. Further dissatisfied as she always was by actuality, she grew soon dissatisfied with the actualities of wedded life. She loved William as much as she could love anybody except herself, and at first she found she could fulfil her dreams by playing the unaccustomed roles of his wife and pupil. But when the glamour of novelty wore off, to be succeeded by the light of common day, she grew restless and discontented.

This discontent was increased by the environment in which she now lived. The Lambs were the last people with whom she could feel at home. She was flustered by their loud voices, offended by their casual manners, and shocked by their cynicism. Their penetration made her vanity uneasy; and their commonsense was always bringing her down to earth with an uncomfortable bump.

Worst of all, the atmosphere they created was one in which she felt herself unable to shine. The Lambs did not believe in heroines and had no taste for whimsicality. Temper and insincerity on the other hand were to them the most unpardonable of faults. Indeed they found their new relation maddening. "What is the eleventh commandment?" she once asked George Lamb. "Thou shalt not bother," he replied in a spasm of exasperation. Among themselves the brothers and sisters alluded to her frankly as "the little beast". Even Lord Melbourne complained that she fidgeted; as for Lady Melbourne, she found Caroline even more tiresome than her mother. Two dominating personalities both absorbed in the same man, the relations between them were bound to be strained. But they could not have got on in any circumstances. Earth and fire, sense and sensibility, realism and fantasy, the eighteenth century and the nineteenth, each was in every respect the other's antithesis; Lady Melbourne, whose first principle it was to accept facts, Caroline, who rejected such few facts as she managed to recognize. Within a short time of William's marriage, war had broken out between them, which was to last till death. The battle swayed this way and that. In open combat Caroline was worsted; she had not the self-command to conduct an engagement with any tactics. Lady Melbourne took every advantage of her opponent's mistakes; crafty and relentless, she contrived to put her even more in the wrong than she was. Yet to her annoyance she found she did not reap the usual reward of her victories. Caroline, though defeated, was unsubdued. Before a week had passed, she was behaving more outrageously than ever; and apparently unaware that she had ever been to blame. During the first three or four years no serious cause of quarrel arose between them. And for the time being Lady Melbourne, followed by the rest of her family, acted on her customary principle of making the best of things. The Lambs treated Caroline as a child, laughing at her vagaries when she was in a good temper; when she was cross, ignoring them. This was not, in her view, the way in which a heroine had a right to be treated. She grew more discontented than ever.

William did not annoy her in the same way. He at least could be trusted to appreciate her. But even William, she began to discover as time went on, was not all she required. He was not distinguished enough for one thing. The man of her choice must be admired by all: William seemed quite happy to follow his tastes unnoticed by anyone. Caroline heard people say that he was never going to do anything; and influenced as she always was by her company, she began to think they must be right. This might not have mattered if he had been completely satisfactory in his relation to her. But he was not. The realist in him made him incapable of playing up to her romantic conception of what a lover should be. As early as 1807 we find her contrasting his behaviour to her at a theatre unfavourably with that of George, newly engaged to Lady Elizabeth Foster's daughter, Caroline. "I could not help remarking the difference between a husband and a lover!" she commented. "George had been an hour and a half at the play before William appeared." Once the honeymoon excitement was over, William's affection had settled down into a tranquil sunshiny sentiment in keeping with his personality. This was so unlike Caroline's idea of love that she began to doubt if he was in love at all.

Here she was wrong. But it was true that William was not ideally suited to her. In spite of all her faults, Caroline was not altogether to blame for the failure of her marriage. At nineteen years old the good in her was still partly uncorrupted by her egotism: and someone who understood how to foster its development, might have managed to make her a possible if not a perfect wife. But this needed a very special type of man, at once firm, tender, and magnetic, prepared to guide her every step, and endowed with a moral majesty that could fire her hero-worship, while keeping her in healthy fear of his disapproval. Poor William! He was the last man to fill this role. Apart from anything else he was far too young. Love had inveigled him into matrimony before he was ready for it. He was still too preoccupied with forming his own tastes, and discovering his own point of view, to assume the responsibilities of a husband. But at no age would he have been the right husband for Caroline. For it was not in him to be an autocrat. The masterfulness he had shown on his honeymoon was the unique effect of an unprecedented burst of emotion. When this cooled, he relapsed into the man his temperament and

Lady Melbourne had made him; passive, self-protective, indulgent, his first principle to let people alone, his first instinct to avoid trouble. Nor was he able to encourage Caroline's idealism. He did not believe in it. Attractive though they might be, at bottom he thought her high-flown fancies great nonsense; and he could not resist telling her so. His dark eyes agleam with mischief, he twitched aside, one by one, the veils of rose-coloured sentimentalism with which Devonshire House sought to hide the seamy side of life; exposed the weaknesses of the characters she had been brought up to revere; pointed out the fallacies involved in the religious and moral systems that commanded the respect of average mankind. Even his own relation to her was not protected from the disillusioning light of his realism. At the same time he assured her that he loved her, it amused him also to tell her that he had loved before, to recount the chronicles of earlier and less reputable amours. All this had its effect on Caroline. It did not make her cynical herself; this was too much against her nature. But it undermined the force of the few restraining principles of conduct implanted in her by native refinement and schoolroom education. If it was true—and William said it was—that everyone really did as they liked, and that it was silly to be shocked by them, there was clearly no reason why she should not do as she liked; and no one had the right to be shocked by her.

In these circumstances it was only a question of time when their marriage came to grief. During its first few years it was kept together by the ardour of their youthful passion. Even then they sometimes quarrelled; but they delighted so much in each other that they were always able to make it up. But as passion faded, a change came. The differences between them rose more and more to the surface, showing themselves in a continuous mutual irritation. They were always having rows. At first they tried to make them up in the old way:

"I think lately, my dear William," writes Caroline in 1809, "we have been very troublesome to each other; which I take wholesale to my own account and mean to correct, leaving you in retail a few little things which I know you will correct. . . . Condemn me not to silence and assist my imperfect memory. I will, on the other hand, be silent of a morning, entertaining after dinner; docile, fearless as a heroine in the last volume of her troubles, strong as a mountain tiger, and active as those young savages, Basil's boys."

It needed a harder heart than William's to resist so engaging an appeal as this: he responded to her overtures with a will. But it was no use. Caroline was a tiger all right, but not docile. However warm their reconciliations, they soon quarrelled again; more and more frequently and with growing bitterness; till gradually they abandoned the struggle to restore their marriage to its pristine harmony. Indeed the spirit needed to unite them was no longer there. Caroline went on saying she adored William: but, in fact, once her vanity was no longer involved in her love, once she had realized that William would never be able to play the part she had assigned him in her scheme of life, she ceased to care for him very much. He was more faithful. On him the Fairy Queen's spell could never lose its power. But he had grown equally disheartened about their marriage. If it were not Caroline's fault—and he hated to think it was—it must be a fault inherent in the nature of the relationship. He became profoundly disillusioned about marriage itself. In his Commonplace Book he noted down with caustic melancholy the conclusions forced on him by his experience of the matrimonial state:

"The general reason against marriage is this—that two minds, however congenial they may be, or however submissive the one may be to the other, can never act like one.

"By taking a wife a man certainly adds to the list of those who have a right to interfere with and advise him, and he runs the risk of putting in his own way another very strong and perhaps insuperable obstacle to his acting according to his own opinions and inclinations.

"By marrying you place yourself upon the defensive instead of the offensive in society, which latter is admitted to be in all contentions the most advantageous mode of proceeding.

"Before marriage the shape, the figure, the complexion carry all before them; after marriage the mind and character unexpectedly claim their share, and that the largest, of importance.

"Before I was married, whenever I saw the children and the dogs allowed, or rather caused, to be troublesome in any family, I used to lay it all to the fault of the master of it, who might at once put a stop to it if he pleased. Since I have married, I find that this was a very rash and premature judgment."

No—experience had proved his old philosophy of detachment only too true. His first attempt to leave his patch of neutrality had turned out as disastrous as he could have feared: trying to combine one's life with that of someone else ended inevitably in failure. Further, he found that it had a deplorable effect on his character. Under the unprecedented strain imposed by the intimacy of married life, his naturally hot temper broke through the smooth surface under which he had, since childhood, managed to conceal it. Caroline began the rows; but, once his patience was exhausted, William raged even more violently than she did. Lack of control shocked his most sacred convictions: each time he lost his temper he apologized to her in horror-stricken remorse. But he began to find out that he could not restrain himself except by avoiding the occasion of anger; and that the only way to do this was to keep out of Caroline's way. By 1810 their relationship had insensibly slipped on to a new footing. They still had jokes in common, still wrote and talked to one another about books and politics. But they went their own ways; each had begun elsewhere than in the other to seek his chief satisfaction in life.

## CHAPTER V

# THE HOUSE OF COMMONS

WILLIAM, like most men, turned for consolation to his work. Whether it was the sort of work best suited to him is doubtful. The speculative mind finds little opportunity to exercise itself in the humdrum mixture of compromise and practical business, which is Parliamentary life. William was interested not in getting things done, but in discovering truth. Faced with a political problem, his mind sought instinctively less to solve it than to divine its causes: and thence to discern what light they cast on the general laws governing human affairs. Where others proposed a plan of action, he made a generalization. Further, English politics are party politics. And William recognized facts far too clearly to imagine that any single party could ever be wholly in the right. He might stick to a leader from loyalty or affection, but never with that blind conviction which makes party warfare a pleasure.

However, he had always made it his practice to fall in gracefully with whatever destiny circumstances indicated for him. It was universally accepted that the eldest son of a great family should go into the House of Commons; into the House of Commons, therefore, he went. As a matter of fact he did it with a very good will. If politics were not the best profession for him, they were far from being the worst. He had been brought up in the world of affairs; it came naturally to him to take a part in it. His chief interest, too, was human nature, and politics exhibited this on the most spectacular scale. Even if he had never taken an active part in them, they would always have formed a chief subject of his thought. Nor were they without their appeal to his imaginative side. He was acutely responsive to the romance of history in the making, to the drama of great events: and to national sentiment. Among the many contradictory elements of his complex nature lurked a strain of mystical patriotism. The thought of England—her great destiny, her majestic and immemorial past—sent a mysterious thrill of awe and veneration vibrating through the deepest fibres of his being.

He was further encouraged to like politics, by the privileged conditions in which he entered them. The society into which he was born might force eldest sons into public life: but in return it admitted them under special advantages. In those pre-democratic days, members of influential families had a prior claim on all the prizes of the profession. Even a stupid Whig magnate had a considerable place in his Party. One as clever as William was almost certain of achieving a commanding position at an early age. From the first, he was treated in a manner to make the mouths of ambitious young politicians of to-day water with envy. There was no need to make himself known. He had lived among the leaders of his Party since childhood. And as soon as he entered the House, they took him into their confidence, told him their private views; and, what was still more flattering, asked him his. Already in 1807 Lord Holland was writing to consult him about the choice of a leader: he was invited to informal councils at Holland House, where he would sit listening to Lord Grey and his host, as they discussed over the port who should speak for the Opposition in a forthcoming debate. Altogether there was a great deal to please him in his profession. When in 1809 he began to throw his full energies into it, he did so without effort.

It was lucky he could. For the state of affairs that confronted him was not in itself one to inspire enthusiasm. During the first years of the nineteenth century, the Whig party was in a state of chaotic frustration. It was long indeed since it had stood for any active policy. Originally formed to support Parliament in its struggle with the King for ultimate sovereignty in the Constitution, it had achieved its essential object nearly a hundred years before, by expelling the Stuarts. During the long period of placid prosperity which followed, it had nothing to do but sit back and consolidate its victory. Now and again this involved a little work. Under the direction of Sir Robert Walpole, the Whigs established the Cabinet system: they also resisted the misguided efforts of George III to retrieve the lost powers of the Crown. But in the main they found themselves sufficiently occupied in drawing large sinecures, and extolling the principles of the glorious revolution of 1688. Nor was their inertia unpopular. The people of England were glad enough of a period unvexed by fundamental issues. But towards the end of the century a change came. The industrial revolution, by turning England from an agricultural to a manufacturing country, began to disturb that balance which must exist in any society between political and economic power. No longer were the land and its aristocratic owners the sole masters of the country's wealth. This position was shared by a new and rising class, part manufacturers, part workmen; who now demanded a voice in the government of the nation, proportionate to their economic influence. Nonconformists, free-traders, and of humble birth, they noted with irritation that the country was run in the interests of Protectionists, Anglicans and Lords. They clamoured for legal reform, fiscal reform, religious emancipation; above all they asked for that Parliamentary reform which, by destroying the aristocratic monopoly of seats, would readjust the balance of government in their favour. And they invoked all manner of novel and alarming doctrines, Equality, the Rights of Man, the Principle of Utility, to give moral justification to their claims. How far and in what manner these claims might be granted, by what means existing institutions could be modified in harmony with the new balance of power, were to be the problems that occupied the next forty years of English history.

Once more fundamental issues were raised. And the old parties had to decide which side they were going to take in the struggle. This was easy enough for the Tories. They had always approved of privilege, and disliked tradesmen. But the Whigs were more ambiguously placed. For, though in theory they considered themselves the upholders of progress and liberty, in fact they had a vested interest in the existing régime. Composed as they were largely of landed proprietors, they did not, any more than the Tories, like the idea of surrendering their power to a set of blackguardly commercials with Yorkshire accents and nonconformist consciences. A few exalted spirits among them threw in their lot with the cause of the future. The Duke of Norfolk drank to Our Sovereign the People; Mr. Whitbread took up Penal Reform; young Mr. Grey developed an interest in the representation question. But they were not enough to carry the Party with them. It was to need the pressure of a powerful public opinion outside Parliament to drive the Whigs as a whole on to the Reform side. For the first thirty years of the century Whig opinion was bewildered, divided and wavering.

Anyway, before these new problems had come clearly to the front, before indeed the average M.P. had realized their existence, all forward movement was suddenly checked by two events abroad. First the French Revolution frightened the respectable people of every party to such a degree as to put them for the time being against any drastic changes: and then the Napoleonic War disposed them to shelve all domestic problems, till victory was won. At its beginning, some advanced Whigs had opposed the war; but by 1807 all the most influential were united to resist the common enemy. The natural outcome of such a situation should have been a Coalition between Whig and Tory. And after Pitt's death it was tried. But it collapsed within two years of William's entry into Parliament. The aged George III took the opportunity of one of his rare intervals of sanity to perform the last of his many acts of political folly. Obsessed by a confused idea that his right to the throne depended on the penal laws against Roman Catholics, he suddenly demanded that all his ministers should pledge themselves not to bring in Catholic emancipation. Catholic emancipation was one of the few measures that all the Whigs were agreed in approving; the Whig Ministers therefore had to go out of office.

The effect of this combination of circumstances was to leave the Whigs in a parlous condition indeed. It was bad enough to find themselves indefinitely in opposition. But what made it far worse was that they could discover nothing they could agree to oppose. The chief question of the day was the war: and on this, most important Whigs sympathized with the Government. The problems of home affairs were in abeyance: in any case on every one of them, except the forbidden topic of Catholic emancipation, they were at odds with one another. As long as Charles Fox was alive, people had been prepared to sink their differences out of loyalty to him. But after his death no one was left with sufficient personality to impose his will on the party. For the time being the Whigs were kept together only by their family and social traditions. Though they disagreed on every political issue, they continued all the same to marry one another's daughters, to dine at Holland House and to spend their leisure hours at Brooks's. These practices however, delightful though they might be, were not in themselves enough to supply the want of a faith or a leader. Gradually party spirit weakened, party organization disintegrated; till by 1809 it had become such a smoky confusion of shifting opinions, bickering factions and competing individuals, as to plunge the unfortunate historian, who tries to disentangle it, into baffled despair.

Three groups dominated the general chaos: the Grenvillites, the Foxites and the Mountain. Of these the Grenvillites, composed of the powerful Grenville family and their hangers-on, represented Whiggism in its strictly dynastic aspect. They abhorred change as much as the Tories; from whom they differed mainly in their conviction that only the great Whig families, and more especially the Grenville family, had the right to govern England. The Foxites, on the other hand, led by Lords Holland and Grey, regarded themselves as the repository of the pure milk of Whig doctrine. Academic, intransigent and tremendously aristocratic, they rejected all proposals not in accordance with the principles of Charles Fox; scorned economics; approved reform in theory, but shrank from it in practice; and made it a matter of conscience not to work with anyone with whom they disagreed about anything. The Mountain was a more heterogeneous body, made up, partly of lively young patricians with a taste for advanced ideas, and partly of clever members of the middle class, brought into Parliament by noble patrons. They were openly against the war, vociferously in favour of any kind of reform; such vigour as remained in the party resided in them.

Around these main groups hovered a motley mob of smaller combinations and isolated personalities. All sections quarrelled with each other, and among themselves. Some were for the Whigs taking a strong line, some for their retiring from Parliament altogether, some for their coming to terms with the Tories. Connections were all the time crumbling and reshaping themselves; all the time, ambitious men flitted from one group to another, according as each seemed more likely to retrieve the fortunes of the Party. The Whig lobbies buzzed with a continual rumour of baseless hopes and abortive intrigues. By the time William was ready to turn his full attention to his Party, it presented a deplorable spectacle; an army in rout, without order, purpose or morale.

He approached it in a detached spirit. Long before he entered the House of Commons, he had begun to outgrow his youthful idealism. And by now his attitude to politics had matured, to be of a piece with his attitude to everything else; sceptical, realistic, cautious. Natural prudence was intensified by the age in which he lived. It is very difficult for us, hardened as we are by the daily spectacle of catastrophes far more appalling, to realize the extraordinary shock given to our forefathers by the French Revolution. Just across the Channel they saw what seemed at first to be no more than a mild constitutional movement, change within four years to a bloody terror, in which people just like themselves, whom they had dined with on their visits abroad, were stripped destitute of all their possessions, and often horribly murdered. These events undermined their root confidence in the stability of civilization. If such things happened in France, why not in England? The idea that they might, began to obsess them.

To such an obsession William was peculiarly susceptible. Detached hedonism is not less dependent on material circumstance than other human philosophies. Its sunny suavity, its easy broadmindedness, can flourish only in security. During mortal conflicts people inevitably grow morose and partisan. Once he had come to years of political discretion, William saw only too clearly that revolution would mean the end of all that made his life worth living, the destruction of the foundation on which his precariously adjusted peace of mind was built. Fear of popular violence loomed ever at the back of his consciousness. It was the single thing that was able to throw his poised judgment off its balance: throughout his life it was a determining motive in his political views. Yet it did not drive him into blind reaction. Belief in liberty, in toleration, was of the very fibre of his thought. Moreover, his vigorous understanding had combined with his Glasgow education, to make him a man of his time. He realized that the world he lived in was changing, and that there was no use in trying to stop it. Poised between two extremes, his point of view was necessarily impartial. And this impartiality was increased both by his intellectual self-confidence and by his lack of ambition. He did not particularly want to get on; he did not care if others agreed with him. And he had no interest in politics except in so far as he was able to speak his honest opinion about them. Thus, disinterested and unenthusiastic, inquisitive and unprejudiced, the corners of his mouth turned down in ironic amusement, he stepped on to the political stage.

One wonders what the other actors thought of him. For he differed strikingly from the ordinary member. William, like most philosophical persons, was not naturally an orator. He was too self-critical to be able to let himself go in public. Stammering and colloquial, as if he were thinking aloud, his words would trickle forth; wandering away into generalization, or pausing as with fastidiousness, he sought out the phrase that might most precisely express his shade of meaning. Moreover, the line he took was generally so unexpected, as to make it difficult to know precisely where his political sympathies lay. "I know he will be reckoned too scrupulous and conscientious for a good Party man," said Lady Bessborough, "but I cannot help admiring the firm integrity of his character." This was a friendly way of putting it. To those less personally prejudiced in his favour, William's conduct, during his first few years in Parliament, might well have seemed a mere exhibition of caprice. At one time we find him refusing to back his Party in their attack on Lord Ellenborough's position in the Ministry; on another, voting in favour of the advanced Sir Samuel Romilly's proposals on Penal Reform. He was strongly against the Government over Catholic emancipation, strongly on their side about the war. When the Duke of York was assailed by the extreme Whigs for selling commissions in the Army through the convenient agency of his mistress, Mary Ann Clarke, William followed them. But not, he was careful to say, because he was certain of the Duke's guilt, but for reasons of public policy. And two years later he voted for the Duke's reinstatement.

He kept a journal of his early Parliamentary impressions. And this also reveals a contradictory spirit. He seems to take an impish pleasure in discovering the disillusioning paradoxes of public life:

the harm done by good intentions, the weaknesses of revered institutions. It amused him to note that Napoleon, one of the worst men in the world, made his subjects happier than most virtuous rulers; that human beings, so it appeared from the Peninsular War, seemed more likely to get what they wanted by behaving violently than by being reasonable. Nor could he feel much respect for the wisdom of the Sovereign People. "It is impossible not to laugh," he said, "at their blunders, ignorance and fury; at the same time it is impossible not to be struck with the most serious alarm upon the subject."

None the less, his opinions were not so negative, nor his actions so capricious, as appearances might suggest. Coming fresh to the game, it was inevitable that he should roam inquisitively around from one set of views to another; getting a sort of wilful enjoyment from finding out the faults of each. But as he lived, he learned. Bit by bit, a store of experience accumulated itself in his mind; and on the strength of it his own political ideas began to take shape. They were not those of the Party to which he was officially attached. His detached mind was unlikely to be impressed by the welter of squabble and wobble, in which the Whigs floundered. William thought them factious. "The fault of opposition," he remarked, "is a determination to make differences where few exist and those trifling." Nor, in point of fact, did he agree with any of the main groups of Whig opinion. The Grenvillites had nothing to offer a man who liked ideas; for they had none. The Foxites, on the other hand, bristled with them. But theirs were obsolete. Of what interest was it to William to preserve the purity of a creed formulated forty years before? As for the Mountain, they were the worst of the lot; against the war, and in favour of all sorts of risky changes. He could agree with the Tories sooner than with them. Yet he was against the Tories too. Their views were out of date, and they themselves stupid. William was still young enough to have a horror of being thought stupid.

As usual, he found himself adopting a middle course. He wanted a policy moderate and rational; that faced modern problems, but involved no threat to that aristocratic supremacy on which in his view the security of civilization depended. He soon found he was not alone. Similar thoughts had been circulating among a number of young men from both parties, headed, ironically enough, by that peculiar object of William's youthful contempt, Canning. Canning is an ambiguous personality. Few people liked him in his lifetime; nor is it possible to feel enthusiastic about him to-day. There is something indefinably charlatanish about the impression he makes, with his flashy eloquence, his restless intriguing ambition, his sharp, arrogant, egotistic face. Yet, as is so often the case in this mysterious world, he was more genuinely creative than many sincerer persons. It was he who, first among English statesmen of the nineteenth century, offered conservative-minded people a constructive political creed. Himself, he was against Parliamentary reform. England in his view did very well under an aristocracy. Besides, he thought the whole democratic philosophy great nonsense. "It is the business of the legislature," he once said, "to remedy practical grievances, not to run after theoretical perfection." On the other hand he thought some of the practical measures demanded by the reforming parties reasonable. He was all for legal reform and emancipation, and considered that many people had taken up Democracy, because they thought it the only means of getting these measures through. And the way to prevent this, in his opinion, was to show that the old system could be made to do the same work equally well. "Those who resist improvements as innovations," so he put it, "will soon have to accept innovations that are not improvements."

Such were the ideas that he propounded over the dinner table, or in conversation with his fellow members as they walked home from the House in the early hours of the morning. And he presented them in a sparkling up-to-date style, nicely calculated to take the fancy of the bright young spirits of the day. What a comfort to find that one could be anti-revolutionary without appearing stodgy or old-fashioned! It was no wonder that he soon had a troop of followers. Two of them, Ward and Huskisson, were already well acquainted with William. Ward was one of his regular boon companions, a handsome young aristocrat, all brilliance and sensibility, and the height of fashion. Huskisson was a relation by marriage. As such he had never appealed to William. Earnest, middle class, and with an unfortunate habit of falling down on the most embarrassing occasions, he was the sort of man whom the Lambs thought a great joke. But he had a massive, well-trained mind and an extraordinary knowledge of finance; and when William saw him at work in Parliament he began to conceive a great respect for him. With such connections, William was quickly admitted into the inner circle of the Canningites. Once there he was captivated.

For their part the Canningites were only too pleased to have him. In spite of his youthful contradictiousness, and his halting way of speaking, William's reputation had steadily grown throughout his time in Parliament. Indeed, his speeches were better worth listening to than those of many more accomplished orators. They were continually lit up by flashes of insight, pungent turns of wit. Besides, everybody liked him so much. As at Cambridge and the Bar, people were delighted to work with anyone so good-natured, so intelligent, so patently innocent of any desire to push himself. "I hardly know anyone," says Ward affectionately, "of whom everybody entertains so favourable an opinion." And the barometer of fame at Holland House told the same tale. "William Lamb," writes Lady Holland, "is certainly one of the most rising men in public."

Yet his situation was not so comfortable as it looked. Once more his circumstances impeded the true development of his talents. If he really agreed with Canning, he should have thrown in his lot with him whole-heartedly; openly joined him, devoted his every effort to forwarding his cause. But this meant difficulties. Canning was officially a Tory. For one brought up in the inner circle of Whig society, it was an extremely unpleasant step to put himself publicly under Tory leadership. Every prejudice of William's home, of the houses he visited, of the clubs where he spent his mornings, was against it. Further, though he might think poorly of the Whigs as politicians, personally they were his greatest friends. To leave them, when they were so obviously in a bad way, seemed an odious disloyalty. It would have been easy only to someone with a passionate conviction in the rightness of his cause. William's upbringing had been such as to make him question every conviction. His sense of personal obligation, on the other hand, was peculiarly strong. In a world of illusion, individual affections, and the loyalties consequent on them, alone seemed solid. Leaving the Whigs was simply one of the things William felt he could not do. He therefore took a temporizing line. In public he never supported his Party against Canning; in private he pressed his claims. But he called himself a Whig; and when early in 1812 the Prime Minister, anxious to strengthen his administration by the infusion of young blood, offered William a post in the administration, he refused.

With an agitated ingenuity he tried to persuade himself that he was fulfilling a moral duty. He could do more good where he was; changing one's party set a demoralizing example to others; it was subversive of the very principles of loyalty. In the ardour of self-defence he even went so far as to say that a man was only justified in doing it, if he thought that otherwise he would go to Hell. But no amount of argument could alter the fact that William was in a thoroughly false position. All he could do was to wait; uncertainly hoping for some sudden change in the political situation, by which it might be possible for a coalition of moderate men of both sides, led by Canning, to come into power.

In the spring of 1812 there was a chance that this might occur. The Government had been doing so badly that it looked as if they would not be able to go on much longer. Political London was in a hubbub of excitement; George III had gone mad again, and anything might happen. In the lobbies of the Houses of Parliament, in the drawing-rooms of great houses, people arrived every moment, bursting with new rumours. Canningite hopes grew high. Alas, they were to be disappointed. In the wavering balance of competing factions, the deciding factor was the line taken by the Prince Regent. Since he had always called himself a Whig, the Canningites imagined that he would look with favour on a more liberal administration. This only showed that they did not know the Prince Regent. He did ask Lord Wellesley to form a Coalition; but after days of havering and intrigue, in which the Prince tearfully reiterated his unalterable fidelity to his old friends, he threw them over in favour of their opponents. This turned the scale. On 19th March, 1812, a petition was brought forward in the House of Lords asking for an all-party Government. Late in the evening, amid the gilt and candlelight of Melbourne House,

Lady Melbourne and a crowd of Whig ladies waited anxiously to hear the result. At last, long after midnight, William and his friends trailed in, glum and crestfallen; the petition had been decisively defeated. This defeat was confirmed a month or two later in the House of Commons. The extreme Tories were safe for ten years more. The hopes of the Canningites were indefinitely postponed.

This set-back to his friends need not have been a check to William's own career. His reputation was now so high that the Prince of Wales wrote himself in the most pressing way, to offer him a place in the Cabinet. But William felt he could not accept it. The failure of Canning had hit him particularly hard. For it meant that he felt himself condemned to a false position for ever. Since he disagreed with his own Party, but yet could not bring himself to leave it, all his hopes had been pinned on the chance of Coalition. Now that this proved impossible, there seemed no place for him in politics. A deep discouragement spread over his spirit; which swelled into a wider disillusionment with public life as a whole. Surveying his Parliamentary career in the clear sunless light of his present disappointment, he wondered if he was not essentially unsuited to the career of statesman. He could not speak as he wished in the House, he could not even think there. The ideas which stirred in him at home, found there no channel for expression. His profession had turned out as great a disappointment as his marriage:

"Sir Edward Coke says, somewhere or another," he noted in his journal, "that he is certain that God enlarges and enlightens the understanding of men when they are sitting in Courts of Justice. Such is the difference between a man who by his habits and feelings is formed for public affairs, and one who is unfitted for them. The former finds himself encouraged, invigorated, and strengthened by the consciousness that he is acting upon the spur of the occasion before the eyes of men, subject to their censure in his failure, but sure to reap their approbation by his success. All these circumstances oppress and overwhelm the latter, and deprive him of the use of those powers which perhaps he possesses in an eminent degree. By this (Sir E. Coke's saying) we must of course, understand that he found in that situation his own mental perceptions more quick and clear, and his judgment more settled and distinct, than upon other occasions. For myself, I must own the House of Commons has upon me quite a different effect. I can walk in the shrubbery here at Brocket Hall and reason and enlarge upon almost any topic; but in the House of Commons, whether it be from apprehension, or heat, or long waiting, or the tediousness of much of what I hear, a torpor of all my faculties almost always comes upon me, and I feel as if I had neither ideas nor opinions, even upon the subjects which interest me the most deeply."

And now more sordid cares arose to complete his discouragement with his profession. £2,000 a year was not much on which to keep up the position of a man of fashion and a member of Parliament; especially for the husband of Caroline. The young Lambs consistently overspent themselves. If there was a General Election—elections in those pre-Reform days cost anything up to £50,000—William did not see what he was going to do. He was resolved not to go to his parents for money. What with Lady Melbourne's parties, Lord Melbourne's card debts, and the joyous expenses of their children, the family income was nothing like as big as it had been. From every point of view, William's immediate political prospects looked black. When in July, 1812, the Government did declare for an election, William reluctantly decided not to stand. Lady Melbourne, deeply distressed at this set-back to her ambitions for him, besought him to reconsider his position, and offered him all the money he would want. But it was one of the occasions when she found herself up against a force in him that she could not move. In August, William was, for the first time for fourteen years, a man of leisure.

## CHAPTER VI

# BYRON

A S A MATTER of fact, if he had stayed in politics, he would have found it hard to give his mind to them. Since 1809 the disturbing elements in his married life had steadily intensified, till now in 1812 they had burst out in a storm that was deafening London. While William was hobnobbing with the Canningites, Caroline had also found new interests. Since the role of wife had proved an inadequate vehicle for her dreams, she turned to other fields. Her first activities were social; it might be pleasant to be the centre of an intellectual circle. She never had any difficulty in attracting people, when she wanted to. Within a short time she was the friend of most of those men of letters who were sufficiently presentable socially to have achieved the entrance to the best houses. Rogers, Monk Lewis, Tom Moore, any or all of them might be found of an afternoon in her sitting-room, reading aloud their works to her while she sketched their portraits. She also made some new female friends. These were of a less desirable kind. Partly in order to annoy her relations-in-law, partly from a desire to impress the world by her emancipation of mind, she struck up with two of the few women of position who had contrived to put themselves outside the lax limits of Whig convention, Lady Wellesley and Lady Oxford. Neither can have been very attractive in herself, to one brought up at Devonshire House. Lady Wellesley was a Frenchwoman of very shady reputation, who had borne her husband several children before she married him; Lady Oxford, a tarnished siren of uncertain age, who pursued a life of promiscuous amours on the fringes of society, in an atmosphere of tawdry eroticism and tawdrier culture. Reclining on a sofa, with ringlets disposed about her neck in seductive disarray, she would rhapsodize to her lovers on the beauties of Pindar and the hypocrisy of the world. Caroline laughed at her affectations: her aristocratic eye also noted that Lady Oxford was a trifle common. But there was something in Caroline that responded to her luscious sentimentalizings. It was undeniably agreeable to a person of sensibility to receive a letter beginning, "Let us, my sweetest friend, improve the passing hour and with its help turn to the contemplation of true wisdom. . . . We will defy the censorious"; or inviting her opinion as to whether learning Greek purified or inflamed the passions. "Caroline seems to have more faith in theory than in practice," remarked her caustic cousin Harriet, "to judge, at least, by those she consults on these nice points of morality."

Indeed, her new friends did not please her relations. William himself implored her not to risk her good name by mixing in such worthless company; Lady Bessborough was distressed; and Lady Melbourne perfectly furious. Whatever the failings of her own friends, they had always been delightful, interesting people, and duchesses as well.

"As you love singularity," she wrote to Caroline, "it may be some satisfaction to you to know you are the only woman who has any pretensions to character whoever courted Lady Wellesley's acquaintance, that I never saw anyone sup in her party. . . . A married woman should consider that by such laxity she not only compromises her own honour and character but also that of her husband—but you seek only to please yourself."

Nor, as Lady Melbourne had already discovered, was having supper with Lady Wellesley the worst of Caroline's indiscretions. Social success did not satisfy her ambitions. A heroine's life, as she conceived it, included drama as well as admiration; and drama to Caroline meant love affairs. In 1810 her name began to be mentioned in connection with Lady Holland's son by her first marriage, Sir Godfrey Webster. Personally he had even less to recommend him than Lady Oxford; a coarse, handsome young rake, whose chief boast it was that he never went to bed till nine in the morning, and whose sporting reputation was so dingy, that even the Whips Club—a very easy-going body—would have nothing to do with him. Caroline, however, chose to regard him as a fine example of dashing manliness, unpopular only on account of his admirable contempt for vulgar opinion. Looked at in such a light, he made an adequate, if not an ideal hero for her purposes.

She flung herself into a violent flirtation with him, which she took care to make as public as possible. They went everywhere together. Ward, calling one afternoon at Melbourne House to see William, was surprised to find himself taken up to Lady Caroline's room; where, pacing the floor in theatrical agitation, she poured forth the story of her unfortunate passion.

It was not surprising that she soon had Lady Bessborough and Lady Melbourne on her track again, this time reinforced by Lady Holland. As usual, when faced with disapproval, Caroline lost her nerve. She deluged Lady Holland with a flood of incoherent and unpunctuated letters, in which she alternately denied with scorn, and penitently admitted, that there was anything between her and Sir Godfrey. Lady Holland was not impressed. However, she told Caroline she was willing to believe that the whole thing was a pretence, worked up to attract attention. These were not at all the sort of grounds on which Caroline wished to be acquitted. Lady Holland's words, so she picturesquely expressed it, lay "like a weight on her stomach", and she performed the most prodigious feats of intellectual contortionism, in her efforts to prove that she was at the same time a blameless and adoring wife to William and the victim of an irresistible infatuation for Sir Godfrey.

Lady Holland remained sceptical; Caroline then lost her temper. "As to the gnats and mites that dare to peck at me," she fulminated, "let them look to themselves. If I choose, you shall see them lick the dust I tread on. Lady Holland, if this is the case, I shall be courted by you. . . . I remain more sincerely than you deserve, Caroline Lamb."

To Lady Melbourne she defended herself by saying that the whole thing was William's fault: his cynicism had destroyed her moral sense. This was the last excuse likely to mollify Lady Melbourne, already seething with indignation on William's behalf. They continued to wrangle till May, when Lady Melbourne got a letter from Caroline saying all was at an end. She had been sitting in her morning-room—so ran her story—with her child, "on the brink of perdition", when suddenly her dog, a present from Sir Godfrey, snapped at the baby and shortly afterwards fell down foaming at the mouth. It flashed upon her that as a judgment for her sins it had gone mad and was going to bite the baby. So dread-

HENRIETTA SPENCER Countess of Bessborough

LADY CAROLINE LAMB in page's costume

WILLIAM LAMB in middle-life

ful an idea brought her to her senses. Tearing from her arm a
bracelet made of Sir Godfrey's hair, she rushed to her writing
table and wrote off to William, confessing all and imploring forgiveness. Whether there was a word of truth in this sensational
piece of autobiography, it is impossible to say. Certainly, if there
was, it produced a less decisive effect than might have been anticipated. The flirtation lingered on until the end of the summer, and
then it was Sir Godfrey who called it off. Caroline seems to have
taken his defection with unexpected calm. Her mood had
changed: she was absorbed in social life, in reading, in the new
dance, the Waltz. Its pulsing lilt was exquisitely in tune with her
spirit: and during the early part of 1812 she might have been
found any morning along with the rest of the smart set of the
period, the gentlemen in swathed neckcloths, the ladies in their
filmy, high-waisted dresses, practising her steps in the painted
ballroom of Melbourne House, to the sprightly strains of *Ah du
lieber Augustin*. In the intoxication of these whirling delights, Sir
Godfrey and his virile charms were forgotten.

But her passage with him had left a mark on her life that no
amount of forgetfulness on her part could efface. Her reputation
was seriously damaged by her choice of a lover, and still more by
the way she had advertised her relationship with him. She had
overstepped, as Lady Melbourne for instance had never done, the
subtle line which separates what society condemned from what it
condoned. From this time she could no longer afford to take any
risk with her good name. More serious, she had widened the gulf
between herself and William. William does not seem to have been
jealous; he knew her well enough by this time to realize, like Lady
Holland, that the whole thing was most likely a pretence and would
soon pass. But even if her actual infidelity was fictitious, his sensitive spirit was deeply wounded to discover that she now had so
little regard for his feelings as to be willing to flaunt it publicly.
Once—it was at a ball on the evening of 11th July—his pent-up
emotions broke forth. Caroline would not go home: and as William was turning to leave alone, he reminded her that it was the
anniversary of their wedding-day, passionately recalled to her the
thousand vows of constancy she had then made—now to all
appearances utterly forgotten. For the moment Caroline was

D

unmoved; but driving home by herself in the grey light of the summer dawn, her naturally generous heart was overcome by an agonizing wave of self-reproach; lying sleepless on her bed, she resolved to reform. She was sincere—only she could not keep it up. Within a few days William watched her behaving as impossibly as ever. And though even now he could not help loving her, for the first time a strain of hard bitterness began to enter his disillusioned heart.

It was to grow stronger during the years that followed. The Webster episode was only the rehearsal of a far more distressing exhibition. In March, 1812, the first part of *Childe Harold* was published to the world. Its success was instantaneous and colossal. The sweep of its rhetoric, its full-blooded romantic pessimism, its glowing Turneresque landscapes, all torrents and ruins, and patches of picturesque foreign colour, alike hit the taste of the time. And so still more did the personality behind them; the figure of the author who, melancholy, detached and scornful, his heart turned to marble by a career of sin and sightseeing in every part of Europe, stood out in melodramatic silhouette against the sublimities of nature and the wreckage of empires. Besides, he was a lord, and, it was rumoured, as beautiful as an angel: such a lion had not appeared in London within living memory. His book became the fashion as no poem ever has before or since. Listening at the dinner table one heard the words "Childe Harold" coming from every mouth; in St. James's Street, where its author lived, the traffic was held up by the press of carriages bearing notes of invitation for him; before a month had passed, the doors of every modish house in the capital had been flung open to announce—"Lord Byron".

On an unprejudiced observer he must have made an unexpected impression. There limped into the room a self-conscious youth, with a handsome sulky head, fidgety movements, showy, ill-fitting clothes and a manner conspicuously lacking in the ease and naturalness usual in a man of his rank. Indeed, Byron at twenty-four was, in almost every respect, the opposite of the version of himself he sought to impose on the world. No one could have been less detached. By nature acutely sensitive to the opinion of others, his confidence had been early undermined by his lame leg, his bullying, drunken mother and the poverty-stricken and provincial circumstances of his childhood. A gnawing, resentful mistrust of all men, and more especially of all women, warred continuously in his breast with an obsessing desire to make an impression on anyone by any means. There was nothing he would not do to score a hit or avoid a humiliation. Nor was he at heart a romantic. Fundamentally, Byron had a robust eighteenth-century mocking kind of outlook. But the romantic attitude, by the scope it gave for individual self-glorification, gratified his egotism: and he could not resist adopting it. His sophistication was equally false; a mask assumed to hide a torturing shyness. He trembled every time he had to enter a drawing-room; his conversation was that of a clever undergraduate, all impish brilliance, and wilful moods, and naïve affectations: and if he failed to please, he flung off in a pet. So far from being the experienced and disillusioned Childe Harold, he was a raw, nerve-ridden boy of genius, whose divine fire gleamed fitfully forth through an undignified turmoil of suspicion and awkwardness, theatrical pose and crude vanity.

Such was the real Byron. But the hostesses of London saw him as Childe Harold. And none more than Caroline. As might have been expected, she caught the Byron fever in a particularly virulent form. "I must meet him—I am dying to meet him," she told Rogers. "He has a club foot and bites his nails," Rogers replied. "If he is as ugly as Æsop," she insisted, "I must see him." A few days later her wish was gratified at a ball. Caroline staged the meeting with her usual sense of the theatre. When Byron was led up to her to be introduced, she gazed for a moment intently into his face, and then silently turned on her heel. That night she wrote in her diary, "Bad, mad and dangerous to know". This was equivalent to saying she had determined to know him very well. They met again two days later during an afternoon call at Holland House. This time as he was presented, Byron, thoroughly piqued by her behaviour at their first interview, began straight away: "This offer was made to you the other day. May I ask why you declined it?" History does not record her reply; but before they parted he had promised to come and see her. The affair between them was launched on its tumultuous course.

The events of this celebrated serio-comedy, as Byron called it, have been told and re-told, analysed and argued about, in a hundred different books. Yet much about it remains obscure. For the chief evidence on the subject is that of Caroline and Byron themselves: and they were both such confirmed liars, both so bent at all costs on making out a good case for themselves, that it is impossible to trust a word that either says. Further, their behaviour was so abnormally capricious as to make it hard, even when the facts are unquestioned, to divine their import. In Caroline, contradictory moods and different dramatic poses succeeded one another with the eye-deceiving rapidity of a quick-change act. While Byron was blown from his course at every turn, now by weakness, now by vanity.

However, from the welter of conflicting statements and inconsistent actions, one fact emerges. Neither was, in any true sense, in love. Caroline of course thought she was—more than anyone had ever been in love before. And it is true that her emotions were violently agitated. But it was not Byron she cared for: it was his reputation, and still more the idea of herself in love with him. Beautiful, brilliant, seared with the flames of exotic passion, and the most lionized man in England, he was everything she had all her life been seeking. Here at last was a hero worthy of such a heroine. Firmly shutting her eyes to everything but her own visions, she made up her mind that she had found the love of her life. Byron was less self-deceived. He knew quite well he was not in love. Caroline was everything he liked least in women, stormy, clever, and unfashionably thin; "I am haunted by a skeleton," he once remarked. But he had not the strength to withstand her; and he never could refuse the chance of a conquest. Moreover, young as he was, and dazzled by the new and glittering world into which his fame had so suddenly flung him, the prospect of an amour with one of its reigning queens flattered him in a way he was unable to resist. Once entangled, he played his part with all the spirit he could muster. Society was presented with the extraordinary spectacle of a love drama, performed in the most flamboyant, romantic manner by two raging egotists, each of whom was in fact wholly absorbed in self.

They did not do it very well. Caroline over-acted her part, and

Byron could not keep his up. Under the glaring spotlight of the public attention, they postured about the stage, getting in each other's way, tripping each other up, turning on one another in childish abuse, pausing to explain to the audience how abominably the other was behaving. Indeed, it would have been an ignominious exhibition enough, but for the personalities of the performers. But both in their varying degrees were people of genius: and in the most ludicrous postures, the most farcical contretemps, they managed somehow to remain magnetic and picturesque. Byron's most flagrant disloyalties sparkle with infectious humour: Caroline's wildest insincerity throbs with an eloquence that brings tears to the eyes. It is this ironic contrast between the glamour of its characters and the unseemly absurdity of the situations in which they were involved, that gives their story its peculiar piquancy to an amateur of the human comedy.

Caroline took the initiative, at once striking the high romantic note on which she intended the relationship to be conducted. "That beautiful pale face will be my fate," she noted, some time during the first week or so of their acquaintance. And she proceeded with a magnificent gesture of generosity to offer Byron all her jewels to sell, if he were hard up. He replied by sending her a rose accompanied by a note, couched in the best Childe Harold strain of insolent allurement: "Your Ladyship, I am told," it ran, "likes all that is new and rare—for a moment." This was only following her lead; how far he had decided to go, in these early days, is uncertain. However, any lingering hesitations he may have felt were soon dispelled by Lady Bessborough. She, fearing a repetition of the Webster affair, tried to discourage Byron by telling him that Caroline's infatuation was only assumed to pique another admirer. This roused all Byron's latent competitiveness: he determined not to rest till he was the acknowledged master of Caroline's heart.

From this time the affair rushed onwards in a gathering crescendo. Byron spent the greater part of every day in Caroline's room at Melbourne House; during the rare moments they were apart they communicated by means of letters and verses. Whether they ever became lovers in the fullest sense of the term is one of the unsolved problems of the whole mysterious business. Rogers, who knew them both well, denied it: and his denial is made more probable by the fact that Caroline was of that cerebral temperament to which the pleasures of the imagination always mean more than the pleasures of the senses. On the other hand it is almost incredible that Byron should have been satisfied without this most practical proof of her subjugation. Whatever the truth may be, it is certain that some time in the summer they went through an odd mock marriage ceremony, exchanging rings and writing mutual vows in a book which they signed Byron and Caroline Byron.

Indeed, every stage of their passionate pilgrimage was marked by some theatrical gesture. Caroline was chiefly concerned to parade her tremendous conquest before the world. Throughout all the brilliant crowding activities of the London season, between the red festooned curtains of an opera box, amid the diadems and bare shoulders of a ball, driving round the park in the level evening sunshine, the lowering dark head and the ecstatic blonde one were conspicuous, side by side. They left every party together in Byron's carriage; if by chance only he was invited, Caroline would hang about outside among the link-boys to greet him with demonstrative ardour when he came out. She also created scandal by appearing at unexpected moments in his rooms, imperfectly disguised as a page, in a plumed hat, silver-laced jacket and tight scarlet pantaloons. He, for his part, ran through all the gamut of the Byronic attitudes: was by turns enigmatic, passionate, mocking and tragic. Sitting in her room, he would declaim with melodramatic desolation on the unparalleled iniquity of his own character; compared with him, he cried, William Lamb was as Hyperion to a satyr. On other occasions, with eyes lurid with jealousy, he would require Caroline to swear that she loved him better than William. And when she hesitated, "My God, you shall pay for this," he thundered. "I'll wring that little obstinate heart." He even made her give up waltzing on the ground that he could not bear to see her in the arms of another man. Caroline was jealous, too, and showed it in an even more spectacular fashion. Little Lord John Russell, at dinner at Spencer House, was startled to notice that Lady Caroline Lamb, seized by a fit of uncontrollable agitation, had bitten through the glass that she

held in her hand; following her gaze across the table, he saw Lord
Byron bending attentively over a beautiful woman next him.

Certainly the course of their love was the reverse of smooth.
Rogers used often to arrive home in the afternoon to find the pair
pacing his garden: they had quarrelled all day and wanted him to
reconcile them. To Caroline, suffering had its compensations:
existence was for the first time as exciting as she had always desired
it. But Byron felt differently. At heart he liked life to move
calmly and sensibly. It was only his desire to conquer Caroline
that had made him play up to her heroics. Once his victory was
won, he grew bored. Besides, he had an uncomfortable feeling
that all this sensational exhibitionism made him look ridiculous.
He grew more and more restive; by July he was longing to be quit
of the whole affair.

Now, a new and powerful influence arose to encourage his longing. Byron had not taken to Lady Melbourne when he first met
her. He only liked those who liked him: and Caroline's mother-in-
law, he suspected, must be his enemy. As a matter of fact, Lady
Melbourne was not ill-disposed towards Byron. Caroline's
troubles, she had long ago made up her mind, were always Caroline's fault. On this occasion she had simply flung herself unasked at a young man's head. And, according to Lady Melbourne's
code, a young man was perfectly justified in making love to a
married woman if she showed herself willing. In himself, Byron
struck Lady Melbourne as extremely agreeable; she therefore
made herself as pleasant to him as she could. Her success was
immediate. Mistress as she was of the art of pleasing men, she
made him feel more at ease than he had since his entry into London society. Moreover, he had a great deal in common with her—
much more than with Caroline. Her worldly wisdom, her caustic
agreeability and her equable temper, alike appealed to him; so for
the matter of that did her cynicism and her lack of refinement.
The Melbourne atmosphere was far more to Byron's taste than the
Devonshire. After the delicacies and exaltations of an interview
with Caroline, what a relief it was, what an indescribable relief, to
turn into Lady Melbourne's rooms on the ground floor; where
one could be as outspoken and flippant and disloyal as one liked,
with no risk of being thought unkind or ungentlemanly. Besides,

Lady Melbourne was so helpful: on her sofa she would sit, advising one in the most terse and entertaining way about how to manage a woman or how to save one's income. "The best friend I ever had in my life," he was to write later, "and the cleverest of women. If she had been a few years younger, what a fool she would have made of me had she thought it worth her while."

Lady Melbourne enjoyed his company as much as he did hers. At sixty-two it was gratifying indeed to be the favourite companion of the most sought-after young man in London—especially when it involved stealing him from Caroline. Nor had she so far outgrown her youth, as to be insensible to his attractions. It would be misleading to say that she was in love with him. Her friendship with Byron was at most an agreeable diversion from the serious business of her ambition. But she felt sufficiently warm towards him to acquire a strong bias in his favour. No doubt he was selfish and fickle—most men were in her experience. But he was sensible enough at bottom, as far as she could see. Discreetly managed, he should give no trouble.

Here she was wrong. The wild fire of genius that burned unsteadily in Byron's bosom made him at once more formidable and more unstable than she realized. But she can hardly be blamed for her mistake. Possessed as he was by the wish to make a good impression, Byron was incapable of showing himself with complete honesty to anyone. And he had achieved an extraordinary dexterity at guessing the version of his character best calculated to win over the person he happened to be talking to. The Childe Harold pose he saw would be no good with Lady Melbourne; if she believed in it, she would not like it. Laughingly, therefore, and with an artful frankness, he represented himself as a straightforward, sensual male, weak, a trifle mischievous, and with no high-flown ideals about him, but essentially good-natured; the victim, not the master of others; anxious only for a quiet life and a little fun. It was not quite the truth. But it was close enough to it to be irresistibly convincing. Lady Melbourne was convinced. However, she did not lose her head. Her demeanour towards Byron was a masterpiece in the delicate art of friendship between older woman and younger man; easy, intimate and with a pleasant touch of flirtation about it, but never so ardent or so familiar as to be unsuitable to her age and position. She received his declarations of admiration with a teasing, flattering irony exactly calculated to keep the relationship between them at that comfortable temperature which would make it firm.

"You say 'I admire you certainly as much as ever you were admired,' " she says on one occasion, "and a great deal more I assure you than ever I was. I have been beloved—but Love is not admiration. Lovers admire, of course, without knowing why. Yours therefore is much more flattering as I sd. the other day—but you quite astonished me when I found your usual playfulness chang'd into such a formal tirade. I have hardly yet recover'd my surprise—now I have told you everything & have shown myself truly to you; I can not see why you should wish that you had not known me. It can not lead to any regret and if circumstances should not stop it entirely our Friendship will be very pleasant to both as any sentiment must be where all is sunshine—and where love does not introduce itself, there can be no jealousys, torments & quarrels. . . . Once you told me you did not understand Friendship. I told you I would teach it you, & so I will, if you do not allow C. to take you quite away."

In reality it was she who was taking him away from C. She made use of the friendship to engineer a break. Far too intelligent to take a solemn line about the matter, she constituted herself Byron's confidante; listened sympathetically to his complaints of Caroline's tantrums, laughed heartily when he made fun of them; and was herself in return very amusing about Caroline. "Really she seems inclined to behave better," she writes once, "and is only troublesome in private and a great bore in public. This I know you never *could* believe. But I hope some day to see you undergo a dinner when she is trying to show off." Subtly she tried to discredit Caroline in his eyes; sensibly she pointed out how awkward the connection was likely to prove in the future. Would it not be better—and kinder too—to make an end of it at once?

Lady Melbourne was not alone in her efforts. Lady Bessborough, beside herself with worry, was even more active. But her very amiability made her less effective. Refined and tender-hearted, her only policy in such cases was to appeal to people's better feelings. From Caroline to Byron, from Byron to Byron's friends she hurried, protesting with tears that she knew what a sacrifice she was asking; but that she was sure they would see it was the right thing to do. Further, she could not bear that Caroline should be wounded more than necessary. Let her if possible make the first move: and let them part in no sordid squabble, but with the dignity and considerateness befitting the end of a great love. Such an attitude showed a complete failure to grasp the unbridled irresponsibility of the two people with whom she was dealing. Far rougher measures were needed to make any impression on Caroline; while Byron merely thought Lady Bessborough, or Lady Blarney, as he called her, a foolish sentimentalist. "I am sure Lady B.," he told Lady Melbourne, "will be a little provoked, if I am the first to change, for, like the Governor of Tilbury Fort, although the Countess is resolved, the mother *intenerisce un poco*, and doubtless will expect her daughter to be adored (like an Irish lease) for a term of 99 years."

Behind the two mothers-in-law clamoured a host of secondary advisers. Caroline's conduct had created so resounding a scandal that everyone remotely connected with her—from her brother down to her mother's maid—considered they had a right to interfere. Even Lord Melbourne was roused. As usual a little muddled, he got hold of the idea that Lady Bessborough as well as Caroline was in love with Byron. "They make a fool of me by forcing me to ask him to my house," he lamented to the Prince Regent. Lady Bessborough, informed of the remark, forgot her worries for a moment in a fit of uncontrollable laughter.

Amid all this hullabaloo, one person remained quiet, William. Alone among those closely concerned, he realized the essential unreality of the situation. It was long since he had believed in Caroline's grand passions; and his sharp eye soon perceived that Byron's was no more sincere. The famous Byronic charm had not worked on him. He admitted Byron was handsome and amusing. But he thought his expression unpleasant and his agreeability an uncertain quantity: while himself genuinely well-bred, genuinely detached, genuinely disillusioned, he was not taken in by Byron's pretence of these qualities. As for his Childe Harold airs, William thought them ludicrous affectations: he enjoyed making fun of them to the infuriated Caroline. But he was sure that two such poseurs would never do anything that would seriously endanger their popularity with their public. The idea that they might elope —which haunted Lady Bessborough—did not worry him for a moment. "They neither wish nor intend going," he said, "but both like the fear and interest they create." It was only a repetition of the Webster affair. In indolent, mocking silence, William waited for it to end as quickly.

However, even without his assistance, the family pressure soon grew so strong as to plunge the hero and heroine of the drama into a tumult of perturbation. Byron felt torn in two. By now he cursed the day he ever met Caroline: but he could not face the idea of a clean break. It meant surrendering a conquest, and it would involve a painful scene. Besides, he did not like being unkind if he could help it. All he could bring himself to do was to try and cool her down by urging self-control. Nothing could have been more futile. Caroline was even more divided against herself than he was. Every breath of disapproval stung her like the lash of a whip; on the other hand she was prepared to suffer anything, rather than lose Byron. Under the strain of her mingled feelings, her words took on the wild intensity of tragic poetry. "You think me weak and selfish, you think I did not struggle to withstand my feelings. But it is indeed expecting more than human nature can bear. When I came in last night—when I heard your name announced—the moment after I heard nothing more. . . . How very pale you are, a statue of white marble, and the dark hair and brow, such a contrast. I could never see you without wishing to cry."

At home she acted as though frantic. Lady Melbourne, summoned upstairs by the sound of Caroline's cries, would find her prone on the floor in hysterical sobs. The climax was reached on the morning of 13th August. Lady Bessborough, calling at Melbourne House, found Lord Melbourne deathly pale, screaming to the servants to stop Caroline. She had, it appeared, in a fit of temper, told him she intended to go to Byron. "Go and be damned," he had retorted, "but I don't think he'll take you." Before he had finished speaking, she had rushed, hatless and without a penny, into the street. Poor Lady Bessborough, almost out of her mind, drove all day up and down London searching for Caroline—in vain. It was not till late that night that Caroline was brought home by Byron, who had found her in a surgeon's house at Kensington; preparing, on the proceeds of a ring she had pawned, immediately to set sail she did not know where, on the first ship she could find.

Clearly such an episode must not be repeated. After a hasty consultation between the two families, it was decided that her family should take her and William on a round of visits to Ireland. Alas, it was easier said than done. Caroline, now to all appearance abjectly repentant, professed complete submission. But when it actually came to making a move, at once she began to raise difficulties. She was too ill, her mother was too ill, wouldn't it do as well if she just went to Brocket? And though promising again and again not to communicate with Byron, she met him secretly, and wrote to him three times a day. He, for his part, while assuring Lady Melbourne that he never wished to see Caroline again, lingered on in London; and answered her letters with protestations of constancy, in which he explained that any apparent coldness was only assumed, to quiet the suspicions of her relations. Lady Bessborough, now almost desperate, demanded that William should act. But William provokingly still refused to take the affair seriously. At heart he did not want to. Much suffering at Caroline's hands had forced him to grow a shell of smiling indifference, which he shrank from breaking. Besides, though he saw through her completely, she still had the power to get round him. After a little cajoling, she had him laughing and reading her mother's letters aloud to her.

There was also a more serious reason for his inertia. Caroline's conduct had not been the only sorrow of his married life. His child, Augustus, within two or three years of his birth, had begun to show unmistakable signs of mental deficiency. Since then Caroline had twice had a miscarriage. To William, so dependent on family affection and so tragically disappointed of it in his wife, all this came as a great blow. Now Caroline—whether seriously or as an excuse to stay in England, it would be uncharitable for posterity to decide—told him that she was once more with child. Rather than risk an accident to the unborn baby, William was prepared to yield to her everything she asked. It seemed as if they would never get away. However, at last Byron announced that he was leaving for Cheltenham. Caroline's motive for staying was removed: her interesting condition mysteriously disappeared: by the end of August the whole party was safely across the Irish Channel.

They were far from the end of their troubles though. Caroline was the most trying holiday companion that can be imagined. The wear and tear of the last few months had intensified her nervous instability as never before; her moods now changed, not every day but every hour. Sometimes she seemed completely her old enchanting self.

"Hart and C.," writes Lady Bessborough from Lismore Castle, where they were staying with her cousin Hartington, "had many disputes on the damp, when last night she suddenly opened the door very wide, saying, 'pray walk in, Sir. I have no doubt that you are the rightful possessor, and my cousin only an interloper, usurping your usual habitation.' For a long time nothing came, when at last with great solemnity and many poses, in hopped a *frog*, Caroline following with two candles to treat the master of the castle with proper respect, she said."

Elsewhere she was the breath and soul of the social life of the neighbourhood, flirting outrageously with the local men and foot-ing it in the Irish jig with untiring spirit. But the very same even-ing the household might be kept up ministering to her, as she screamed and swooned and lay drumming with her heels on the floor. At one moment she would lament her torturing incurable love for Byron; the next, with equal vehemence, she asserted that it was William alone who had always possessed her heart; and she delighted to caress him in front of other people. The whole countryside talked of how fond Lady Caroline seemed of her hus-band. "When they say this to me," remarked the exasperated Lady Bessborough, "I want to bellow."

The unfortunate William might well have bellowed too. For on him fell the brunt of Caroline's hysteria. If she could not sleep, she woke him up; when he suggested going alone to Dublin for a few days, she fell into transports of agitation, swearing that, if he did, she would never see him again. However, he rose to the occasion. In the sustained intimacy of country life he began to realize how serious her condition was. And, with this realization, the unselfish tenderness of his nature came to the surface. He devoted himself to her with a patience and sympathy that brought tears to Lady Bessborough's eyes; gave up going to Dublin without a word of protest; sat up till daybreak three nights running, holding her head in order to soothe her. On one occasion only is he recorded to have betrayed the strain he was feeling. During one of Caroline's nocturnal paroxysms, a deafening thunder-storm burst out. "The storm outside," said William to her with a rueful humour, "is hardly more than that inside."

Meanwhile Byron, on the other side of the sea, was showing himself equally unstable. He had bidden farewell to Caroline with words of undying fidelity. "All will be done to make you change," he said, "but it is only you I am afraid for; for myself there is no fear." And for the first few weeks after she had left he wrote to her lovingly. But by the same post he also sent letters to Lady Melbourne saying that all was finally over between them, and talking airily of other flirtations. Lady Melbourne, always anxious to make trouble between them, duly reported his words to Caroline. Immediately torrents of accusation, lamentings, and abuse began to pour over from Ireland on his head. From force of habit he denied Lady Melbourne's reports. But as a matter of fact he was glad enough of an occasion for quarrel. Caroline's absence had made him realize how delightfully quiet life could be without her. By the end of August he had made up his mind he must be free of her before she came back.

His best method seemed to be to involve himself with another woman. Accordingly, prompted partly by Lady Melbourne, he sent a proposal of marriage to her niece, Miss Annabella Milbanke. Miss Milbanke refused him: with a certain relief, Byron turned to less responsible forms of love. And by the middle of October he was up to the neck in an affair with Caroline's old friend, Lady

Oxford. It seems odd that he should have left one professional romantic for another. But Lady Oxford's romanticism was very different from Caroline's, a fashionable pose that had no connection with the cool and easy-going sensuality which in fact directed her conduct. "A broken heart is nothing but a bad digestion," she told Byron; and in her company he could relax to enjoy the pleasures of the body, safe from fear of subsequent scenes and heart-burnings. Only Lady Oxford exacted one condition in return for her favours. Relations with Caroline must be broken off finally, and at once.

Byron did not hesitate. Apart from his own irritation with Caroline, the same weakness that had kept him so long tied to her, now made him wax in Lady Oxford's hands. But, like all weak people when driven at last to take a strong line, he lost his head and acted far too violently. In a tremble of fear lest he should lose his new-found tranquillity, and determined by one blow to save himself from any further trouble with Caroline, he wrote off to her, without any preliminary warning, the most unforgivable letter he could concoct. "As to yourself, Lady Caroline," it ended, "correct your vanity which has become ridiculous—exert your caprices on others, enjoy the excellent flow of spirits which make you so delightful in the eyes of others, and leave me in peace." Caroline, receiving this incredible document at the Dolphin Hotel, Dublin, whence she was preparing to set sail for England, took to her bed for a fortnight in a state of nervous convulsions.

It was the end, as far as any hope for her was concerned. Byron, once free, was never going to allow himself to fall into her clutches again. But it was not in Caroline to face an unpleasant fact. And for the next six months she fought a desperate rearguard action, if not to win him back, at any rate to remain a leading figure in his life. Indeed, even less than usual was she in a condition to listen to reason. Byron's letter had thrown her already tottering mind, for the time being, completely off its balance. Ghastly pale, bone-thin and with eyes starting from her head, she looked insane; and throughout the winter, derangement also betrayed itself in a series of actions, fantastic, ludicrous and distressing. She offered herself to young men on condition that they challenged Byron to a duel;

she forged a letter from Byron to a picture-dealer in order to get possession of his portrait; she put her men servants into a new livery, on the buttons of which were engraved "Ne crede Byron" —Do not believe Byron. But her most singular performance was a bonfire at Brocket, on which Byron's presents to her were solemnly burnt; whilst some village girls dressed in white capered round the flames in a ritual dance of triumph, and a page recited verses composed by Caroline for the occasion.

> "Ah look not thus on me," so they adjured her audience,
>     "So grave and sad.
> Shake not your heads nor say the lady's mad."

They did say so, nevertheless.

Meanwhile she continued to bombard Byron with menaces of vengeance—"Very like the style of Lucy in the Beggar's Opera," said Byron, "and by no means having the merit of novelty in my ears"—incoherently interspersed with agonized pleadings for some sign of relenting; a letter, a bracelet of his hair, above all an interview.

Some time in the spring the interview did take place. According to Caroline it was very affecting; Byron, bathed in tears, implored her forgiveness. But it is difficult to believe this in the light of the letters he wrote about her to others. For the time being at any rate he positively hated her. Exasperation at her persecution of him had called up all that ultimate antagonism to women which childish misfortunate had implanted at the root of his character. On Caroline he visited all the sins of her worthless and predatory sex. He replied to her appeals with studied cruelty, and answered her request for a bracelet, first by sending one made of Lady Oxford's hair, which happened to be the same colour as his own; and then by relating the deception as an excellent joke to all his friends, including Lady Melbourne. What made him particularly angry was that the noise created by the affair was doing him harm socially. Caroline abused him as loudly as he abused her: some people believed her; as the year advanced, Byron, always sensitive to public opinion, began to notice a party was forming against him.

"With regard to the miseries of 'this correct and animated waltzer', as *The Morning Post* entitles her," he complained to Lady Melbourne, "I wish she would not call in the aid of so many compassionate countesses. There is Lady W. (with a tongue, too) conceives me to be the greatest barbarian since the days of Bacchus; and all who hate Lady Oxford—consisting of one half of the world, and all who abominate me—that is the other half—will tear the last rag of my tattered reputation into shreds, filaments and atoms."

Scandal had yet to reach its climax. On 5th July, Byron and Caroline met at a ball given by Lady Heathcote. It was the first time they had been together in society, since the previous summer: and Caroline arrived, determined to make one last effort to rekindle Byron's flame. She went straight up to him; and in order to pique his jealousy, said, "I presume *now* I am allowed to waltz." He replied, with contempt, that she could do as she liked, as far as he was concerned. And a few dances later, brushing past her in a doorway, "I have been admiring your dexterity," he whispered sarcastically. Wild with rage, and resolved in revenge to bring him to public shame at whatever cost to herself, she rushed into the supper-room; and, breaking a glass, began to gash her naked arms with the pieces. Immediately the place was in a tumult; women screamed; only Lady Melbourne, with her usual presence of mind, seized Caroline's hands and held her down. A few minutes later, still jabbing at herself with a pair of scissors, she was carried from the room.[1] Lady Melbourne reserved her comments for Byron's ears.

"She is now like a Barrel of Gunpowder and takes fire with the most trifling spark. She has been in a dreadfull—I was interrupted & obliged to put my paper into my drawer, & now I cannot for my life recollect what I was going to say—oh now

[1] There are several accounts of this celebrated episode—by Byron, by Caroline, by Lady Melbourne and by various social gossips of the period —agreeing in the main but differing in detail. When in doubt I follow Lady Melbourne. She had more chance of knowing the truth than the gossips and less motive than Byron or Caroline for misrepresenting it.

I have it!—I was stating tht. she had been in a dreadful bad humour this last week. With her, when the fermentation begins there is no stopping it till it burst forth. . . . I must do Ly. Bessborough the justice to say that her representation of her violence in these paroxysms was not at all exaggerated. I could not have believed it possible for any one to carry absurdity to such a pitch. I call it so, for I am convinced she knows perfectly what she is about all the time, but she has no idea of controlling her fury."

Byron was quick to reply to this communication in a similarly scornful strain. But secretly he could not help feeling gratified at having been the occasion of so memorable a scene. After his death, carefully preserved among his papers, was found a faded invitation card to the party. "This card I keep as a curiosity," he had scribbled on it, "for it was at this ball that Lady C.L. performed ye dagger scene—of indifferent memory."

Next day London was ringing with the incident. A scandal was just what was needed to revive the excitement of a dying season; and such a scandal! Everywhere the story was told and re-told, each time with some new dramatic detail added; letters of condolence poured in on the outraged Lamb family; a scurrilous paper, *The Satirist*, published a leading article on the subject. The uproar grew so violent that it became impossible for Caroline to remain in London. She was packed off to spend the rest of the summer at Brocket.

It was a turning point in her life. Up till now, though she had shocked public opinion, she had always managed not to put herself outside the pale of society. The cousin of the Duke of Devonshire, the wife of William Lamb, was allowed to get away with a great deal that would have ruined a less glorious personage. Caroline's paroxysms of actual violence, too, had always been kept relatively private. But now she had given way to one in public; she had also published her infidelity to her husband in a way that not even Lady Oxford had ever done. And though the influence of her friends still kept her from being made an open outcast, for the rest of her life she was a marked woman.

She felt it with all the force of her nature. "I see the sharp cen-

sures ready to start into words in every cold, formal face I meet,"
she cried. And people noted that for the first time she showed
genuine signs of shame. It was not only that she was tormented
by the consciousness of other people's disapproval; a death-blow
had been struck at the security of that palace of illusions in which
alone she could happily live. At last she had managed to involve
herself in a scene as spectacular as any in poetry or romance. And
what had been the effect on the world? Not admiration, not even
sympathy; but harsh disapprobation and derisive contempt. Such
a catastrophe made its impression. No longer could she persuade
herself that the world thought her the heroine she wished to be.
A subtle change began to penetrate her outlook. That supreme
self-confidence, which had enabled her to survive so many set-
backs, for the first time began to give way.

It was left to William to administer such comfort as could be
found. Poor William! One wonders what his thoughts were. But
history tantalizingly is silent; and perhaps he never gave them
utterance. Throughout the long ordeal of the preceding winter he
had maintained to the outward world his shell of apparent indifference. "William Lamb laughs, and eats like a trooper," said
an observer who saw him on their return from Ireland. And during the events that followed, during all Caroline's bonfires and
forgeries, he continued, as far as we can gather, to eat and laugh.
Caroline professed herself very much hurt, that he, in particular,
should not have fought a duel on her behalf; she said that it
would have brought her back to him. And it is possible that some
such picturesque gesture might for a moment have revived her
romantic interest. But it was not in William to make gestures.
And besides, he did not think they would do any good. By now
he had few illusions left about her; certainly he thought it was no
use trying to control her vagaries. All the same, he would not cut
himself completely free from her. His family wanted him to.
Furious at the disgrace which "the little beast" had brought upon
them, from this time on they were always pressing him to get a
separation. But he refused. It came partly from the same apathy
that stopped him trying to influence her actions: it came also from
pity. Ever since Ireland, he had felt so sorry for her that he could
not help being lenient. After all, he tried to persuade himself, she

should not be blamed too much; the trouble was chiefly Byron's fault.

William's pent-up feelings showed themselves in a bitter, steadily growing hatred of Byron. That he should have seduced Caroline was bad enough; but that he should turn against her afterwards was even more shocking to his honourable spirit. When he heard that Byron was threatening to cut her publicly, all William's own injuries at her hands were forgotten in a sudden flare of indignation. Byron thought this very inconsistent of him. But it was Byron's misfortune not to appreciate the workings of a generous nature. Nor would he have understood why William resented his relationship to Lady Melbourne. To William it was acutely painful that his own mother should have so little sense of his feelings as to conspire against his wife with that wife's lover. Only here again affection made him put the chief responsibility on Byron. With the sharp eye of hatred, he penetrated, as Lady Melbourne had failed to do, the essential duplicity of Byron's character. "He was treacherous beyond conception," he said in later years. "I believe he was fond of treachery. He dazzled everybody and deceived them: for he could tell his own story very well." To desert the victim of such a ruffian, at the moment when she was desolate, was against William's most sacred instincts. If he could not leave the Whig Party when its fortunes were at a low ebb, how much less could he leave his own wife. For the next two years he hardly quitted her side.

People noticed that grey streaks were appearing in his black curls. No wonder; it must have been a dreadful strain. Caroline, though at first a little subdued by misfortune, was no more rational than before; her moods still varied between wild gaiety, fits of rage and bursts of tears. Miss Webb, a companion who had been engaged to help look after her, recommended that she should play the harp, which she considered a sovereign remedy for mental disorders. Whether she was right must remain doubtful. For Caroline would not look at the harp. She preferred the organ, on which she would play all night, till she was frozen with cold. She also kept the house awake, by stalking the passages like a ghost, till the early hours of the morning. In the daytime she often refused to eat. William bore it all as best he could. Sometimes his temper broke out. "It is too bad of you," he would cry out. "If you fret so, I will send you to live with your grandmother." The graceful rooms which had provided so harmonious a setting for the careless sunshine of their honeymoon hours, now re-sounded all too often with Caroline's wails, with William's oaths and exasperated laughter. And from his relations at any rate he no longer tried to hide what he thought of Caroline's character. "When Mr. C. spoke to Caroline about the road," we find him writing to his mother, "she was too happy in the opportunity of at once abusing them, and making an excuse for herself."

But on the whole he was extraordinarily patient and sym-pathetic. He made the most of her rare moments of good humour; if her depression became intense, he could be absolutely depended upon to give support and comfort. And for the rest he took advan-tage of his leisure to meditate and study.

Now and again they made a brief excursion into the great world. We catch a sight of them during the summer of 1814 at a masquerade ball given in honour of the victory over Napoleon, at Wattier's Club; William handsome, but a little self-conscious, in a costume of conspicuous splendour; Caroline prancing about in green pantaloons—"masked," said Byron, a sardonic observer of the couple, "but always trying to indicate who she was to every-body." The following year they were abroad for several months. Caroline's brother, Frederick, had been wounded at Waterloo; so she hurried out to Brussels, her fancy fired by the picture of her-self as ministering angel at the bedside of a hero. In practice, however, she found it boring; and preferred to promenade the streets of Brussels; where she shocked Miss Burney, by appearing with arms, shoulders and back bare, but for a floating scarf of gauze.

We next hear of the Lambs in Paris, during its triumphant occupation by the allies.

"Nobody is agissant but Caroline William in a purple riding habit, tormenting everybody," writes her cousin Harriet, now wife of the English Ambassador, Lord Granville, "but, I am convinced, ready primed for an attack on the Duke of Wellington; and I have no doubt but that she will to a certain extent succeed, as no dose of flattery is too strong for him to swallow or her to administer. Poor William hides in a small room, while she assembles lovers and tradespeople in another. He looks worn to the bone."

Lady Granville was right in her prophecies. Caroline was still sufficiently her old self to be stirred to instant pursuit of the acknowledged hero of Europe: the Duke was at once gratified by her adulation and amused by her oddness. The next glimpse we get of her, she is giving occasional "screams of delight" as she dines alone with him and Sir Walter Scott.

Indeed the whole world seemed to be in Paris. Every night the Lambs were out meeting distinguished personages, Talleyrand, Metternich, Lord Castlereagh, Kings, and Queens. William enjoyed it all. It appealed to his interest both in historic events and public characters. He sought to improve his appearance by having his grey hairs pulled out: and never went to bed before four in the morning. Caroline, too, was in a good humour with him. "Whom do you imagine I consider the most distinguished man I ever met?" she suddenly asked a neighbour at dinner. "Lord Byron," he replied tentatively. "No, my own husband, William Lamb," said Caroline.

Her good humour, however, was not to be depended upon. A Mr. and Mrs. Kemble met the Lambs at dinner one night with Lord Holland,

". . . when accidentally the expected arrival of Lord Byron was mentioned," writes their daughter. "Mr. Lamb had just named the next day as the one fixed for their departure, but Lady Caroline immediately announced her intention of prolonging her stay, which created what would be called in French chambers 'sensation'. When the party broke up, my father and mother, who occupied apartments in the same hotel as the Lambs—Meurice's—were driven into the courtyard, just as Lady Caroline's carriage had drawn up before the staircase leading to her rooms. . . . A *ruisseau*, or gutter, ran round the courtyard, and intervened between the carriage step and the door of the vestibule, and Mr. Lamb, taking Lady Caroline, as she alighted in his arms (she had a very pretty, slight, graceful figure) gallantly lifted her over the wet stones. . . . My mother's sitting-room faced that of Lady Caroline and before lights were brought into it she and my father had the full benefit of a curious scene in the room of their opposite neighbours. Mr. Lamb, on entering the room, sat down on the sofa, and his wife perched herself on the end of it, with her arm round his neck, which engaging attitude she presently exchanged for a still more persuasive air, by kneeling at his feet, but upon his getting up, the lively lady did so also, and in a moment began flying round the room, seizing and flinging on the floor, cups, saucers, plates—the whole cabaret, vases, candlesticks, etc., her poor husband pursuing and attempting to restrain his mad moiety, in the midst of which extraordinary scene the curtains were abruptly closed, and the domestic drama finished behind them, leaving no doubt, however, in my father and mother's minds, that the question of Lady Caroline's prolonged stay till Lord Byron's arrival in Paris had caused the disturbance they had witnessed."

Indeed, for all she might say, she had never brought herself to give up hope of getting Byron back. At times the scales did fall from her eyes. Byron, she told a friend, would have stuck to her, if she had been celebrated enough as a beauty to be a credit to him. But such moments of insight into his true nature were fleeting; she could not for long give up her intoxicating dream. He was still deluged at intervals with spates of letters from her: during her visit to London in the summer of 1814, she once more took to haunting his rooms. On one occasion she created a great deal of embarrassment by suddenly bursting in dressed up as a carman, at a moment when he was intimately entertaining another lady. On another he came home to find the words "Remember me" scrawled in Caroline's hand on a book that lay on the writing table.

> "Remember thee," he wrote, "remember thee!
> Till Lethe quench life's burning streams
> Remorse and shame shall cling to thee
> And haunt thee like a feverish dream.

Remember thee! Ay, doubt it not,
  Thy husband too shall think of thee,
By neither shalt thou be forgot,
  Thou false to him, thou fiend to me!"

To Lady Melbourne he lamented in a less stormy strain, but
with equal irritation. "You talk to me about keeping her out. It
is impossible, she comes in at all times, at any time; the moment
the door is open, in she walks. I cannot throw her out of the
window."

He felt very much inclined to. When she was badgering him,
he hated her as much as ever. But he was inconstant in hate as in
love. If Caroline was quiet for a month or two, dislike of losing
his power over her would combine with a genuine impulse of
affection, to produce a fitful revulsion in his feelings. He
wrote to her kindly; he even felt a curious desire to see her
again.

In such circumstances they continued to meet on and off, for at
least eight months more. In the spring of 1814 they had a scene of
farewell at his rooms; when, so Caroline says, Byron confided to
her such dreadful revelations about himself, that she vowed never
to see him again. But, in view of her previous history, it is extremely unlikely she would have kept this vow, had not Byron a
few months later got engaged to Miss Milbanke. Certainly he
was in a fever lest the announcement of the engagement should
provoke one of Caroline's old explosions. However, for a wonder
she kept fairly quiet, contenting herself with telling other people
that "Byron would never pull together with a woman who went
to church punctually, understood statistics, and had a bad
figure".

She was quite right, it needed less than a year to prove it. The
crash, when it came, gave Caroline a last chance to display to her
lover the bewildering contradictions of her nature. There is reason
for thinking that it was she who spread abroad those reports of
Byron's intrigue with his sister, which made any reconciliation
with his wife finally impossible. On the other hand, to Byron
himself Caroline wrote urging moderation and magnanimity; and
even offered to tell Lady Byron that any stories she was told

against Byron had been invented by herself—Caroline—out of jealousy. Was this offer just a final theatrical gesture: or did she, confronted for once by a real tragedy, rise above her egotism to that level of heroic self-sacrifice to which she professed to aspire? Either is possible. As it was the last communication she ever held with Byron, we may be allowed to give her the benefit of the doubt.

## CHAPTER VII

# FRUSTRATION

ALAS, THERE was no doubt about her behaviour to the rest of the world. In spite of William and Miss Webb, Caroline's condition of mind during the last two years had progressively deteriorated. The disaster at Lady Heathcote's ball had finally undermined her belief in her illusions; she had realized her failure there, too keenly for her to be able ever again to play the role of heroine with her old confidence in its success. Yet her vanity was too fundamental for her to be able to profit by the stern lessons of experience. She could not face the fact that she was wrong; so she was unable to reform herself. Instead, bewildered, terrified and resentful, she rushed blindly about, seeking, she hardly knew how, to put her shattered day-dreams together again. At times, as we have seen, she made futile efforts to behave with her former self-assurance; chased after the Duke of Wellington, paraded the streets of Brussels half naked. But for the most part, she stayed at home, where, surrounded by a swarm of page-boys whom she alternately spoiled and bullied, she tried to forget her gnawing sense of shame by indulging every whim of fancy, yielding to every gust of distraught temper. Her eccentricities grew more and more marked, her tantrums wilder than ever before. It became growingly impossible to live with her. The breaking-point was reached in April, 1816, when, provoked by some trifling act of mischief on the part of one of her pages, she flung a ball so hard at his head that it drew blood. "Oh, my Lady, you've killed me!" he cried out. "Oh, God!" she yelled, tearing out into the hall, "I have murdered the page."

As a matter of fact he was hardly hurt. But there was no telling, the Lambs felt, what might happen next time. Caroline was certainly a lunatic, and probably a dangerous one. They made up their minds that it was impossible for William to live with her any longer. In a body they went to William and once more demanded a separation. This time he did not refuse.

Formal separations, however, entail lengthy preliminaries. For three weeks Melbourne House was made hideous by a succession of appalling scenes, in which the Lambs told Caroline, with brutal frankness, that she was mad, and she in return now stormed, now pleaded. Neither was of any avail: the arrangements went inexorably on. Beside herself with fury and despair, Caroline resolved on revenge. Before she was cast out of the house, she would at least publish her story to the world in such a way as to justify herself and confound her enemies. Accordingly, dressed for some mysterious reason in page's costume, she proceeded to sit up day and night writing. Some weeks later an old copyist called Woodhouse was summoned to Melbourne House, where, to his astonishment, he was confronted by what he took at first to be a boy of fourteen, who presented him with the manuscript of a novel. Before the end of May this novel, *Glenarvon*, made its appearance on the booksellers' tables.

It is a deplorable production: an incoherent cross between a realistic novel of fashionable life and a fantastic tale of terror, made preposterous by every absurd device—assassins, spectres, manacled maniacs, children changed at birth—that an imagination nurtured on mock-Gothic romance could suggest. But it has its interest, as revealing the way that Caroline contrived to reshape her story so as to please her vanity. She appears as Calantha, a heroine, noble, innocent, fascinating, but too impulsive for success in a hard-hearted world. Her husband, Lord Avondale, otherwise William, in spite of the fact that he too is unusually noble-hearted, neglects her, and corrupts her morals by his cynical views. In consequence, she yields to the temptations of a depraved society and finally, though only after heroic resistance on her part, is seduced by Byron, here called Glenarvon. He is Byronism incarnate; beautiful and gifted beyond belief, but driven by the pangs of a conscience burdened with inexpiable crimes, to go about betraying and ruining people in a spirit of gloomy desperation. Though Calantha is the love of his life, he deserts her out of pure devilry. The heartless world turns against her; she dies of a broken heart: Avondale dies shortly afterwards out of sympathy. For Glenarvon a more sensational fate is reserved. He jumps off a ship into the sea after sailing about for days, pursued by a phantom vessel manned by revengeful demons of gigantic size.

The tension of this dramatic tale is relieved by some thinly veiled satirical portraits of the Lamb family, the Devonshire family, Lady Oxford, Lady Holland, and a number of other leading social figures, notably the influential Lady Jersey. Its moral is that Caroline's misfortunes were Byron's fault, William's fault, society's fault—anyone's fault, in fact, but her own.

The world did not accept this view. *Glenarvon* had a success of scandal; three editions were called for within a few weeks. But it dealt the death-blow to what remained of Caroline's social position. Ever since Lady Heathcote's ball she had kept it on sufferance; certain people had continued to countenance her out of affection for her relations. Now she had set out deliberately, and in print, to insult these last of her supporters. It is not surprising that they too turned against her. In desperate bravado she had continued to go into society, at the time the book was appearing; only to find that her cousins avoided her, Lord Holland cut her dead, and Lady Jersey scratched her name off the list of Almack's Club. At last she had succeeded in putting herself completely outside the pale. And she was never to get inside it again.

As for the Lambs, they were almost out of their minds. For many years, so they not unjustifiably considered, they had endured Caroline's goings-on with singular patience. And in return she had chosen to wound them in their two tenderest points, family loyalty and regard for appearances. To people brought up with Lady Melbourne's tradition of discretion, no worse torment can be imagined, than to have the intimacies of family life displayed in public. And in such an unfavourable light! What cause for odious triumph would the book not give to that dowdy and envious section of society which had always maligned them? While, when they thought what their beloved William must be feeling as he saw *Glenarvon* lying open on the tables of every house he entered, their fury almost suffocated them.

Caroline was impenitent. William, she asserted, had enjoyed the book very much. That she should have succeeded in persuading herself of this, is the most extraordinary of all her extraordinary feats of self-deception. In fact William was utterly crushed. He had heard nothing of the book till the morning of its appearance. "Caroline," he said, coming into her room, "I have stood your friend till now—I even think you were ill-used: but if it is true that this novel is published—and as they say against us all—I will never see you more."

That all the long-concealed shames and sorrows of his marriage should be dragged out for the world to see, was torture to a man of his sensitive reserve; it was also acutely distressing that one, closely connected with him, should behave with such treacherous ingratitude to those he loved. Sunk in black gloom he sat all day in Melbourne House; "I wish I was dead," he muttered. "I wish I was dead." And to his old friends the Hollands he wrote off such halting words of apology as he could find:

"Dear Holland,

It must have appeared strange to you that I have not been to see you. And you may perhaps put a wrong construction on it—it is nothing but the embarrassment which the late events have not unnaturally revived. They have given me great trouble and vexation, and produced an unwillingness to see anybody and more particularly those who have been the objects of so wanton and unprofitable an attack. I did not write, because, what could I say? I could only exculpate myself from any previous knowledge, the effect of which must be to throw a heavier burden on the offending party—I am sure you will feel for my situation. I should like to see you some morning. Yours W.L."

The grounds for separation seemed stronger than ever. Indeed, several people wrote to William saying that if he did not now break with Caroline, they would consider it a sign that he connived at her book. By the middle of the summer the arrangements were pretty well completed. The evening before the final signature, William, leaving Caroline, as he thought, in safe hands, went down to Brocket for a night's quiet. What was his dismay, while he was undressing, to hear a scuffling noise outside his room. It was Caroline, who had escaped, followed him down, and was preparing to make a last desperate effort to melt his stony heart by spending the night stretched out on his door-mat. What transpired between them is unknown. But next morning the lawyers, arriving with the papers, found her sitting on his knee in fits of laughter, feeding him with small scraps of bread and butter. The Deed of Separation was a dead letter.

What was the reason for this surprising change of heart? Caroline no doubt thought it was simply love. And it is true that all his sufferings at her hands had not succeeded in driving her image wholly from William's heart. The same incurable immaturity of spirit which made her behave so childishly, also kept her charm fresh. When for a moment the storm-clouds of hysteria parted, it sparkled out as waywardly captivating as ever: and against his will, William responded to it. But it would seem that his volte-face was due primarily to other and more complex motives. Dislike of the unpleasant had something to do with it; he could not bring himself to face the agonizing ordeal of a final scene of farewell. He felt guilty too; at the back of his mind lurked an uneasy feeling that his carelessness during the early days of their marriage was partly responsible for her present collapse. But strangely enough, he was most of all affected by *Glenarvon*. He might say, in the first heat of anger, that he never meant to see her again: but when the full storm broke, when he saw everyone cutting her, when he read the outrageous personal attacks on her published in the newspapers, his mood underwent a revulsion. Bad as Caroline might be, she was not so bad as to deserve such persecution. Besides, if he had felt it shabby to leave her before, how much more now! Except for him, she had not a friend in the world. Every chivalrous instinct, every touching memory of his old love, revolted against deserting her in such a plight. Once more personal obligation showed itself the one strong motive for action in his frustrated nature. "Caroline," he told her, "we will stand or fall together."

Most likely they would fall. It is not to be imagined that William entered on this new chapter of his wedded life with rosy expectations. However, he had long ago given up expecting much of anything. Drama, as usually happens in real life, had ended not in tragic *dénouement*, but in lassitude and anti-climax. In pity, in exasperation, in ironical apathy, he settled down to his accustomed round.

Elsewhere also he was beginning to pick up old threads again. In the spring he had re-entered the House of Commons. Ever since he had left, his friends had been urging him to come back; and in 1815 Lord Holland had written offering him a seat. But for the time being William had lost his zest for Parliamentary life. The more philosophical outlook afforded by the windows of Brocket library made the bustle of party politics look a futile waste of energy. Anyhow, he did not want to come back as a Holland House man. Since peace had been signed, the Foxites had shown themselves more academically out of touch with reality than ever. Though Europe was still shaking, they wanted most of the Army dismissed at once, for fear it might lead to a Cromwellian military despotism; they worried lest by helping to restore the French king, the English Government had implied belief in the divine right of kings. Worst of all in William's eyes, at a time when every sensible person was longing only for peace and quiet, they were toying with subversive schemes of reform. The detachment in which William had been living made him more confident in his independent views. In a letter of refusal to Lord Holland, he made his position thoroughly clear.

"In the present state of politics with no one in either House of Parliament whom I should choose to follow, with questions, certain to occur, so numerous and so various, so perplexed by circumstances and complicated in the detail, that it is almost impossible for any two persons to come to the same conclusion upon all of them, it would be very disagreeable and embarrassing for me to have a seat in the House of Commons which should not allow me the fullest and most unquestioned liberty of acting upon any subject according to my own particular opinion—I cannot also conceal from myself that the having been three years without taking any part in public affairs has had the natural effect to a certain degree of diminishing the eagerness of the interest which I once felt in them; and consideration and reflection have had the equally natural effect of altering and, in my view, amending some of the opinions which I fancied myself to hold. . . . In Europe I am for an immediate settlement even though that settlement be full of errors and imperfections; because I cannot but think I perceive that every fresh struggle and convulsion in France or Spain or elsewhere, only terminates in impairing and diminishing justice, liberty and all real rights, or rather the real interests of mankind. Such being my opinions . . . I apprehend they will force you to come to the same conclusion as myself, that such a political connection would only lead to mutual dissatisfaction and reproach . . . my principles are I believe the Whig principles of the Revolution; the main foundation of these is the irresponsibility of the crown, the consequent responsibility of Ministers, the preservation of the power and dignity of Parliament as constituted by Law and Custom. With the heap of modern additions and interpolations I have nothing to do—with those who maintain those principles and against those who either do or appear to be ready to sacrifice them, I shall always act: but I must always lament when I see the advocates of freedom injure their own cause by raising objections which are inapplicable or extravagant or impracticable as I do beg you to consider. . . . 'τα λιαν δημοτικα απολυει την δημοκρατιαιν'."

However, when a year later he was offered a seat at Northampton that did not commit him to strict party orthodoxy, he accepted it. He had nothing else to do; his family wanted him to; and a vague rumour was afloat that Canning might at last be coming into office.

A doubtful flicker of light illuminated the political horizon. All the same, looked at as a whole, his situation was a cheerless one. And he felt it. This period, and still more the four years preceding it, were the most melancholy of his active life. Brooding aimlessly in the book-lined seclusion of Brocket library, pacing the turfy

solitudes of its park in the fading summer twilight, he would be
overwhelmed by a leaden sensation of failure, of emptiness, of the
fleeting vanity of things human, his own existence most of all. It
is not surprising. He was now thirty-seven; and the perspective
of his past life that met his eyes as he turned to survey it from the
gathering shadows of middle age was, for all its surface glitter,
a profoundly disheartening spectacle. The world, and his own
weaknesses, victorious over him in early years, had now in his
maturity more decisively defeated him. He had yielded to the
inhibiting pressure of convention and tradition; his creative individuality had forced for itself no outlet; the conflict that lay at the
root of his nature had ended by effectively frustrating his power of
action. He had indeed gone into Parliament and married. But
his marriage, so far from providing him with an independent base
from which his personality might develop unhampered, had
merely served to sap his spirit and confirm his cynicism. Love
had turned out the most painful of all his disillusionments.
Further, the misfortunes of his wedded life had intensified that
morbid self-protectiveness, that propensity at all costs to avoid
trouble, which was a major defect of his character. Nor was his
political career a more encouraging subject of contemplation. The
most valuable part of him had found no means of expression in
the atmosphere of Parliament: while, though he sympathized too
little with his Party to combat usefully in its cause, he shrank too
much from wounding his friends to leave them, and throw in his
lot openly with that leader in whom at heart he believed. Alike in
public and in private life, he recognized himself as a failure: and
there seemed no reason to suppose he would ever be anything
else.

It is true that in neither had he ostensibly given up the struggle.
He had gone back into the House of Commons: he had reconciled
himself with Caroline. But these acts are evidence of his defeat
rather than of his fighting spirit. For he was not proposing to
attack his old problems with new vigour and by new methods. It
was just that he lacked sufficient faith in himself, or in anything
else, to try and rebuild his life on fresh lines. Better, in a world of
deception and disappointment, to acquiesce in the line of least
resistance. If Caroline wanted him, he would stay with her; if

E

Lady Melbourne liked him to be a member of Parliament, a member of Parliament he would be. A distinguished creative intelligence, he resigned himself, unless fortune changed, to live the unfertile life of a commonplace man of his rank. An onlooker in youth, in middle age he settled down to be an onlooker, if need be, for the rest of his days.

Only not with the old zest. He had not lost his curiosity about the world: he could entertain himself with the passing moment pleasantly enough. But with the dissolution of his youthful dreams and aspirations, had vanished also the keen savour of his youthful joys. The rapture of first love, the burning, exultant thirst for truth, the stir of the heart quickened by the tumult and trumpet call of great events—where were they now? Nor had life supplied him with any compensating source of happiness to take their place. William still scribbled verses to while away a vacant hour: and in a paraphrase from the Latin, made apparently about this time, we may catch a hint of the emotions that welled up in his tired spirit as, pausing at this sad milestone of his life's pilgrimage, he mused on times gone by:

> 'Tis late, and I must haste away,
> My usual hour of rest is near;
> And do you press me, youths, to stay—
> To stay and revel longer here?
>
> Then give me back the scorn of care
> Which spirits light in health allow;
> And give me back the dark brown hair
> Which curled upon my even brow.
>
> And give me back the sportive jest
> Which once could midnight hours beguile,
> The life that bounded in my breast,
> And joyous youth's becoming smile!
>
> And give me back the fervid soul
> Which love inflamed with strange delight,
> When erst I sorrowed o'er the bowl
> At Chloe's coy and wanton flight.

'Tis late, and I must haste away,
My usual hour of rest is near;
But give me these and I will stay—
Will stay till morn—and revel here!

With regret, with resignation, with hopeless bitter-sweet yearning, he gazed back at his memories of the irretrievable past. There seemed nothing much worth looking at in the future.

## Part Three

## CHAPTER VIII

## TEN YEARS LATER

O N 20TH JUNE, 1826, Emily Lamb, now Countess Cowper, sat writing the family news to her brother Frederick at Madrid, where he was Minister Plenipotentiary. "William," ran her letter, "looks cheeerful and gay, but is much too fat."

This brief sentence sums up the main changes that were to be observed in him during the years that had elapsed since 1816. William was in better spirits and his figure had begun to fill out; but that was all. The melancholy prognostications of ten years back had been fulfilled; fate had not seen fit to rescue him from the frustrated and stagnant situation in which he had then found himself; at forty-seven his prospects and his position were substantially the same as at thirty-seven.

Politically he was still poised uneasily between Whig and Tory. Those rumours of Canning's imminent triumph, which had raised his hopes on his re-entry into Parliament, had proved illusory. And William settled down to pursue his usual and lonely middle course. During the anxious years that followed the conclusion of peace, he had sometimes supported Government, sometimes Opposition. The riotings and rick-burnings which had disturbed the countryside roused his fear of revolution; and he agreed in 1816 to become a member of the committee appointed to devise means of repressing disorder. Later he voted both for the suspension of Habeas Corpus and for the Six Acts. On the other hand, unlike the Tories, he had been in favour of an enquiry into the Peterloo massacre and had voted for Mackintosh's bill for modifying the rigours of the penal code. Moreover in economic matters he had taken the Whig side; arguing vigorously on behalf of economy and no income tax. As regards foreign affairs he was for keeping quiet. Above all, England should not be so silly as to set up as the moral arbiter of Europe, either on the side of authority or freedom. In 1820 public life was diversified by the unedifying farce of Queen

Caroline's divorce. William, along with his fellow Whigs, was against the King, and voted for retaining the Queen's name in the liturgy. But he was too worldly-wise to persuade himself into any romantic belief in her innocence. It would be better for her, he said, to act magnanimously; and he took the trouble to write to the virtuous Mr. Wilberforce asking him to come up in order to try and persuade the King to any compromise which might compose the situation, and so avoid the risk of popular tumults. The juxtaposition of two such incongruous characters as William and Wilberforce provides an entertaining spectacle. Wilberforce liked William, but had a horror of getting mixed up in so disreputable an affair; "Oh, the corrupted currents of this world," he confided to his diary, "oh, for that better world where there is no shuffling!" William for his part, though diplomatically polite to so formidable a pillar of respectability, did not find him sympathetic. "I believe he has good motives," he said, "but they are very uncomfortable for those he has to act with." Wilberforce's inner life as revealed a few years later in his published diary William thought ridiculous; "perpetually vexing himself, because he amused himself too well".

In 1822 Canning at last got office; but, by bad luck, it was in such circumstances as to make it no advantage to William. What he wanted was a Whig–Tory Coalition. Canning was now the Tory member of an exclusively Tory administration. Nothing had occurred since William had re-entered Parliament to loosen those bonds of personal loyalty which held him to his old Party. And when in 1824 Canning offered him a place, once again he felt bound to refuse. However, though he could not himself join Canning he was all for anyone else doing so. Three years earlier he had strongly urged his friend Ward to accept a similar office. "It would have the effect of supporting and assisting Canning," he remarked, "at this moment, and it might enable you to be of essential service to the Ministry. At the same time," he adds characteristically, "do not take it, unless you can make up your mind to bear every species of abuse and misrepresentation and the imputation of the most sordid and interested motives." Himself, both at home and in the lobbies of the House, he consorted more and more with the Canningites. Huskisson, who followed Canning into the Government, was always coming down to Brocket.

He combined profound knowledge of practical affairs with an antipathy to doctrinaire theory. This exactly harmonized with William's own point of view. His previous respect for Huskisson's judgment grew to unbounded admiration. "The greatest *practical* statesman I ever knew," he said of him in later years; and he set himself to learn all he could from such a wellspring of wisdom. Practical knowledge had always been the weakest part of William's intellectual equipment. The instruction acquired from Huskisson was to be of great service to him. Meanwhile in Parliament he steadily gave Canning such support as was possible from Whig benches. Apart from the fact that he agreed with him, he thought it important that Tory policy should be modified by more Liberal ideas, lest it should relapse into hopeless obscurantism. Since William admired him so much, it is not surprising that Canning was struck by his talents. Lamb, he declared, was unusually eloquent and able. Nor was Canning William's only admirer. During the second period of his Parliamentary life his reputation steadily increased. For all that his Canningite sympathies were by now universally recognized, he was accepted as a necessary member of the inner group of Whig leaders; when they met to talk things over at Lansdowne or Holland House, William was always asked. In Tory circles too, he was an object of approbation. Lord Castlereagh was heard to say that "William Lamb could do anything if he shook off carelessness, and set about it"; while George IV, expatiating over the wine at Windsor Castle, went so far as to prophesy that William would one day be Prime Minister.

Such tributes were extremely gratifying. But they did not give much cause for encouragement. To be Prime Minister, to be a Minister of any kind, William required a party with which he could associate himself. And the prospect of any such party coming into power looked small indeed. The Tories seemed more safely in the saddle than ever. For the country, terrified by the ominous threat of revolution that muttered round the horizon, was more than ever suspicious of any administration likely to embark on a forward policy. And anyway the Whigs were in no condition to take office. Till they were prepared to adopt a progressive programme publicly they had no alternative to offer to the existing Government. And so far from agreeing on such a policy, they were more divided than ever. The Grenvillites, now merely a fossilized remnant of eighteenth-century aristocratic domination, were against all reform. The Foxites, at heart nervous of change, said they must wait till the respectable classes of the community showed themselves anxious for it; headed by Lord Grey, they had pretty well retired from politics. The more active younger group had disintegrated into a rout of quarrelling factions. Some rushed to the extreme left; others, led by Brougham, bustled agitatedly about, now flirting with the extremists, now devising elaborate programmes of moderate change, now courting Canning's favour—all in vain effort to find some effective cry with which to rally party and country to their support. As for a Canningite Coalition, there seemed little chance of that. The Government was mainly composed of diehard Tories like Lord Eldon and the Duke of Wellington. And they felt themselves too strong to need to concede anything to the more liberalizing elements in public life.

What was poor William to do? With an ironical smile and a despondent heart, he did as little as he could. Frustration and disappointment found expression in a prevailing mood of inertia. He was lax in his attendance at the House; when he was there he seldom made a speech. It was pleasanter and more profitable to stay at Brocket looking through old family letters, walking out with a gun after duck, and reading Sophocles in the library. As the years passed and no prospect of political influence appeared, his indolence grew stronger. Hope deferred maketh the heart lazy. He now sat for the local borough of Hertford: by the election of 1825, he found himself almost unable to face the effort required to ingratiate himself anew with his constituency. "William," said the irritated Emily, "canvasses very idly and says constantly that it won't do; sees everything in the light of his adversaries so that he disheartens all his own friends; and yet does not make up his mind to give up, but is always shilly shally." It was thought at first that the seat would be uncontested. But suddenly the opposition put up a disreputable young rake called Duncombe, who plunged into the fray, scattering guineas on all sides, accusing William in a striking metaphor, drawn from the racecourse, of "being unsound in both forelegs", and seeking to discredit his personal character by raking up the hoary scandals of his married life. With relief William seized the opportunity to retire from the fight. In the summer of 1826 London saw him once more a man of leisure. "In very good spirits," it was noted, "at being out of things again."

It might have been expected that his frustrated energy would have found some other outlet. And in fact he did toy with the idea of literary composition. He contributed an occasional review to the *Literary Gazette*; and when in 1819 it was proposed to him to write the life of Sheridan, he accepted; began studying documents, making notes, and sketching out preliminary plans for chapters. However, within a year he had resigned the task to Tom Moore. History gives no reason. It seems likely to have been self-distrust. "I have read too much and too little," he notes in his common-place book somewhere about this time, "so much, that it has extinguished all the original fire of my genius, and yet not enough, to furnish me with the power of writing works of mature thinking and solid instruction." Moreover, it was late for a man of his indolent temperament to set himself to learn a new profession. Politics might not be the occupation that best suited him; but he had been immersed in them for fifteen years. By now it needed the pressure of public life to make him concentrate on a given task. To keep his mind to the effort of sustained literary composition sufficiently to achieve anything like the standard required by his exacting taste, was perhaps beyond him. At all events, after giving up Sheridan's biography he attempted nothing more. The period is as barren of literary achievement as it is of political.

Meanwhile his private life pursued a grey and unprofitable course. Here indeed there had been changes. But time had made them, not William. The eighteenth century was a memory by now: and by 1826 the last of the figures which had irradiated its setting with so incomparable a splendour, had followed it into the shadow. Lady Bessborough had died suddenly in 1821, from a chill caught while travelling in Italy. Worn out by a life of tempest and disillusion, she was glad enough to quit the world; and though racked with pain, met her end with a gentle serenity, only ruffled a little by anxiety, lest her departure might distress those whom she loved. Three years before, she had been preceded to the grave by Lady Melbourne. Her end was melancholy and unlooked for. Up till 1816 her matchless vitality had shown no signs of flagging: indomitable as ever, she continued to direct her household, entertain her friends, and plot her children's advancement. Then suddenly a change came. She, who had triumphed relentlessly over so many enemies, fell herself a victim to the relentless force of mortality. Miserable, horribly fat, and doped with laudanum, she lay, at last deaf to the enticements of the world, in the clutches of a fatal disease. Only on her deathbed did the clouds lift to reveal a glimmer of her old self. She summoned Emily, now launched on a career of romance as varied as her own, to her bedside; and besought her as a last request to be true—not to her husband Lord Cowper, Lady Melbourne had too much sense to expect that—but to her first and most distinguished admirer, Lord Palmerston. And with her last breath she sought to fire William with the energy needed to achieve the great position for which from childhood she had designed him. What were his feelings, as he looked on her features, fixed in the enigmatic stillness of death? What ironical epitaph, mingling love and regret and disenchantment, rose to his lips as he took a last farewell of her who had played the chief part in moulding his disillusioning destiny? . . . No expression of his thoughts is recorded at the time; probably they were of a kind best kept to himself. Only as a very old man at Brocket, he was once found, lost in meditation, before her portrait. "A remarkable woman," he murmured to himself, "a devoted mother, an excellent wife—but not chaste, not chaste."

Lady Melbourne's place in the family was taken by Emily. Her personality was less compelling than her mother's. Bewitchingly pretty in a soft dark style, she was a charming sunshiny worldling, born with an instinctive shrewdness and social accomplishment, but spontaneous and warm-hearted, moved by no fiercer ambition than to make life as pleasant as possible for herself and everyone else. As a hostess, however, she was equally successful. Panshanger, her country seat, was as famous a fashionable centre as Melbourne House had been: and life there carried on the same tradition, disorderly and elegant, brilliant and unedifying, "full," says a visitor, "of vice and agreeableness, foreigners and *roués*."

Emily had also inherited her mother's family sense. It was natural to her to gather her brothers round her, to keep an eye on their healths, their careers, and their affairs of the heart. William, she did find a little hard to manage; he was, she complained, so lazy and undecided—besides he ate too much. But she was devoted to him, and delighted in his company. He on his side took great pleasure in her; the beauty and success of "that little devil Emily" remained, all through life, his pride and joy. Even when he was sixty-one and she fifty-three he could not forbear asking Queen Victoria if she did not think Emily was wearing "a very dashing gown". And when the Queen expressed her admiration, "She beats any of them now," he broke out, "she was always like a pale rose." After his mother died, he spent much of his time at Panshanger: lounging, arguing, and being late for meals, as in a second home.

He needed one. There was little domestic amenity to be enjoyed at his own house. *Glenarvon* and Lady Heathcote's ball between them had done for Caroline. Admiration had grown to be as necessary to her as air; nothing had any interest to her except in so far as it helped her to make an impression on other people. The fact that she was now an outcast dependent solely on solitary and impersonal interests for her satisfaction meant that the backbone of her life was broken. There was nothing for her to do but disintegrate into oblivion.

Alas, it was a slow and painful process. For she was too vital to accept defeat. Instead, with the fitful energy of despair, she cast about for any means by which she might once more compel the attention and applause of mankind. Like an actress who has outlived her popularity, she continued, with unquenchable hope, again and again to try her luck before the footlights. Sometimes she appeared as a woman of intellect. During this period she published two novels and a number of poems, notably one to her husband which opened with the surprising couplet

> "Oh, I adore thee, William Lamb,
> But hate to hear thee say God damn."

She also presented herself to the public as a sportswoman. At the time of George IV's Coronation she wrote offering her services as riding master to the official champion, whose task it was to ride into Westminster Hall and fling down a challenge to anyone who might dispute the King's right to his throne. At home, Caroline sought to make an impression by playing the more modest role of efficient housewife. Fashionable visitors to Brighton one spring were astonished to see Lady Caroline Lamb on horseback in the public street spiritedly haggling with the grocer about the price of cheese: her table at Brocket was piled with elaborately worked-out schemes for the economical regulation of her household. The elections of 1819 gave her a chance to blossom forth in yet another character, that of political woman. George Lamb was standing for Westminster; and Caroline, though protesting that she was at death's door, at once drove up to London and invaded the local taverns, where she diced and drank with the voters in order to win them to the good cause. One day, driving through the streets in her carriage, she was assaulted with a volley of stones by a mob of angry opponents. Here was an opportunity indeed for a heroine to display her quality. Stepping out with head held high, "I am not afraid of you," cried Caroline magnificently; "I know you will not hurt a woman—for you are Englishmen!"

In other moods she studied less to discover effective roles, than to collect an appreciative audience. Within a few months of the publication of *Glenarvon* we find her inviting her cousin Harriet Granville to pay her a visit of reconciliation at Melbourne House. "I went yesterday to Whitehall," writes Harriet, "and followed the page through the dark and winding passages and staircases. I was received with rapturous joy, embraces and tremendous spirits. I expected she would put on an appearance of something, but to do her justice she only displayed a total want of shame and consummate impudence, which whatever they may be in themselves are at least better or rather less disgusting than pretending or acting a more interesting part. I was dragged to the unresisting William and dismissed with a repetition of embrassades and professions. And this is the guilty broken-hearted Calantha who could only expiate her crimes with her death!"

In later years Caroline made sporadic attempts to recover her place in London society; wrote beseeching the Duke of Wellington to use his influence to get her re-admitted to Almack's, suddenly sent out invitations for an evening party at Brocket. But for the most part she fought shy of her old friends. And, like many other people who have failed to obtain a footing in fashionable society, she fell back on intellectual. It was not the great world that was deserting her, so she put it to herself, it was she who was leaving the great world, in pursuit of the higher satisfactions of the spirit. Accordingly, she made friends with Godwin, the philosopher, with Lady Morgan, the novelist, and Miss Benger, the historian: and was to be found, an exotic figure, at little reunions up three pairs of stairs, where, refreshed by cups of tea carried in by the solitary maidservant, the genteel intelligentsia of the Metropolis discoursed to one another on Truth and Beauty. In return she took the opportunity to display herself in the agreeable character of fairy godmother; showered her new friends with unexpected gifts of fruit and opera tickets, and invited them to Melbourne House. There on her sofa she would lie, swathed in becoming folds of muslin and surrounded by souvenirs of Lord Byron, talking by the hour of the great people she had known, and the ardours and endurances of her life of passion.

Sometimes she asked her new friends to meet her old. There is a comical account of a dinner she gave in 1820 consisting of a number of artists and writers—notably William Blake and Sir Thomas Lawrence—some humble country acquaintances and a few persons of *ton*, whom she had managed to entice into her house. It was not a success. Naïve Blake, it is true, was happy enough. "There is a great deal of kindness in that lady," he said looking at Caroline. But the ambitious Lawrence was not at all pleased at being seen by his fashionable patrons in such dingy-looking company: while the grandees, after taking one look at the extraordinary people they had been asked to meet, relapsed into disgusted silence. Caroline herself added to the general awkwardness by commenting loudly and unfavourably on the rest of her guests, to whichever one of them she happened to be talking to.

Friends, however, had never been enough for her; to be a queen of hearts remained her most cherished aspiration; and she snatched at the slightest chance of a love affair. They were not glorious chances. She was now too notorious and eccentric to attract anyone much worth attracting. The wife of William Lamb, the lover of Byron, had to make do with hardened *roués*, ready to take up with any woman, or callow youths, glad to have their names connected with so celebrated a personality. However, beggars cannot be choosers. And Caroline set all her powers to the task of making the best of a bad job; represented the most trivial intrigue to herself as a passionate romantic drama; and threw herself into it with an extravagance of melodramatic gesture all the more preposterous by contrast with the ignominious un-reality of the emotions involved. Every few months saw the repetition in caricature of the Byron love affair. The old limelight was switched on: the old tricks played out: she swooned, she rhapsodized, she pounded the organ all night; she made scenes of jealousy and scenes of reconciliation. Each lover, during the period of his reign, was awarded the privilege of wearing a ring, given her by Byron. For the most presentable of her conquests, the twenty-one-year old Bulwer Lytton, she even staged a death scene, summoning him to her bedside, where with pathetic falter-ing accents she sought to move him by a last declaration of love.

Such exhibitions could not be kept secret. Caroline did not wish them to be; besides, the sort of men she was now entangled with liked to brag of their conquest. By 1821 her reputation had sunk so low that she was suspected of an intrigue with any man she was seen with, down to her son's tutor and the family doctor, Mr. Walker. One of her stockings, so ran scandalous rumour, had been found at the end of Mr. Walker's bed. This seems to have been a libel; but London society was only too pleased to accept any evidence justifying their hostility towards her. While the Lamb family believed everything against her, and were pro-portionately disgusted. "It is such a low-lived thing to take a Scotch doctor for a lover," commented Emily viciously.

Nor did her affairs afford Caroline herself much compensating satisfaction. The old romantic properties were grown dreadfully faded by this time; in the hands of inferior players, the Byronic drama showed fustian indeed. She pursued her quarries with the effrontery of desperation. But try as she might she could not re-capture the thrill of the past; and she quickly tired of the chase. Within a short time she dropped it; and, restless and disappointed, turned in search of some new victim to persecute with her feverish attentions.

But indeed, poor Caroline, any effort she made to mend her broken life ended equally in disaster. Each new part she appeared in was a failure. Her later novels made no hit: the Coronation champion preferred to employ a more conventional instructor: and her electioneering vagaries merely made her the laughing-stock of London. Her housewifely activities were also unsuccessful— "What is the use of saving on the one hand, if you squander all away on the other?" exclaimed William in despair. While the only effect of her intricate domestic schemes was to make the servants leave. "The servants at Brocket," says Emily, "still continue to pass through, like figures in a magic lantern. A new cook whom Haggard [1] was delighted to secure from her great character and fifty guineas wages, stopped only a week. . . . Haggard, talking of Caroline, is so good. He says she cannot get any worse, so one hopes she may get better."

Caroline did not succeed in making friends either. The *beau monde* had done with her for good. Emily, out of affection for William, got her re-admitted to Almack's: but the doors of the great houses remained closed. As for her evening party at Brocket, it was a fiasco. The rooms shone with a galaxy of candles; the tables were spread with supper for eighty people; Caroline sent her own carriage to fetch those guests who lived far off. But only ten people came. Her excursions into other social spheres were less openly disastrous. Then, as always, the intelligentsia were susceptible to the charms of rank and fashion; while Caroline was delighted at first to find people who gazed at her with awe, and believed every word she said. All the same there was a gulf between them and her that no amount of snobbery on their part, or vanity on hers, could overspan. Serious, stiff and middle class, they were bewildered alike by the splendour of her surroundings, the candour of her confidences and the modish effusiveness of her manners. She was equally at sea with them. That Lady Morgan should not be able to afford to keep a groom of the chambers!— Caroline had not imagined that such sordid poverty was possible. And she consternated Miss Benger, by suddenly bursting in on

[1] The agent at Brocket.

her one morning while she was occupied in the plebeian task of
counting the washing. Poor Miss Benger! she thought she would
die of shame when Lady Caroline's dog pulled out a heap of dirty
handkerchiefs and stockings from under the sofa, where she had
hastily shoved them on the arrival of her distinguished visitor.
Moreover, after the first fun of impressing them was over, Caroline was bored with her new friends. Intellectual persons for the
most part are less socially accomplished than fashionable ones;
their conversation may have more stuff in it, but it is not so graceful. Caroline, accustomed to Devonshire House, grew conscious
of this. "These sort of people," she confided to a friend, "are not
always agreeable, but vulgar, quaint and formal. Still I feel in-
debted to them, for they have one and all treated me with kindness
. . . when I was turned out." In plain words she only associated
with them because those she liked better would have nothing to do
with her. It was the devastating truth, and she recognized it.

For this was the most distressing feature of her predicament.
She realized her failures even though she refused to accept them.
Her natural acuteness was always at war with her power of self-
deception. Though she could persuade herself of anything, it was
never for long. In consequence, the logic of facts forced her
gradually, reluctantly, agonizingly, to relinquish her illusions; step
by step she found herself compelled to recognize that her literary
powers were small, that the intelligentsia bored her, that her lovers
were a poor lot. At last she actually admitted that her misfortunes
were mainly her own fault. Even then it was impossible for her to
regard herself in an unsympathetic light. And she fell back on a
last desperate pose of pitiful victim; a fragile butterfly, worthless
and shallow perhaps, but punished far beyond her deserts by the
harsh decrees of destiny.

"I am like the wreck of a little boat," she wrote to Godwin,
"for I never come up to the sublime and beautiful—merely a
little gay merry boat which perhaps stranded itself at Vauxhall
or London Bridge; or wounded without killing itself, as a
butterfly does in a tallow candle. There is nothing marked
sentimental or interesting in my career; all I know is that I was
happy, well, rich, surrounded by friends. I have now one

faithful friend in William Lamb, two more in my father, brother, but health, spirits and all else is gone—gone how? O assuredly not by the visitation of God but slowly gradually by my own fault."

And again:

"It were all very well one died at the end of a tragic scene, after playing a desperate part, but if one lives and instead of growing wiser remains the same victim of every folly and passion, without the excuse of youth and inexperience what then? There is no particular reason I should exist, it conduces to no one's happiness and on the contrary I stand in the way of many. Besides I seem to have lived a thousand years and feel I am neither wiser, better nor worse than when I began . . . this is probably the case of millions but that does not mend the matter; and while a fly exists, it seeks to save itself."

The appropriate end of such a character was clearly to die. And, in order to squeeze the last tear of pity from her audience, Caroline now took every few weeks or so to announcing her speedily approaching death.

In 1821 the spectre of her tumultuous past rose, in a succession of dramatic events, to trouble her distracted spirit still further.

"I was taken ill in March," she told a friend, "in the middle of the night, I fancied I saw Lord Byron—I screamed, jumped out of bed . . . he looked horrible, and ground his teeth at me, he did not speak; his hair was straight; he was fatter than when I knew him and not near so handsome. . . . I am glad to think that it occurred before his death, as I never did and hope I never shall see a ghost. I even avoided enquiring about the exact day for fear I should believe it—it made enough impression as it was. . . . Judge what my horror was as well as grief when long after, the news came of his death; it was conveyed to me in two or three words—'Caroline behave properly, I know it will shock you, Lord Byron is dead.' This letter I received, when laughing at Brocket Hall."

As a consequence she took to her bed with a serious attack of hysterical fever. Three months later, when she was just beginning

to recover, she went out driving. As her carriage emerged through
the park gates it was met by a funeral cortège, grim with all the
murky pageantry of plumes and mourning coaches, wending its
way through the serene summer landscape. William, who was
riding beside her, trotted on to ask whose it was. "Lord Byron's,"
was the answer. Fearful of the effect of the sudden shock on
Caroline, he did not tell her at the time: but when she heard it
that night, once more she collapsed.

Such a collapse was only the intensification of what was now a
chronic condition. Caroline was not the woman to rise superior to
misfortune. Her self-respect was broken, and under the repeated
batterings of fate her character gradually went to pieces. She began to exhibit all the painful, pitiable traits of the *déclassée* person;
thrusting herself defiantly forward when she was not wanted, yet
on edge, all the time, to take offence at insults real or imagined.
Blinding herself to her present situation, she talked continually
of the famous people she had known, with an embarrassing and unsuccessful pretence that she was as intimate with them as ever.
Meanwhile her nerves were now permanently at the same pitch of
irritability as at the height of the Byron episode. Not a week
passed without some dreadful scene when she sobbed and kicked
and screamed insane abuse at anyone who came near her. As for
breaking things, it had become a habit: it was computed on one
occasion that she had destroyed £200 worth of china in a morning.
Rather than face the torture of her solitary thoughts, she took to
galloping frantically round the park all day, and sitting up all
night, holding forth to anyone who could be persuaded to listen.
When all else failed she sought oblivion in laudanum and brandy.
Loss of self-respect also showed itself in the ordering of her life.
Unequal to the discipline of regular meals, she had food placed
about the house that she might snatch a bite when and where she
felt inclined: she grew squalid and careless in her person; while
her bedroom presented a curious image of moral and mental disintegration. It was decked out with every fantastic caprice of the
romantic fancy. An altar cloth, a portrait of Byron, and "an elegant crucifix" hung conspicuous on the walls. But the curtains
were in holes: the furniture was scattered with half-finished plates
of cake and pickles. While on the dressing-table, flanked by a

prayer-book on one side and on the other by a flask of lavender water, stood shamelessly the brandy bottle.

It was not an auspicious setting for domestic happiness. William's married life after 1816 was even more disagreeable than before. In a sense he was better equipped to bear it. For he entered on it with open eyes. He recognized himself as the lunatic's guardian, which in fact he was; and strove to approach his task with the firm but kindly detachment suitable to it. There was no question of his pretending, either to Caroline or to anyone else, that he thought marriage a pleasant state. One day when the family were gathered round the Brocket dinner-table the conversation turned on matrimony. Caroline opined that husband and wife should live in separate houses; while William, though admitting that people had better marry, said that only the very rich could expect to be happier by so doing. "People who are forced to live together," he declared, "and are confined to the same rooms and the same bed are like two pigeons under a basket, who must fight." He was also completely hardened by now to Caroline's making a public exhibition of herself. Emily was outraged when, at the height of the Mr. Walker scandal, she saw William at a concert in company with Caroline and her reputed lover. "William looked such a fool arriving with them," she said, "and looking as pleased as Punch, and she looking so disgusting with her white cross and dirty gown as if she had been rolled in a kennel." As a matter of fact, so far from her lovers annoying him, he looked on them as fellow victims for whose sufferings he could feel nothing but sympathy. "William Lamb was particularly kind to me," said Bulwer Lytton after describing an appalling series of scenes with Caroline, while staying at Brocket. "I think he saw my feelings. He is a singularly fine character for a man of the world."

At the same time William still felt a responsibility towards her: and did all he could to alleviate her unhappiness. Such of her activities as seemed comparatively harmless had all his encouragement. He was always pressing Emily to try and get her asked about in London society; at Caroline's request he assisted Godwin in his career. And he took an immense amount of trouble to help her in her novels; going over every sentence with her, and himself sending the finished manuscript to the publisher with a covering letter. Consistent with his new attitude to her, he made no attempt to recommend them above their merits.

"The incongruity of, and objection to, the story of 'Ada Reis' can only be got over by power of writing, beauty of sentiment, striking and effective situation, etc. If Mr. Gifford thinks there is in the first two volumes anything of excellence sufficient to overbalance their manifest faults, I still hope that he will press upon Lady Caroline the absolute necessity of carefully reconsidering and revising the third volume, and particularly the conclusion of the novel. . . . I think, if it were thought that anything could be done with the novel, and that the fault of its design and structure can be got over, that I could put her in the way of writing up this part a little, and giving it something of strength, spirit, and novelty, and of making it at once more moral and more interesting. I wish you would communicate these my hasty suggestions to Mr. Gifford, and he will see the propriety of pressing Lady Caroline to take a little more time to this part of the novel. She will be guided by his authority, and her fault at present is to be too hasty and too impatient of the trouble of correcting and recasting what is faulty."

He also did his best to soothe her nerves. It was to William that everyone turned, if Caroline became more than usually unmanageable. One day she was making arrangements for a dinner-party at Brocket. Exasperated at what she considered the stupidity of the butler in failing to grasp her ideas of decoration, she suddenly leapt on to the dinner table, and fixed herself in a fantastic attitude which she requested him to take as the model from which to arrange the centrepiece. The poor man, terrified by her extraordinary appearance, ran to William for help. He came immediately. "Caroline, Caroline," he said in tranquillizing tones, and gently lifting her from the table carried her from the room.

Caroline was not his only care at Brocket. He also concerned himself with his son. Augustus was now in his teens; but mentally he remained a child of seven. A strong well-grown boy, he caused dismay by romping half-dressed into the drawing-room when the housekeeper was setting it to rights, tumbling her over and sitting on her. But William never faced the fact that his deficiency was incurable. Despairing of his wife, he clung all the more desperately to the hope that something might be made of his child. No stone was left unturned; he consulted every kind of doctor and psychological expert, and procured a special tutor, for whom he had prepared an elaborate scheme of education, including lessons in logic, moral philosophy and metaphysics. All of course in vain; it was as much as the tutor could do to teach Augustus to read and write. But William obstinately, pathetically, refused to despair.

About Caroline he showed less fortitude. In spite of all his resolution he was unable to make even a modified success of his relationship with her. For he was in a false position. It was all very well to try and behave as the guardian of a lunatic. But William had neither the taste nor the talent for such a part. He had embarked on it mainly from weakness; because he could not face the unpleasantness of breaking with her. In consequence he was not supported in his ordeal by any conviction that he was doing right. And he could not stand the strain. As the years went by his patience progressively crumbled. He went away from Brocket as often as he could. During the time he spent there, he lived in a state of nervous tension, morbidly apprehensive of an outburst; when it came, he flew out into a violent passion; and then in the end gave way to her completely for the sake of peace. Such a situation could not last. By 1825 William at last admitted he had made a mistake in trying to settle down with her again. Once more he decided on a separation.

The process of its accomplishment was a caricature of all the least admirable features in their relationship. Never had he been weaker or she more intolerable. He was still too frightened to face breaking the news to her in person; so in March he went off to Brighton, where he wrote to her saying he was never coming back. This provoked the storm that might have been expected. However, by May her letters had grown so much calmer that he decided to go down to Brocket to discuss the necessary arrangements. It was a mad risk to take. To begin with Caroline was all right; quiet, sensible, and at moments so entertaining that she kept

William in fits of laughter. But, when he began to talk business, the other Caroline appeared. She wanted an allowance of £3,000 a year: he, though his family offered to help him, could not see his way to giving her more than the £2,000 on which they had lived up till then. In the twinkling of an eye she had become a fury, "relapsed," he said bitterly, "into her usual course of abuse, invective and the most unrestrained violence." She wrote round to her relations alleging that he beat her; and accusing him in the same breath of ruining her character by over-indulgence and driving her to desperation by his cruelty. She was the more unbridled, because for once she had a supporter. Her brother, William Ponsonby, "reckoned an ass and a jackanapes by everybody," said Emily tartly, was sufficiently convinced by Caroline's reports to write off to William in the strain of Lady Catherine de Bourgh; saying that he could not allow his sister to be trampled on by William, who owed her a great deal for deigning to marry someone of such inferior social position. Not trusting himself to answer such a communication with discretion, William went away and left the affair in Emily's hands. She, to use her own words, "bullied the bully" by telling Caroline that rather than give way William would take the whole thing into court. Caroline was always ready for publicity, even of an undesirable kind: but her relations were more reasonable. In the end the matter was referred to the arbitration of her cousins Lord Althorp and the Duke of Devonshire, who proposed a compromise of £2,500 a year. Both parties accepted the settlement; neither was pleased with it. William thought he would never be able to afford so large a sum; Caroline, on the other hand, informed her friends that she was going to be so poor, as to be in danger of dying of starvation. Indeed the version of this particular passage in her history, which she published to the world, had even less relation to the truth than usual. At the same time that she was squabbling with William over money and accusing him of every vice under heaven, she told Lady Morgan that she loved him more than anyone in the world, and that he was being forced away from her against his will by the machinations of his family. Her letter ended with the usual announcement of her imminent demise. "If I would but sign a paper," she said, with bitter sarcasm, "all my rich relations will protect me, and I shall no doubt go with an Almack's ticket to heaven."

Trouble was not yet at an end. It was one thing to persuade Caroline to sign; it was another to get her out of the house. She refused to move till she had decided what to do.

"Shall I go abroad?" she asks Lady Morgan. "Shall I throw myself upon those who no longer want me, or shall I live a good sort of half kind of life in some cheap street a little way off, the City Road, Shoreditch, Camberwell or upon the top of a shop— or shall I give lectures to little children, and keep a seminary and thus earn my bread? Or shall I write a kind of quiet every-day sort of novel full of wholesome truths, or shall I attempt to be poetical, and failing beg my friends for a guinea a-piece, and their name, to sell my work upon the best foolscap paper; or shall I fret, fret and die; or shall I be dignified and fancy myself as Richard the Second did when he picked the nettle up—upon a thorn?"

Faced with such variety of sensational alternatives to choose from, there seemed no reason she should ever make up her mind. And William, exhausted by the unnatural energy of purpose he had exerted during the first part of the year, now reacted into a listless indolence, in which he refused to put any pressure on her. On the contrary, to his family's irritation, he was always paying her visits in order to keep her in a good humour. At last in August Caroline decided that she wanted to go to Paris. A tremendous farewell scene was staged at Brocket, in which Caroline played her part so affectingly that even the butler—so she noted with satisfaction—was bathed in tears. By the 14th she was over the Channel. It was a very bad crossing: "She will, I trust," writes Emily, "have been so sick as to feel little anxiety to cross the water again directly."

This pious hope proved vain. Within two months her relations-in-law were dismayed to learn that Caroline had reappeared at an inn in Dover; whence she wrote to all and sundry giving a heart-rending picture of the poverty-stricken state to which she was re-duced; "in a little dreary apartment", made drearier by the peals of heartless laughter that rose from the neighbouring smoking-room, destitute, she complained, of such necessities of life as pages, carriages, horses, and fine rooms; and accusing the Lambs, with a wild disregard for truth, of conspiring with her doctor to say that she was mad, in order that they might withhold from her her meagre allowance. "William," she asserted, "is enchanted at the prospect of giving me nothing." The plain fact was that she was far too unbalanced to be able to manage life on her own. And there was no knowing the trouble in which she would involve herself and everyone else, unless she was looked after. Since no one else offered, the Lambs reluctantly took on the task again. Just three months after taking a last farewell of Brocket, she was settled there once more. William, clinging to the outward form of separation, still had his official home in London. But since he felt himself obliged to pay her frequent visits in order to see how she was getting on, his situation, with regard to her, was not essentially altered. It seemed as if, in personal life as in public, all his efforts to free himself ended equally in frustration.

In reality, however, the long-drawn-out drama was near its close. Unknown alike to William and to Caroline, the fates had decided to cut the coil which for so many years had bound them, one to another, in wretched conjunction. The ordeal of the separation marked an epoch in Caroline's life. For the agitations it involved had put a fatal final strain on her already worn-out constitution. At last her amazing vitality began to ebb. From this time on, in a dying fall, a strange muted tranquillity, her storm-tossed career declined swiftly to its period. Once, during the first few months after her return to Brocket, a glimpse of the old Caroline showed itself. Bulwer had become engaged to a Miss Wheeler. And Caroline, partly from pique at his fickleness, partly because she saw the theatrical possibilities inherent in the situation, invited Miss Wheeler to Brocket, where she staged a little scene: Caroline, an experienced woman of the world, with kindly wisdom warns Miss Wheeler, an innocent girl, against the perfidy of men. "Don't let Edward Bulwer let you down," she adjured her ominously; "they are a bad set." This piece of sentimental comedy, however, was a faint echo indeed of the thundering melodramas of Caroline's prime. And it was the last echo. After this her days passed in eventless rural monotony.

"How can I write?" she tells a friend. "Even imagination must have some material on which to work. I have none. Passion might produce sentiment of some sort. But mine are all calmed or extinct. . . . Memory—a waste with nothing in it worth recording! Happy, healthy, contented, quiet, I get up at half past four, ride about with Hazard, see harvesters at work in the pretty green confined country; read a few old books, see no one, hear from no one."

No longer did her spirit leap out at the call of fame; no longer did she combat hostile fate in baffled rage, or seek to forget it in the brandy bottle. Instead, profoundly weary, she lay back clinging to the comfort of safe homely innocent things, conscious only of a numbed longing to be at peace. So great a change in the direction of her desires brought with it an equal change in her character. The fury of her egotism dwindled with the vitality of which it was the expression. A child always, she was now a tired child, gentle and submissive, pathetically terrified of annoying people, stretching out her arms to be soothed and cherished. Frederick and Emily, driving over from Panshanger to pay her a visit, found all their age-old hostility towards her melting away: Caroline appeared so sincerely, so touchingly anxious to behave as they wanted. Still more did she want to behave as William wanted. For, as the fever of her maturity left her, so also did the memory of its preoccupations. Bulwer, Webster, Byron himself were as though they had never been: and the old first love, fresh and single as in honeymoon days, brimmed back into her heart. By this time William's life had begun to change; in April, 1827, he was given an official appointment in Ireland. While he was there she wrote to him continually, naïve careful letters, asking him assiduously about his life, detailing the little facts of hers, and without a word about her own feelings. Alas, he had suffered too deeply at her hands to be able to respond with the same ardour. She had broken something in him that could never be mended. But when he saw the change in her, a generous tenderness welled up in his spirit that washed away any trace of bitterness that might lurk there. He answered her letters with affectionate kindness, saved up such scraps of news as he thought might entertain her, encouraged any plan of hers that seemed likely to give her pleasure.

"My dear Caroline," runs a typical letter, "I am very much obliged to you for your letters—and much pleased with them—I never knew you more rational or quiet, and you say nothing which doesn't give me great pleasure—Matters are a little uncertain in the political world, but at any rate I think a tour to Paris would do you good, provided you can avoid making scamps of acquaintance, which is your great fault and danger—I went down to dine at Bellevue; where I saw Mr. Peter La Touche, 94 years old past—he dined with us. Mrs. La Touche had tried to persuade him not, but he was determined upon it. They keep him on a strict regimen of sherry and water, but if he can get at a bottle of wine now he drinks it off in a crack—there is a fine old cod for you." . . .

It is significant of the strength of the bond that bound him to her, that now Caroline was no longer provoking him, he began at once to try and excuse her to himself on the old plea. Other people, not she, were responsible for her errors: Let her avoid making friends with scamps, and he was only too anxious for her to go herself to Paris or anywhere else if she fancied it might make her happy. But there was to be no more travelling for her in this world. As the year advanced, her health began to exhibit alarming symptoms. In October, 1827, the doctors reported her to be dangerously ill of dropsy. From the first Caroline was sure her case was hopeless. But the conviction did not disperse her calm. On the contrary, her spirit rose to meet its stern ordeal; and, face to face with death, that streak of genuine nobility, which a lifetime of folly had not succeeded in wholly eradicating from her nature, showed itself as never before. She did not, indeed, give up dramatizing herself; she would not have been Caroline if she had. Appreciating to the full the pathos of her situation, she rallied all her strength in the effort to stage a death scene which should do her credit. Still, there is something heroic in a sense of the stage that is unquelled by the presence of death itself; and moreover the role, in which Caroline chose to make her last appearance before the world, was for once worthy of the heroine she had so long aspired to be. She showed no fear; she sought refuge neither in self-deception nor self-pity. Though racked with suffering, she lay hour by hour through the darkening autumn days, quiet and unmurmuring; her chief concern to convince others, in the short time that remained to her, how sorry she was for the needless suffering she had brought on them.

"Dearest Maria," she writes to Lady Duncannon, her eldest brother's wife, "as I cannot sit up, I am obliged to use a pencil. . . . I consider my painful illness as a great blessing—I feel returned to my God and duty and my dearest husband: and my heart which was so proud and insensible is quite overcome with the great kindness I receive—I have brought myself to be quite another person and broke that hard spell which prevented me saying my prayers; so that if I were better, I would go with you and your dear children to church. I say all this, dearest Maria, lest you should think I flew to Religion because I was in danger —it is no such thing, my heart is softened, I see how good and kind others are, and I am quite resigned to die. I do not myself think there is a chance for me."

And to Lady Morgan, with a flash of her old bewitching whimsicality, she says:

"I am on my death-bed: say I might have died by a diamond, I die now by a brickbat: but remember the only noble fellow I ever met with is William Lamb. He is to me what Shore was to Jane Shore."

For, now at this final crisis of her troubled history, it was William who more than ever filled her thoughts. His name was always on her lips; she still wrote to him regularly and with no word of complaint—she who was used to complain so often and so groundlessly—and she besought the doctors not to tell him of her condition lest it might be a worry to him. There was no concealing it however. Lady Morgan, visiting Ireland, saw him one evening sunk in black depression at the news. A day or two later, he sent her the doctor's report with a covering note. "It is with great pain

I send you the enclosed. It is some consolation that she is now
relieved from pain: but illness is a terrible thing." To Caroline
herself, when she rallied a little, he wrote with an emotion all the
more poignant for the reserve with which it is expressed.

"My dear C, I received your little line yesterday; and later
received with great pleasure Dr. Goddard's account that you
were a little better. My heart is almost broken that I cannot
come over directly: but your brother, to whom I have written,
will explain to you the difficult situation in which I am placed.
How unfortunate and melancholy that you should be so ill now,
and that it should be at a time when I, who have had so many
years of idleness, am so fixed and held down by circumstances."

His ordeal was not to be protracted. In December Caroline,
now removed by medical advice to London, was visibly sinking.
It was noticed that she spoke with difficulty and that she seemed
unable to take in what was going on round her. By the middle of
January, it became clear that the end was near. Then only "Send
for William," she whispered with a last effort of her spent forces,
"he is the only person who has never failed me." He did not fail
her now. Within a few days he had arrived at Melbourne House.
And alone behind closed doors, they spoke to one another for the
last time. It was for this only she had waited. A day or two later,
her sister-in-law, Mrs. George Lamb, watching by her still
form, heard a little sigh. She looked more closely: Caroline was
dead.

William was out of the room at the time. When he was told the
news he was sunk for a day or two in grief. Then, to all appearance
his usual self, he went back to work. But this was no sign of in-
sensibility. Sad experience had taught him that no purpose is
served by unavailing lamentation: "solitude and retirement
cherish grief," he once wrote to a bereaved friend, "employment
and exertion are the only means of dissipating it". In reality
Caroline's death affected him profoundly. Detached from her as
he had learnt to make himself, painful and frustrated as his feeling
towards her had grown to be, it yet remained different in kind from
what he felt towards anyone else. "In spite of all," he was to say

in later days, "she was more to me than anyone ever was, or ever will be." For years afterward the mere mention of her name brought tears into his eyes; and plunged him into melancholy reverie. "Shall we meet?" he would be heard murmuring to himself, "shall we meet in another world?"

CHAPTER IX

## THE FINISHED PRODUCT

BUT THIS is to anticipate. In 1826 William's life was still at a standstill. So far as outward circumstances were concerned, it was unchanged since 1816. All the same these ten years had not been unimportant in his history. Frustrated of active outlet, his energies concentrated themselves on the development of his inner man. It was high time. For though he had been a precocious youth, at about twenty-six he had begun to mark time. The perturbations of his marriage, the preoccupations of his social and political life, required so much of his vitality as to leave little over for the maturing of mind and personality. Besides, he was the sort of character that, in any circumstances, does not come of age till middle life. His nature was composed of such diverse elements that it took a long time to fuse them into a stable whole. Certainly he needed some slow blank period in which to digest his experience. These ten years were a bit of luck for him, whether he realized it or not.

In the first place they gave his intelligence space to develop. During this period he read omnivorously. No more than at Cambridge was it an orderly sort of reading. From Pindar to Shakespeare, from Thucydides to St. Augustine, from French to Latin, from philosophy to novels, he turned as the fancy took him. But the very diversity of his fancy meant that he covered a great deal of ground. And if his reading was unsystematic, it was the very opposite of superficial. He pondered, he compared, he memorized; the Elizabethan drama, for instance, he knew so well that he could repeat by heart whole scenes not only of Shakespeare but of Massinger; the margins of his books were black with the markings of his flowing illegible hand. He educated himself outside the library as well. When he was shooting—he loved the sport and was often out six hours a day—he took the opportunity to observe the habits of the wild creatures and note them down. On a landlord's ride round his father's property he would pick up

143

information about agriculture, committing it to his memory for future reference. And he thought as much as he observed. More, in fact; for, to William, information was only interesting in so far as it illustrated a universal law. It was the nature of his mind to argue from the particular to the general; and he kept a common-place book, in which he noted down the generalizations that were always springing to his mind. Sometimes they were the fruit of his reading:

"Never disregard a book because the author of it is a foolish fellow."

"A curious book might be made of the great actions performed by actors whose names had not been preserved, the glories of the anonymous."

We find him speculating as to why it is, that the spirit of a past period, so vivid in an original document, evaporates completely in the process of translation; or comparing the attitude of the Greeks to Alcibiades, with that of the English to Fox. He made it a rule, if a passage in a book started a train of thought in his mind, to pursue it to its conclusion, and then jot this down before he forgot it: At other times his reflections are the product of his personal experience. He had seen a great deal of human nature in his time. Now he began to meditate on it. Why did people get married? How did they manage their incomes? What was the secret of their success or failure? What fundamentally are the prevailing forces in public and private life? The pages of his book are littered with questionings and generalizations on these subjects. As time passed the different aspects of his thought began to connect themselves one with another; the wisdom he had acquired from books, to relate itself to the wisdom he had acquired from life. Gradually his scattered reflections composed themselves into a philosophy, his unconsciously acquired point of view built up for itself a conscious intellectual basis and justification.

Along with this mental development, went a development of character. The lessons of experience sank in and began to modify his native disposition; insensibly he began to control such impulses in himself as were inconsistent with what he believed, to give rein to those that his intelligence approved. Time, too, did its work on him; stripping his nature of such characteristics as were merely youthful and superficial, sharpening and stabilizing those that were of its essence. Slowly, the difficult process of maturity accomplished itself; bit by bit William's temperament and his intelligence, the influence of his heredity and his education, of his married life, his social life, and his public life, integrated themselves into a completed personality. At forty-seven he was at last the William Lamb, Lord Melbourne, of later days. As it is in this character that he cuts a figure in English history, it may be permitted to us to pause for a moment, and examine it in greater detail.

To look at he was extremely prepossessing, "handsome, verging to portly," said an observer, "with a sweet countenance and an expression of refined, easy, careless good humour. He was too well-bred to seem unpleasantly sensual; but his whole person, expression and manner showed a pleasure-loving nature, indulgent to himself and to others." Indeed, age, while abating little of the sparkle of his youthful good looks, had enriched them with a new mellowness. His well-cut countenance radiated the comfortable glow that comes from years of good living; beneath his thick greying brows the eyes gleamed out, brilliant as ever, but with an added softness of geniality. His demeanour was of a piece with his appearance. There is no more talk of his arrogance or self-consciousness. Natural talent had united with long experience to make him the perfect man of the world, whose manners, at once unobtrusive and accomplished, could handle the most delicate situation with light-handed mastery, and shed round every conversation an atmosphere of delightful ease. Yet there was nothing studied about him. On the contrary, the first thing that struck most people meeting him was that he was surprisingly, eccentrically natural. Abrupt and casual, he seemed to saunter through life, swearing when he pleased, laughing when he pleased —with an odd infectious explosive "ha, ha!"—sprawling about in chairs, taking his meals with unashamed relish, and jerking out anything apparently that came into his head. It was his frankness that, above all, astonished. On the most dignified occasions, solemn political councils, stiff social gatherings, when everybody else was guarded or stilted, William Lamb talked exactly as if he were at home; came out, in lazy, flippant, colloquial tones, with some candid comment that made the whole pompous pretence immediately ridiculous.

His habits were equally unconventional. He was full of queer idiosyncrasies of behaviour: gleeful rubbings together of his hands if he were amused, odd ejaculations, "eh, eh!", before he made a remark; and, a curious gesture, passing a finger to the back of his head while he was talking. His letters were folded and sealed anyhow; the pockets of his beautifully-cut coats bulged with a confusion of papers and bank notes; he never could be bothered with a watch, but would just shout to a passing servant to tell him the time; he went to sleep when and wherever the mood took him; in a fit of absent-mindedness he would start talking to himself in the midst of a company of strangers. Indeed, though they liked him, people found him perplexing in more ways than one. Here we come to his third salient characteristic. He was mysterious. It was partly that, for all his apparent frankness, he was discreet. Persons coming away from an interview with him, in which he had seemed to talk with complete candour, would suddenly realize that he had not given himself away on any point that really mattered. On the contrary, they wondered nervously if they had not given themselves away to him. His air of idle nonchalance lulled them at first into thinking he noticed little. But then, looking up at him by chance, they would perceive, darting out beneath the half-closed lids, a keen glance that seemed to penetrate to their very hearts.

But most of all his point of view baffled them. His conversation was fascinating; the fine flower of Whig agreeability, at once light and learned, civilized and spontaneous, but made individual by the play of his whimsical fancy and the gusto of his good spirits— "There was a glee in his mirth," it was remarked, "indescribably charming." But the spirit, the intention behind the discourse— ah, that was elusive. Was William Lamb serious? Certainly he sometimes seemed to be. He would talk ardently on the most solemn subjects, political principle, the doctrines of Christianity. Yet within a few minutes he was conversing with equal animation in a different and less edifying strain. He had the typical eighteenth-century enjoyment of animal humour; "Now," he would say with zest as the dining-room doors shut on the ladies, leaving the gentlemen to their wine, "now we can talk broad." And even on serious subjects his tone was ambiguous. Its salient characteristic was irony, a mischievous, enigmatic irony, that played audaciously over the most sacred topics, leaving its hearer very much in doubt whether William Lamb thought them sacred at all. Paradox, too, was of the fibre of his talk. He loved to defend the indefensible. "What I like about the Order of the Garter," he once remarked, "is that there is no damned merit about it." Much as he appreciated poetry, he professed to welcome the news of a poet's death. "It is a good thing when these authors die," he confided, "for then one gets their works, and is done with them." His paradoxes grew bolder the more astonishment they created. If he was talking to anyone who struck him as a prig or a humbug, they would pile themselves wickedly one on the other, till his bewildered interlocutor relapsed into shocked silence. Indeed, William's whole personality was a paradox. Racy and refined, sensible and eccentric, cynical and full of sentiment, direct and secretive, each successive impression he made seemed to contradict the last.

Yet each impression was a true one. The outward paradox mirrored accurately the paradox within. His new mildness of demeanour, for example, was no pretence. As with age he grew more independent of other people's opinions, native fastidiousness began to modify family custom. The Lamb robustness remained, but refined into a charming brusquerie. Experience, too, had softened him. It is the proof of his essential fineness of disposition, that he profited by suffering. The difficulties of his private, the disappointments of his public life, so far from hardening him, had taught him to be tolerant in practice as well as in theory. Further, the unsatisfactory spectacle of his own career disposed him to look kindly on the shortcomings of others. Profoundly unegotistic, he judged the rest of the world as he would judge himself.

F

But he was not at one with himself.  On the contrary, maturity had only intensified the discord within him.  His intellectual judgment was more cynically realistic than ever.  All he had seen of the world confirmed him in his view that it was ruled mainly by folly, vanity, and selfishness.  This is the burden of almost every observation on human nature in his notebook:

"Your friends praise your abilities to the skies, submit to you in argument, and seem to have the greatest deference for you; but, though they may ask it, you never find them following your advice upon their own affairs; nor allowing you to manage your own, without thinking that you should follow theirs.  Thus, in fact, they all think themselves wiser than you, whatever they may say."

"It wounds a man less to confess that he has failed in any pursuit through idleness, neglect, the love of pleasure, etc., etc., which are his own faults, than through incapacity and unfitness, which are the faults of his nature."

"Persons in general are sufficiently ready to set themselves off by communicating their knowledge, but they are not so willing to communicate their ignorance.  They are apt, both in writing and conversation, to stop when they come to the precise difficulty of the subject, which they are unable to get over, with such common phrases as 'it were easy to push these considerations much further', or 'with the rest you are perfectly well acquainted'."

"When a man is determined by his own inclination either to act or not to act in a particular manner, he invariably sets about devising an argument by which he may justify himself to himself for the line he is about to pursue."

"If you make an estimate of your expenses for the coming year, and upon that estimate you find that they exactly amount to or fall little short of your income, you may be sure that you are an embarrassed, if not a ruined man."

"Wealth is so much the greatest good that Fortune has to bestow that in the Latin and English languages it has usurped her name."

"You should never assume contempt for that which it is not very manifest that you have it in your power to possess, nor does a wit ever make a more contemptible figure than when, in attempting satire, he shows that he does not understand that which he would make the subject of his ridicule."

And when someone quoted to him an old observation of his own to the effect that man could only learn by experience, "No, no," he returned sadly, "nobody learns anything by experience; everybody does the same thing over and over again."

This last reflects, indirectly, as much on himself as on others. It was the measure of his detachment, that he never excepted himself from his condemnation of human beings in general. His contempt was not arrogant. This makes it more amiable; but it shows how thoroughly disillusioned he was. As for the ideal motives by which people professed to be actuated, he thought them the most fantastic illusions of all; smoke-screens raised by men in order to hide from themselves the fact of their own selfishness. If, by any rare chance, idealists were sincere, it could only be because they were too stupid to understand the nature of things. "A doctrinaire," he used to say, "is a fool but an honest man." Or again, "Nobody ever did anything very foolish except from some strong principle."

Yet his heart continued to rebel against the conclusions of his reason. His sensibility was as tremblingly keen as in youth. He did not believe in human virtue: but he recognized goodness when he saw it; and he loved it. Even if public life was in fact a shoddy, self-seeking affair, how heart-stirring a pageant did it contrive to present! A moving tale still brought the tears to William's eyes, an heroic deed still fired him to a glow of generous admiration. The grace of girlhood, the sweetness of friendship, the charm of garden solitude, vain and ephemeral though they might be, set him throbbing with exquisite and poignant emotions. And now and again his spirit was touched by sublimer visitations.

Suddenly there would sweep over him a mysterious sense of some august and unearthly power behind the show of things, governing human destiny. "I consider," he once broke out, unexpectedly and with emotion, to an embarrassed Cabinet meeting, "that England has been under the special protection of Divine Providence at certain periods of her history; the Spanish Armada, for instance, and the retirement of the French squadron from Bantry Bay." And on another occasion, "I do not approve," he said, "of the condemnation in Fénelon, of those whom he is pleased to call mystics—to which persuasion I belong." Indeed these curious spiritual intimations of his were in the nature of direct mystical experience. They did not lead him to adopt a thoroughgoing mystical philosophy; for they came too seldom and too fleetingly for him to feel justified in founding an intellectual structure on them. Besides, he could find no logical ground for believing in their truth. But he was too sincere not to recognize their convincing reality as long as they lasted. And though they did not displace his rationalism, they undermined its security. Uneasily he hung suspended between two opinions.

No wonder he was paradoxical! What was life but a bundle of contradictions? No wonder he was ironical; faced by the preposterous incongruity of experience, the only thing a reasonable person could do was to shrug his shoulders and smile. His duality of vision appears in his attitude to every sort of subject. No one appreciated better the achievements of culture: but he did not believe they had ever seriously influenced mankind. "Raphael was employed to decorate the Vatican," he said, "not because he was a great painter but because his uncle was architect to the Pope." In politics he united a mystical patriotism and a disinterested wish to do the best for his country, to a scornful disbelief in the sacredness of any human institution, the good sense of any political ideal. Again, though his heart was so abnormally tender that he could hardly hear a tale of suffering without tears, humanitarian schemes raised in him a violent antagonism. "I am not a subscribing sort of fellow," he would reply breezily to earnest persons asking him to contribute to a philanthropic cause. Educational reformers, factory reformers—the only result of their efforts, he alleged, would be to worry the poor. As for the anti-slavery fanatics, he thought them perfectly futile. "I say, Archbishop," he once remarked to Archbishop Whately, "what do you think I would have done about this slavery business if I had my own way? I would have done nothing at all. I would have left it all alone. It is all a pack of nonsense. There always have been slaves in most civilized countries, the Greeks, the Romans. However, they *would* have their own way and we have abolished slavery. But it is all great folly." It was their confidence in their own ability to do good that put him off humanitarians so much. Little did they realize humanity's gigantic propensity to error. "Try to do no good," he asserted trenchantly, "and then you won't get into any scrapes."

But it was in his attitude to religion that his duality of mind appeared most significantly. Many people thought he was an atheist. Certainly he talked flippantly about the most holy topics; he seldom went to church himself, and he did not like other people going often; "No, my Lord," he replied to the disconcerted Archbishop of York, who had invited him to attend the evening service, "once is orthodox, twice is puritanical." And he had a horror of pious emotionalism—"Things are coming to a pretty pass," he exclaimed, after listening to an evangelical sermon on the consequences of sin, "when religion is allowed to invade private life." Roman Catholicism, in his view, was insufficiently calm, and he recommended the Church of England on the ground it was the "least meddlesome". Yet the subject of religion exercised over him a strange compelling fascination. For hours he would sit studying the controversies of the early fathers; every new theological work found its way to his shelves, its margins scrawled with his notes. No doubt this was partly due to historical interest. Religion, he once said, had played so prominent a role in human history, that every educated man should investigate it. Perhaps he also found an ironical amusement in contemplating the extraordinary figments of fancy with which, according to his ideas, human beings had seen fit still further to confuse their already perplexed lives. But there was, all the same, a serious side to his religious preoccupations. The imaginative element in him cried out against a purely rationalistic interpretation of the universe. And the mystical strain, stirring always in the hinterland of his consciousness, set him wondering if there was not something in religion after all. Certainly there were things in his experience inexplicable by rationalist theory. If he searched the records of religion long enough, might he not discover an explanation of them—might he not even find grounds for that faith for which, in spite of himself, his spirit yearned? Anyway there was no harm in trying. In a world where all was obscure, the speculations of the theologians had as good a chance of being true as anything else.

For this was the final result of his cogitations; a scepticism more complete, because more considered, even than that of his youth. When the evidence of heart and head, of reason and imagination, contradicted each other at every turn, he could put no certain trust in his judgment. And the opinions of others, so far as he had studied them, provided no more satisfactory solution to the riddle. How could one trust the judgment of beings, the essential condition of whose nature it was to be limited and biased and ignorant?

"Neither man nor woman," he noted, "can be worth any-thing until they have discovered that they are fools. This is the first step towards becoming either estimable or agreeable; and until it be taken there is no hope. The sooner the discovery is made the better, as there is more time and power for taking advantage of it. Sometimes the great truth is found out too late to apply to it any effectual remedy. Sometimes it is never found at all; and these form the desperate and inveterate causes of folly, self-conceit, and impertinence."

No, life was an insoluble conundrum; and all that a sensible man could do was to try and get through it with as little un-pleasantness to himself, and everyone else, as possible; in private to be considerate and detached, in public to do what little he could to guide the world down its uncharted course with the minimum of friction. This generally involved doing very little. It certainly meant refusing to risk an immediate disturbance for the sake of a problematical future good. As for ultimate truth, the nearest an honest man could hope to get to that, was to be vigilantly faith-ful to the conclusions of his own reason and experience; not to let his candid impressions be distorted by convention or cowardice or the deceptions of his own vanity. Probably, these personal conclusions were as far from the truth as everything else. But they were the only things of which he had first-hand evidence. Anyway only good could come of speaking one's mind, even if it did shock people. "It is a good thing to surprise," he once said. By shaking others out of their complacency one might make them realize how ill-founded human convictions are.

He reaped the reward of his courage. William got closer to truth, pierced far deeper into the significance of things, than the majority of his hustling contemporaries. All the same his creed was not an inspiriting one. And there was a strong undercurrent of melancholy in him. "To those who think," he was fond of quoting, "life is a comedy, to those who feel, a tragedy." William was far too sensitive not to feel its tragic implications more often than was comfortable for him. Fits of depression overtook him, in which he sat silent and remote, overwhelmed by a sense of the barren fleetingness of existence; and even his brightest moods were shot through by grey streaks of disillusionment. Yet he was not so unhappy as might have been expected. For one thing he was no longer at open war with himself. Though the discordant elements in him were as discordant as ever, he had given up trying to reconcile them. He had imposed an armistice on his inner struggle, he had come to terms with his difficulties. Besides, happiness is an affair of temperament rather than opinions. And William's temperament was all salt and sunshine. The depression of 1816 was too alien from his spirit to last long; when the immediate cloud passed, willy-nilly he began to respond to life again; by the time he was forty-six he had recovered nearly all his youthful capacity for enjoyment. The world might be a futile place; but how odd it was, how fascinating, how endlessly full of interest! By now he had acquired the skill of a life-long hedonist in extracting every drop of pleasure from life that it had to offer. "Lord Melbourne looked as if he enjoyed himself," said a surprised observer who had watched him beaming at some tedious city banquet. "There is nothing Lord Melbourne does not enjoy," was the reply. Along with his pleasure in life went a pleasure in his fellow creatures. Most cynics have a fundamental antipathy to their kind; not so William. "The worst of the present day," he once said to a friend, "is that men hate one another so damnably. For my part I love them all!" This was a slight exaggeration. Arrogant people irritated him profoundly, and pretentious ones still more. "There now, that fellow has been trying for half-an-hour to make me believe he knows a great deal of what he knows nothing," he commented after listening to a literary man holding forth at his table, "we won't have him again." But though he did not love everybody, he liked most and hated none. Himself normal in his tastes, he felt at home with the normal run of humanity; sympathized with their aspirations, shared their pleasures, understood their weaknesses. Perhaps human beings were not very dignified; but then, he did not feel dignified himself. Besides, their absurdities and inconsistencies only made them the more entertaining. And if he liked men as a whole, certain individuals among them he loved. Experience had only confirmed the strength of his personal affections. For Emily, for Fred, for his closest friends, he felt an ardent unselfish love that overrode all his deliberately cultivated detachment. Unquenchable beacons of comfort and joy they shone out, radiating a little circle of light in the huge darkness of the universe, warming the shivering heart. Indeed the very paradox of his nature made him a happy man on the whole. A cynic who loved mankind, a sceptic who found life thoroughly worth living, he contrived to face the worthlessness of things, cheerfully enough.

Only there was a chink in the armour of his serenity. It depended too much on keeping in the sun. Since he relied for happiness on the passing joys of pleasure and affection, he must manage his life so that these were always at his disposal. A threat to the amenity of his mode of existence was deeply disturbing to him. As we have seen he was terrified of revolution. And in private life, too, he avoided the disagreeable as much as he could. He had a horror of seeing a corpse, for instance. Even in books, he refused to read anything that dealt with the grim or the sordid. Crabbe, he said, degraded everything he touched; and in later years he put aside *Oliver Twist* after one glance. "It is all among workhouses and pickpockets and coffin-makers," he said, "I do not *like* those things: I wish to avoid them. I do not like them in reality and therefore I do not like to see them represented."

Indeed there was a flaw in his philosophy, a radical defect, implicit in this shrinking from the unpleasant. The happiness that is an expression only of an instinctive mood has no certainty of continuance; William's serenity rested on no reasoned foundation, but only on a precariously-adjusted equilibrium. For the present his sanguine temperament was strong enough to provide a counterweight to the melancholy of his scepticism. But supposing his mood changed, supposing that, stricken by sorrow or by the failure of vitality, he lost his faculty of enjoyment—at once he would be flung into that slough of despond to which his intellectual convictions might logically seem to consign him. Only as long as he kept his balance was he safe; and in a world of chance and catastrophe, at any moment it might begin to waver.

The truth was that William's mature character, like his youthful, was a compromise. In a sense he had made far more of a success of it than most people. For he was that rare phenomenon, a genuinely independent personality. From the turmoil of warring influences which, from cradle to middle age, had fought for possession of him, he had emerged dominated by none, his every opinion the honest conclusion of his own experience; his every utterance and habit, down to the way he ate, and folded his letters, the unqualified expression of his own individuality. But, though he was enslaved to nothing else, he was not master of himself. Strong enough to reject any faith that his own reason did not think convincing, he had not the strength to form a faith of his own. His spiritual security was at the mercy of circumstances.

And the course of his life too. His philosophy hampered his power of action. It was not that he was weak, as his friends, from Emily down, were always complaining. On the contrary, no one could act more vigorously once he was convinced he was right. The trouble was that he was seldom so convinced. He saw every question from so many sides, most problems seemed to him so hopeless of solution, that he was generally for doing nothing at all. Still less could he direct his various actions to a chosen end: he had never made up his mind as to whether any end was worth achieving. If circumstances should happen to push him into a position of power, he was perfectly ready to take it on: for men and their affairs inspired him with far too little respect for him to shrink from assuming responsibility for them. But, on the other hand, he did not think it worth while stirring a finger to mould circumstances to his will. Smiling, indolent, and inscrutable he lay, a pawn in the hands of fortune.

# LORD M

*or the Later Life of Lord Melbourne*

LORD MELBOURNE IN 1836

LORD MELBOURNE in 1838

## CHAPTER I

## IN OFFICE

### (1)

AT LONG last fortune favoured him. In February, 1827, Lord Liverpool, the Prime Minister, had a stroke. Bereft of his placid and reconciling hand, the Government split into two opposing sections: the Ultra-Tories and the Canningite-Tories. Which of the two was to obtain control depended on the unpredictable caprice of George IV. After the usual hesitations, he asked Canning to form a Government. Rather than serve under him, the Ultras, led by the Duke of Wellington, resigned. Canning therefore, in order to fill the gap left by their secession, turned to his Whig followers, notably Palmerston and William Lamb. Even now it seemed as if William's ironical lazy indifference might lose him his chance. To his sister Emily's exasperation, he chose to leave London at the very moment the Government was forming. However, when the list of candidates for office was placed before the King—"William Lamb!" he exclaimed, his memory aglow with pleasing recollections of old Carlton House convivialities. "William Lamb—put *him* anywhere you like!" In May he was appointed Chief Secretary for Ireland. It was the turning point in William's life. At last, at forty-six years of age, his luck had changed: and for good. William stepped on to the public stage, an official ruler of England.

It was a very different England from that of his youth. The lucid leisured eighteenth century was vanished; and in its place, to the thunder of a thousand factory wheels, surged forward the murky and tumultuous era which was its successor. All was movement; the industrial movement, the democratic movement, the Romantic movement, the Irish National movement. All was confusion; religious neo-medievalists jostled progressive rationalists; hard-fisted capitalists clashed with enthusiastic humanitarians; destitution and stupendous wealth dwelled side by side; in England the young Mill hailed the dawn of the age of enlightenment, in Scotland the young Carlyle brooded darkly on the imminent eclipse of human virtue. And the spirit that infused the age was of a piece with its preoccupations; earnest, hopeful, strenuous and foggy—pulsating with energy, aglow with hope, tormented by conscience. The smoke and flame of the factories found their counterpart in the smoke and flame that swirled in the hearts of the people who lived under their shadow.

The new spirit showed itself in the world of politics. Signs were visible on every side that the struggle between the old aristocratic landed régime and the new individualist democratic forces could not be delayed much longer. Till 1815 it had been held up by the Napoleonic Wars, in the disturbed years, which followed, by the fear of revolution. But now Europe seemed settled down into steady peace; for the time being the country was prosperous. And the restless discontent of those classes who were shut out from political power began to make itself felt; seeping up from the world of revolutionary agitators to infuse itself into the respectable middle and professional classes. Everywhere the cry was reform: law reform, educational reform, fiscal reform of the laws against Nonconformists and Roman Catholics, Parliamentary reform. Parliamentary reform was the crucial issue. For, by destroying the aristocracy's monopoly of seats in the House of Commons, it wrested from it at one stroke the control of government. With it, the men of the new age would be in a position to impose any other change they wanted; without it, they could move only by permission of their opponents.

Such were the questions canvassed at reunions of provincial kings of industry, at gatherings of serious thinkers, in working men's clubs. Only in the lordly drawing-rooms of the politicians themselves was the atmosphere less excited. Belonging as they did, Tory and Whig alike, to the old régime, they had no personal interest in a change. However, they could not altogether escape feeling the pressure of the time-spirit. It was becoming clear to them that something new would have to be done; and that, since they alone possessed political power, they would have to do it. Confronted by this new situation, the old party divisions began to lose whatever binding power they still possessed; people began to range themselves into new groups. There were, roughly speaking, three positions that they could take up; that of the Ultra-Tories, that of the Canningite-Tories, and that of the large body of opinion whom, anticipating the terminology of a later age, we may call the Liberals. The Ultras were against all reform; the Liberals in favour of it in varying degrees; the Canningites stood between them. Strongly against the surrender of aristocratic power, implied in Parliamentary Reform, they yet believed that administration was in need of much modification and improvement; and moreover that by making such practical and executive reform, they would allay the discontent that created the demand for Parliamentary Reform. If, so they contended, people had a better police and poor law and a fairer system of taxation, they would be quite happy to go on being governed by the gentlemen of England.

In 1827 the Canningites got a chance to try their policy. The Ultras, in power for the last thirty odd years, were clearly out of tune with the temper of the times. The Liberals were not yet in a condition to take their place officially. They belonged, most of them, to the Whig Party; and the Whigs were still in confusion. A few like William agreed with Canning; the old orthodox Whigs, led by Lords Grey and Holland, secretly nervous of change and personally distrustful of Canning, shrank from committing themselves in any direction. The professional politicians, led by the brilliant and changeable Brougham, still tacked about in a seething turmoil of intrigue, now to the right, now left, according as either seemed likely to bring them office. Anyway, for the time being, the crucial issue of Parliamentary Reform was in abeyance. The reformers quarrelled among themselves, while the public was not yet completely convinced that reform was necessary. Now, if ever, was the time to try the Canningite middle way.

It came naturally to William to support it. Not that he was much of a reformer, even in the modified Canningite sense. The spirit of the new age left him singularly unimpressed. He did not like earnestness, he did not like energy, he did not like muddle-headedness. And he had the aristocrat's antipathy to the middle classes. "I don't like the middle classes," he once observed; "the higher and lower classes, there's some good in them, but the middle class are all affectation and conceit and pretence and concealment." Further, he thought change always ran the risk of disturbing the security of society; while convinced as he was of the futility of most human effort, he did not believe it ever did the good it intended. On the contrary sensational reforms, like Parliamentary Reform, did positive harm. For by raising hopes that could never be fulfilled they left people more discontented than ever. "I like what is tranquil and stable," he once remarked. This sentence sums up his political creed.

On the other hand, he recognized that the world, unfortunately, was a changing place; and that political institutions, make-shift affairs at best, must change along with it. Tranquillity and stability can only be preserved by a continuous process of adaptation. If a large section of the people were dissatisfied with the existing system, it meant that it was out of date. And, however silly their demands might be, there would be no peace till they were in some degree conceded. Finally since administrative reforms affected their actual lives the most, they were the kind most likely to pacify them. Holding these views, he could follow Canning if not with enthusiasm yet with an honest conviction that it was the best thing to do.

Himself he had only a minor part to play. The Irish Secretaryship carried with it no seat in the Cabinet; though Ireland, as usual, was in a state of furious unrest, there was nothing much for the time being to be done about it. The Irish were agitating for Catholic Emancipation. Canning was in favour of giving it to them; but the King, reverting in a misguided moment to the ideas of his father, refused. All that Canning could do was to send for William and tell him to go over there and try and convince the Irish of the Government's good intentions, until such time as the King's mind might change. In August he arrived in Dublin.

It was a great change from go-ahead England. Under a frail veneer of eighteenth-century manners, the country wallowed in bloodstained medieval chaos. The Protestant governing-class divided their time between bullying the natives, wild Hibernian rollickings and killing each other in duels. The mass of the people, savage, superstitious and on the edge of starvation, now fawned on their masters in oriental servility, now gathered together in secret societies with fantastic names—Caffees, Bootashees, Whiteboys and Ribbonmen—to plot their overthrow by means of atrocity and assassination. The administration itself was a clotted tangle of corruption and inefficiency. While round the general confusion hovered the Irish nationalist politicians led by the flamboyant O'Connell, seizing every chance to exacerbate the situation. The humane and sophisticated William made an incongruous figure in such a place. But he was not daunted. His commission suited him very well. Catholic Emancipation was one of the few reforms of which he thoroughly approved; both from a deep-seated dislike of religious intolerance and because he thought that discontent in Ireland had grown so widespread as to show, according to his theory of politics, that it was necessary. On the other hand he did not mind its being put off for the moment: temperamentally he was always inclined for inaction. Surveying the scene with calm sardonic detachment he set himself to his task.

The Irish political scene soon began to feel the impact of a new personality. Former Chief Secretaries, fettered by the conventions of their position, had associated mostly with that Irish Protestant circle who led Dublin Society. Not so William: "The great means by which the Orange gentry have drawn over everyone who has come here," he writes to a colleague, "was by assuming that their set was the only one worth associating with, quite the first company. You, who know Almacks, know that this is one of the strongest, if not the very strongest passions of the human mind." Himself he saw everyone; kept open house to a mixed crowd of every party and creed, and took particular pains to make the acquaintance of seditious opponents. Such behaviour shocked the old officials very much. "Mr. Lamb," lamented one of them, "keeps a lot of bad company!" Indeed William was an unorthodox head of a department in every way. The free and easy habits of the Lamb family, transported into official life, produced a surprising spectacle. Every rule of precedent and routine was set aside. Seated in his room with the door open, William would write his letters and interview a deputation at the same time; while around him, a crowd of underlings sauntered through their work amid a hubbub of conversation. If a message was sent in that someone had asked to see him—"Show him in!" he would shout. When the visitor was admitted, "Now," William would begin genially, "don't go too fast, don't ask for impossibilities and don't do anything damn foolish." Even the Irish were surprised by his methods of conducting business; but, unlike the officials, they liked them. Here at any rate was a change from the formal frigid Englishman they had been accustomed to expect. Nor did William just talk pleasantly to them: he went out of his way to treat Catholics on an equality with Protestants, appointed them in preference to posts open to each; openly proclaimed his disgust at the prejudiced way in which Catholics were treated in the law-courts, set himself against all pro-Protestant agitation and shut the door against informers.

He also threw himself into the study of the Irish problems. It was soon clear that all talk of his laziness was nonsense. Given a job, he worked unusually hard. Every post to England carried with it elaborate memoranda from him; on the Tithe question, the local government question, the land question, the Education question. It must be admitted that these were seldom constructive. The upshot of William's researches was that each problem bristled with difficulties, that most solutions would do more harm than good and that the wisest policy seemed to leave things alone at any rate for the time being. "One is sorry," he observes with caustic melancholy at the end of one of these dispatches, "to trouble anything that is quiet here." Anyway his own time was fully occupied in keeping Lord Wellesley, the Lord Lieutenant, in a good humour and warding off the never-slackening throng of persons clamouring angrily to have a job done for them. Sometimes their importunities strained William's patience to breaking-point. "I can't give away a place of fifty pounds without making fifty enemies," he exclaimed: and again, "Lord Clare and Mr. Fitz-gibbon want a living for a Mr. Westhorpe whose principal merit is that his is the only family in the county of Limerick that will receive Mrs. Fitzgibbon. Tho' I have the greatest toleration and even partiality for ladies of that description, yet I cannot go so far as to say that associating with them in compliance with the wishes of a patron is the best possible recommendation for a clergyman . . . that damned little man milliner Clare!—he knows that I promised him nothing: but, like all Irishmen, if you put one single civil word in your communication with them, they immediately construe it into a promise; and charge you with a breach of faith if they don't get what they have asked."

On the whole, however, he got a good deal of fun out of the spectacle of human infirmity afforded by the Irish scene. One day a little boy, the son of a subordinate, was brought in to be shown his room at the office. "Is there anything you would like here?" William asked him kindly. The child chose a stick of sealing-wax. "That's right, my boy," said William, pressing a bundle of pens as well into his hand, "begin life early. All these things belong to the public; and your business is to get out of the public as much as you can."

He was not to enjoy Ireland long. By the end of January, 1828, political affairs in England were so unsettled as to bring him back for good. Canning had died the previous August. But the King, incensed at what he considered his desertion by the Duke of Wellington, had kept the Canningites in power under the leadership of Lord Goderich, a fussy, timorous politician, hen-pecked by his wife, terrified of responsibility, and often on the verge of tears. Such a man could not long conduct the government of England through a critical period. In January, after an ignominious scene of resignation, in which he was forced to borrow his royal master's pocket handkerchief in order to assuage the effects of his own agitation, Lord Goderich disappeared from the scene.

His departure produced a crisis of the first order. It was clear that no government, not confessedly Whig, could now go on without the help of the Duke of Wellington. Accordingly George IV appointed him Prime Minister; and the declared Whig ministers, led by Lord Lansdowne, then resigned. What should the Canningites do? The Duke, in order to keep them, promised to modify his policy to suit their views. After hours of indecision they decided to remain for fear, they said, lest otherwise Canning's policy might be completely reversed.

William, out of personal loyalty—always his ruling motive—stayed along with his friends. But he thought it a mistake. He was right. Whatever the Duke might say, he differed fundamentally from the Canningites on every important issue: and they found that in practice they could only work with him by constantly acting against their true opinion. This mattered to William less than to most, for few political views were to him a matter of principle. Only once, when he voted against the repeal of the Test Act excluding nonconformists from government posts, did he go against a strong conviction. But no amount of laxity on his part or that of anyone else could keep so divided a ministry going for long. "The Cabinet," said Palmerston, the Canningite Minister for War, "has gone on differing about every question of importance that has come under consideration—meeting to debate and dispute and separating without deciding." Twice in three months the Government came within an inch of splitting. In May the crash came; on the question as to what should be done with the seat left vacant by the disfranchisement of the borough of East Retford. Most of the Canningites, led by Huskisson, were for giving it to a manufacturing town, as a sop to the reformers: the Duke and Peel, fearing this might prove the thin end of the wedge, proposed giving it to a county. After a deplorable exhibition of clumsy vacillation on his own part and unscrupulous strategy on that of the Duke, Huskisson was forced to resign. His followers had to make up their minds whether to go with him. The chief of them were Palmerston, William's old friend Ward, now Lord Dudley and William himself. On the afternoon of Sunday, 25th May, Palmerston, walking along the Horse Guards, saw Ward beckoning him from the balcony of Melbourne House. He went up to find discussion raging. William was for resignation and Palmerston supported him: but Ward, who passionately enjoyed being in office, hung back, "stroked his chin, counted the squares of the carpet three times down and then went off in the agony of doubt and hesitation". That night decision could be delayed no longer. The three went to see Huskisson and then, leaving their cabriolets to follow slowly behind them, strolled back through the balmy stillness of the spring night for a final consultation. Ward walked between the two others. "Well," he began, "now that we are by ourselves in the street and no one but the sentry to hear, let me know right and left what is next to be done—in or out?"

"Out," said Palmerston and William echoed him. Ward was still reluctant. "There is a rumour," he said, "that Huskisson's place is to be filled by a moderate Tory, a young man of promise from a noble Tory family." "I do not know any young man of

Tory family who is a man of promise," replied William discouragingly; and then went on to point out with chilling good sense that the fact that Huskisson was to be replaced by an official Tory of any kind meant a change in the character of the Government; and that he himself, unable as he was to state his views in Cabinet, could not feel justified in associating himself with it in its new form. Poor Ward made a last try. "There is something in attaching oneself to so great a man as the Duke," he observed wistfully. "For my part," retorted William, unmoved, "I do not happen to think he is so great a man. But that is a matter of opinion." Next day they were all three out.

It was a little hard on William. For, on the East Retford question, he agreed with the Duke. Still there was no question he had to go. In general he had no confidence in the Duke: and anyway the same loyalty that had kept him in now sent him out. "I have always thought," he once said, "that it is more necessary to stand by my friends when they are in the wrong than when they are in the right."

## (2)

Nevertheless it was a depressing time for him. After years of doing nothing he had at last obtained work; and found that he enjoyed it. Now within a few months it was snatched away with no visible prospect of return. However, he had long ago learnt not to cry over spilt milk. Soon he was setting to work to distract himself by corresponding with Lady Holland about Greek poetry and writing reviews of theological works for the *Literary Gazette*.

His private life too required attention. Since August it had been at least as eventful as his public. All the old ties were breaking. Lady Caroline had died in January, 1828. Their only child, poor Augustus, still lived, a half-witted youth of twenty-one. But William, though still far too solicitous for his welfare to let him leave home, must by now have given up all hope of his becoming normal. In July of the same year Lord Melbourne's unimpressive life had come to an end at last. It is not to be supposed that this occasioned much sorrow to anyone. But it was a landmark in William's life. With his father and mother and Caroline gone, the chapter of his youth was completely finished. Moreover he was now head of the family. The Melbourne fortune though still large was somewhat reduced by this time. Melbourne House was sold, as too expensive to keep up; and—taking a new house in South Street, Mayfair—William, or Melbourne as we must now learn to call him, settled down to face the future.

Already, as a matter of fact, his private life was involved in a new disturbance. Feminine society was a necessity to him. And while in Ireland he had made the acquaintance of a certain Lady Branden, the wife of an Irish peer in holy orders. Nothing is known of her, beyond the fact that she was young, lovely, and that she lived apart from her husband. Melbourne spent almost every evening with her when in Dublin: in the following year she settled in London, where he continued to visit her. In the summer of 1828, trouble began to raise its head. If scandal was to be believed, the Reverend Lord Branden was not a credit to his cloth. It was rumoured that he had written to Lady Branden, alleging that he had got some compromising evidence about her relations with Melbourne, but that he would overlook the matter, if she would persuade her lover to get him made a bishop. Lady Branden very properly rejected this unseemly proposal. Accordingly in the summer of 1829 Lord Branden brought an action. When it came into court, however, Melbourne turned out to have little to worry about. All the evidence Lord Branden could produce was first, that Lord Melbourne had sent Lady Branden some grapes and pineapples and, secondly, that a gentleman, alleged to be Melbourne, had been seen leaving her house in Lisson Grove in the early hours of the morning. This was not much: it proved to be even less when the only witness who professed to have seen the gentleman in question, said that he was short, whereas Melbourne was unusually tall. "Pray call someone who will prove something to the purpose," said the judge testily; "you must get him a good deal nearer than this. You have not got him to the lady's house yet": while the Attorney-General remarked facetiously that if there was any suspicion, it attached to the short gentleman. The case was dismissed.

The truth about the matter will never be known for certain. Possibly that Lord Branden had more ground for his suspicions than he was able to justify. It is significant that in his will Melbourne left annuities to two ladies with whom his name had been connected; Lady Branden and Mrs. Norton. But whereas he categorically stated that there had been no guilty connection between himself and Mrs. Norton, he made no similar statement about his relations with Lady Branden. Anyway the affair does not seem to have engaged Melbourne's heart deeply. He made Lady Branden an allowance which he arranged to be continued to her after his death: and he kept sufficiently in touch with her to be worried five years later because he had not heard from her for some months. But she had before this ceased to play an important part in his life. With the dismissal of the case, the shadowy figure of Lady Branden vanishes from this history.

Meanwhile in the political world, momentous events were crowding thick on one another. Freed from the incubus of the Canningites, the old régime, under the Duke's leadership, made a last bid to assure and maintain its domination. It failed. The first blow came from Ireland. By 1829 the agitation for Catholic Emancipation had swelled to a pitch of violence which, it seemed, must explode in open rebellion. Rather than face such a disaster, the Duke threw over the principles of a life-time and himself repealed the Anti-Catholic laws. The consequence was that he lost another section of his supporters, the irreconcilable anti-papists of the extreme right. However, weak as his position had now become, the Duke was preparing to carry on, apparently unperturbed, when he was again assailed by a new and even more formidable popular agitation. An industrial depression had made people discontented again: and now that the Canningite middle way had been tried and had failed, they turned to drastic change as the only alternative to blind reaction. At the beginning of 1830 the movement for Parliamentary Reform flared up with new and extraordinary fury.

At Birmingham, Thomas Attwood organized a huge association for Reform: his example was followed in other great towns: meetings were held all over England: the most celebrated of contemporary agitators, Cobbett, rode round the country on a cob exhorting people to take action. As the year advanced, so did the Cause. George IV's death removed a powerful obstacle to reform: while in Paris, the bloodless revolution of July showed timid reformers that drastic change could be accomplished without catastrophe. By the end of the summer, feeling in the country was stirred to a pitch of excitement unknown since the days of the Long Parliament one hundred and ninety years before. In the houses of the great and the clubs of St. James's, an atmosphere as before a thunderstorm, tense with ominous expectancy, hung heavy over the political scene. Everybody felt something tremendous was going to happen, nobody quite knew what. Obsessed by their youthful memories of the French Revolution, people murmured nervously to one another of the ruin and bloodshed that must ensue, unless popular discontent was conciliated. "It was just like France in 1789," said an elderly French visitor.

In August it seemed as if rebellion was already starting. The poverty-stricken labourers of southern England, roused to frenzy by Cobbett's eloquence, broke out in riot and outrage. Night after night, respectable householders looked out of their windows to see the quiet Kentish countryside lurid in the light of blazing ricks; bands of men roamed the lanes, breaking machines and manhandling the agents of the great landlords; placid Mr. Eltons and Mr. Collinses in sequestered rural vicarages found letters thrust under their doors threatening them with assassination unless they remitted tithes; a party of rioters broke into a duke's house and had to be dispersed by force.

Fear increased the strength of the reforming party. Some people who had wavered turned to it as the one means of avoiding disaster. The question was whether the Duke of Wellington would once more forswear his principles and go with them. In November, when Parliament met, he gave his answer. Our existing constitution, he said, was so perfect that he could never take the responsibility of tampering with it. Within a fortnight his Government had fallen; and a Whig ministry under Lord Grey, pledged to bring in Reform, had taken its place.

It was the crisis of the century. At last that decisive battle between the old order and the new, imminent for the last forty years, was openly joined: and all the varied strains of political opinion, for so long indefinite and fluctuating, rushed to range themselves on one side or the other. The anti-reformers were a solid block of the Tory landed interest and the Established Church. The reformers were a more heterogeneous body. There were the radical democrats, the political theorists, the dissenters, and the bulk of the manufacturers: all those believed in reform and liked it. There were also a number of people who disliked it, but thought it inevitable. Among these were the Canningites.

Since their resignation their position had been an uncomfortable one. The Tories thought them too Whig; the Whigs thought them too Tory. Now, however, Lord Grey, anxious for all the support he could find in his formidable task, pressed them to join his administration. The Canningites hesitated. They had no one to direct them: for their recognized leader, Huskisson, notorious all his life for his physical clumsiness, had recently let himself be run over by a railway train going twelve miles an hour. Further, the Canningites had hitherto opposed reform. It made a great difference to them though that it now appeared the only alternative to revolution and as such the lesser of two evils. After a long consultation, they agreed to join. Melbourne joined with them. Since he had resigned he had taken no prominent part in politics. Once early in 1829 he had spoken against an Irish Coercion Act: he said very sensibly that, until the Irish were conciliated by Catholic Emancipation, coercion would do more harm than good. Later, and more unfortunately, he had, out of affection for his brother Frederick, addressed the House of Lords in favour of a more adventurous policy in Portugal. It was against his better judgment— adventurous policies always were—and he made a very bad speech. Otherwise he had kept discreetly quiet. His reputation had grown in consequence. Twice the Duke had tried to inveigle him back into the Government; in 1829 too he was asked to Windsor, where he was amused to note that George IV took particular pains to be attentive to him. On the other hand the Whig leaders felt friendlier to him than they did to most Canningites. He had always kept himself a little detached. When he had joined the Wellington Ministry he took care to declare that he did it "purely as an individual", and so could not be accused of compromising the Whig party by his action. Nor did it in fact stop him throughout the next two years from spending as much time as ever at Holland House and Lansdowne House with his old friends. His personality it was that gave him his position. People liked him so much that they wanted him in the Government, whatever his opinions. Further, during his short period of office he had acquired a good name as a colleague. Then as now it was rare to find a minister who got on with everyone and was always in a good humour. So precious indeed did these qualifications appear to a harassed Prime Minister, that on Melbourne's very first entry into a Cabinet, he was given the important post of Home Secretary.

### (3)

Those, however, who did not move in Cabinet circles, found the appointment astonishing. By the world in general he was still looked on as an agreeable idle man of fashion—far too inconsiderable for the job, said Greville, the Clerk of the Council. He was wide of the mark. Though Melbourne presented a less professional appearance than most of his colleagues, his mind was more penetrating and more original than theirs. And he was only lazy as long as he had nothing to do. All the same it cannot be denied that the world had something to be surprised at. Fortune, to whom Melbourne had resigned the direction of his life, had become infected with his own irony when she made him a Cabinet Minister. Whimsical, speculative and pessimistic, he had never, for all he had been so long mixed up in them, been able to bring himself to take political affairs wholly seriously: and to the end of his life, he remained an alien element in them. He had learnt to play the political game with practised skill; but like a grown-up person playing hide-and-seek with children, he never entered completely into the spirit of the thing. His thought moved from a different centre and on different lines. And he was much too candid not to show it.

Ordinary people, bewildered by him at all times, were still more bewildered when he talked politics—when the Home Secretary commented on the policy of his Government with a mischievous and philosophic detachment, as of a spectator himself unconnected with it and out to get as much fun from watching as he could. Still less was Melbourne in place in a reforming Government. Temperamentally an eighteenth-century aristocrat and profoundly sceptical as to the value of human activity of any kind, politics most of all, he seemed the last man one would expect to find assisting in the inauguration of a golden age of progressive legislation. As to Parliamentary Reform itself, he was unenthusiastic about it, even for a Canningite. Early in his career he had noted down his reasons for disapproving of it. One of these was unusual.

"I anticipate the total destruction of freedom of speech from a reformation of the Parliament, and for this reason. The present House, knowing that there are popular, plausible and prima facie objections to its formation, will endure to hear its conduct arraigned and condemned because it does not wish to stir dangerous questions, but a House of Commons elected according to what is called theory and principle will never bear to hear itself freely and violently censured, though its acts may possibly be such as to deserve the most acrimonious censure."

His other objections to Reform were less paradoxical. As an aristocrat, he did not think the country was likely to be well governed by a Parliament of middle-class commercial persons, such as were likely to be elected under a reformed system. As a student of history he had no confidence in the will of the majority. And as a man of prudence, he feared Reform might lead to disaster. For since it would inevitably fail to produce all the benefits hoped from it, its disappointed supporters would insist on more and more drastic changes, till the whole constitution collapsed in ruins; to be succeeded, as the recent history of France indicated, by a Napoleonic despotism, in which the liberty and tolerance which Melbourne valued more than anything else in the world would be extinguished. However, it was one of his fundamental principles not to stand out against a widespread popular movement. And as early as 1821 we find him saying that reform might turn out to be unavoidable. Now in 1830 he was sure it was. His realistic commonsense also told him that unless reform was fairly extreme, it would not satisfy people enough to be worth while. "I am for a low figure," he said at a preliminary Cabinet held on the subject; "unless we have a large basis to work on, we shall do nothing." All the same at heart he still disliked it thoroughly.

In fact he was not called upon to play much part in passing the Bill. The Home Secretary's role was rather to keep the country calm and orderly while it was going through. This was a heavy

enough task for one man. The accession of the Whigs had not
eased the tension of the last few months. In the South the ricks
still burst into flames nightly: and hordes of marauders marched
about carrying banners ominously inscribed "Bread or Blood".
Moreover unrest had now spread to the North: the hungry
workers of the industrial towns were, it was reported, forming
themselves into sinister communal organizations called Trades
Unions, who spent their nights secretly drilling and who had the
purpose of ousting employers from the rightful command of their
labour. Strikes and riots broke out in which one employer was
actually murdered. What made the situation especially alarming
was that outside London there was as yet no regular police force,
and that the army which alone filled its place was a mere handful
of men. To the propertied classes it seemed as if the very foundations of civilized life were crumbling beneath their feet. A wave
of panic swept over them. Every day Melbourne's post-bag at the
Home Office arrived heavy with fantastic alarmist tales: that the
disturbances were part of a deep-laid Jesuit plot, that they had
been worked up by the French preparatory to invasion, that the
ricks were set alight by fireballs, projected from a great distance by
guns cunningly disguised as umbrellas. Melbourne preserved his
calm in face of these dreadful suggestions: but he threw himself
into his task with unexpected energy. For once he felt no hesitation. To preserve order had always, in his view, been the first
function of government. And he acted with a vigour and decision
that left his critics gasping. Within a month people were heard
saying that Lord Melbourne was the one strong man in the
Government.

The trouble in the South was the most urgent. Melbourne
posted soldiers in the most disturbed areas: gingered up the
magistrates to act firmly: and in order to enforce the law more
quickly appointed a special commission of judges to go down and
immediately try such persons as had been arrested. The effect of
these measures was instantaneous. Order was restored in three
months.

(4)

At a cost though: the tale of the repression of the labourers' re-volt of 1830 is dark and terrible; a stark Hardy-like tragedy of ele-mental blood and anguish and man's inhumanity to helpless man, all the more shocking to the imagination when we find it occurring in the cheerful, urbane England of Brooks's Club and Holland House. The law, which the judges were called upon to enforce, was so appallingly harsh for one thing. A man could be hanged for setting fire to a rick or for demanding food with menaces: he could be transported for life for writing a threatening letter, and for seven years for breaking up a piece of agricultural machinery. And the cruelty of this code seems intensified when we consider who were some of its victims; ignorant, illiterate rustics, struggling to support ten children on six shillings a week, misled by crude agita-tors and their own despair, into striking out blindly at those who they were told were the authors of their misery and starvation. In fact the law was not carried out in its full rigour; of several hun-dred men condemned to death only a handful were actually exe-cuted. But what happened was sufficiently dreadful. The reader's blood runs cold at the reports of the scenes outside the Court rooms at Salisbury and Winchester; the ragged, wailing wives and mothers watching boys of nineteen dragged to the gallows, fathers of young families, manacled and hustled into the carts that were to take them to the grim hulks in which they were to be transported to a lifetime of slavery in the convict settlements of Australia.

It is painful and disturbing to think of the tender-hearted Mel-bourne as involved in such events at all, let alone as responsible for setting them in motion. But in fact his conduct in the matter is not so uncharacteristic or so unjustifiable as might at first be supposed. After all it was not he who had made the laws. Or who tried the cases; that was the judges' affair. And he had no reason to suppose that the judges did not carry out their duties correctly and conscientiously. Melbourne's concern was with general policy. That policy was in harmony with his whole political out-look. He had always thought civil disorder the worst of all evils. "To force," he said, "nothing but force can be successfully opposed. It is evident that all legislation is impotent and ridiculous, unless the public peace can be preserved and the liberty and property of individuals saved from outrage and invasion.'' If this were true at any time, it was especially true in 1830. Melbourne, in common with most responsible people in England, was sure the country was tottering on the edge of bloodstained chaos. Not unnaturally, when they woke every morning to hear of mobs burning down houses and robbing harmless citizens, without anyone being able, apparently, to stop them! What made these events more ominous was that the men who composed the mobs were no worse off than they had often been during recent years; yet never before had they broken out in this sinister fashion. It looked as if these disturbances must be deliberately provoked by some revolutionary plot. Now if ever, Melbourne felt, was the time for a Government to act strongly. Above all, a reforming Government! He thought reform a risky business at best: the risk was only justified if the country was kept under iron control while it was going through. The surest, and ultimately the most humane way to do this, was to stamp hard and at once on the first stirrings of rebellion. People needed a fright. Even when he did not intend that a prisoner should be executed, Melbourne approved of sentencing him to death. ''The death sentence,'' he remarked, ''is an example more strict.''

In all this he showed thorough good sense. Only too often have Governments of moderate change brought catastrophe on a nation by a weak, timid inability to control the disruptive forces which they themselves have let loose. Melbourne deserves some of the credit for the fact that England, alone of European countries in the nineteenth century, succeeded in getting rid of the old régime without a revolution. Nor indeed, by the standards of his age, was he unusually severe. On the contrary, many people thought he was not nearly severe enough. William IV in particular was always writing him endless agitated letters urging him to forbid Trades Unions, to increase the legal penalties for rioting, to call out the military. And many persons more intelligent than William IV said the same things. To their excited urgings, Melbourne remained blandly impervious. The existing law, he said with truth, was quite severe enough if it was properly enforced. Trades Unions were no doubt undesirable institutions; but to suppress them was illegal and a dangerous blow at liberty. Calling out the soldiers was an hysterical, tyrannous proposal. And when one of his colleagues suggested employing spies and *agent provocateurs* in order to discover the ringleaders of revolt, Melbourne sent him away with a polite flea in his ear.

> "I am sure you must feel," he wrote, "that in our anxiety to discover the perpetrators of these most dangerous and atrocious acts we should run as little risk as possible of involving innocent persons in accusations, and still less of adopting measures which may encourage the seduction of persons now innocent, into the commission of crime."

Firmly and unsentimentally, he chose as usual to follow a rational and middle way.

All the same, it is disconcerting to find him so very unhesitating and unruffled about it all. Surely so kind a man should have had more qualms about applying, however moderately, a criminal code of this ferocity. There are moments when an air of philosophic detachment is out of place. Here we come up against the limitations alike of Melbourne's circumstances and his outlook. A man born in 1779 was all too used to people being hanged and transported for small offences: if, in addition, his life moved on the Olympian heights of Melbourne House and Brooks's Club, he was unlikely to enter imaginatively into the sufferings of agricultural labourers, unless he made a considerable effort. Melbourne did not make the effort. No doubt this was partly due to his good sense. He knew that all statesmen had to do disagreeable things sometimes; having decided a disagreeable thing was necessary, why make it worse by fruitless worrying? But his apparent imperturbability was also, paradoxically, the defect of his very softheartedness. Just because he hated the painful so much, he tended to shut his eyes to it. He shrank from imagining the labourers' feelings for the same reasons that he was later to shrink from reading *Oliver Twist*. And of course his sympathies were further frozen by secret fear: that stab of uncontrollable fear which always attacked him at a serious threat to the tranquillity and stability which he valued more than anything else in the world.

Anyway, if he had felt a qualm, it might well have been stifled by the chorus of congratulations with which his policy was greeted. Everyone whose opinion he could possibly be expected to value, thought he had done admirably. The Tories were profoundly relieved to discover that a Whig Minister could be as firm against revolution as they were: Liberals were delighted the country should realize that Reform could be carried through without disorder. Macaulay, the typical man of the new progressive middle-class, asserted that the sins of reactionary landlords were no excuse for Jacobin outrage. Even Miss Harriet Martineau, stern pioneer of feminism and popular economics—though in general she disapproved of Melbourne as a reprehensible example of aristocratic frivolity—felt bound to praise him for the mingled firmness and moderation with which, in her view, he had dealt with the disturbances of 1830. His colleagues backed him to a man. And when the Radical Hunt proposed a general pardon for offenders in the House of Commons, his motion was rejected by a huge majority. Melbourne's reputation as a statesman was growing steadily higher.

Besides putting down disorders, he also took steps to see they should not break out. Highly characteristic steps; into the Home Office in London he imported the free and easy methods of conducting business which surprised the officials of Dublin. He was ready to see people at the most unconventional times and places—notably in his dressing-room when he was getting up in the morning. His eyes concentrated on his shaving glass and his chin white with soap, he would listen inscrutably to what his visitor had to say. From time to time he jerked out a brusque, acute question. After he had found out what he wanted to know, genially he brought the interview to a close. People were disconcerted too by the men he employed. What were they to think, for instance, of his secretary Tom Young, a sharp vulgarian of dubious connections and breezy over-familiar manners, whom Melbourne had somehow managed to pick up when he, Young, was acting as Purser on the Duke of Devonshire's yacht. Melbourne, however, was too sure of his own dignity to mind his familiarities; while Young's doubtful connections he found a positive advantage. "He's my weather gauge," Melbourne remarked, "through him I am able to look down below; which is for me more important than all I can learn from the fine gentlemen clerks about me."

He had special need of information from below at this period. The revolutionary movement was not confined to the countryside. Beneath a smooth and orderly surface, London was seething with unrest, murmurous with discontent. Every evening that autumn when dusk had fallen on the great city, groups radical and revolutionary would meet in shops and obscure upper rooms, to discuss schemes, sometimes legal, sometimes illegal, by which the defeat of the anti-reformers might be assured. Melbourne wanted some first-hand information about these people; to find out what they were really plotting and, if possible, to influence them towards lawful courses. As at Dublin, he saw that it was hopeless to try and do this through official channels and by means of decorous civil servants. What he wanted was a man like Tom Young, accustomed to knocking about in all sorts of queer company and who did not take no for an answer.

Conspicuous among these radical groups was one which gathered at a sort of combined bookshop and political club called the Charing Cross Library and was dominated by Francis Place, a maker of leather breeches who has left his name in history as a pioneer of democratic radicalism. A dour-faced, bristle-haired person, capable, aggressive, self-educated and self-satisfied, he represented that important middle section of his Party which combined a bitter hostility to lords and landowners with an equally bitter contempt for unpractical extremists on his own side. In the days of his festive youth, Melbourne had bought his breeches from him; in fact Place had once dunned him for an unpaid bill. This inauspicious circumstance, however, did not now stop Melbourne from picking him out to be the means by which he might get into contact with the working-class movement. Accordingly in November he sent his brother George Lamb to ask Place to appeal publicly to the agricultural labourers to stop rioting; he also set up regular communications with him through the medium of Tom Young. Place received these overtures with shrewdness and suspicion; he refused to have anything to do with George Lamb's proposals and was not taken in by Young's false joviality; "A cleverish sort of fellow who has a vulgar air of frankness which may put

G

some people off their guard," he noted caustically. On his side, Melbourne did not put much confidence in Place. That type of man in his experience was always, in fact, ready to break the law, whatever he may say to the contrary beforehand. He also noted that Place's information always seemed to support the policy Place wanted the Government to adopt. However, each felt he had something to gain from the other. On a healthy basis of mutual distrust, the connection established itself.

Meanwhile, the battle for Reform thundered on. After passing its Second Reading in the House of Commons by one vote, it was beaten in Committee. Clearly the Whigs would never get it through without a larger Parliamentary representation. Prompted by Lord Grey, William IV therefore hurried down to Westminster and cramming his crown hastily on to one side of his head, entered the Chamber and dissolved Parliament. A stormy general election followed in which the Whigs got their increased majority. Once again, the Bill was brought in: this time it passed the Commons and proceeded to the House of Lords. Its first appearance there was the occasion of a memorable full-dress debate. The outstanding speakers were Lord Grey, who revived for the wonder and delight of a new generation the stately splendours of eighteenth-century oratory; and Lord Chancellor Brougham, a master of the more trenchant modern style. His speech culminated in a peroration in which, falling on his knees and with outstretched hands, he implored the peers not to throw out the Bill. Unluckily, in order to stimulate his eloquence, he had during his speech drunk a whole bottle of mulled port, with the result that once on his knees he found he was unable to get up until assisted to do so by his embarrassed colleagues.

Melbourne did not emulate the rhetorical feats of his leaders. But he supported the Bill in a characteristic speech, full of detachment and digression and apt quotations from Livy and Lord Bacon; and in which he frankly explained the reasons for his changed attitude to Reform. He did not believe in it any more than before, he said; certainly its results were likely to disappoint its more enthusiastic advocates. But the popular demand for it had become so widespread that, according to his theory of statesmanship, there was less danger in passing it than in turning it down.

These cool and prudent reflections did not succeed in convert-ing their Tory-minded lordships. On the morning of 9th October, the pro-reform papers announced, in an edition specially printed on black-edged paper, the House of Lords had thrown the Reform Bill out. The effect of this news on the country seemed to justify Melbourne's reading of the public mind; and his belief in the dan-ger of revolution as well. Riot and outrage broke out even more violently than the year before; and this was not only in the country, but also in the great centres of population. Towns blazed as well as ricks. In Derby the jail was broken into and several people killed; Nottingham Castle was destroyed; Bristol was a scene of spectacular destruction, with the red-coated soldiers firing on the crowd and the Bishop's palace in flames against the dim November dawn.

More alarming to those in power, because more generally for-midable, were the signs of organized revolution which were begin-ning to show themselves. The Political Unions for instance; they protested that their only function was to maintain law and order while Reform was going through. But they were disciplined, they had the advantage of efficient middle-class leadership, and their moving spirit, Attwood, was as bitter a radical as Place himself. What purpose might not he turn them to, if he began to think that the cause of Reform was in danger! Moreover, in the North work-ing-men's unions had sprung up, whose aims were openly revolu-tionary. There were the usual sinister rumours of secret drilling and arms practice after dark. Civil War looked close. In the polite circles of London feeling reached a new height of tension. Ladies in drawing-rooms repeated to each other horrific reports of re-spectable squires' wives torn brutally from their beds by savage mobs, who broke up their furniture and made merry in their cel-lars; in clubs gentlemen had it on good authority that a rebellious army was at that very instant marching on the capital. The King's letters to his Ministers grew more and more frantic. Even Lord Grey wondered if the Government had taken the Trades Union movement seriously enough. Indeed almost alone among Minis-ters, Melbourne appeared his ordinary smiling self. People were even more struck by his coolness than they had been the year before.

This was the more remarkable because the times were more anxious. Once more it was his responsibility to repress disorder. Once more he rose to the occasion. London was the chief danger spot; the seat of government must at all costs not be allowed to get out of hand. Nonchalantly, unconventionally, effectively Melbourne took his steps. Troops and private negotiations were his means. He posted soldiers at strategic points, forbade public meetings, and sent Young off to see Place. Within a week or two all danger of disturbances in London had passed. In the country, with equally successful results, he got into touch with Attwood and dispatched military detachments to especially unruly districts. For the rest, his time was taken up with soothing down the King and his colleagues and with dealing with his official correspondence. Panic had started a new flood of letters to the Home Office, passionately adjuring the Minister to do something drastic and to do it at once. Melbourne noticed they seldom said what. He was not impressed. "When in doubt what should be done," he reflected, "do nothing."

But he was not as calm as he looked. How should he be, when the strife and chaos he dreaded loomed apparently ever nearer! Underneath his indolent surface, throbbed a growing nervous tension. Once for an instant it betrayed itself. There was in September a debate in the House of Lords about the spring-guns which some landowners had set up in their fields to keep off rick burners. Melbourne defended them in a speech marked by a strange and uncharacteristic note of hysteria. "Rick burning," he cried, "seems to have no object or motive; but to arise from a pure unmixed and diabolical feeling of senseless malignity." His heightened state of emotion also showed itself in a change of attitude towards the Reform Bill. What with the House of Lords on the one side and the Political Unions on the other, it was clear that it was not going through as easily as the Government had once hoped. A crisis was approaching in which Ministers would have to decide whether to pacify the Lords by modifying the Bill or satisfy the reformers by creating enough peers to force it through. They began to divide themselves into two groups according as to how far at heart they really wanted to reform. Melbourne inevitably inclined to that group which did not want it. Indeed the effect of his anxiety was to bring out all his latent prejudice against it. What nonsense it all was! What a nuisance that anyone should ever have raised the question! Secretly he would not have been sorry to see the Government go out and the whole issue drop. He found himself feeling suddenly exacerbated by those of his colleagues who clamoured that the Bill be put through at all costs. The excitable Lord Durham in particular, shouting abuse at Lord Grey in Cabinet for what he considered his weakness in hesitating to create peers at once—"If I'd been Lord Grey," said Melbourne, "I'd have knocked him down." And again when Durham fulminated against any proposals to alter the Bill in order to conciliate its opponents. "I doubt if he knows what the alterations are," commented Melbourne tartly, "as he will not let anyone tell him."

On the other hand Melbourne's emotions were not so out of control as to silence the voice of that good sense which had previously brought him round to agree to Reform. In some ways it had been reinforced by the disturbances in the autumn. Melbourne had been quite right in thinking that the popular demand for Reform was now so strong as to make it risky to refuse it. More risky than before as their hopes had now been raised! "It is a very dangerous way of dealing to retract what you have once offered to concede," he said.

In the end these considerations triumphed; good sense generally did with Melbourne. The proposals for modifying the Bill came from a group of moderate Tory peers—the Waverers, they were nicknamed. These wanted the recall of Parliament put off in order to give time for their plans to be thoroughly considered. Melbourne was against this: a delay would rouse public suspicion. Riots and rick burning would begin again, and he would have to put them down. Besides, though he sympathized with the Waverers' intentions, he did not think their policy likely to do any good. Rather would it lead to the break up of the Government, he told Palmerston, and to a general exacerbation of feeling. The Ministers' chief aim should be to keep things together until people had a chance to cool down. Besides, it would be letting down Lord Grey to assist in breaking up his Government. As often before in Melbourne's history, he felt strongly about personal obligations because he was so uncertain about any others.

Doubtfully, reluctantly, resignedly he reverted to his old accept-
ance of Reform. The complex contradiction of his sentiments on
the subject showed in his demeanour. The tone of his talk became
even more bewildering than usual to simple-minded persons. By
turns flippant and pessimistic, frank and enigmatic, he seemed
wholly detached from the Government of which he was a member. Of course Reform was folly, he would say. Yet, when anyone
suggested resisting it, he would burst out laughing, rub his hands
and turn the subject. One observer was especially mystified by
him. Charles Greville, the Clerk of the Council, had constituted
himself an unofficial intermediary between the Waverers and the
Ministers. He was always buttonholing Melbourne, in the Park,
in South Street, at the Home Office, in order to extract from him
some statement of his views. Greville was ingratiating, persistent
and conceited—"The most conceited man I ever met," said Disraeli, "though I have read Cicero and known Bulwer Lytton"—
the very type Melbourne most enjoyed teasing. Sometimes he set
out to shock Greville by openly mocking the whole idea of Reform,
sometimes he tantalized his curiosity with half confidences about
his colleagues, sometimes he lounged back "in his lazy, listening,
silent humour, disposed to hear everything and to say very little".
Never, though, did he quite commit himself. Greville found these
interviews extremely unsatisfactory. What a pity it was, he reflected, that at this important moment in English history, one of
His Majesty's chief Ministers should be no better than a frivolous
cynic; and a dissipated spendthrift into the bargain. Leaving
South Street one morning he noticed with a pleasurable sense of
moral disapproval, a Jew waiting in the hall and a valet de cham-
bre sweeping away a bonnet and shawl.

With the new years events began to move towards their culmina-
tion. It became obvious that the Whigs would not get the Bill
through without at any rate pledging themselves to make peers.
Were they prepared to do this? Many hated the idea, Melbourne
most of all. What a dangerous precedent would it provide for
forcing all sorts of other odious reforms through Parliament in the
future! For a moment he was moved from his attitude of detached
resignation; and protested so strongly that in January it was
thought he might resign. In the end, however, common sense and

loyalty once more prevailed. When the final crisis came in May, Melbourne in Cabinet voted for demanding from the King the power to make peers. But up to the last he was in a queer uncertain mood. Greville met him in April at a ball at the French Embassy. Melbourne suddenly said to him, "I don't believe there is a strong feeling in the country for the measure . . . might it not be thrown out?" "Do your colleagues agree?" asked the astonished Greville. "No," said Melbourne. Greville said that he ought to persuade them. "What difficulty can they have in swallowing the rest?" replied Melbourne. "After they have given up the rotten boroughs . . . I don't see how the Government is to be carried on without them. Some means may be found; a remedy may possibly present itself but I am not aware of any." No doubt he was still teasing Greville by a display of cynicism. But he was also giving voice to his secret convictions. When it came, the glorious triumph of the Reform cause left Melbourne noticeably unexhilarated. Reluctantly he had supported it as the only means of pacifying popular discontent. Now he began to wonder if it would produce the desired effect. After all they had been led to hope, the people would certainly be disappointed by the results of Reform; with the consequence that they would get more angrily discontented than ever. One day soon after the Bill had passed, he met Attwood. "If the people don't get their belly-full after this," Attwood said, "I shall be torn in pieces." "And so much the better, you deserve it," retorted Melbourne with unwonted bitterness. Moreover, even if by a stroke of luck the people did stay quiet, the new Parliament would not. Gloomily Melbourne envisaged the prospect of a House of Commons full of earnest, strenuous middle-class persons insatiably clamouring for more and more reforms; and with the power to get them. One thing he was sure of: they were not easily going to persuade him to help them again. "There is no knowing to what one may be led by circumstance," he wrote to his brother Fred, "but at present I am determined to make my stand here and not to advance any further."

However, it was not in him to give way to depression. Perhaps things were not as bad as he feared; anyway it was never any use worrying. Ruefully and philosophically he shrugged his shoulders at the future and went off to dine at Holland House.

# MRS. NORTON

FOR LUCKILY he had other resources to fall back upon, when affairs looked melancholy. He was able to take things philo-sophically because he was detached; and he was detached partly because politics were never to him the be all and the end all of existence. Though he had thrown himself with such surpris-ing energy into his work, his character was not so far changed as to make him forgo his old enjoyments. He still read enormously. At the height of the disturbances of 1831 he contrived to find time to study the subject of the Druids and to explore the obscurer by-paths of Elizabethan dramatic literature—Heywood's *Apology for Actors* and Rumbold's *Collection of Stage Plays*.

He re-read old favourites, too, notably *As You Like It*. "It is the prettiest play in the world," he once said. Moreover he liked it because he seems to have felt an affinity with the character of the melancholy Jaques. Into his commonplace book he copied Jaques' remark after hearing Touchstone talk of Ovid,

"Oh knowledge ill inhabited, worse than Jove in a thatched house!"

"A man," comments Melbourne, "may be master of the ancient and modern languages, and yet his mind and his manners shall not be in the least degree softened or harmonized by discipline and by force and beauty of example. The elegance, grace and feeling which he is continually contemplating, cannot mix with his thoughts or insinuate itself into their expression: but he remains as coarse, as rude and as awkward, and often more so than the illiterate and the ill-instructed."

Such a passage illustrates typically Melbourne's attitude to literature. Books appealed to him primarily not for their learning or as a source of artistic pleasure but for the light they threw on experience. Always he relates what he reads to what he himself has observed. For—and here he is unlike most men of affairs—he never lost his interest and his curiosity as to life in general. His mind did not grow so tired and pre-occupied as to stop him questioning and reflecting. Seated in Cabinet, gossiping at a dinner party, he continued to notice and draw his characteristic conclusions. When he was back in his library at South Street he pulled out his commonplace book and jotted these conclusions down. They were varied, according to what aspect of life had stimulated them. Sometimes they arose from his political experience.

"People complain of the instability of human affairs, but in fact the state of man, if fixed and certain, would not be endured."

Sometimes they are the results of his classical reading.

"Greek and Latin literature is thought so good because so much of it is lost."

Social life was for him a great stimulus to reflection.

"A well-looking man should dress himself more carefully because his appearance attracts attention to his attire, and if the latter sits ill or be ungraceful it points out and strengthens the contrast: whereas an ill-looking fellow and an ill-made suit appear both of a piece."

"Wit of all things suffers most by time."

"Nothing hurts the character or degrades the understanding so much as suffering wit and humour to dominate and hold the first place in discussion . . . the ludicrous is an admirable auxiliary but it should not be depended upon as a principle."

"Labour is so necessary to the health and vigour of the body, and consequently of the mind, that those who by their wealth are exempted from it as a means of subsistence are yet compelled to seek it as a diversion."

"Persons who are foolish enough to do that which requires admonition are rarely wise enough to refrain from the practice for which they are admonished."

His own character was another favourite object of his curious contemplations. He viewed it with an impartial detachment.

"I am very good-tempered if I have my own way; and that is not saying little for myself. For many are just as ill-tempered when their wishes are complied with as when they are thwarted."

Such modified self-approval, however, as is implied in this saying is rare. The melancholy and sceptical view which Melbourne took of human life in general extended to himself; all the more as with advancing years he grew aware of the incurable nature of his own weaknesses and of the failure of his youthful hopes.

"Misfortunes are often accidents, yet the calamities inflicted on us by the hand of God are very few in proportion to those which come from our own errors."

"The advantages of youth are those which we prize least and employ most when we possess them: and regret most when we lose them. There is no man who, at an advanced period of his life were he able to choose, would not at once ask for the restoration of the strength and health of his early years."

"In youth we are anxious to affect the gravity and experience of age, and in age, still more vainly, the spirit and gaiety of youth."

The best of these entries in Melbourne's commonplace book are interesting as showing how his circumstances frustrated the full development of his talents. Why, with a mind so penetrating and individual, was he not one of the great aphorists, an English La Rochefoucauld, a nineteenth-century Halifax? The answer is surely that he did not write well enough: his mode of expression

is as a rule improvised and diffuse. This was not because he lacked
a gift for words. The phrases he tossed off in conversation are un-
forgettably pithy and racy. But he never took trouble to acquire
that sustained art which is needed to turn good conversation into
good literature. His literary energy had been weakened and dispersed by too much politics and too many parties.

For he kept up his social life too: dined out, went to the club,
above all took trouble to satisfy his need for feminine society. The
bonnet and shawl, which Greville noticed with such interest in the
hall of South Street, indicates that he sometimes took the opportunity to gratify his more agreeable passions. But passion in itself
never meant very much to Melbourne. What he required from
women was companionship of mind and sentiment; and these he
could only find in his own civilized world. During the Reform
years two new female characters make their appearance in his
story. One was not his usual type. Miss Emily Eden, the thirty-
five-year-old sister of Lord Auckland, was an aristocratic example
of the kind of English lady whose most distinguished representative is Jane Austen; a clever, sensible, delightful spinster, combining a rational belief in orthodox, solid virtue with a zestful
worldly-wise interest in her fellows and a sparkling satirical
humour. Melbourne used to meet her staying with his sister Lady
Cowper at Panshanger; he found her charming company; and she,
though she could not bring herself wholly to approve of him, was
peculiarly qualified to appreciate his oddness and his wit. Soon
they were close friends, meeting often and writing to each other
about politics, theological points and the foibles of their acquaintances. Naturally enough, Lady Cowper and others soon began to
talk of their marrying. Miss Eden would obviously be better off
with a husband and what an excellent wife she would be to Melbourne! At once intelligent, pleasant and good, was she not exactly the woman he had all his life been in need of? Perhaps she was!
Perhaps she and Melbourne would both have been happier if they
had had the wisdom to marry each other! Alas, love is not the
child of wisdom; and neither of them wanted to. Miss Eden was
of a cool prudent temperament and had long ago decided that she
much preferred staying at home and looking after her brother to
running the risks of matrimony. Certainly not with Melbourne:

"He bewilders me and frightens me and swears too much," she said laughingly when she heard of the suggestion. Anyway, she was sure that she was not the sort of woman he could ever feel romantic about. "I stand very low on the list of his loves," she re-marked, "and as for his thinking well of my principles, it would be rather hard if he did not, considering the society he lives in." These comments show her shrewdness. Cool and rational himself, Melbourne did not look for these qualities in his wife: his heart could only be set on fire by a personality that glowed with the pas-sion and enthusiasm he lacked.

His other new woman friend was not deficient in this respect. In December, 1830, he got a letter from a Mrs. Norton, the grand-daughter of the great Sheridan, asking him, on the strength of his old acquaintance with her family, if he could find a job for her husband. Since he had heard she was an attractive woman, he re-solved to answer her letter in person. And one evening he called on her at her house in Storey's Gate, Westminster. He was ushered up into a minute drawing-room, bright with flowers and muslin curtains and almost filled by a large blue sofa, from which rose to greet him a young woman of glittering beauty—all opulent shoulder and raven's wing hair, who bending forward a little, looked up at him meltingly from under sweeping lashes and whose blood, as she spoke, mantled delicately under a clear olive skin.

Her conversation was as vivid as her appearance. Her counten-ance alive with changing and dramatic expressions, and speaking in a softly modulated contralto, she poured forth a flood of words in which ardent opinions and flights of high-flown sentiments were interspersed by flattering attentive pauses and lightened by a free-spoken rollicking Irish humour. Melbourne found her society agreeable enough to make him want very much to see her again. Accordingly he set about getting Mr. Norton made a police court magistrate. Soon all London was gossiping about this Home Secretary's new entanglement. Every morning, it was said, Mrs. Norton could be seen waving to Lord Melbourne from her bal-cony as he walked by to his office; and every evening on his way home, he called in to see her.

She cannot much have minded the gossip. Caroline Norton was a natural *prima donna*, born it would seem to move through life under a spotlight of publicity. She had in a high degree the characteristics of her type; was vital, warm-hearted, impulsive, temperamental, egotistic and not quite a lady. It would have been a wonder if she had been, considering her history. At twenty-two years old she had already seen a remarkable amount of the seamy side of human existence. The Sheridan family hovered on the fringes of society, showy and impoverished, and surrounded always by a faint aura of scandal. For three generations they had set the world talking of their brilliance, their debts and their elopements. Mrs. Sheridan, worried to death about the future of her penurious daughters—there were three of them all beautiful—had married them off as quickly as she could. At the age of nineteen Caroline became the wife of George Norton, the younger brother of Lord Grantley. From the first, the marriage had been a failure. It was not Caroline's fault. Even her enemies—and she was to have many—have not a word to say for George Norton; a coarse, shifty cad, pathologically mean about money, subject to fits of brutal ill-temper and always talking about the state of his stomach. Within a few weeks of the honeymoon, he had thrown an ink-bottle at his wife's head. He followed this up later by kicking her, setting fire to her writing table and scalding her with a tea kettle. Caroline was not the woman to take such treatment lying down. On the contrary, she now and again vented her outraged feelings by doing whatever she thought might most annoy him. With some skill; on one occasion, when they had returned squabbling very late from a ball and George Norton flung himself dog-tired into bed, she kept him awake by refusing to join him and instead standing at the window apparently in exalted contemplation of the dawn. For once we can hardly blame him for leaping up and throwing her heavily to the ground. She also retaliated on him by insulting his Scotch family pride, mocking at the dowdy dullness of the Nortons and pointing out their ludicrous inferiority to the radiant Sheridans.

However, she was neither sensitive nor spiritless enough to let her matrimonial troubles obsess her. If for once in a way Norton was in a friendlier humour, she was always ready to respond. For the rest, she turned her mind to other things. This was not difficult for her. Passionately she thirsted for pleasure, achievement,

admiration. She also wanted money. George Norton had no fortune to compensate for his lack of other attractions. And since he
was incapable of earning much himself, Caroline soon decided
that, if they were to live in anything like the style she liked, she it
was who must provide the means. Settling in London, she opened
her campaign. Her chosen weapon was her pen. With some of her
grandfather's literary gift, she had inherited all his professional
facility; that ability to master the tricks of the trade which later
enabled her to turn out a well-made lively novel or pour out her
feelings in fluent Byronic verse with a competent effectiveness
which put her work from the first in quite a different category
from that of the lady amateur. Already by 1830, she had with some
success published two books of poems and had a play produced at
Covent Garden. She also added to her income by writing articles
and editing a fashionable magazine.

But writing, though it filled her pocket, did not satisfy her
dreams. It was as a woman, a queen of fashion and the salons, that
she aspired to shine. What with her looks and her wit, she found
it easy. By the time Melbourne got to know her, we find her name
in every social record of the day; at dinners, at balls, notably at a
masquerade where she dazzled all beholders in the costume of a
Greek slave. In fact, her position in society was not as good as it
looked to an outsider. Most of the great ladies who were its rulers
thought her altogether too flashy and theatrical—Miss Eden, we
note with interest, did not take to her—and they never admitted
her into the inner circle of their acquaintance. The gentlemen,
however, were less particular. "A superb lump of flesh," said one
of them, "looking as if made of precious stones, diamonds, emer-
alds, rubies, sapphires." When they discovered that her talk was
as scintillating as her beauty, they gathered round her.

They also went to her house. The little drawing-room in
Storey's Gate—so conveniently close to the Houses of Parliament
—became a centre where the cream of masculine London, statesmen and authors, artists and journalists, distinguished old gentlemen and rising young ones, met to relax and converse and sparkle.
Caroline was well able to hold her own with them. Indeed she was
not a woman to be trifled with. If interrupted while telling a story,
or if anyone dared to raise a laugh at her expense, she was liable to

lose her temper. But more often she sat on her sofa making animated contributions to a political or literary discussion: and when discussion lapsed, she would rise to entertain the company with an improvisation on the piano or a humorous song in the Irish brogue.

It was a delightful place for Melbourne to spend his evenings. There, forgetful for a blessed moment of bloodthirsty trade unionists and irascible Cabinet Ministers, he sat observing with amused curiosity the clever young men. Now and again his hostess would bring one up to be introduced and he would say a friendly word to him. "Well now, tell me—what do you want to be?" he asked the youthful Disraeli, flamboyant in satin trousers and ornate black ringlets. "I want to be Prime Minister," replied Disraeli gravely. Melbourne was taken aback; odd as he realized that the new England was likely to be, he could not conceive of it being so odd as to make such an eventuality at all possible. Genially he tried to warn the queer entertaining young man not to place his ambitions quite so high.

Often there were no young men; and he saw Caroline *tête à tête*. She also visited him alone at South Street. Soon the relationship was a feature of importance in both their lives. It was natural. Intelligent, ambitious, at sea in a difficult world, Caroline was the sort of woman who always feels drawn to clever and older men. She delighted to learn from Melbourne's knowledge and civilized wisdom; and she turned to his experience for advice. Soon he had heard the whole story of George Norton's misdemeanours. These had not ceased with the improvement of his fortunes. He seems to have been one of those men who think that the best way to accept favours without incurring loss of self-respect, is to receive them with a bad grace. He did not cut much of a figure at his wife's parties: when he did speak, he was truculent and uneasy. In the Spring of 1831 he caused a new trouble by insisting on having his sister to stay for a few months. Miss Augusta Norton was an unpleasing person of eccentric manners who wore her hair cropped short, and dressed in bloomers. Poor Caroline felt her social position too insecure for her to be able to face appearing in public with so unpresentable a companion. She refused to take Miss Norton about with her. Thereupon her brother said that she too must stay at home; otherwise, he declared, he would cut the traces of her carriage. The house rang with rows of ever-growing intensity, until the time came for Miss Norton and her bloomers to take their departure.

Politics too were a source of dispute between husband and wife. Caroline was a Whig; temperament and family tradition alike disposed her to take the progressive adventurous side. So also did the fact that the Norton family was Tory. She threw herself actively into the campaign for Reform, talking, writing and canvassing Members of Parliament. Norton stormed at her for publicly acting against his opinions. All these troubles were poured out to Melbourne, who was amused and sympathetic and counselled patience.

Caroline felt the more warmly towards him because she was sorry for him. Lonely, burdened with responsibilities and with no home life of his own, he was not, she soon perceived, as happy as he looked. There was a strongly maternal streak in her emotional nature and she particularly sympathized with his anxieties about Augustus. The doctors had ordered that he should never be left alone for long and Melbourne was never sure whether his attendants obeyed this command when he himself was not there. In the middle of a conversation with her at South Street, he would suddenly become silent and inattentive; she realized he was listening tensely to hear if there was any ominous sound from Augustus's room. Her impulsive heart welled out in pity.

She also entered into his other difficulties; listened if he was worried about what was happening to Lady Branden and took an interest in his political future. Since with her interest meant action, she also did what she could to help him. She brought him into contact with people who might be useful to him and tried to pick up information he might want to hear; so efficiently that he began to make use of her as a go-between when he wanted to get into unofficial communication with a member of the opposition. She also gave him advice herself. "Don't dine with Ellice,[1] and drink and say Damn Politics!" she writes on one occasion. "It hurts your Government and your reputation." These were wise words. When her judgment was not clouded by her egotism Caroline Norton was both sharp-eyed and clear-sighted. It did not

[1] Edward Ellice was a Government Whip in the Grey Administration.

take her long to grasp the main facts about Melbourne's character and the English political scene. Indeed she was unusually suited to satisfy his imperative need for a woman in his life. The difference of age did not matter. He had always enjoyed the role of mentor to the young; now more than ever when he was growing older and could drink in from his pupil some of the invigorating freshness of her youth. Caroline also knew just how to amuse him. How entertaining it was when she was away on a visit at a country house to open a letter from her describing gay evenings when "Mrs. Heneage was never out of Lord Edward Thynne's arms and Lady Augusta Baring never off Mr. Heneage's knee", and Lord Edward said something to Caroline at which George Norton took offence so that everyone thought they were going to fight a duel on the spot; or giving a racy account of young Lord Ossulston bursting into her own bedroom in the middle of the night "with his large blue eyes opening and shutting like the wings of a Cashmere butterfly", and so aflame with dishonourable intentions that it took her some time and all her tact to get rid of him without anybody hearing. In these lively communications Melbourne breathed once more the scandalous delightful atmosphere of that Regency world in which he had grown up.

But there was a more intimate reason why he was drawn to her. She possessed the one quality common to all the women he cared for most in his life; the zestful positiveness of nature, blending spontaneous joy in living with an inability to doubt or hesitate about anything, which was the antidote to his own sad questioning scepticism. It was this partly he had loved in that other Caroline who was his wife. Indeed the two women were not unlike. Caroline Norton was, in every sense of the word, a less uncommon phenomenon. She was not exquisite or elfin or mad. But she also loved the limelight; she also was dynamic and restless; she also was an incurable self-dramatist in the high romantic style. And in her, as in her namesake, these qualities exhilarated Melbourne and made him laugh and touched him.

Did they do more? Did he love her? Not certainly as he had loved Caroline Lamb. He was not young enough for one thing. And moreover with so much that appealed to him, Caroline Norton lacked the untarnished childlike quality that was needed to kindle his heart and his imagination into full flame. And the refinement. "All the Sheridans are a little vulgar," he said to Queen Victoria some years later, in an unguarded moment. We remember that the Sheridan he knew best was Caroline Norton.

He grew very fond of her though, and there was something of the lover in his feeling. He was too much a man for it to be otherwise. The relationship between them was pitched in a slightly raised emotional key: it had its flirtatious gaiety, its moments of tender sweetness and its spasms of jealousy. "You, I suppose, will be happy at Panshanger with the virtuous Stanhope and the virgin Eden," she writes tartly to him. He equally could not help complaining a little when Caroline seemed to be enjoying herself wholeheartedly, away from him. She hastened to reassure him.

"My dear Lord,
 Do not be angry with me if I say that it is selfish to be discontented with me for being amused here—you talk of my romping and flirting—and forgetting everything else. I have not forgotten anything. I am sure your name is always on my lips and there is hardly anything they can say or do that does not bring back some of your opinions or expressions. If I could be always with you, if you were with me in any country house you would find that you would seem the one person to talk to. But I cannot be with you always and therefore I amuse myself as I can—or rather I amuse others—for they come and coax me out of my room if I attempt to write there or sit by myself and they will do nothing without me . . . I can assure you I should much rather sit by your sofa in South Street than be Queen of the Revels here. You won't believe me and yet it is true. God bless you.
 Your affectionate,
 Caroline."

The tone of this letter, though light, is not that of a mere sensible sexless friendship.

Yet their relationship remained platonic.[1] Nor, in the circum-

[1] Cynical persons have questioned this—not unnaturally in view of the character of the parties concerned. But for once cynicism appears unjustified. Mrs. Norton in a self-justifying pamphlet on English Laws for Women, published in 1854, quotes a letter from Melbourne, written

stances, was this so curious as a censorious world may suppose.
Caroline had always professed a strict regard for virtue. "Adultery is a crime, not a recreation"—thus she had firmly repulsed the
attentions of the blue-eyed Lord Ossulston. Moreover she always
maintained that it was friendship, not love, she wanted from men.
"The saddest moment for me," she confided to a friend, "is when
a man seems uneasy at being left alone with me, when his voice
lowers and he draws his chair nearer; I know then that I am about
to lose a friend I love and to get a lover I don't want."

This remark does not ring absolutely true. In it, Caroline
shows herself a little too obviously anxious to appear superior to
the petty vanity of commonplace women and also to prove that
she was not so fast as the malicious world liked to make out. But
there is something in what she said. For all her temperament, she
was not the amorous type. *Prima donnas* dream first of influence
and admiration, not of love.

If she was unwilling, Melbourne, on his side, was not the man to
compel her inclinations. Thirty years older than her and scrupu-
lously honourable and considerate in personal relations, he might
well hesitate before involving her in the possibility of a scandal
which, with a husband and a reputation like hers, would have
meant her certain ruin. There was a streak too of the paternal in
his sentiment for one young enough to be his daughter, inconsistent with violent passion: and after all, sympathy of spirit, not
sensual satisfaction, had always been what he wanted most from
the other sex. Now in the cooler calm of his middle age, he was
contented to ask no more of fate than pleasant evenings alone with
beautiful Caroline in her drawing-room; evenings of lively talk, of
easy laughter, of warm confidential intimacy; and caressed deli-
ciously at moments by a light breath of romance.

---

in April, 1836, when her husband's action against her was pending, in
which he tells her she need have no fear since she is innocent. As the
context shows this to be a private informal letter in which Melbourne has
no need to disguise the truth, this would seem to settle the question. This
conclusion is further confirmed by the fact, alluded to on page 177, that at
his death Melbourne left a note asking his brother to continue the allow-
ances he made to Lady Branden and Mrs. Norton, and reasserting his
innocence in regard to Mrs. Norton.

## CHAPTER III

## AFTER REFORM

H E HAD need of consolation during the next few years. For the political scene was not such as to cheer his foreboding spirit. To anyone, but especially to any member of the governing class, the atmosphere of England after the passing of the Reform Bill was tense, dark and uneasy. It was obscurely realized that the Bill marked the beginning of a completely new epoch; but what that epoch was going to be like, no one could tell. In consequence, those who had anything to lose felt all the time jumpy and apprehensive. The pessimists among them, like the Duke of Wellington, even took the view that they were in for a period of violent revolution, that now, with the citadel of aristocratic power surrendered, it would only be a few years before King, peers and private property were swept away in a storm of bloodshed. Certainly, as Melbourne had expected, extreme parties were already showing themselves angrily disappointed by the results of Reform. The Home Office still got reports of secret plots to overthrow the Constitution: from time to time there were still outbreaks of riots and violence. Now loud, now soft, the murmur of popular discontent was ominously audible.

Whether or not it could be quieted depended on Parliament. But Parliament, in its new reformed state, had itself become an unknown quantity. Not only was it largely made up of what Melbourne called "the blackguardly interest"—manufacturers, nonconformists and other dingy and unpredictable persons—but they and their fellow members were susceptible, as never before, to the pressure of their constituents, who could threaten to turn them out if they did not approve of their actions. Could they be relied on to stand firm, if firmness was likely to be unpopular? Besides, every day that passed revealed the Reform Party, which formed the majority of members, as very divided. Reform had been passed by a combination of people who wanted it for widely different reasons. The Radicals looked on it as the first necessary step in a general reform; reform of the Church, reform of local government, reform in Ireland, reform of the House of Lords, reform of the Corn Laws. The old-fashioned Whigs and the Canningites, on the other hand, hoped that by granting Parliamentary Reform, they would pacify discontent sufficiently to stop the demand for any other reforms. In between these two extremes hovered a crowd of people, willing for more reform than the Canningites, though not for so much as the Radicals, but who could not agree as to what particular reforms they each desired. All these different groups had united together to fight for Parliamentary Reform. Now that they had got it, however, their differences began to show. It looked as if these might become so sharp as to break up the party and bring down the Government. And who was to succeed them? Not the Tories; for the time being they were a beaten, punch-drunk rout with no confidence in themselves and no hope of getting a majority in the country. The result might well be that, for want of an alternative, the Radicals would sweep in and effect by constitutional means changes almost as extreme as those proposed by the agitators for revolution. To avoid this, strong and skilful leadership was needed. It did not look as if this was going to be obtained from the existing Government.

Indeed, they were an odd set of men to be guiding England along the path of progress at this crucial moment. A scratch team of aristocrats gathered hastily together to pass the Reform Bill, they were, for the most part, themselves men of the past; who, whatever their theoretical opinions, were unqualified alike by tradition and experience to envisage the new bourgeois and industrial epoch which it was their fate to inaugurate. Moreover, as much as their followers, they were divided as to what they wanted to happen. They, too, had supported reform for diverse reasons: and now they, too, reacted differently to the prospect of the future. Every shade of opinion except that of the extreme left was represented in their ranks.

So variously-minded a body could only have worked together easily if its individual members had been themselves conciliatory persons. This, however, was far from being the case. Some of them, like Melbourne himself or Lord Holland, were reasonable enough. But there were others who would have been troublesome members of a team at any period. To be born and bred a ruler does not encourage a man to be accommodating; and the high-nosed, be-chokered countenances that gaze down at one so arrogantly from the portraits of the Reform ministers exhibit them as possessed of all the wilful and idiosyncratic independence of their Whig blue blood.

The two most influential members in deciding the course of policy were Lord Grey, the Prime Minister and Lord Althorp, the Chancellor of the Exchequer. Grey was a shy, reserved, formidable *grand seigneur* of unbending principles and distinguished manners, who had become celebrated in his younger days as a pioneer of Reform. Since he would never join an administration not specifically Whig he had kept out of politics for many years. Now, brought back to lend the authority of his name and his character to the Reform Government, he found himself, like Rip Van Winkle, in a world utterly unlike that of his youth. He did not like it. The age of enlightenment and progress, for which he had once fought so ardently, turned out, now it had arrived, to be a vulgar, restless affair. Not a day passed that Grey did not yearn to be back in the quiet and freedom of his country home at Howick Hall, Northumberland, with his books and his grandchildren and his sporting guns: and, though a stern sense of duty kept him at his post, the strain of living in so uncongenial an atmosphere kept him permanently irritable and ill at ease. At the slightest extra friction —and this occurred almost monthly—Grey threatened to resign.

Lord Althorp, though easier-tempered than his chief, was also liable to proffer his resignation on small excuse. He was a curious and lovable character of a peculiarly English type. With his heavy figure and plain red weather-beaten face, he looked like a farmer; and in fact there was a lot of the farmer about him. Country pursuits were the only things he enjoyed; even during the crisis of the Reform Bill, he always opened letters from his bailiff before looking at the rest of his post. Yet beneath this John Bull exterior lurked a quixotic strain of enthusiastic idealism which led him far from the path Nature would seem to have marked out for him. He had loved his wife with so romantic a passion that when she died he gave up fox hunting, which he enjoyed more than anything else in life, for ever; no less a sacrifice could, he felt, express his utter desolation at her loss. He also threw himself into the cause of Reform against all his natural instincts as a landowner, simply because he thought Reform was the cause of justice. The same motive kept him still in office afterwards, though he had no ambition and was as miserable in London as a sporting dog. Not that he could feel that he did much good there. "I am nothing in Cabinet," he remarked with humorous humility, "I have no great talent nor ill temper, so nobody cares for me." It was not true. Althorp's influence with his colleagues was considerable. With the House of Commons it was more. Who could resist so endearing a mixture of honesty and modesty and homeliness? The fact that he was a poor, halting speaker somehow only made members like him more. He could do anything he liked with them. Once when an opponent had raised a point against the Government, Althorp replied that he had some facts with which he was sure he could answer it, but for the moment he had mislaid them. Both sides of the House at once accepted his answer as perfectly satisfactory. Indeed, so far as the management of Parliament was concerned, Althorp was the most important member of the Government. "He is the tortoise," said Melbourne, "on whose back the world reposes."

Four other personalities stand out especially in the history of those years; the Hon. Edward Stanley, Secretary for Ireland; Lord John Russell, the Privy Seal; Lord Durham, the Paymaster General, and Lord Chancellor Brougham. Stanley represented the extreme right wing. Only family tradition put him on the Whig side. By temperament a despotic oligarch, he had been a leading Waverer over Reform; and now ruled Ireland by a policy of ruthless coercion in the interests of the Protestant Ascendancy. For the rest, he was youthful, brilliant and combative with an extraordinary gift for aggressive, effective debating, and off-hand patrician manners which induced a disagreeable sense of social inferiority among the more bourgeois members of his party. They were mystified by the race-course metaphors with which he sprinkled his discourses, and resented his habit of lounging back on the Treasury bench with his feet propped up on the table in front of him, for all the world as if he were taking his ease at Brooks's Club.

Lord John Russell also lacked the common touch. A small, prim young man, with a large head and a precise, old-fashioned mode of speech, he often failed to recognize a follower of ten years' standing and conversed in a strain of cold, flat candour that was the reverse of winning. On one occasion he described to a friend how at a party he had left the Duchess of Inverness to talk to the Duchess of Sutherland because she was sitting farther from the fire and he felt too hot. "I hope you told the Duchess of Inverness why you left her," said the friend. "No," said John Russell after a pause. "But I did tell the Duchess of Sutherland." All the same, if John Russell was not loved he was, unlike Stanley, deeply and growingly trusted by his Party. This is a little surprising because, in addition to his lack of social charm, there was something depressingly commonplace about John Russell's mind. Perhaps, though, this was an advantage to him. Intellectual originality does not make for popularity in English politics. What the average member likes are ordinary ideas supported by brains and character stronger than the ordinary. This was just what John Russell possessed. His outlook was the orthodox Whig outlook of the new generation, who believed in adapting old institutions to a new situation by a process of cautious reform. But John Russell did not hold this in a vague, instinctive, amateurish fashion. Intellectual and highly educated, he never rested till he had clarified and ordered his opinions in relation to a system of defined and rigid political principles. He was a doctrinaire of the middle way. With a doctrinaire's certainty, too; here we come to the final cause of his influence. A strong, narrow character, fortified by the unhesitating self-confidence which was the inheritance of every member of the august house of Russell, he never doubted that he was always in the right about everything. "There is not a better man in England than Lord John Russell," said Sydney Smith, "but he is utterly ignorant of moral fear: there is nothing he would not undertake. I believe he would perform the operation for the stone —build St. Peter's—or assume, with or without ten minutes' notice, the command of the Channel Fleet: and no-one would discover by his manner that the patient had died, the church tumbled down and the Channel Fleet been knocked to atoms." Self-confidence on this scale, though irritating to his acquaintance, was a great help to John Russell in imposing his will on more hesitant persons.

Black-browed, "Radical Jack" Durham, the champion of left-wing ideas in the Government, was equally sure he was right. But he was less successful at persuading others to share his belief. The rich Radical seldom carries conviction, especially if he is as fantastically rich as Durham. Justly or not, it is hard to accept, as spokesman of the poor, a man who is reported to have spent £900,000 on doing up his house. Besides, Durham's character was even more paradoxical than his political position. Independent, courageous and with fitful gleams of political vision, he was also a theatrical, unbalanced egotist whose infirmities of temper had been developed to the highest pitch by bad health, bad nerves and too much money. Accustomed to indulge every changing mood and follow every impulse, his character was a bundle of inconsistencies. He was an autocrat at home and a democrat abroad, spoiled his children and cuffed his servants, was delightful to his friends one moment and insulted them the next, gave magnificent dinner parties through which he himself sat in sullen silence, risked his reputation to serve the cause of liberty and equality at the same time as he was pulling every string he could lay hands on to get himself made an earl—"shall the richest commoner in England be no more than the last of her barons?" he demanded furiously. As a member of a Cabinet Durham was impossible. Not only did he deliberately provoke his less progressive colleagues by the revolutionary violence of his proposals, but he advocated them with a lack of self-control that made discussion with him impossible. He stormed, he sulked, he made scenes, he burst into tears, he flung out of the room, he squabbled incessantly with Stanley; and he bullied Lord Grey—who, incidentally, was his father-in-law—so unmercifully that the poor gentleman, losing all his patrician poise, cowered in a corner, while kindly Althorp sat with his face buried in his hands out of sheer embarrassment. Outside the Cabinet Durham intrigued with disaffected members of his Party against his own leaders and made public speeches of extreme indiscretion. In the autumn of 1832, to the general relief it was arranged he should go on a mission to Russia. Russia sounded comfortably far off. But before many months were over he was back, and the scenes were raging away as intolerably as ever. By 1834 there were few of his colleagues with whom Lord Durham had not personally quarrelled.

All the same it is doubtful if he was quite such a nuisance as Lord Brougham. Durham's views kept fairly steady, even if his temper did not. Not so Brougham's. He was the one important Minister who was not an aristocrat; a middle-class Scottish lawyer who, from the time he had entered political life twenty odd years before, had, by the sheer brilliance of his personal gifts, established himself in the forefront of the Whig Party. During its long period of eclipse he had done more than any other one man to modernize its appeal and keep up its fighting spirit. By 1830 he was generally considered the most dynamic single force in politics and possibly the cleverest man alive. Certainly Brougham was a phenomenon; as flamboyantly eccentric as a character of Dickens—and as preternaturally vital. The queer, lanky figure with the baleful, restless eyes and twitching, inquisitive nose was never still for an instant. Across the page of history he strides, fidgeting, posturing, scratching his head, picking his nose and incessantly pouring forth a flood of talk in which ideas and scurrility, jokes and voluminous learning were strangely and sparklingly blended. No one could help listening to Brougham when he really got going. "Lord Brougham," writes a fashionable lady, "kept us spellbound at breakfast talking about the habits of bees, as charming as a fairy tale." In serious conclave with his colleagues, he was equally riveting: the one member of the Government with expert knowledge of the special problems of the new age—educational problems, legal problems, economic problems—and with projects for solving them all. "This morning," remarked the sardonic Rogers about him, "Solon, Lycurgus, Demosthenes, Archimedes, Sir Isaac Newton, Lord Chesterfield and a good many others went away in one post-chaise!"

But what lay behind this astonishing display? Not profound thought. Examined today and unassisted by the magnetic light of Brougham's personal presence, his learning shows up as superficial and his ideas as no more than commonplace. Morally he was even less impressive—undignified, boastful, drunken and directed by no consistent principles whatsoever. His days passed in a turmoil of plot and counter-plot, trickery and double-dealing in which he tacked about so often and so quick from section to section of his Party, according as to which seemed most likely to further his career of self-advancement, that it was impossible to be sure at any one moment which side he was on. To complete the confusion he created, there was a streak in him of sheer irresponsibility. Out of jealousy or temper, or just from an impish delight in stirring up trouble, he was always liable to do or say something which set everyone by the ears. Indeed, the more Brougham is studied, the more surprising it becomes that he should have succeeded in getting where he did. For there was nothing constant in him, but an unsleeping egotism and a wonderful skill in showing off. Upwards rushed the rocket, deafening the ears with its roar and lighting up the whole sky with a shower of stars. But when they had faded, all that remained was a bit of charred stick and a faint ominous whiff of sulphur.

His contemporaries were dazzled by the stars, but they smelt the sulphur all right. "Beelzebub", "the Arch-Fiend", "old Wickedshifts"—such were his nicknames. None of the Whig leaders trusted him enough to want him in the Government; but they feared he might be more dangerous outside it. So Grey made him Lord Chancellor. He soon regretted it. Perhaps in an unusually disciplined and united Ministry Brougham's energy and brains might have been subdued to serve some useful purpose; but not in the Whig Ministry of 1831! The Arch-Fiend used his great position only as a platform from which to make his personality felt by his own characteristic methods, which included meddling in other Ministers' business behind their backs, and conducting his own without any reference to the lines of policy laid down by his leaders. Like an elderly and malignant Puck, incongruously clothed in Lord Chancellor's robes and wig, Brougham flitted about leaving a trail of bad faith and bad blood wherever he went.

With such a team to drive it is no wonder that poor Grey longed to be back at Howick Hall. He himself did not feel inclined for further reforms; only as much of them as would keep the Radicals quiet without annoying the old Whigs so much that they withdrew their support from him. Helped by Althorp and in a less degree by

John Russell, he managed to pursue this middle course more successfully than might have been expected. Some substantial measures were passed in those years, notably those dealing with banking, legal, factory and poor law reform. But the Government was too divided to settle down into any kind of stability. Hardly two months went by without someone threatening to resign; Durham and Brougham from temper, Stanley and John Russell from principle, Althorp and Grey from the simple desire for a quiet life. The Cabinet lurched on from dangerous crisis to dangerous crisis; and, though for a time catastrophe was averted by a succession of hastily patched-up compromises, yet each crisis left the Government weaker in itself and more discredited in the eyes of the world. At last the left and right extremes broke off. Durham went in the spring of 1833; Stanley followed him in May, 1834. It was clear that one more rumpus, and the whole thing would fall to pieces.

From his customary position of detachment Melbourne surveyed its decline and approaching fall. Himself he was in favour of Grey's middle-way policy. It was not that he liked reforms any better than he had done: or that he was less apprehensive about the future. So far as he could judge from the reports that came into the Home Office, popular feeling was still very disturbed. He was appalled, so he told Greville, driving up with him to London from a country house visit in the autumn of 1832, by the desire for change and general restlessness which prevailed, and he judged violent revolution to be likely enough to insist on the Commander-in-Chief being a non-party appointment. If it came to fighting, he thought, it was essential that the forces of order should have the confidence of all respectable people behind them. Melbourne's very fear of disorder, however, modified his instinctive conservatism. Better concession than civil war, he would agree after some grumbling. It might pacify people for a bit at any rate; and it would help to keep the Government united. As much as ever he felt its unity to be more important than anything else; and did all he could to promote it. "I was always exhorting different sections of Lord Grey's Government to shuffle over differences," he related later. Personally he always took care to avoid rows and tried to get on with everyone: so successfully that he was the only

Minister whom all the others liked. This did not mean that he liked them. Coolly and silently, he observed his colleagues and drew conclusions about their characters for future use. As politicians, he esteemed them only in so far as their conduct encouraged what was tranquil and stable. By this test Grey and Althorp, along with some old friends like Lord Holland, came out not too badly—though Melbourne mocked at Grey's reluctance to make the best of anything. "Lord Grey," he said, "in or out, successful or unsuccessful, was never satisfied with anything, least of all with himself." Melbourne got on also with John Russell well enough. Of course John Russell worried too much about his principles, but his views were moderate, his word was to be trusted; and anyway Melbourne had known him all his life. The others were not so satisfactory. Stanley was the best of them. Melbourne sympathized with his dislike of reform and was enthusiastic about his oratory. "He rose like a young eagle above them all," he cried, after listening to one of his star performances in the House of Commons. But Stanley could not be described as a tranquillizer. "He has about him both the faults of great spirit, haste and rashness, and those of being discontented and disgusted," Melbourne told Fred. So also had Brougham and Durham without any of Stanley's compensating virtues. Durham was everything that irritated Melbourne most—idealistic, vain and rude. Besides, it was impossible to believe a word he said. All that fuss about his ill health for instance!—Melbourne noticed that he was only ill when he wanted to get out of doing something. He could not bear Durham. About Brougham, he was not able to bring himself to feel so strongly. Melbourne always had a soft spot for amusing ruffians, and all the more if they were eccentric. He even went so far as to say that Brougham had a good heart lurking about him somewhere. This did not mean that he liked having him in the Government. As early as the autumn of 1832 he had made up his mind that he was an untrustworthy nuisance. Three years later he declared, "Brougham is mad and will one day, by sacrificing everything to his personal whim, end by sacrificing himself." Melbourne thought that the sooner this happened the better.

Altogether the spectacle of cabinet life served to confirm him in his general sense of the infirmity of human beings and their institutions.

"A Cabinet is a delicate and fragile machine," he writes tartly in the summer of 1834, "this is still more the case when it has recently been shaken and broken, and repaired with new materials. Those who remain are anxious not to have to concede anything to their new allies: those who join are equally desirous of obtaining as much concession as possible, in order to justify themselves for having accepted office. . . . Such a body is not to be approached without the utmost care and even alarm!"

For the rest, his colleagues provided abundant food for his sense of comedy. He was especially entertained by the way they—like Ministers in all periods—insisted on believing themselves to be both indispensable and popular. "They think themselves fixtures," he exclaimed in comic wonderment; "I cannot think why!" Yet, he reflected, his irony taking another turn, they might be right. When did unpopularity ever bring a Government down? Perhaps, on the contrary, it kept it in! "Now we are as unpopular as the Tories," he remarked after the passing of the Bank Bill, "we may stay in as long as they did." Certainly he got a lot of fun out of being a Minister, in spite of his gloomy views. By a characteristic paradox, he was at once the most pessimistic and the most cheerful member of the Government. During the next three years every glimpse we get of his figure reveals him in some joyous attitude; writing to Miss Eden "in tearing spirits", lounging back with a look of arch amusement at a Guildhall banquet, swilling wine joyfully with John Russell, giving jocose infectious grunts of pleasure as he browses in the Holland House library, genially relaxing with his feet up on Lady Holland's elegant drawing-room chairs; and everywhere loudly laughing. "Lord Melbourne," said Tom Moore, "laughs more and at less than ever."

We get a more extended view of him in those moments of relaxation through the eyes of Benjamin Haydon, diarist and painter. Haydon, naïve, acute, egotistic, idealistic and preposterous, made Melbourne's acquaintance in the autumn of 1832. After a lifetime's unsuccessful struggle to persuade the public and the Royal Academy that he was a great artist, his luck had turned. He was

commissioned to paint a picture of the official banquet to celebrate the triumph of Reform. The Ministers came down to his
studio to sit for their likenesses. Their patrician grace of manner
appealed alike to Haydon's snobbishness and his æsthetic sense.
He was enchanted by them all, but especially by Melbourne. "A
fine head," he noted, "a delightfully frank, easy, unaffected man of
fashion. There is nothing like them when they add intelligence to
breeding."

Melbourne, on his side, was very much entertained by Haydon
—here was a new type to be added to his collection of human oddi-
ties—and he encouraged him to display his eccentricities to the
full. He asked him questions about himself and his queer friends,
Keats, Shelley, Hazlitt and so on; and in his turn regaled Haydon
with anecdotes about Charles Fox and Sir Joshua Reynolds.
"Reynolds was a hard-working old dog," he said. "He worked
too hard to be happy." The two also had long discussions on politics, art and religion, in which Melbourne listened with apparent
gravity to Haydon's exalted rhapsodizings. Now and again he
pulled him up by a shrewd well-informed comment; but never in
such a way as to make him ill at ease. On the contrary—"I am always brilliant with him," Haydon noted complacently. Indeed,
he found Melbourne so sympathetic that he was soon trying to enlist his help in what was the most cherished object of his heart,
namely to persuade the State to become an active patron of historical paintings and more especially of the historical painting of
Benjamin Haydon. Alas, he had mistaken his man! Melbourne
was against the State taking on any task that was not a necessity;
he did not look on historical painting as a necessity. Moreover, it is
likely that he realized that Haydon was far from being the great
artist he fancied himself. Accordingly, when Haydon mentioned
the subject of State patronage, Melbourne gazed at him with a
mischievous look and answered evasively. A dreadful doubt began
to steal into Haydon's mind. Could it be that Lord Melbourne
did not take him seriously? "His manner suggested that I was a
disappointed enthusiast," he noted, "whom he found it amusing
to listen to, however absurd it might be to adopt my plans."

This was pretty near the truth. But Haydon had never been one
to let truth get in the way of his dreams, without a struggle. In

1834 he returned to the charge and called on Melbourne at his house. Melbourne, just out of bed, appeared delighted to see him. But the upshot of this, and of subsequent interviews, was to confirm Haydon in his disillusionment. Not that he ceased to respond to Melbourne's charm. How graceful his gestures were, he noticed, how infectious his laugh, how like an antique statue's was his neck revealed by the open collar of his grey dressing-gown! All the same, his attitude to Historical Art was, so far as Haydon could see, nothing short of lamentable. "God help the Minister that meddles with art!" he had remarked shockingly. Indeed, he seemed to take a positive pleasure in bantering and tantalizing Haydon on the subject. One day he would be maintaining perversely that State patronage was harmful to painters; on another that the Government was against paintings in public buildings because they wanted to emulate "the simplicity of the ancients". Sometimes he did not even bother to answer Haydon's eloquent adjurations; but merely rubbed his hands, burst out laughing and, turning to the looking glass, began to brush his hair.

Haydon's patience was finally exhausted when the question of decorating the new House of Lords came up; and Melbourne, simply to tease, suggested employing the academician Callcott, a noted enemy of Haydon's. A man who could make such a proposal even as a joke, reflected Haydon, was, it was clear, hopelessly frivolous. Sadly he decided that talking to Melbourne, seductive though it might be, was a waste of time. This did not prevent him from writing to Melbourne a year later to ask for some money. Melbourne sent a cheque for seventy pounds at once, adding, kindly but firmly, that Haydon must not expect any more. After this, we notice, communication between them seems to have ceased.

Laughing at Holland House and listening to Haydon, however, only occupied Melbourne's leisure hours. These were more limited than he liked. He still had plenty of work. His main duties were two-fold; answering for the Government in the House of Lords and performing his functions as Home Secretary. In the House of Lords he was only moderately effective. Since he was shrewd and tactful he could be trusted not to let the Government down; but no amount of practice could make him an orator. The last thing he felt inclined to do was to cajole other people into adopting his opinions, let alone those of his Party. All too well he realized how doubtfully right these were. Moreover he never learned to concentrate his thoughts in a purposive flow. Now and again, provoked by some unusually foolish or unjust remark from the other side, he would gather his wits together to make a sharp-edged effective reply; but for the most part he let himself wander along, now and again touching on the practical point at issue, but soon drifting off to pursue some curious train of generalizing thought, the upshot of which was always that since no one really knew anything about the matter, it was better to take no action on it, beyond allowing people to do what they liked. The only measures he enthusiastically approved were those for removing restrictions. Certainly let the Jews be relieved from their civil disabilities—"all disabilities are injurious," he declared, "and most are ineffectual." He was also against stopping Trades Unions from holding meetings on Sundays, and poured scorn on the idea that you could make people more law-abiding by controlling the sale of drink. Indeed, all new-fangled schemes for checking crime struck him as futile. Perhaps some good might be done by insisting that convicts should keep themselves clean—they would be sure to dislike that. But do not try to educate them. "Recollect that crime has existed in all ages," he remarked; "all attempts at eradication have hitherto proved useless. Education will not help, for education is knowledge . . . which can be good or bad." Indeed, he once suggested that the criminal law involved issues so obscure and deep as to be a subject for the philosopher rather than the statesman. It was part of the science of man; and "the science of man, if it is a science," he said, "is one of the most unsettling and at the same time most curious lines presented for our investigation". Such speculations led the peers of England into mental regions in which they were not at home. Melbourne's speeches left them more bewildered than impressed.

As Home Secretary he was also bewildering. Strangers continued to be startled by Tom Young's manners, and disconcerted to find themselves being interviewed by Melbourne shaving in his dressing-room at midday. Even when he did get down to the Office he carried his own atmosphere of eccentric informality with

H

him. This was especially startling to deputations—those deputations of public-spirited persons keen to advocate some cause, which were a new and characteristic phenomenon of the age of Reform. What were they to make of a Minister who received them lounging back nursing a sofa cushion; who, while they ponderously delivered their carefully prepared recitals of cogent argument and authenticated fact, pulled a feather out of the cushion and began blowing it about the room; and who after they had finished, answered briefly and with a bland smile that he was afraid he could not help them as he knew nothing about the matter in question? Was the Home Secretary an irresponsible ignoramus, they wondered?

Of course Melbourne was nothing of the kind. Anyone who worked for him could have told the deputation that most likely he had sat up half the night before, reading up the subject of their discourse. But he had no intention of letting them know this. This was partly out of mischief. Earnest well-informed persons with liberal ideals and nonconformist consciences are always powerful stimulants to the comic spirit. Melbourne could not resist the temptation to tease them. But there were more sober motives for his behaviour. Often he did not wish to commit the Government; to pretend ignorance was an easy way of doing this. There was generally a method in Melbourne's madness. Queer and haphazard though his way of doing things might seem, his work got finished and his ends achieved. If efficiency is the art of getting what one wants, Melbourne was an efficient man.

As far as the Home Office was concerned his efficiency was limited by his political views. These were not constructive; for them to be so would have involved his taking an interest in social reform. Social reform bored Melbourne and he did not think it did any good. During his long period of leisure he had read some economics. His reading had converted him to the new doctrine of *laissez-faire*. It seemed to him proved beyond doubt that the problems of poverty could only be solved by allowing the forces of supply and demand to take their course. He realized that this process involved considerable suffering for the poor: and since even the study of economics could not transform Melbourne into a hard-hearted man, this disposed him more than ever to avert his mind from the subject. Here was yet another painful aspect of existence which he preferred not to think about.

His point of view appears vividly in an account of some conversations a few years earlier. In November, 1830, Lord Suffield, an enthusiastic peer of humane ideals, approached the Government with a scheme for relieving distressed agricultural labourers by settling them on waste lands as smallholders. In vain: to the orthodox opinion of the period all such schemes were cranky nonsense. So they were to Melbourne. He told Suffield he could have nothing to do with his plans. "I fear you have not devoted much attention to the subject," said Suffield. "I understand it perfectly," replied Melbourne crisply, "and that is my reason for saying nothing about it." "How is this to be explained?" asked Suffield. "Because I consider it hopeless," retorted Melbourne. Suffield said hotly that he supposed Melbourne agreed with Malthus that vice and misery were the only cure for the evils of poverty. Melbourne shrank from accepting so harsh and bald a version of his opinions. "No," he said, "the evil is in numbers and the competition that ensues, etc." "Well then," said Suffield, "I have means to propose to meet that difficulty." "Of that I know nothing," said Melbourne, and changed the subject. Suffield could get nothing more out of him.

The same mixed uneasy state of feeling showed itself in his attitude towards the new reform measures. The Poor Law for instance; in so far as it was grounded on sound economic theory, he was in its favour. But both as a conservative and a man of heart he disliked it. The fact that it put power into the hand of commissioners to act without the permission of the Secretary of State, struck him as a dangerous bureaucratic innovation; and he was repelled by the idea of dragooning the poor into thrift and industry by stopping the old easy-going system of outdoor relief. The consequence was that he defended it in a lukewarm speech, and was heard swearing in a loud, angry undertone as he gave his vote for it. His mind was similarly divided over the Factory Acts for the protection of working children. He felt sorry enough for the children to sponsor the Bill in the House of Lords. On the other hand, in his view any legislation of this kind meant interfering with the action of economic laws; and as such was futile. The result was he could not throw himself into the fight for it with the enthusiasm which is born of faith. One afternoon, a member called Denison stopped him, just as he was getting on his horse outside the Home Office about to start home, and proposed some improvements in the Bill. Irritably Melbourne told him to go and see his brother George Lamb, who was working out the details for him. "I have been with him half-an-hour," said Denison, "but I could get no way with him; he damned me, damned the clauses and damned the Bill." "Well, damn it all," said the exasperated Melbourne, "what more could he say?" Then an impulse of compunction swept over him. "But I will see what I can do about it," he added. No doubt he did; he was a man of his word. But the story shows that he was not at heart a believer in social reform. On the contrary. "The whole duty of government," he said, "is to prevent crime and to preserve contracts."

In consequence his activities as Home Secretary were confined to the same object as in 1830: namely to maintaining order without infringing existing traditional liberties. This meant that he had to fight on two fronts. On the one hand he must see that the law was in fact properly enforced: on the other he had to resist proposals to introduce new and tyrannical legislation which was still urged on him by a large number of people, including the King and the Duke of Wellington. Of these the King was the most tiresome. Since the passage of the Reform Bill he had become yet another source of bother to an already harassed Government. William IV was a classic example of a man not up to his job. As a prince he had been merely harmless and comical; a bustling, chattering old buffoon of a sailor, with a head shaped like a pineapple, and a large troop of illegitimate children. As a King he made a more disturbing impression. On the throne of England a buffoon is no laughing matter. The glory of his position is likely to turn his head; it also gives him greater scope for displaying his folly unchecked. So it was with William IV. The mere prospect of becoming King began to throw him off his balance. When he heard George IV was dying and the crown within his grasp, he took to wearing overshoes and gargling every morning in front of an open window, for fear he might be carried off by a sudden chill before the splendid prize was actually his. Once King, he took steps to make his personality felt. At first he set up as a democratic monarch suitable to the new democratic age; and dismayed his subjects by spitting in a plebeian manner out of the window of the State Coach, and by walking about the streets unattended and followed by a crowd who jostled and pushed him with unseemly familiarity. His democratic sympathies, however, were not deeply grounded enough to survive the disturbances of the Reform Bill period. These left him so frightened that he turned into a panicky reactionary who smelt bloody revolution in every breath of popular feeling. His nerves were further irritated by a justified suspicion that his Ministers did not take him very seriously. Altogether he found that being King was not the pleasure he had hoped it was going to be: with the result that the jolly old buffoon became a surly, touchy, bewildered old buffoon, who sought to compensate for a sense of impotence by bombarding his Ministers with reams of futile complainings and inept advice. Since his chief worry was popular unrest, the brunt of his agitation fell on the Home Secretary. Melbourne dealt dexterously with him. To his communications he replied with a judicious blend of respectfulness, firmness and good humour. Now and again he allowed himself a note of irony, too discreetly worded to penetrate the intelligence of his royal correspondent. When William clamoured for legislation to stop workmen combining, Melbourne replied by sending him a list of thirty-six Acts beginning in Edward I's time that had been passed for this very purpose—all of which, he added gravely, had been since repealed as ineffective. "Upon the whole," he concluded, "Viscount Melbourne humbly trusts that Your Majesty will rest assured that the subject will be considered by His Majesty's servants with that circumspection which is suggested by its evident difficulty, and at the same time with the firmness and determination which are required by its dangerous and formidable character." Such replies did not stop the King from writing. Nor did they make him like Melbourne very much. He had grown incurably suspicious of all Whigs by this time. Moreover, Melbourne's mind was too subtle, and his personality too aristocratically confident and stylish, for the silly, homely old sailor King to feel really at home in his company. Melbourne said of him, "He hasn't the feelings of a gentleman; he knows what they are, but he hasn't them." However, the King found Melbourne more genial than most of his other Ministers; and he was quite incapable of standing up to his diplomatic skill. Melbourne was always able to manage him in the end: he was also able to manage the Duke of Wellington and other complaining correspondents. With them his tone was different. He was not so respectful, he let himself go a little more. But his terse, caustic notes generally succeeded in quietening them.

The most important topic of these different correspondences was the rise of the Trades Union Movement. As Melbourne had expected, the working class found themselves no better off as the result of the Reform Bill. In order to improve their conditions, therefore, they turned to industrial agitation. Trades Unions were the means by which they hoped to achieve their ends. Unions of the workers in individual trades were already in existence, when the Reform Government came in. After 1832 they increased by leaps and bounds. Towards the end of 1833 Robert Owen started a scheme for still further strengthening their bargaining power by uniting them into one organization entitled the Grand National Consolidated Trade Union. The aims of this body were political as well as economic. Not only was it to be concerned with practical day-to-day questions of wages and hours, but it declared itself out to establish "a different order of things, in which the really useful and intelligent part of society only shall have the direction of its affairs; in which industry and virtue shall meet their just distinction and reward, and vicious idleness its merited contempt and destruction." The Grand National Consolidated Trade Union caught on even more quickly than had the individual Trades Unions. Within a few months an enormous number of town labourers belonged to it. Early in 1834 it began to gain adherents in the country districts as well.

The middle and upper classes viewed these events with growing alarm. The name Trades Union, we must remember, did not suggest to them the established and respectable bodies that it does to us, but rather dangerous and sinister secret societies of a kind happily unknown in England before, round which hovered a murky atmosphere of violence and conspiracy. Admission to them, it was reported, was accompanied by all sorts of melodramatic initiation ceremonies involving skulls and oaths of silence and names signed in human blood. Nor did the middle classes in the least sympathize with their aims. In so far as the Trades Unions tried to modify labour conditions they were interfering with what was thought by the best opinion to be the natural and healthy working of economic law, while their political professions had an ominous whiff of revolution about them. It was enough to make the prosperous citizens' flesh creep to think of "a different order of things", in which property was apparently to be redistributed in accordance with what the more discontented members of the working class happened to think morally just.

Melbourne shared the general disapproval of Trades Unions. How could he do otherwise considering his fear of disorder and his belief in *laissez-faire*? So far from benefiting the oppressed poor, he thought they would only make their lot worse. Trades Unions, he told a manufacturer in 1833, were "inconsistent, impossible and contrary to the law of nature". From the time he took office he had been sufficiently worried about them to appoint a commission under Nassau Senior, the Professor of Economics at Oxford, to investigate their activities. However, his anxieties were not strong enough to modify his natural bias towards liberty and inertia. And, when the commission came out with a report recommending drastic legislation to put the Trades Unions down, Melbourne opposed it. Apart from the fact that he was sure the House of Commons would never be persuaded to pass such a measure, he himself thought it unnecessary. He had already remarked to an anxious correspondent on the subject, "I recommend above all not being above measure disturbed by new evils and dangers, to which human society is always liable." Trying to tamper with the inevitable working of economic law was so futile, he said, that it could not be long before even the stupidest working man would realize it; and then the Trades Union Movement would collapse of itself.

When, however, it showed signs of spreading to rural England Melbourne's mood began to change. His fear of revolution grew stronger, and his dislike of doing anything weakened. Men of his age could never forget that the French Revolution had started in the country. Though he was still against new legislation he began

to wonder if everything possible was being done within the existing law to put the Unions down; and he consulted the crown
lawyers on the subject. After foraging about, they discovered an
Act passed at the time of the Nore Mutiny in 1799, but since pretty
well forgotten, making it an offence to administer secret oaths.
Trades Union Societies often took secret oaths: here was a new
weapon against them. Melbourne instructed magistrates to take
every opportunity to use it. "Perhaps you will be able to make an
example by such means," he wrote.

The result of his words was an episode which was to become
famous in history. In March, 1834, it was discovered that a new
Trades Union at Tolpuddle in Dorset had administered secret
oaths, as part of its ceremony of admission. Accordingly several
of its members were arrested. A Commission was sent down to
try them, and they were condemned to the maximum penalty of
seven year's transportation. Before confirming the sentence, Melbourne asked the local magistrates what sort of men the prisoners
were. They told him that they were thoroughly bad characters.
Relieved that he could carry out his policy of making an example
without doing any injustice to individuals, Melbourne confirmed
the sentence. Meanwhile he told the local authorities not to penal-
ise the prisoners' families in any way; nor, he said, should employers take advantage of the sentence to dismiss workmen just
because they belong to a Trades Union. Trades Unions remained
perfectly legal if they did not administer secret oaths. Finally he
warned farmers against trying to reduce wages below their just
economic level.

In spite of these conciliatory gestures, however, the trial of the
Dorset labourers produced a storm. Seven years' transportation
did seem a very severe punishment for breaking a law of which
many people had forgotten the very existence. The whole working-class movement broke out in furious protest; it was supported
by the radical intelligentsia and by an important section of the
Press. Melbourne paid no attention. He would have been disinclined to do so, even if he had felt himself in the wrong; for he
thought it in the last degree contemptible to yield to popular
clamour. In fact he had never felt more in the right. It was the
plain duty of any Government to discourage Trades Unions so far

as it could do so legally. From all over the country he got letters telling him that agricultural workers were waiting to see what penalty was inflicted in Dorset before deciding whether or not to join a Union. Clearly it was a crucial moment. Now or never was the time to make an example. Melbourne's firmness did not at first stop the protests. A petition demanding pardon for the labourers was signed by a quarter of a million people. On 21st April a crowd, thirty thousand strong, headed by a clergyman in full canonicals, marched down with it to Whitehall. Melbourne, smiling and unperturbed, watched them from the window of the Home Office. When the leaders asked leave to present the petition to him he refused to see them. If it were brought by a reasonable number of persons, he said, he would be willing to read it; but he was going to do nothing that might give the impression that he was overawed by a display of force. The procession dispersed and soon the violence of the agitation began to die down. More important, the Trades Union Movement received a check from which it took years to recover. Melbourne's policy had proved triumphantly right. The existing law as it manifested itself in the trial of the Dorset labourers, turned out to be strong enough to make any further legislation unnecessary. Once again, as after the disturbances of 1830, the large majority of educated Englishmen united to congratulate the Home Secretary on the quiet effectiveness with which he had maintained the cause of order.

Once again posterity has not shared that satisfaction. As in 1830, one finds oneself brought up with a jarring shock against the contradictions of the period, the discrepancy between the civilized humanity of upper class private life, and the blood and iron harshness which was accepted as a necessary feature of the criminal law. What makes the story of the Dorset labourers especially distressing is that the victims themselves seem to have been undeserving of their fate. Prejudice or panic had led the local authorities to mislead Melbourne about their characters. So far from being criminals and revolutionaries, they were sober, respectable men enough, driven into lawless courses largely by ignorance and hunger and by the struggle to bring up their families on wages lately reduced to seven shillings a week. Melbourne was not to blame for not realizing their true characters. He was not there, and he had to trust to the reports of his subordinates. Moreover, all along he had done his best to follow his usual course of combining firmness with moderation. But it is true that the affair, like so many of his dealings with working class agitation, does curiously reveal his limitations. For all his superior breadth of vision, he did not see further into the lives of the poor than the average intelligent man of his circle, especially when his fear of revolution was aroused. The same fear united with his dislike of unnecessary trouble to move him from his characteristic attitude of impartial detachment. His letters show him a little over-ready impatiently to brush aside anything that might be urged on the labourers' behalf. Further, his moral scepticism led him to adopt too exclusively a deterrent view of punishment. For some obscure reason retributive punishment is often looked upon as likely to be crueller than deterrent. The reverse is the truth. According to the retributive theory a man can only be punished as much as he deserves; which, unless he is accused of some unusually heinous crime, does not mean anything unbearably severe. The exponent of deterrent punishment, on the other hand, regards himself as justified in going to any lengths required to deter effectively: and in fact the most notorious persecutors ancient and modern have sought to justify their actions on deterrent grounds. Poor Melbourne was far from being a persecutor. All the same he did look on himself as the guardian of order rather than the instrument of ideal justice; and was too dominated by the determination to get the law obeyed at all costs to consider sufficiently whether he was in fact being morally just to the labourers.

However, it was not a matter about which he felt strongly, as subsequent events showed. For the story of the Dorset labourers did not end with the procession of April, 1834. As time passed and tempers cooled, more and more people began to doubt the justice of the sentence. A year later John Russell wrote to Melbourne asking him to pardon the labourers. Melbourne's first impulse was to resist. He was sure the labourers deserved all they got, he said. Anyway, the matter was settled; why, oh why bring it up again? John Russell, however, his conscientiously held principles now vigorously in operation, returned to the attack. Melbourne began to think that resistance would involve more trouble than concession. Immediately he gave in. "I myself do not care what is done about the labourers," he remarked with cheerful impatience.

As a matter of fact the affair occupied his mind very little. To him it was at worst a disagreeable episode in the ordinary routine of his Home Office work. Besides he had other and to him more important things to think about. The Reform Government, tottering for so long, was now on the point of final collapse. It was the Irish question that finished it. Ever since 1830 it had threatened to do so. There had been a hope that Catholic Emancipation would pacify the Irish. And it is just possible that it might have done so, had it been followed by a policy of bold conciliation designed to satisfy the national and religious aspirations of the Irish people. But the Government was too frightened and too prejudiced to risk such a policy. Protestants, not Catholics, were still given the important jobs in Ireland; and they used them to maintain their ascendancy. The Irish, therefore, as discontented as ever, entered under the guidance of O'Connell on a fresh campaign; this time for the repeal of the Act of Union. They were able to do this the more effectively because they were now represented in the English Parliament; and were thus in a position to make difficulties for any Government there, if they were not given their way.

Meanwhile in Ireland O'Connell encouraged a new outbreak of violence and disorder. The Irish began burning, pillaging and rioting as merrily as in the days before Emancipation. Clearly any English Government must make up its mind to do something about Ireland. Either it must subdue her by force or try to win her over by concession. Here was yet another issue for the Ministers to quarrel about. Quarrel they did—and far more bitterly than over home affairs! For Ireland raised, as home affairs did not, questions of religion and patriotism; two topics about which mankind has always been peculiarly unreasonable. Stanley and Grey both thought that the dignity of England would be fatally outraged if concessions were made, before law and order was restored. To Althorp and Durham, on the other hand, coercion unaccompanied by concession seemed an act of indefensible tyranny. The question of appropriating Church endowments raised another issue of principle. Since the Irish were overwhelmingly Roman

Catholic, John Russell considered that they ought not to be made to pay high taxes, for keeping up the Protestant Church: some of the money should surely be appropriated for secular purposes. Stanley, an ardent Protestant, looked on such a proposal as a direct attack on the cause of true religion. With Ministers thus divided and angry it was clear that the Irish question was a perpetual danger to the stability of the Government. At first Grey tried to tide things over by never mentioning it himself, and changing the subject if anybody else did. His efforts were vain. Inevitably Ireland cropped up. Whenever this happened, someone felt it their duty to make a conscientious stand on one side or the other. The result was a major political crisis. It was over Ireland that first Durham and then Stanley had in turn resigned.

Now in the spring of 1834, a new crisis loomed up. Stanley's Coercion Act had run its course. Since Ireland was still unsettled, Wellesley, the Lord Lieutenant, wrote to Grey pressing that it should be re-enacted *in toto*, including some clauses forbidding public meetings, which were especially hated by the Irish. At this Brougham made one of his fatal interventions. The Arch-Fiend had begun to notice that he was unpopular. He fancied he might win some of the progressive Whigs to him, by setting up as a friend of Irish freedom. He therefore embarked on a secret intrigue with the new Irish Secretary Littleton, by which Wellesley was persuaded to write a second letter to Grey asking that the obnoxious clauses should be, after all, omitted from the Coercion Act. Brougham also arranged that O'Connell should be told of his services to the Irish in this matter; and by concocting some false version of the negotiations, tricked Althorp into giving his approval of his part in them. He had reckoned without Grey, who flatly refused to have the clauses touched. The Act was therefore introduced unchanged into the House of Commons. O'Connell rose and publicly accused Brougham, Littleton and Althorp of cheating him. The upright Althorp sat listening to this attack on his honour. "The pig is killed," he said to John Russell; and he resigned. Overjoyed at last to find a decent excuse for retiring to Howick, Grey said he could not carry on the Government without him, and resigned too.

Though Irish affairs in those days were under the Home Office, Melbourne had taken little part in all these manœuvres. His mind was even more divided over Ireland than over most things. His belief in tolerance had united with his own experience as Chief Secretary to make him for once genuinely in favour of a reform policy. But the results of Catholic Emancipation, though they had not exactly reversed his views, had cooled his enthusiasm. In spite of the fact that the Irish had been given what they asked for, there did not seem much prospect of tranquillity and stability in Ireland. "What all the wise promised has not happened," he said, "and what all the damned fools said would happen has come to pass." He found this thought more depressing than surprising. Only too well did it harmonize with his general sense of the baffling irony of human affairs. Perhaps giving men what they wanted was the best way to make them discontented! If the men were Irishmen, he was pretty sure this was so. In dispassionate mood he meditated on the root causes of Irish discontent. "The dependencies and provinces of great monarchies," he concluded, "have always been apt to grow too great and too strong to be governed by the mother state; and that, perhaps, exactly in proportion to the degree in which their true interest has been consulted and their prosperity has been allowed to develop itself." This reflection reveals a far more searching vision into the nature of the forces governing political affairs than is vouchsafed to many professional statesmen. But it was a vision that left Melbourne—so far as Ireland was concerned—passive and fatalistic.

Over the immediate crisis preceding the collapse of the Government, Melbourne, with occasional hesitations, backed Grey. After the troubles of the Reform Bill years, he was all against seditious persons being allowed to hold public meetings. Besides, he was very much annoyed with Brougham and Wellesley for trying to manage Irish affairs behind the Home Secretary's back. He was not, however, so upset by the affair to be moved from his customary detachment. On the day the Government fell, an observer noticed that Lord Melbourne, going off to join a party of ladies on the river, wore an air of philosophical calm.

All the same, it turned out to be one of the most important days of his life. The departure of Grey did not mean the departure of the Whigs. For the Tories, though gaining in power, were not yet strong enough in the country to take on the Government. Much against his will, therefore, William IV had to find another Whig Prime Minister. Clearly, it had to be someone sufficiently on good terms with the differing sections of the Party to have some hope of holding it together. This excluded Brougham and John Russell. Althorp would have done, or a great Whig magnate like Lord Lansdowne. But Lansdowne refused, and the King distrusted Althorp as too radical for his taste. Melbourne, on the other hand, was known to be on the right of the Party: and the King, though he did not like him much, liked him better than he did his rivals. Accordingly on the following morning, when the Cabinet met to take formal leave of one another, Grey handed Melbourne a sealed letter. In it was a letter from the King asking him to come and see him to discuss the formation of a government under his leadership. True to form in this, the supreme decision of his career, Melbourne hesitated. He thought himself unlikely to enjoy being Prime Minister. It meant more work and responsibility and committees and deputations; it meant humouring the King and keeping Brougham in order; it meant less time than ever to read the early Christian Fathers and flirt with Mrs. Norton. And to what end? Melbourne had long ago given up the idea that governments could do much good. On the other hand he did not like to let down his friends and his Party by refusing. Wavering and doubtful, he spoke his thoughts aloud to Tom Young. "I think it's a damned bore," he said. "I am in many minds as to what to do." "Why, damn it all," answered Young, "such a position was never held by any Greek or Roman: and if it only lasts three months, it will be worth while to have been Prime Minister of England." There are moments when a hair will turn the balance; "By God, that's true," exclaimed Melbourne. "I'll go!"[1]

Thus casually, unexpectedly, through a transient combination of circumstances—a chance turn of the political wheel, a whim of William IV, an unconsidered remark of Tom Young and without effort or inclination on his part—Melbourne at the age of fifty-five became ruler of England. The year before he had copied, into his commonplace book, a couplet of Voltaire's.

[1] We have this story second-hand from Greville. Hayward, who claimed to know Melbourne well, does not believe it. But it is in character.

"Mais Henri s'avançait à sa grandeur suprême
Par des chemins cachés, inconnus à lui-même!"

"The case with every great man," Melbourne commented, "much of what is attributed to design is accident; the unknown cause leading to the unknown end." As he wrote the words, was he peering into the dark mirror of the future to discern his own destiny?

## CHAPTER IV

# PRIME MINISTER

## (1)

"Everybody wonders what Melbourne will do. He is certainly a queer fellow to be Prime Minister." So wrote Greville in June, 1834: so thought a lot of people. In spite of his success as Home Secretary, Melbourne's reputation, outside the circle of his immediate colleagues, was not of the sort that befits a Prime Minister. Queen Adelaide found his views on religion lax and his conversation disagreeably paradoxical. Many of her subjects agreed with her. To their solemn sensitive nineteenth-century nostrils there was a disquieting whiff of the Regency about him. However, they could comfort themselves with the thought that his Government could not possibly last for long.

Melbourne drew comfort from this too. The weak Whig Government was weaker than ever now. Not only was it bereft of some of its more distinguished members, but it looked as though the time for an emergency Government of this kind was over. If the people wanted Reform, they wanted it more radical than the old Whigs offered. If—and this seemed more like the truth—they were reacting against Reform, they inclined to the Tories. Melbourne himself did not mind this. Privately, he said that he hoped the Tories would come in. The King agreed with him: so much so, that he suggested Melbourne should try to form a Tory-Whig coalition. The feelings of the Whig Party, however, put this out of the question. All Melbourne could do was, for the time being, to try and carry on as before. With the help of Althorp, who reluctantly agreed to rejoin the Government, he patched up a new administration out of the remnants of the old: and unhopefully set himself to his task.

It proved as thankless as he could possibly have feared. All the same questions began making trouble again; and all the same people. William IV, now convinced that England was on the slippery slope to an atheistic republic, wanted Melbourne to pledge himself first never to give a Radical office; and secondly not in any way to suggest altering the existing constitution of the Irish Protestant Church. Melbourne managed to parry both these attacks, but only after many letters and some painful interviews, each of which lasted several hours. Hardly less trying than the King, were his colleagues. There was Lord Lansdowne, nearly resigning in a pet because two protégés of his had not been given jobs; and there was John Russell who chose this of all moments to suggest that O'Connell should be given office in order to drive a wedge between him and his Irish supporters. Apart from the fact that the very idea of such an appointment was certain to throw both the King and the more cautious Whigs into a panic, Melbourne thought it would obviously fail of its object. "Taking office would not shake O'Connell's influence with the people of Ireland one jot," he wrote sharply. "The people of Ireland are not such damn fools as the people of England. When they place confidence, they don't withdraw it the next instant." A new stormy petrel too had appeared on Melbourne's horizon in the shape of Lord Palmerston, the Foreign Secretary. Personally, Melbourne got on with him well enough. For Palmerston—jaunty, plain-spoken and unchaste—was also a survival from the Regency. But he was a vulgar version of the Regency type, marked, as Melbourne was not, by its characteristic blemishes of arrogance and insensitiveness. Melbourne learnt with dismay that he seemed likely to antagonize every foreign diplomat in London by the casual bluntness of his words and manners. Palmerston's manners were not his only defect; Melbourne was also suspicious of his policy. Europe during this period was divided by what, for want of a more agreeable phrase, must be called an ideological split. On one side lay the autocratic Eastern powers, Russia, Austria, Prussia, who wished to suppress within their own and other people's countries that Liberal Movement which was the child of the French Revolution. On the other there were the Western powers, France and England, who were its supporters, so long at any rate as it showed no signs of growing dangerously revolutionary. Palmerston vigorously espoused the Liberal cause. His steady aim, pursued sometimes in action and always in words, was to make England its active leader. This came partly from the fact that he was a man of adventurous and domineering temperament whose instinct it was to intervene in other people's disputes and partly because he thought that Liberalism, and those middle classes, who everywhere were its chief supporters, was far more likely than despotism to produce governments stable, pacific and friendly to England and English trade. This was not a point of view to commend itself to Melbourne. His attitude to foreign affairs was of a piece with his attitude to home affairs. As at home, tranquillity was his first object; and, as at home, his sense of reality taught him that Liberalism was now so strong a force that refusal to meet its claims in some degree could only end in disturbance. On the other hand he never could like Liberal progressives of any nationality, nor did he see any reason to suppose that they would be more friendly to England than the autocrats were. "All these chambers and free presses in other countries are very fine things," he said, "but depend upon it they are still as hostile to England as the old governments." Let not Palmerston think that they would be grateful to him for intervening on their behalf. "The case with all foreign powers," he remarked crisply to him, "is that they never take our advice on any of their previous steps; they treat us with the utmost contempt; they take every measure hostile to our interests; they are anxious to prove that we have not the least influence on them. And then when by their misconduct they have got themselves into an inextricable difficulty, they throw themselves upon our mercy and say, 'For God's sake re-establish us . . . that we may run again the same course of domestic error and hostility to England'." Melbourne, too, did not share Palmerston's belief in the middle classes as a bulwark against revolution. "The bourgeois are timid always," he said, "I should have some fear, if difficult times were to arrive, of our own boasted middle classes." Finally, his temperamental dislike of adventurous courses in general was as strong as Palmerston's liking for them. The world was quite full enough of trouble as it was; why stir up more? As Melbourne watched Palmerston bombarding foreign powers with scoldings and unasked-for advice he felt sceptical, irritable, anxious.

But, as might have been expected, the greatest nuisance among his colleagues was Brougham. Rage that he had not been made Prime Minister swept away any vestige of self-control that may have remained with him. To soothe his vanity he gave out that Melbourne was his creature, whom, for some mysterious reason of his own, he had chosen to put in office: he introduced a highly controversial Bill about a judicial matter in the House of Lords without mentioning a word about it to his colleagues: and he besieged the King—who detested him—with impertinent and unasked-for letters of advice. His most sensational performance, however, took place during the August Recess when he embarked on a sort of public progress round Scotland, making speeches in which he openly attacked his colleagues, and infuriated the King still further by representing himself as his only confidential friend among his Ministers. In his intervals of relaxation he created scandal by playing Hunt the Thimble with the Great Seal in an Edinburgh lady's drawing-room, and arriving at the local races dressed in the full regalia of Lord Chancellor's wig and gown and roaring drunk.

To outward appearance Melbourne was unperturbed by all these disturbing events. He still ate enormously, saw a great deal of Miss Eden and Mrs. Norton, and found time to spend pleasant evenings at Holland House; where he awed the unwilling Greville by the breadth of his learning—he seemed equally conversant with Greek history, etymology and the details of the texts of Shakespeare's plays—and dazzled him by the lively boldness of his views. "Henry VIII was the greatest man that ever lived," he asserted with a cheerful oath. "Melbourne loves dashing opinions," noted Greville.

But beneath his smiling exterior, Melbourne during these months was apprehensive and despondent. He did not see how he was to keep the Government going. He was also depressed by the general mental atmosphere of the age. On the night of 16th October, the Houses of Parliament were burnt down. Melbourne watched the huge conflagration as it reflected itself in the dark waters of the Thames. He looked cool and jocose, but in reality his heart was filled with strange and mournful emotions. The spectacle was symbolic. Thus also was the England he had always known being destroyed before his eyes. And no one seemed to mind: even *The Times* shocked him by the practical and utilitarian tone in which it spoke of the event. It seemed nothing to the men of today that the time-hallowed scene of so much of England's past and England's glory, the place where in the hopeful ardour of his youth—now alas so irrevocably distant—his heart had thrilled to the eloquence of Pitt and of Fox, should be a heap of ashes. In so alien a world, he felt little spirit to proceed with his anxious and thankless task, even had he thought that there was much prospect of his making a success of it.

Now an event took place which rendered success more unlikely than ever. On the 10th November Lord Spencer died. This meant that his heir, Althorp, was translated to the House of Lords; and the Whig Party lost its leader and most influential member in the Commons. Melbourne did not want to carry on in these reduced circumstances; he pretty well told William IV so in a letter. But he felt that he owed it to his Party to agree to stay if required, and went down to Brighton where the King was at that time residing, to talk the matter over with him. After a lengthy dinner, in which William IV regaled his Prime Minister with naval anecdotes and did not mention politics at all, he suddenly said: "By the way, Lord Spencer is dead I hear. So is the Government, of course: where the head is dead, the body cannot go on at all. Therefore there is no help for it, you must all resign. Here, my Lord, is a letter I have written to the Duke of Wellington, directing him to form a Government. Be sure you give it to him directly you arrive in town." Melbourne suggested John Russell as a possible successor to Althorp. The King repudiated the proposal violently. "That young man"—it was in this disparaging phrase that he always referred to John Russell—was associated in his mind with those alterations in the Irish Church which had become to him a symbol of all that it was his royal duty to resist. Indeed it was his feeling about the Irish Church, coupled with his dislike of Brougham, which had just decided him to get rid of the Whigs. After more fruitless and interminable conversations both that night and the next day, Melbourne arrived in London late in the evening. Just before he went to bed, Brougham burst in asking for news. Melbourne told him what had happened: but asked him not to say anything about it till he had had time to inform the rest of the Ministers. Brougham promised: but on leaving the house hurried off as fast as he could to give the news to *The Times*. Most of the

Ministers woke up to learn of their dismissal from the morning paper.

They were extremely indignant at the King's behaviour; and surprised that Melbourne was not more so. They could hardly believe their ears when they heard that he had been seen at the theatre the very next night laughing heartily at a farce about the dismissal of a Minister. As a matter of fact, though he was a little nettled by William IV's brusqueness and high-handedness, Melbourne was relieved to be out. He had conducted the whole negotiation in a detached, take-it-or-leave-it tone, which was not calculated to persuade the King to change his mind. But he did not choose to risk undermining his Party's confidence in his loyalty to their cause by admitting his true feelings even to his intimate friends. Rather let them think that his calm was the expression of a proper pride that scorned to parade its injuries in public. "I have always considered complaints of ill usage contemptible," he told Miss Eden, "whether from a seduced, disappointed girl or a turned-out Prime Minister." Once more we note that Melbourne was a good deal more discreet than he appeared.[1]

He needed all his discretion during the months that followed. The left wing of his Party—in order to revive that reforming enthusiasm in the nation which had swept them to victory four years before—wanted the Whigs to come out at once with a provocative programme of bold drastic reform. Melbourne was against this. Apart from the fact that he thoroughly disliked drastic reforms, he thought, with reason, that they were the last thing to appeal to an electorate obviously swinging to the right. On the other hand he had to avoid revealing himself as so unsympathetic with his Party's aspirations as to shake their faith in him. Accordingly he made a couple of vague, moderate-sounding, reassuring public speeches, and then, retiring to the country where no one could get at him, refused to make any definite statement about future policy at all. In January there was a general election. The Tories under Peel

[1] There are various conflicting accounts of the Government's actual dismissal. Croker says that Melbourne resigned voluntarily. The account in Lord Holland's unpublished diary shows that if this was so, he concealed the truth, not only from the world but from his closest colleagues. This is not in keeping with his character. Besides they must have found out: and would have lost all confidence in him in consequence.

returned considerably stronger, but not in sufficient numbers to
have a majority over the combined votes of Whigs, Radicals and
Irish. After a month or two of minority government Peel was
beaten on the crucial question of what was to be done with the
revenues of the Irish Church. In March the Whigs were in office
again. Melbourne was not surprised: he had doubted whether the
pendulum had swung far enough yet to bring the Tories back.
But he was far from pleased. He had resisted any proposal to turn
the Government out till a question of fundamental principle like
that of the Irish Church had arisen. And even then he did his best
to avoid taking on the full responsibility of the Government himself. First he made some secret enquiries, using Mrs. Norton as
go-between to find out if there was any possibility of arranging a
coalition with some of the more moderate Tories. Then he tried
to persuade Grey to take his place once more as leader of the Whig
Party. It was only after both these attempts had failed, that Melbourne reluctantly resigned himself to taking up his burden again.

(2)

One can understand why he was unwilling. The prospect facing
the Prime Minister in the second Melbourne Government was not
an inviting one. The Party's position could hardly have seemed
worse. It was virtually in a minority. The King and the House of
Lords were solidly against it. In the House of Commons it held
its majority largely by favour of the Irish: this was a very uncertain quantity. Further, the Whig Party itself was more acrimoni-
ously divided than ever. Its right wing had been weakened by the
loss of Grey and Stanley, with the result that the Radicals had become more confident, more unmanageable and more unwilling
than ever to submit to what they considered the reactionary tendencies of their official leaders. All this meant that the life of the
Government was perpetually in danger from three sides. If the
Radicals or the Irish felt they were not getting what they wanted,
they could either of them vote it out of office: if, on the other hand,
the Tories considered that the Government was giving in too
much to the Irish and the Radicals, they were able, with the help
of the House of Lords, to make themselves so obstructive as to
render the Government's continued existence impossible. Mel-

bourne's only hope of carrying on, therefore, lay in a balancing, trimming, procrastinating policy, yielding a little to the left here and to the right there, according to which happened at the moment to be the greatest threat to him: and also in creating a generally relaxed and reassuring personal atmosphere in which differences of opinion lost their sharpness.

Luckily such a policy had more chance of success than might have appeared on the surface. For one thing none of the three potential sources of danger really wanted the Government to fall. The Radicals and Irish both knew that the alternative to the Whigs was the Tories, under whom they would fare far worse. Peel, for his part, did not want to come in until such time as he could be sure of having a solid majority of the country on his side. Moreover, Melbourne was admirably equipped for his particular task. It is paradoxical that the most suitable head for a supposedly progressive Government should have been a man who disbelieved in progress. But in fact Melbourne's scepticism was a help to him. For it meant that his conscience was not upset if he had to make concessions to the Tories. As a matter of fact he often agreed with Peel more than with most of his own colleagues. Yet scepticism equally prevented him from being too dogmatically unprogressive. He was quite willing to agree to a reform if it seemed likely to stop a row and was thus the lesser of two evils. On the other hand, just because he feared unrest so much, he was not at all sceptical as to the importance of keeping the Government together. And he knew just how to do it. Friendly and easy-going, he easily liked people and easily made them like him. Yet no one could dominate him and no one could take him in. With negligent mastery he maintained his detachment amid the clamouring crowd of idealists, careerists and wire-pullers by whom he was surrounded. And, if he felt it necessary, he could put his foot down unhesitatingly and very hard.

This appears in his choice of his Cabinet. Four years of keen observation and harsh experience had taught him that this was a matter of critical importance. Never again, if he could help it, was he going to make a hard task harder by saddling himself with troublesome colleagues. What he wanted from them first of all was loyalty; he must be able to depend on them to back him up.

"I will support you as long as you are in the right," said a politician to him on one occasion. "That is no use at all," replied Melbourne; "what I want is men who will support me when I am in the wrong." A whole team of such self-sacrificing persons was, he realized, too much to hope for in an imperfect world. But certainly he was determined to have Ministers who could be trusted not to work actively against him, or without consulting his aims and feelings. He would not have any avowed Radicals. Most of them were doctrinaire Benthamites, and, said Melbourne, "Benthamites are all fools." No—let Radicals join deputations and sit on Royal Commissions if they wished: deputations and Royal Commissions, thank God, seldom accomplished anything. But there must be no Radical ministers. There were certain individuals also whom Melbourne meant to keep out if he could. He did not want to have Durham, or Wellesley, or Brougham—at any rate, not in positions of influence. And he wanted to keep Palmerston out of the Foreign Office. These were bold decisions, for, if they were offended, all these men could give a great deal of trouble. Lords Grey, Holland and Spencer agitatedly implored him not to take the risk of antagonizing them. Smiling and immovable, Melbourne disregarded their warnings. Over Palmerston he was beaten. Palmerston said if he could not be Foreign Secretary he would not join the Government at all: and Melbourne thought him too important to be prepared to lose him. Back to the Foreign Office, therefore, stepped Palmerston, jaunty as ever. But Melbourne got his way about all the others. Durham was packed off to Russia again: Wellesley was fobbed off with a Court appointment; and Brougham was not offered a job at all. The last two protested violently. Wellesley even talked of challenging Melbourne to a duel. Melbourne went to see him. "His language," related the outraged Wellesley afterwards, "was rough, vulgar and such as has never been employed from a person in his station to one in mine." However, in spite of this, there was no more talk of a duel; nor was Lord Wellesley promoted.

Brougham was a harder nut to crack. The trouble with him had started soon after Melbourne left office. Brougham had heard that his late colleagues were talking against him; he wrote angrily to Melbourne to ask why. He got a plain answer.

"It is a very disagreeable task," Melbourne said, "to have to say to a statesman that his character is injured in the public estimation: it is still more unpleasant to have to add that you consider this to be his own fault; and it is idle to expect to be able to convince almost any man, and more particularly a man of very superior abilities, and with unbounded confidence in these abilities, that this is true. I must, however, state plainly that your conduct was one of the principal causes of the dismissal of the late ministry; and that it forms the most popular justification of that step."

Brougham demanded details. Not without zest, Melbourne provided them.

"You ask for specific charges. Allow me to observe that there may be a course and series of very objectionable conduct, there may be a succession of acts which destroy confidence and add offence to offence, and yet it would be difficult to point to any marked delinquency. I will, however, tell you fairly, that, in my opinion, you domineered too much, you interfered too much with other departments, you encroached upon the provinces of the Prime Minister, you worked, as I believe, with the Press in a manner unbecoming to the dignity of your station, and you formed political views of your own and pursued them by means which were unfair towards your colleagues. . . . Nobody knows and appreciates your natural vigour better than I do. I know also that those who are weak for good are strong for mischief. You are strong for both, and I should both dread and lament to see those gigantic powers which should be directed to the support of the State exerted in the contrary and opposite direction."

To soften the blow, he ended his letter on a friendlier note. "I can only add that whatever may be your determination, no political difference will make any change in the friendship and affection which I have always felt and will continue to feel for you." However, he had already decided not to take Brougham back. "If left out he would be dangerous," he said, "but if taken in, he would be simply destructive." Brougham was so obsessedly vain that despite all Melbourne's home-truths, he was dumbfounded when he actually heard he was not going to get a place. His nose twitching more violently than ever, he strode round to Melbourne's house, fulminating wrath and demanding redress. "Do you think I am mad?" he kept on shouting furiously, "do you think I am mad?" "God damn you," said Melbourne, "you won't get the Great Seal, and that's the end of it." Brougham left the house routed.

It was for ever, too. He never got office again; and he proved too crazy and too distrusted to be much danger to the Government in opposition. At last the Arch-Fiend's bluff had been called. And it had been the easy-going Melbourne who had done it. Here was more evidence that he avoided rows, not because they frightened him, but because he thought them useless. No one could make a row with more thundering effect, when he judged a row was needed.

(3)

The result of his firmness was that the first months of the new Government were the calmest for a long time. And if the calm did not last, the Government did. Though apparently always on the verge of sinking, the leaky, rickety vessel under the command of its flippant and indolent-seeming Captain, kept afloat for six years. It had, it must be admitted, an uncomfortable thwarted voyage. Events followed a recurrent pattern. The Whigs brought in first one and then another measure of reform—the most important were those concerned with Church finance, Irish tithe and the reformation of the municipal corporations of England and Ireland. Each Bill passed the House of Commons and proceeded to the House of Lords, who either held it up or threw it out. Then followed an interim period in which Melbourne and Peel strove to persuade the extreme members of their respective parties to agree to some compromise. This interim period was marked by crisis, sometimes of sufficient intensity to threaten the very existence of the Government. In the end most of the Bills were passed, but often in so modified a form as to defeat the intention of their original promoters.

It was not a satisfactory state of things for people who believed in the measures. John Russell in particular was in a continual state of exasperation. Could not they create peers, he said, in order to force the bills through the House of Lords? If this was impossible, then better go out; even opposition was preferable to staying in checked at every turn. Melbourne soothed him. What would be the good of going out, if the other side could not form a Government? Back the Whigs would have to come again. "It is no use popping in and out like a rabbit!" he observed sensibly. Himself, he saw no reason for resigning. In his heart of hearts he was pleased rather than otherwise when a reform was stopped: and he still feared that resignation might lead to a situation in which neither of the great parties could form a Government. "Perhaps it is a chimerical fear," he told John Russell, "and one which vanity and self-opinion very much minister to, and therefore should not be entertained. But I—being somewhat of an alarmist on this side, not having quite the confidence in the stability of popular and constitutional forms of government which others have, and thinking them very likely to break up of themselves and from the exaggeration of their own principles—cannot feel quite free from it." Do what he might, the spectre of possible civil war and revolution still hovered, dimly menacing, in the hinterland of his mind.

These various considerations conditioned his outlook on political affairs during these years. In general, he was for standing still. "I am for holding the ground already taken, but not for occupying new ground rashly," he announced to his colleagues. He set himself to act as a brake in the machinery of government. The words "delay", "put off", "postpone", echo through his letters and speeches like a series of Wagnerian *leit-motifs*. Of course, if the Radicals got dangerously restive, it was right to pacify them by some concessions: in practice, Melbourne showed himself surprisingly ready to do this. But he did not like doing it; and always felt bound to justify himself on the ground that it was the only means of keeping things quiet. He even grew irritated with John Russell for mentioning the Reform Bill without saying it was a necessary measure. "If it was not absolutely necessary," he remarked sharply, "it was the foolishest thing ever done." As for encouraging people to bring forward new reforms, it was simply laying up trouble for the future. They would get the habit of asking for more and more; in the end they would have to be stopped; by which time it would be an almost impossible task. "My esoteric doctrine," he proclaimed, "is that if you entertain any doubt, it is safest to take the unpopular side in the first instance. Transit from the unpopular, is easy . . . but from the popular to the unpopular the ascent is so steep and rugged that it is impossible to maintain it." So far as specific measures were concerned he approved of them only in so far as they seemed likely to make things calm. He was against the secret ballot, for example, because he suspected that it would encourage subversive persons to express their preferences more boldly than before. He was against admitting nonconformists to the University as he thought it would put Anglicans in a bad temper. He was against schemes for popular education because they seemed likely to create a new class of semi-educated discontented people. "You may fill a person's head with nonsense which may be impossible ever to get out again," he said. He also thought such schemes were futile in themselves. For one thing, no one could ever agree what form they should take. "All are agreed about the benefits of education, but are unable to agree as to the means of carrying them into effect," he told the House of Lords, "I am afraid this will afford those satirists, who disparage human nature, some matter on which to plume themselves." Besides, only the intelligent in Melbourne's view, were susceptible to real education, and surely the intelligent always educated themselves. Anyway, he sometimes wondered if education was really of any use, so far as success in life was concerned. The careers of his acquaintance seemed to indicate the reverse. "I do not know why there is all this fuss about education," he once remarked to Queen Victoria, "none of the Paget family can read or write and they do very well."

On the other hand, he was not against the Act that proposed reforming the municipal councils. For one thing, he thought there was a strong feeling in the country in favour of it: and he considered, as he had over the Reform Bill, that a wise statesman defers to such a feeling even if he does not happen to share it, in order to keep things peaceful. Secondly, the Bill seemed likely to give more local influence to the middle classes. Melbourne rightly judged that the middle classes, whether or not they called them-

selves liberal, were a conservative-minded body who would dislike dangerous changes. Even so, he did not feel enthusiastic about
the measure; and was not upset when the House of Lords threw
it out the first time it was introduced there. "What does it matter?" he said. "We have got on tolerably well with the councils
for five hundred years. We may contrive to go on with them for
another few years or so." And when at last it did go through, "It
is a great *bouleversement*, a great experiment," he remarked doubtfully; "we must see how it works!" Certainly he did not feel sure
that the Whigs were especially efficient at running local affairs.
The Tories in the House of Lords made an attack on some magistrates who had recently been appointed by the Home Secretary.
Out of loyalty to a colleague, Melbourne defended these appointments. But after the debate was at an end, he strolled over to the
other side of the House to speak to an opponent. "Have we really
been so bad in our appointments?" he unexpectedly asked him.

His attitude to Irish affairs was of a piece with his attitude to
English. The Irish question was not so troublesome as usual, for
John Russell, with Melbourne's tacit connivance, had negotiated
an unwritten pact with O'Connell by which the Repeal campaign
in Ireland was to be called off in return for promises to administer
Ireland in a more pro-Catholic spirit than before.[1] Melbourne did
not object to doing this. He had always thoroughly disliked the
Irish Protestants. His tolerant spirit was especially irritated by
their bland assumption that, because they owned most of the property in the country, their Church had a right to be supported by
money wrung from the pockets of a poverty-stricken peasantry
who thought them heretics. "Religious establishment," he said
with unusual bitterness, "is for population not property. Its existence is for the poor and needy, not for the opulent who have the
means to provide spiritual instruction for themselves." All the
same, the moment that pro-Catholic action showed signs of
seriously annoying people in England, Melbourne hung back from
it. John Russell, as before, proposed a Bill to reform the Protestant

[1] Melbourne, who both as an Englishman and a gentleman disliked
O'Connell, professed to know nothing of this compact. But he certainly
took advantage of it as indeed was necessary for the success of his own
Irish policy.

Church in Ireland and to strip it of some of its revenues. Uncertain and unwilling, Melbourne agreed. "I am afraid the question of the Irish Church," he said, "can neither be avoided nor postponed. It must therefore be attempted to be solved." However, when the House of Lords threw out this Bill, he wanted to drop it. He was the more reluctant to proceed in the matter because growingly he doubted that it, or any other Bill, could do much to solve the Irish question. The more he saw of the Irish the more he was confirmed in his conviction that their discontent arose from something born in them. "I never thought," he said, "that their crimes and outrages had much to do with former misgovernment and present politics. I believe them to arise from the natural disposition of the people and the natural state of society, which would have been much the same under any dispensation."

As a matter of fact Melbourne did not play much part either in planning or initiating the positive legislation activities of his Government. He left such work to John Russell. Not only did his conservatism of spirit make him dislike new legislation, but it was mostly concerned with administration; and he was still as bored by administration as ever. It needed more than four years as a Minister of the Crown to turn Melbourne into a man of action. The old Melbourne, like the young Melbourne, was interested less in getting things done than in studying why they happened. In so far as active politics did provide a field for his talents, it was on their personal side; in the opportunity they offered him to use his gift for managing individuals. This opportunity involved quite as much work as Melbourne liked. He found his hands full keeping his colleagues together and the King in a good humour. Even over this he was careful to expend his energy economically. He prudently refused to remove from South Street to the Prime Minister's official residence in Downing Street. The last thing he wanted was to be in the thick of things, with his colleagues bursting in at any moment of the day or night, asking awkward questions and urging quick decisions. Nor did he think it the Prime Minister's business to take a hand in the detailed running of every department in his administration. Canning, he noted, always maintained that a Government worked best in which each Minister was allowed to do his own job independently, and where the

Prime Minister only intervened if any specially critical situation arose. Melbourne was pleased to find that his opinions and his inclinations alike led him to agree with Canning. "The companion rather than the guide of his Ministers," so he was described; and he kept just sufficient eye on their activities to notice if they seemed likely to do anything unusually foolish. This, however, with a team like his and the situation so precarious, entailed the exercise of an incessant and vigilant diplomacy. He conducted it in his customary unofficial, undress sort of way—by means of a casual word dropped in the card-room of Brooks's Club or over the port wine at a dinner party; and also by letters. Every day a stream of notes proceeded from South Street; pithy, racy, conversational notes counselling moderation and good sense, couched in a tone that artfully combined subtle tact with an air of friendly frankness. Now and again a glint of his paradoxical humour showed itself; and also his love of bold generalization. "Political dinners are very good things when you can be sure of apparent unanimity," he will say, "when great differences are found, they are dangerous." Or, "People are very fond of stating others to be dead or in a hopeless state and are very much disappointed to find them alive or not so bad as they gave them out to be." Sometimes such sentences disconcerted his correspondents; so much so as to undo the effect of his tact. He realized this. "I observe," he confessed sadly, "that these speculative letters, especially if they are written in an impartial or conciliatory tone, give the greatest offence." The English party system has much to be said for it: but it does not provide a natural home for the detached thinker.

For the rest, Melbourne's working day was occupied with routine activities; leading the House of Lords and dispensing patronage. He was still only moderately successful in the House of Lords. It was not in him to assume that stately and formidable public personality by which a born Leader of the House like Grey awes his opponents and rallies his noble supporters. Melbourne's was incurably a private face. Because the debates bored him he tended to leave the management of many Bills to his deputy, Lord Duncannon; when he did it himself he was often listless and perfunctory.

His individuality showed itself more happily in the dispensing of patronage. The letters he wrote on the subject are some of the most entertaining in his correspondence. Nowhere do the diverse strains in his nature exhibit themselves more curiously. His judgment was extremely detached. The fact that a man had attacked him did not in the least bias him against giving him an honour. And he had an acute eye to perceive genuine merit. On the other hand, he thought it foolish as a rule to waste an honour on a man who could do nothing to help the Whig cause. This disinclined him to reward literary achievement. "Literary men are seldom good for anything," he said. He also had an aristocratic distaste for rewarding successful business men. "Never mind the clamour of the magnates in the city," he told Lord Holland; "they grunt like pigs unless everything is done to suit their convenience." This did not stop Lord Holland pressing for an honour to be given to a Mr. Goldsmith who, he assured Melbourne, was not a vulgar commercial type of man. Melbourne replied, "I wish you would not press Goldsmith upon me. I hate refined Solomons. God knows I hate doing something for these Stock Exchange people; there are as many refined Christians as Goldsmith; and, after all, there is not so much merit in being a Jew as to cause him on that account to be selected in a manner which must provoke much clamour and discontent." The Holland family were a great nuisance to Melbourne where honours were concerned. Lady Holland was so importunate as to come in for an incisive rebuke on the subject. "You seem to have one fixed principle," Melbourne told her, "and that is to choose the man with the worst character in the list of candidates." Certainly none of his friends and colleagues were considerate of him when they wanted a job done for a friend. John Russell himself forgot to be conscientious if there was a chance of promoting the advance of a member of his own family. "The Duke of Bedford and John Russell," Melbourne exclaims on one occasion, "plague me for William Russell, a snuffling Methodist and a foolish fellow. No one has the least sense where their own connections are concerned, and a large family is a greater impediment than riches to a man's entry into the Kingdom of Heaven." And the obscure were just as clamorous as the great. "Turn round," Melbourne whispered hurriedly to a companion when they were riding in Rotten Row. "Is not that Dacres coming? There is no bore so great to a Prime Minister as a country gentleman." All the same—and in spite of the bother that it involved him in—Melbourne got a great deal of amusement out of his job as patron. It was so delightfully revealing of human absurdity and vanity. Who, for instance, could have known that so many men wanted to be baronets? "I did not know that anyone cared any longer for these sort of things," he said. "Now I have a hold on the fellows!" He was also entertained by the self-confident tenacity with which the Scotch nobility claimed honours for themselves. "Give him the Thistle!" he remarked about a notably half-witted Scottish peer. "Why, he'd eat it!" Not that the English Peerage were much better. An Earl came to him demanding to be made a Marquess. "My dear sir," replied Melbourne, "how can you be such a damn fool!"—and about an insatiable applicant, "Confound it! Does he wants a Garter for his other leg?" Sometimes it seemed to him as if people demanded rewards precisely in proportion as they were undeserving of them. "The list of applications which I have," he writes to John Russell about candidates for the Civil List pensions, "comprises Mrs. James, widow of the writer of *The Naval History*; Leigh Hunt, distinguished writer of seditious and treasonable libels; Colonel Napier, historian of the war in Spain, conceited and democratic Radical and grandson of a duke; Mr. Cary, translator of Dante, madman; Sheridan Knowles, man of great genius but not old nor poor enough for a pension. Say what would you think ought to be done." It is to be noted that several of the names on this list did in fact get their pensions. Melbourne's lack of illusions served, if anything, to increase his ironical tolerance. It also had the advantage of making him impervious himself to the temptations to which he perceived so many of his countrymen were susceptible. William IV urged him to accept the Garter; but, said Melbourne, "a Garter may attract to us somebody of consequence which nothing else can reach. But what is the good of my taking it? I cannot bribe myself!"

His most onerous work as patron was that concerned with ecclesiastical appointments. The Church of England was entering upon one of the most strenuous and turmoiled phases of its history. Like other traditional English institutions, it had woken from the

I

placid summer afternoon slumber of the eighteenth century to find itself in a strange and disturbing world. The rise of liberalism, political and intellectual, appeared to be threatening its very existence: on every side the air re-echoed with the menacing cries of atheist radicals, now demanding its disestablishment, now questioning the very foundations of the Christian faith. However, the Church herself was susceptible to the spirit of the new age; romantic mysticism and the moral earnestness of the nineteenth-century middle class flowed together into her veins to reinvigorate her with a fresh vitality; and she energetically rallied all her forces to resist her enemies. Unluckily, these forces could not agree as to how best this was to be done. There was the Liberal school who wanted to bring religion up to date; to strip its creed of what it considered its Medieval anachronisms and re-edit it on progressive "rational" lines. The new High Church party, the Puseyites of Oxford, on the contrary, were out to make the Church much more Medieval; surely she was strongest when she was mysterious and supernatural and authoritarian, as she had been in the great Age of Faith! Meanwhile, the Evangelical party, longer established than its rivals, stuck to its old prescription of philanthropy, puritan morals, and strict adherence to the literal words of the Scripture. All three parties regarded each other with righteous abhorrence. When an important position in the Church fell vacant, each loudly clamoured for it to be given to a candidate of its own persuasion. The unfortunate Prime Minister, in whose gift lay most important Church appointments, had to decide between the claims of these vociferous and intolerant clerics.

Melbourne cut an odd figure in such a role. In one sense, he was better equipped for it than many statesmen; for theology had always been a hobby of his. But this very fact brought out in sharper relief how unlike his attitude to the subject was to that of the people with whom he was dealing. What were Dr. Pusey and the rest of them to think of a man who treated the most awful and momentous preoccupations of the human soul as matter for a hobby—and a whimsical hobby at that? These stiff, grave, conscience-ridden divines were disconcerted indeed to find themselves being tackled as to their views on the Virgin Birth or the Apostolic Succession in the cheerful man-of-the-world accents of a dinner party at Holland House. In 1840, for instance, we find Melbourne interviewing Dr. Thirlwall, a candidate for a bishopric, who had rendered himself a little suspect at Cambridge because he had translated from the German a doubtfully orthodox book on St. Luke's Gospel. Dr. Thirlwall found Melbourne in bed surrounded by heaps of patristic folios. "Very glad to see you," said Melbourne. "Sit down, sit down; hope you are come to say you accept. I only wish you to understand that I don't intend if I know it to make a heterodox bishop. I don't like heterodox bishops. As men they may be very good anywhere else, but I think they have no business on the Bench. I take great interest in theological questions, and I have read a good deal of those old fellows"—pointing to the folio editions of the Fathers—"They are excellent reading and very amusing; sometime or other we must have a talk about them. I sent your edition of Schleiermacher to Lambeth, and asked the Primate to tell me candidly what he thought of it; and look, here are his notes in the margin; pretty copious, you see. He does not concur in all your opinions; but he says there is nothing heterodox in your book."

Dr. Thirlwall was a liberal theologian. Melbourne tended to favour these most. The evangelicals, he thought, were a set of bigoted, uneducated spoil-sports; and as often as not, hypocrites as well. "One good thing," he writes to John Russell after reading Wilberforce's life, "is that it shows the great philanthropist Thomas Clarkson to be a sad fellow." The Puseyites were less objectionable—there was an agreeable odour of antique learning about them—but their mode of thought was so remote from his as to be unintelligible. "I hardly make out what Puseyism is," he told Lord Holland. "Either I am dull or its apostles are very obscure. I have got one of their chief Newman's publications with an appendix of four hundred and forty-four pages. I have read fifty-seven and cannot say I understand a sentence, or any idea whatever." Melbourne certainly had survived into an age remote from that of his youth. It is comically incongruous to think of him in his armchair at South Street, puzzling over the sublime hair-splittings of Newman.

He found the thoughts of the liberal theologians easier to follow. Learned, sensible persons of a kind he expected to meet in academic circles, they were at least commendably open-minded about the mysterious subjects of their cogitations. He was also disposed in their favour by the fact that they were generally on the Whig side politically. This was a fact that the Prime Minister had to consider: the Government's position was so precarious, and bishops had votes in the House of Lords. Indeed, in these days, most important Church appointments carried political implications with them. The realistic Melbourne was the last man to forget this. "I feel myself bound to recommend for promotion clergymen whose general views on political matters coincide with my own," he told the Archbishop of Canterbury firmly. He added, however, that he did not want to advance any man whose views were heterodox, or who, for whatever reason, was unpopular with the main body of the clergy. Peace and quiet, as always, were the things he cared most about; and any sympathy he might personally feel with a man or with his opinions was kept strictly in check by his overriding determination to avoid a fuss. For this reason, he refused to make either Sydney Smith or Dr. Arnold a bishop. In delightful Sydney's case, this was with regret and a certain feeling of guilt. "We shall not be forgiven for not having made Sydney Smith a bishop," he exclaimed in his old age. No such qualms troubled him about Arnold. Humourless, busy and progressive, Arnold represented those aspects of the new age which Melbourne found most uncongenial. Besides, Arnold's manner of preaching struck him as unpleasantly vehement, and he thought that he had very crotchety ideas about education. Alas, all Melbourne's care did not save him from sometimes causing a storm by his ecclesiastical appointments. "I have always had much sympathy with Saul," he once remarked. "He was bullied by the prophets just as I have been by the bishops who would, if they could, have tied me to the horns of the altar and slain me incontinently."[1] Such being his experience, it is not odd that he flinched at the prospect of adding to their number. "Damn it! Another bishop dead!" he would sigh, "I believe they die to vex me."

[1] It must be admitted that Melbourne on his side had no great opinion of the bishops. "What a good, simple-hearted old man the Archbishop of Canterbury is!" said a colleague to him one day. "He is the damnedest fool alive!" replied Melbourne.

In point of fact, the biggest row he got into over a matter of this kind was not concerned with a bishopric. In 1836, the Regius Professorship of Divinity at Oxford fell vacant. After much consideration, Melbourne offered it to Dr. Hampden, a man eminent for his learning, and a Whig. Unluckily, he had also acquired distinction by delivering a course of lectures in which he had betrayed himself as a little dubious about the doctrine of the Holy Trinity. In consequence, his appointment roused a storm of protest. William IV, the Archbishop of Canterbury and Dr. Pusey himself, all wrote agitatedly remonstrating with Melbourne; and some pious peers made angry speeches on the matter in the House of Lords. Dr. Hampden, whose temperament seems to have been less bold than his theological speculations, offered nervously to retire from the field. Melbourne, however, was not the man to let himself be bullied once he had made up his mind. Besides, he was determined to do nothing which looked like a surrender to the spirit of intolerance. Genially he soothed Dr. Hampden's anxieties. "Be easy," he said laying a hand on his arm. "I like an easy man." Himself, he used his usual pacifying tactics with King and Archbishop and wrote a letter to Dr. Pusey suavely putting him in his place.

"I entirely concur with you in the necessity of agreement," he said, "if it can be created consistently with other more important objects, upon the greater points between those who fill the theological chairs in the same university. It is hardly necessary to go to Germany to learn so plain and so obvious a truth; and the theological colloquy and religious belief which prevails in the universities of that country is, if it be such as it is popularly represented, no very favourable testimony to the results of those institutions and to the manner in which they are conducted. Uniformity of opinion, however desirable, may be purchased at too high a price. We must not sacrifice everything to it; soundness of opinion, reasonableness of opinion, extent of knowledge, powers, intellectual and physical, must also be taken into account. . . . I do not myself dread bold enquiry and speculation. I have seen too many new theories spring up and die away to feel much alarm upon such a subject. If they are founded on truth, they establish themselves and become part of the established belief. If they are erroneous, they decay and perish. . . . I return you my thanks for calling my attention to the general state of religious feeling in the country, and to the deep interest which is taken in religious questions and ecclesiastical appointments. Be assured that I am neither unaware of its extent nor of its fervour, and that I have not been a careless observer of its progress. I doubt not that it is working for good, but the best and most holy aspirations are liable to be affected by the weakness of our nature and to be corrupted by our spirit of ill will, hatred and malice, of intolerance and persecution, which in its own warmth and sincerity it is apt to engender; a spirit to which, in whatever form or place it may show itself, I have a decided antipathy, and will oppose at all hazards all the resistance in my power."

The House of Lords had less claim to be treated respectfully in these matters. Melbourne made this clear in a speech. "Very few of your Lordships," he said bluntly, "have the means of forming any sound opinion on such extremely difficult and abstruse points as these. . . . I know very little of the subject and yet I believe I know more than those who have opposed the Doctor's nomination."

Melbourne's dealings with ecclesiastical affairs were not confined to the question of patronage. The spirit of reform was out to make itself felt in every established institution. A great many of these institutions were connected in some way or other with the National Church. Accordingly, during the period of Melbourne's Government, progressive reformers were always coming forward with schemes that affected it; schemes for reforming tithe and church-rate and the constitution of cathedral churches; for legalizing civil marriage and abolishing religious tests at universities. In order to please his colleagues, Melbourne reluctantly agreed to support some of these projects. But he disliked them all. He was a liberal only in matters of thought: so far as practical Church reforms were concerned, he was as conservative as Dr. Pusey himself. He was against schemes for equalizing clerical incomes; "I am all for inequality and rich clergy," he remarked gaily to a committee of the House of Lords. And how could anyone be so sure of anything, he would wonder, as to have conscientious scruples against being married in church, as their fathers and grandfathers had been before them? The same conservatism appeared in his dealings with the Church of Scotland. In 1835, it was proposed that the Government grant to the Scottish Church should be increased. Scottish divines were divided as to whether this would be a good thing. Some held that the cause of religion required financial support: others, that to accept State aid of any kind was sinful and erastian. After listening to their arguments, Melbourne made his comment in a letter to the celebrated Dr. Chalmers.

> "The one party looks to nothing less than a general change in the state of human nature and human society by means of increased pastoral exertion; and the other is dreaming upon the pure and prosperous state of the Christian Church in the first centuries, and the evil and degradation which it has incurred ever since the unfortunate conversion of the Emperor Constantine. You will excuse the plainness of my phrase, but to persons so influenced by heat and enthusiasm, to use no stronger terms, it is vain to expect that any arrangement can be satisfactory."

He was opposed, he concluded, to any alteration in the financial arrangements of the Church of Scotland.

So far as established Churches were concerned, Melbourne's method did not work badly. Established institutions need, first of all, to be kept running smoothly. Melbourne's spirit of civilized moderation helped him to do this. It was not so appropriate when he came into contact with independent and extreme religious bodies. One day a deputation of Dissenters came to see him. "Now, sir," he said after listening to one of them, "you talk like a man of sense. It's these damned Anabaptists who do all the mischief." Another member of the deputation felt impelled to testify to his faith. "I am an Anabaptist," he announced gravely. "The devil you are!" replied Melbourne, laughing and rubbing his hands; "well, you've all done a great deal of mischief—and I should like to hear whether you are wiser than the rest!"

Towards the Church of Rome his manner was more respectful. No doubt it was superstitious and tyrannical, and Melbourne was extremely glad that England was not under its sway. Moreover, he did not like Roman ritual which struck his gentlemanly and English eye as too theatrical to be consistent with a true spirit of devotion. But the Church of Rome was an ancient and venerable institution that appealed to his historic sense and with which he thought it wise the English Government should be on good terms. Melbourne thought that the Whigs had always underrated the importance of the Church of Rome as a factor influence in public opinion. He regretted that Protestant bigotry made it impossible for him to send an ambassador to the Vatican. As it was, he made efforts to get into good unofficial relations there. These were not very successful as far as practical results were concerned. His tone was not quite right. "The present Pope was very rude to me," Melbourne complained on one occasion. "I wrote to him asking him to give a Cardinal's Hat to an Irish bishop who had been of great use to us on the management of the country. But he took no notice of my request." It would have been odd if he had. The Vicar of Christ should not be addressed as if he was a political colleague to be breezily cajoled into doing a job for a harassed Prime Minister.

Indeed, Melbourne's attitude to religion in its corporate manifestations was incorrigibly secular. Not in its personal ones though; here he remained paradoxically ambiguous as ever. He could not be called a believer. Yet he felt himself instinctively opposed to all professional unbelievers. He took a mischievous pleasure, when he found himself staying at Holland House with the atheistic Bentham, in beguiling him into attending Divine service at the local church. This was partly due, no doubt, to a dislike for dogmatic prigs of any kind. But not altogether: Melbourne had a positive feeling for religion that no amount of intellectual scepticism could dispel. He might have been expected to sympathize with Henry IV of France for becoming a Roman Catholic in order to keep his country at peace. On the contrary; "I would have died rather than do it!" he exclaimed to Queen Victoria; and he was seriously concerned lest the dying William IV should not see a clergyman. Moreover, Melbourne's interest in theology, apparently so whimsical, was connected with the deepest movements of his nature. Amid all the distractions of office, his perplexed spirit continued to brood intermittently over the riddle of man's relation to the universe. One day Haydon called to find him reading the Greek Testament. "Is not the world," Haydon asked him, "evidence of a perpetual struggle to remedy a defect?" "Certainly!" mused Melbourne. "If as Milton says," went on Haydon, "we were sufficient to have stood, why then did we fall?" At these words, Melbourne suddenly sat bolt upright. "Ah! That is touching on all our apprehensions," he exclaimed.

This remark betrays a troubled spirit. Indeed, these were not happy years for Melbourne. His forebodings before becoming Prime Minister had proved justified. For all his growing reputation, for all that he was succeeding better than anyone had expected in staving off his Government's defeat, he was usually harassed and often depressed. After all, though his policy might be the wisest in the circumstances, it was not a glorious one. It is not satisfying to be continually compromising and conceding, especially when the best that can be hoped from them is to put off the inevitable coming of some more or less evil day. Even on a short view, their success was precarious: any violent turn of events and the whole careful structure of his diplomatic skill would fall to pieces. Besides, to maintain it was wearing. It meant being constantly watchful and tactful, and patient and good-tempered. Against considerable temptations to the contrary, too: so many people made themselves a nuisance to him so often. "Damn it! Why can't they be quiet?" he would sigh to himself. As always, the King was the greatest trial. Soured by his failure to keep the Whigs out, William IV's temper had become more uncertain than ever. During the first months of the new Government, he refused to speak to his Ministers at all, except on business. "I would rather have the devil than a Whig in the house," he exclaimed, and sat sulking evening after evening, alone with a bottle of sherry. John Russell and Lord Glenelg, the Colonial Secretary, were his particular aversions. He insulted Glenelg so often and so publicly that Melbourne had to remonstrate with him. With good effect; indeed, Melbourne was admirable in dealing with the King who, under the influence of his mingled tact and firmness, did begin to grow friendlier. But his good humour did not last long. By

the following summer, he was once more violently hostile—
"Crazier than ever!" said Melbourne gloomily. Every week, he
received some long, rambling, grumbling complaint from the
Palace; about the Navy, or the Militia, or the shocking behaviour
of the Duchess of Kent—of whom, as the mother of the heir to the
throne, William IV was furiously suspicious.

The King's rudeness annoyed the Ministers. Melbourne then
had to soothe them. "It is best not to quarrel with him," he would
remark. "He is evidently in a state of great excitement." But so,
often, were they! Even without Brougham and Durham, they had
turned out a difficult team to drive. Palmerston was rash and unmanageable, Glenelg feeble and languid; even John Russell,
whom Melbourne looked on as the strong central pillar of his administration, was liable to what the cautious Melbourne considered fits of extreme indiscretion. Without a word of warning,
in the Cabinet or, still worse, in public, he might come out with
some dogmatic statement about his own opinions that was bound
to cause a row. The chance that this might happen made Melbourne nervous. "I hope you have said nothing damn foolish,"
he writes to him on one occasion. "I thought you were teeming
with some imprudence yesterday." Besides, if John Russell found
himself unable to speak his mind as his principles directed, he was
inclined to throw up the sponge. Three times at least, during
these years, he threatened to resign: and had to be cajoled by his
chief into staying in office. This irritated Melbourne. His irritation grew sharper when John Russell took upon himself to tell him
that he ate too much and did not take enough exercise.

The King and his colleagues were not the only people to give
Melbourne trouble. There was the Radical wing of his party ex-
ploding in righteous wrath every time he made a concession to the
Tories: there was the Opposition in the House of Lords, always
on their toes to trip the Government up, factious, carping, asking
awkward questions and exulting in ugly pleasure over any Whig
slip. It was true that Peel, for his own good reasons, did his best
to keep them in check. But Melbourne could not feel that this was
done in a spirit of sporting goodwill. Peel, in his view, was a cold,
ungenerous, ungenial type of man—"Not a horse into whose
stable you should go unadvisedly and without speaking to him be-

fore!" he warned John Russell; and again "he is cross and sarcastic which I take to be the nature of the man: it is only prudence
and calculation which make him otherwise."

Altogether, being Prime Minister was fully as troublesome as he
had feared. Gradually the strain began to tell on his nerves. He
slept very badly, and suffered from rheumatic attacks that kept
him in bed for days at a time. Every month brought some new
abortive crisis: every crisis left the Government a little more discredited. The nadir was reached in the late summer of 1836 after
the Government had suffered a series of defeats in the House of
Lords and every one—King, Irish, Radicals—seemed in a thoroughly bad temper. "It would try the patience of an ass," Melbourne broke out one day. For the first time he began to wonder
whether it might not be wiser to resign.

Dissatisfaction with his immediate situation merged into a more
general sense of sadness and disillusionment. He felt the fleetingness of things mortal more acutely than ever; saw himself more
than ever as an alien in the new age. Especially down in the country at Brocket, where he had time to reflect and the atmosphere
was soaked in memories of his happy childhood and brilliant
youth, regret swept over him like a wave. The golden September
sunlight bathing the stretches of turfy parkland seemed only to
mock by contrast the sunless autumn of his own prevailing mood.

> "Thou bringest the light of pleasure fled,
>     And hopes long dead."

So he would be heard murmuring to himself as he gazed out of the
window.

(4)

The events of his private life contributed to his depression. He
had lost Miss Eden for the time being. In 1835, Miss Eden's
brother, Lord Auckland, was made Governor-General of India;
and she went away with him. No longer could Melbourne look
forward to calling on her each week, for an entertaining talk on the
foibles of his colleagues or the Epistles of St. Paul; no longer could
he relax his taut nerves in the pleasant warmth of her kindness and
her good sense.

"My mother always used to say," he writes in a note of fare-well, "that I was very selfish, both Boy and Man, and I believe she was right—at least I know that I am always anxious to escape from anything of a painful nature, and find every excuse for doing so. Very few events could be more painful to me than your going, and therefore I am not unwilling to avoid wishing you good-bye. Then God bless you—As to health, let us hope for the best. The climate of the East Indies very often re-establishes it. I send you a Milton, which I have had a long time and often read in. I shall be most anxious to hear from you and promise to write. Adieu."

Then in the spring of 1836 he found himself in serious trouble over Mrs. Norton. She had been the central figure in his private life for the last five years. Either in his house or hers, they saw each other nearly every day; often for three hours at a time and often alone. She talked or listened to him about his political work; when he wanted to forget politics, they read poetry together, or flirted and gossiped. Such a relationship, innocent though in fact it might be, was bound to excite censorious comment. One man can steal a horse, says the proverb, while another cannot look over the hedge. Melbourne and Caroline belonged conspicuously to the second category. Both lived in the public eye: Melbourne be-cause he was Prime Minister, Caroline because it was her nature so to do. Moreover, what with Lady Branden and the general amorous reputation of his family, Melbourne could not pay marked attention to a woman without people suspecting the worst. Nor was Caroline the type of woman to disarm their suspicions. She was showily beautiful, her conversation was the opposite of prudish, and she had no sense of decorum. "Met Mrs. Norton at the French Ambassador's," notes the correct Lord Malmesbury in 1835. "She talked in a most extraordinary manner and kicked Lord Melbourne's hat over her head. The whole *corps diplomatique* were amazed." The world in general reacted to such exhibitions in the same way as the *corps diplomatique*: and disapproval mingled with their amazement. Indeed, Caroline had only maintained her precarious footing in respectable society in virtue of the fact that she had not broken its first fundamental law of conduct: she still lived under the same roof as her husband. As time passed, she found this growingly difficult.

The marriage had always been a dog-fight. Neither husband nor wife had the self-control to keep their wrongs to themselves. Gradually, parties were formed on each side. They interfered and made things worse. Caroline's supporters were the first to enter the fray. One evening in 1833, the Nortons had a worse row than usual. George Norton insisted on smoking a cigar in the drawing-room, though Caroline objected to the smell. Accordingly, she flounced upstairs and locked herself in her bedroom. Norton pursued after her, broke down the door, and, after blowing out the candle, proceeded to throw her and the furniture about in an alarming fashion. The next day she took refuge with her family who vehemently espoused her cause. However, things were patched up sufficiently for the Nortons and the Sheridan family— Caroline's sisters and her brother Brinsley—to go on a foreign tour together in the following year. As might have been expected, this only led to more trouble. Once again the worst explosion was occasioned by George Norton's smoking. One day, when driving with his wife in a small closed carriage, he puffed away at a hookah regardless of her entreaties. She tore the mouthpiece from his lips and flung it out of the window; he clutched her so violently by the throat that, in fear of her life, she jumped from the carriage and ran back to her relations. Outraged to see their sister treated in this way, they returned to England, George Norton's implacable enemies who never lost a chance of working up Caroline against him. Now it was his turn to seek for sympathy among his relations. He found it, and especially from Miss Vaughan, an elderly spinster connection of his, to whom he had always taken pains to make himself pleasant as he hoped she might leave him her fortune. Stirred up by Miss Vaughan on the one hand and the Sheridans on the other, the feeling between husband and wife began to increase to a bitterness that made rupture inevitable. It did not come at once only because George Norton was too unstable easily to take decisive action about anything; and because Caroline, partly out of concern for her reputation and her children, and partly out of genuine softheartedness, shrank, when it came to the point, from pushing matters to their extreme conclusion. Some uneasy months followed of recurrent quarrels, apologies and re-conciliations. Each time the quarrel was sharper and the recon-ciliation more half-hearted. In April, 1836, the final break came. Its occasion—a dispute as to whether or not the children should be allowed to pay a visit to Caroline's brother—seems trivial enough. Perhaps George Norton had already thought of the plan by which he hoped he might at once disembarrass himself of his wife and also improve his wretched financial position. Why not take advantage of Caroline's notorious indiscretion to get a divorce and make the co-respondent pay him large damages? He there-fore turned her out of the house, packed his children off to his re-lations, and set about looking for a likely co-respondent. Several celebrated names occurred to him as possible candidates for this important role. For a time his mind wavered between Shelley's corsair friend Trelawny, Harrison Ainsworth, the novelist, and the young Duke of Devonshire. Then an even more spectacular alternative presented itself to his mind; the Prime Minister him-self. It is doubtful whether this was George Norton's own idea or —as was commonly rumoured—it was suggested to him by wire-pullers from the underworld of the Tory Party, who saw in the divorce case a means of discrediting the Whig Government. How George Norton thought he was going to get away with it is hard to imagine. For, up till the very day Caroline left him, he had taken pains to keep on particularly good terms with Melbourne—even better than with Caroline's other rich admirers. So far from ob-jecting to the intimacy, he had ushered Melbourne up to visit her in her bedroom when she was ill and escorted her to South Street when she was going to pay a call there. However, he was intoxi-cated by the prospect of the fortune he was likely to get if he did contrive to win his case; alternatively, he thought Melbourne, for the sake of avoiding a public scandal, might pay up handsomely in order to persuade him to withdraw it. In either case he fancied he stood to win. He proceeded, therefore, to file a petition, accusing him of criminal connection with his wife.

The general sensation stirred can be imagined. It is not every day that the Prime Minister of England is publicly accused of adultery with a reigning beauty. The gutter-press of the day re-sounded with articles in which spicy scandalous rumours were nicely blended with pious reflections on the deplorable prevalence of vice in high places. All this was more agreeable for the newspaper reader than for the parties concerned. Caroline was consternated. It looked like the end of all her ambitions. In those days, divorce meant complete social ruin for a woman. Even if she were exonerated, her good name would be tarnished. Her children, whom she loved with all the unbridled force of her emotional nature, were cut off from her, and in the hands of the odious Nortons. Reports reached her that they ill-treated them. Her dramatic imagination exaggerated these reports till she was nearly out of her mind. Alas, misfortune did not make her prudent! Indeed, it served still further to weaken her self-control and provide a new channel for the expression of her instinct for theatrical gesture. She proclaimed her wrongs at the top of her voice; she did her best to put herself in the wrong with George Norton by writing him letters imploring his forgiveness if he would take her back; she even rushed down to the country house where her children were confined, only to have them torn screaming from her arms and herself thrust ignominiously from the gates. At the same time, she failed to take the opportunity to mend her broken reputation by adopting a soberer and more retired style of living. Instead— either from pride or a desperate longing to forget her troubles— she shocked people by continuing to dine out and to go to parties, gorgeously dressed in pink satin and black lace, and laughing and talking with feverish vivacity.

The one person she could not risk being seen with was Melbourne. However, she communicated with him in a series of letters in which cries of anguish, denunciations of the Nortons, and appeals for comfort and advice were frantically mingled. Poor Melbourne, he must have rued the day he first called at her house! No pleasure he had found there could compensate for the trouble it was now causing him. He had chiefly enjoyed his relationship to Caroline as a delightful distraction from the disturbances of his political life. Now it turned out to be involving him in disturbance itself. And a much more disagreeable kind of disturbance. For it was one that stirred his sense of guilt. Through his own indiscretion, he had done harm to the reputation of his Government and brought acute distress upon a woman he was very fond of. He did

not, indeed, look on himself as primarily to blame for the failure
of the Norton marriage. To his shrewd and worldly-wise eyes it
seemed to have been grossly mismanaged from the start. No
doubt George Norton was the villain of the piece. Melbourne's
personal experience of him made him certain of this. Norton had
proved shockingly unsatisfactory at his job; quarrelsome, shifty,
grossly unpunctual and conceitedly imperious to any word of cor-
rection. "I know very well that a man of that description," Melbourne told Caroline, "who is fully persuaded that he is about to
do something extremely well is on the point of committing some
irretrievable error or of falling into some most ridiculous absurdity." As to Norton's behaviour at home, Melbourne saw quite
enough of it to realize that all Caroline's complaints were justified.
All the same, he did not think she went the right way about dealing
with him. Not thus would his mother have tackled a troublesome
husband. Caroline was at once too violent and too weak; lost her
temper too quickly and too readily forgave an injury. "The fact
is he is a stupid brute," he said to Lord Holland, "and she has
not the temper nor the dissimulation needed to manage him."
Further, he thought that living with Norton had lowered her standards of behaviour so that she had grown content to let her marriage degenerate into a condition of continuous sordid squabble
that must end in catastrophe. For he had no doubt that a breach
was a catastrophe. Far more clearly than Caroline he recognized
how fatal it would be for her reputation openly to be separated
from her husband. All along Melbourne had urged her to put up
with anything in order to keep the home together. As he wrote to
her in his first letter after the final quarrel:

"I hardly know what to write to you, or what comfort to offer.
You know as well as I do, that the best course is to keep yourself
tranquil, and not to give way to feelings of passion which, God
knows, are too natural to be easily resisted. This conduct upon
his part seems perfectly unaccountable, and, depend upon it,
being as you are, in the right, it will be made ultimately to appear, whatever temporary misrepresentations may prevail. You
cannot have better or more affectionate advisers than you have
with you upon the spot, who are well acquainted with the cir-

cumstances of the case and with the characters of those with whom they have to deal. You know that I have always coun- selled you to bear everything and remain to the last. I thought it for the best."

He still thought it for the best. Soon he was pressing her to try and make things up again—even after he got the news that George Norton was trying to find grounds for a divorce.

"Never, to be sure, was there such conduct. To set on foot that sort of inquiry without the slightest real ground for it! But it does not surprise me. I have always known that there was a mixture of folly and violence which might lead to any absurdity or injustice. You know so well my opinion that it is unneces- sary for me to repeat it. I have always told you that a woman should never part from her husband whilst she can remain with him. This is generally the case; particularly in such a case as yours, that is, in the case of a young, handsome woman of lively imagination, fond of company and conversation, and whose celebrity and superiority has necessarily created many enemies. Depend upon it, if a reconciliation is feasible there can be no doubt of the prudence of it."

In spite of all, to make it up would be the best for Caroline, best for her children—and of course best both for Melbourne himself and for the Whig Party.

When all hope of reconciliation was over, Melbourne concen- trated on comforting Caroline and trying to persuade her to keep her head. "I hope you will not take it ill," he said, "if I implore you to try at least to be calm under these trials. You know that whatever is alleged (if it be alleged) is utterly false, and what is false can rarely be made to appear true." And again, "Keep up your spirits; agitate yourself as little as possible; do not be too anxious about rumours and the opinion of the world." Alas, such advice, sensible though it was, had no effect on a woman like Caroline. Rather, it roused her exasperated nerves to an outburst of irritation. To her his whole tone only showed that he was cold and selfish and did not enter into her feelings. How could he expect her to be calm? Nor did she like it when he said that other people agreed

with him. What did he mean by talking of her concerns to other
people. Was it not shockingly disloyal of him? Gently, and with
the patience born of long experience of similar temperamental explosions in his own home, he defended himself. "You describe me
very truly when you say that I am always more annoyed that there
is a row than sorry for the persons engaged in it. But, after all, you
know you can count on me." Indeed, Caroline was wildly mistaken in thinking that he did not feel for her. On the contrary, as
the time for the trial approached, the matter began to prey on his
mind till he became actually ill from disgust and apprehension.
The idea of any woman he was fond of being involved in the
squalor of a public lawsuit on such a subject was almost unbearable to his chivalrous heart. Caroline wrote describing an interview with her lawyers. She had found it odious: they had been so
cold-blooded about the affair, so obviously ready under an air of
superficial politeness to believe her guilty, and, she cried once
more, Melbourne did not realize her sufferings! He was feeling so
worked up by now that this time he burst out in reply.

"I have received your letter," he said, "and given such instruction as I trust will be for the best. I do not wonder at the
impression made upon you. I knew it would be so, and therefore I was most unwilling to have the interview take place at all.
All the attorneys I have ever seen have the same manner: hard,
cold, incredulous, distrustful, sarcastic, sneering. They are said to
be conversant in the worst part of human nature, and with the
most discreditable transactions. They have so many falsehoods
told them, that they place confidence in none.

"I have sent your note, having read it. I daresay you think
me unfeeling; but I declare that since I first heard I was proceeded against I have suffered more intensely than I ever did in
my life. I had neither sleep nor appetite, and I attributed the
whole of my illness (at least the severity of it) to the uneasiness
of my mind. Now what is this uneasiness for? Not for my own
character because, as you justly say, the imputation upon me is
as nothing. It is not for the political consequences to myself,
although I deeply feel the consequences that my indiscretion
may bring upon those who are attached to me or follow my for-

tunes. The real and principal object of my anxiety and solicitude is you, and the situation in which you have been so unjustly placed by the circumstances which have taken place."

It is likely that his passionate desire to convince her of his sympathy made him exaggerate a little. He cannot have suffered so profoundly as at the crisis of his marriage. But he was older now, he could stand these strains less well: and perhaps it is true that never before had he felt his nerves so wretchedly upset. Certainly it is the first occasion in this phase of his life that we find people saying that he looked depressed.

Meanwhile he asked the King if he should resign; he was willing to if it was thought proper. The King said no. He suspected the whole affair of being an underhand political plot: and with all his faults, William IV was not the type of man to connive at underhand plots. Nor had his own private life been of a kind to make him take a censorious view of Melbourne's alleged misconduct. The Duke of Wellington also took steps to let Melbourne know that he saw no cause for resignation. On the contrary, he said he would refuse to take office in any Government that might be formed as a result of it. He too was not the man to be particular in such matters. Besides he was very anxious to dissociate himself from the intrigues of his shadier supporters.

The case came up for trial on 23rd June. Public excitement was tremendous. Couriers waited all day ready to carry the news of the verdict to every important capital in Europe. From early morning, the law courts were besieged by huge crowds trying to get seats: so much so that the Attorney General, Sir John Campbell, who was appearing for Melbourne, had considerable difficulty in pushing his way through the throng. During the whole day before he had been feeling acutely apprehensive. Who knew what apparently damning evidence George Norton might have contrived to concoct in order to gain his ends? Campbell need not have worried. Dickens was to satirize the case a year or two later in the *Pickwick Papers*: and in fact, the proceedings did turn out to be a scene of grotesque Dickensian farce. Hogarthian rather: for much of the evidence offered was of too scandalous a kind to find a place on the chaste pages of a Victorian novel. Melbourne and Caroline were not present, though Melbourne sent an affidavit asserting his innocence. George Norton could not by law go into the witness box himself. Instead, he relied on the evidence of a handful of servants once in his employ, whom he had tracked down after months of search in the underworld of London and then persuaded by means of lavish bribes to come forward on his behalf. They were of a type to cast a lurid light on the character of life below stairs in the Norton household. Two were women who had been discharged on account of their indiscreet familiarities with members of His Majesty's Brigade of Guards; while the chief male witness was a groom called Fluke who had been dismissed for his habitual drunkenness. Fluke was an engaging character. It was reported that he had refused at the last moment to come to court unless he was brought in a chaise and four, and was given both chicken and duckling for breakfast before starting.

"I had had a drop too much," he confided to the court, when relating an incident in his evidence.

"You like to speak the truth sometimes?" said Campbell sarcastically. "You took a drop too much, eh?" Fluke resented the tone of his remark.

"I don't know who does not. We are all alike for that, masters and servants," he answered.

"How often did you take a drop too much while in Mrs. Norton's service?" asked Campbell.

"What, Sir, during four years service!" exclaimed the astonished Fluke. "You have put a very heavy question!" It also transpired during his examination that Fluke had spent the last weeks living at a public house on the Norton family estate and had had several interviews with George Norton. The chief documentary evidence brought forward were three notes from Melbourne. The first ran, "I will call about quarter-past four. Yours, Melbourne."

The second, "How are you? I shall not be able to come today. I shall tomorrow."

The third, "No House today: I will call after the levee. If you wish it later I will let you know."

Norton's Counsel did what he could with these unpromising documents. He said they showed "a great and unwarrantable degree of affection", because they did not begin My Dear Mrs. Norton, and added, "There may be latent love like latent heat in the midst of icy coldness." This mysterious and imaginative reflection failed to make the impression on the court which its author desired. The proceedings, which lasted for nearly thirteen hours, were frequently interrupted by bursts of uproarious laughter. Campbell called no witnesses for the defence. Instead, rising at six o'clock and continuing till the candles guttered low in their sockets, he demolished the evidence offered on behalf of the plaintiff in a speech which all present agreed to be one of the most brilliant exhibitions of legal wit and eloquence ever heard in an English Court of Justice. The case ended just before midnight: the Jury acquitted Melbourne without leaving the box. The verdict was received with thunderous applause. Late as it was, Campbell went down to the House of Commons, where the news of his success had preceded him, and was met with another great outburst of cheering. Even the bitterest Tory did not dare to question the justice of the verdict. "As far as I can see," said one acidly, "Melbourne had more opportunities than any man ever had before and made no use of them."

On the whole the Prime Minister's reputation was affected wonderfully little by the affair. The newspapers indeed, on the morning after the trial, maintained the lofty and censorious tone which, as self-appointed guardians of public morality, they had assumed throughout. *The Times*, though it accepted the verdict, reproved Caroline's conduct as "imprudent, indiscreet, and undignified, and the very last we should hold up as an example to an English wife". As for Melbourne, a man who could waste his own and the lady's time on such "contemptible and unnecessary frivolities" was, it said, utterly unfit for his high office.

This view does not seem to have been shared by anyone in the world of politics and fashion in which Melbourne lived: while, as might have been expected, his own relations, little as they cared for Mrs. Norton—why must William always involve himself with such impossible women?—rallied round him with all that sense of family solidarity which was characteristic of them. "The whole thing seems to leave the lady in a position where, with a little protection, she may do very well," wrote Frederick Lamb to his sister

Emily. "We know them for *canaille*, but we must help her as well as we can. Do not let William think himself invulnerable for having got off again this time. No man's luck can go further."

William did not think himself invulnerable. No doubt it was a great load off his mind. The night of the trial, walking home by Storey's Gate, he saw a young lawyer of his acquaintance staring curiously at Mrs. Norton's house. Melbourne touched him on the shoulder. "What does this mean, Mr. Solicitor?" he asked with a roguish look. But he did not feel so carefree as to imagine he could risk resuming his intimacy with Caroline on anything like the old terms. It was sad; for he had grown in his loneliness to depend on her very much. But it was inevitable. All the same, he still felt responsible for her and very much concerned about her future prospects. Those were not bright. In spite of the fact that she had been exonerated, the trial was a disaster for her. It cut her off indefinitely from her children: and, for all that Frederick Lamb might say to the contrary, it struck a dangerous blow at her precarious social position. Many people still thought her guilty; at the best, she had shown herself extremely indiscreet. Nor did her flamboyant personality enable her to play the role of innocent, injured woman in such a way as to disarm the suspicions of the censorious. Besides, she was very poor. Legally everything she possessed down to her very jewels belonged to George Norton, even if she got a legal separation from him: and he was prepared to claim all his legal rights. Melbourne was all the more worried about her because for some time after the trial he did not hear a word from her, though he had written more than once. He began to wonder if she had not turned against him as one of the authors of her troubles. At last she did answer, miserable and bitter indeed, but against Norton, not himself. He replied in a series of letters in which are apparent the mingled strains of his feelings in regard to her: regret, affection, pity, a sense of personal responsibility and chivalrous indignation with Norton.

"Well, come what may, I will never again from silence or any other symptom think that you can mean anything unkind or averse to me. I have already told you that most of the bitterness which I have felt during this affair was on your account. I do

not think your application to Norton was judicious.[1] Every
communication elates him and encourages him to persevere in
his brutality. You ought to know him better than I do and must
do so. But you seem to me to be hardly aware what a gnome he
is, how perfectly earthy and bestial. He is possessed of a devil,
and that the immensest and basest fiend that disgraces the infernal regions. In my opinion he has made the whole matter
subservient to his pecuniary interests. . . . Now that he has nobody to advise or control or soothe him, what follies or what
abominable conduct he may pursue it is impossible to conjec-
ture. I pity you about the children. . . . It is most melancholy
not to know where they are or with whom. I have never mentioned money to you. I hardly like to do it now. Your feelings
have been so galled that they have naturally become very sore
and sensitive. I know how you might take it. I have had, at
times, a great mind to send you some but I feared to do so. As
I trust we are now upon terms of confidential and affectionate
friendship, I venture to say that you have only to express a wish
and it shall be instantly complied with. I miss you. I miss your
society and conversation every day at the hours at which I was
accustomed to enjoy it: and when you say that your place can be
easily supplied, you indulge in a little vanity and self-conceit.
You know well enough that there is nobody who can fill your
place. . . . I saw Brinsley and his wife the other night at Lord
Hertford's. I thought him rather cold. None of them seemed
really glad to see me, except Charles. But there is no reason
why they should be. If they went upon my principle, or rather
my practice of disliking those who cause trouble, uneasiness,
vexation, without considering why they do it, they certainly
would not rejoice in my presence."

Towards the end of the year his private life was disturbed by yet
another shock. For some months, Augustus Lamb's health had
shown signs of breaking up. The attacks from which he had
suffered since a child came oftener and more violently. In spite of
all his other preoccupations, Melbourne had watched over him as
carefully as he could: had him with him when he was working, and

[1] This appears to have been an application for money.

sat in his room for hours together observing vigilantly every varying symptom of his condition. One evening in November they were together and Melbourne was writing when Augustus suddenly said, "I wish you would give me some franks that I may write to people who have been kind in their enquiries." Words and tone were those of a sane, mature man: Melbourne's pen dropped from his hand in astonishment. "I cannot give any notion of what I felt," he related, "for I believe it to be, as it proved, the summons they call the lightening before death. In a few hours he was gone." Melbourne's words are calm and he went back to work at once, to all outward appearance his usual smiling self. But Augustus was his only child, and he had loved him with the ardour of a starved and tender heart. The event cast a greyer shadow on the last months of 1836.

There was nothing to dissipate it in his professional life. The Government continued, as it had for some months past, to jolt and creak along its accustomed round, checked and harassed as before by King and Peers, Irish and Radicals. The King's moods were various. Violently out of temper during August, he was sufficiently softened by November to send his Ministers an invitation to dinner, accompanied by the alarming proviso that he expected them each to drink two bottles of wine. In December, however, he had turned against them once more: and, though his experiences in 1834 had taught him not to try and get rid of them on his own initiative, he remained for the rest of his reign hostile. The House of Lords, too, was very obstreperous. It threw out the Irish Church Bill at the end of 1836; mainly because it still objected to the clause appropriating Church revenue to secular purposes. Melbourne took the opportunity to persuade his colleagues to drop this clause. The House of Lords was not sufficiently pacified to pass the Bill; and the Irish were very much annoyed. One evening in December sitting at Lord Sefton's, Creevey told Melbourne that he had heard O'Connell was likely to stop supporting the Government.

"God!" remarked Melbourne with placid interest. "It's a curious thing—two or three people have said the same thing to me"—and then after a pause, "God, perhaps it is so!" Creevey was amazed at the detachment with which the Prime Minister seemed to contemplate an event that must lead to the downfall of his Government. In fact O'Connell still preferred the Whigs to the Tories and so did not withdraw his support. His followers, however, were displeased. So were the Radicals. Every concession to the opposition made them harder to control. Meanwhile the Government appeared so weak that moderate opinion in the country was veering more and more round to Peel. The effect of all this was to exhaust the patience of Ministers to breaking point. John Russell began periodically threatening resignation again; and from the beginning of 1836 there was a growing party in the Cabinet who wanted to stop compromise, even if it meant that the Government went out. Melbourne felt a good deal of sympathy with them. The strain of accommodating himself to the King's temper and what he called "Peel's low creeping policy" was becoming more than he could bear. But his view of the general political situation had not altered, and against his private inclinations he still thought the Whigs ought to stick on. "A Minister has no more right to treat a case as desperate than a physician," he remarked, "events are too uncertain and results differ too much from anticipation, to permit such conduct." As late as May, 1837, he is still telling John Russell that he feared lest the fall of the Whigs might throw the country into a dangerous chaos. All the same, he cannot have thought the Government able to hang on much longer.

If it should fall, Melbourne's career might well seem to have come to its end. The Whig wave was spent, the Tories were likely to be in for a considerable time. Melbourne was fifty-seven, and old for his years: it was improbable that he would be Prime Minister again. Dawning late, his difficult, frustrated, unrewarding day of eminence looked as if it would soon be over. In fact his unpredictable fate had yet one more surprise in store for him. The most brilliant phase of his whole history was just round the corner.

## CHAPTER V

# THE QUEEN: FIRST PHASE

## (1)

IN THE middle of May, 1837, political circles in London were thrown into fresh agitation by an unforeseen event. King William IV fell dangerously ill. After several weeks hovering between life and death, he breathed his last in the early hours of 20th June. At nine o'clock of the same morning the Prime Minister, in the full dress uniform of a Privy Councillor, arrived at Kensington Palace to pay his respects to the new Queen. He was ushered into a small room, where he found himself alone in the presence of a round-cheeked, blue-eyed little figure, dressed very plainly in deep mourning, who with an air at once childish and regal held out her hand for him to kiss. In artless words and a sweet, clear treble, she told Melbourne that she wished him and his colleagues to continue in office; and then listened with attention, while he read to her the speech he had written for her to make later in the morning to the Privy Council. He asked if she would like to be supported by the chief officers of her realm on entering the room at this, her first public appearance as a sovereign. The Queen replied, at once and with composure, No—she preferred to come in alone. Melbourne then kissed hands again and withdrew. A short time before the Council, he returned in case she wanted any further advice as to how to conduct herself at it. He need hardly have bothered. Once or twice, the Queen was observed to look enquiringly at her Prime Minister as if in doubt what to do next; but for the most part, she amazed all beholders by the modest and graceful self-possession with which, in the face of a large and august audience, she went through the stately ceremonies of her inauguration. After dinner that night, Melbourne came back once more for an hour's leisurely talk with her. "I had a very important and very *comfortable* conversation with him," wrote the Queen in her diary that evening.

It was to be the first of many such. The eighteen-year-old

Queen needed someone to instruct her as to how to conduct herself in her new and difficult role. In the ordinary way this would have been done by some responsible and experienced person appointed as confidential secretary for the purpose. It was not easy, however, to find the right man; for if he were intelligent enough for the work, he was likely to have ideas of his own about political affairs which might well conflict with those of the Government. The last thing Melbourne wanted was an independent power behind the Throne. Nor did he intend, if he could help it, that the new monarch should be as hostile to the Government as the old had been. All these considerations made him decide to take on the secretary's work himself. This meant that he saw the Queen constantly. He visited her at least twice a day: she saw him alone in her own private sitting-room where she received no other visitor. They also communicated by letter, he wrote to her and she wrote to him sometimes as often as three times a day. Three or four times a week at least he dined. Whoever the guests might be, Melbourne sat on the Queen's left, and after dinner she spent most of her time talking to him. A month or two later she went to take up residence at Windsor. But this change did not mean any break in their association. Melbourne wrote as often as ever and at greater length. He also went down to stay. There, in addition to the daily conference and evening relaxation with each other, he would accompany her out riding. Altogether it can be calculated that in these first years of her reign Melbourne spent four or five hours of every day talking or writing to his royal mistress. No doubt he felt it his duty to do so; but he was not the man to carry out a duty so rigorously, if it went against his inclinations. As a matter of fact, all his inclinations were in its favour; what had begun as a duty very soon turned into an intense pleasure. These months saw the birth and quick maturing of the most precious personal relationship that he had known since the first happy days of his marriage with Caroline thirty-two years before.

It was a very different sort of relationship. For apart from their unlikeness in age and situation, the two women involved were so different. The young Queen's personality, however, was just as compelling as Caroline's and, in its own way, as exceptional. Not that she was complex or eccentric. On the contrary, her simple and formidable character was compounded of a few basic and universal elements. By nature she was almost all the things that the typical woman is alleged to be by those who have the temerity to generalize on the subject; instinctive, personal, unintellectual, partizan, interested in detail, viewing things in the concrete rather than the abstract, and with a profound natural reverence for the secure and the respectable. With these common qualities of her sex, the Queen possessed also those of her age. Like most of the eighteen-year-old girls who were her subjects, she was innocent and enthusiastic, enjoyed dancing and dress, set store by anniversaries and mementoes and celebrations, blushed and burst out laughing, bubbled over with sentiment for her pet dog and her old home. And not in any particularly refined or rarefied way; though regal, she was not aristocratic as the English understand the term. The healthy, homely German blood which coursed through her veins had imparted a commonplace, even a bourgeois tinge to her taste. But if her nature was normal, her character was not. It was too abnormally high-powered for one thing. Her enjoyments were more rapturous than the average girl's, her sentimentality more unbridled, her interest in detail more inexhaustible, her partizanship more violent, her innocence more dewy. Some strain in her —once again it may have come from Germany—had endowed her with an extravagant force of temperament; so that the ordinary in her was magnified to a degree where it became extraordinary.

To this startling fervour of feeling she added a startling simplicity of vision. Through her childlike eyes she saw the world as naïvely, literally and absolutely as a child. All facts came fresh to her. "To hear the people speaking German and to see the German soldiers, etc. seemed to me so singular," she notes a year or two later, on her first visit to Germany. Her judgments were as simple as her vision. They were often shrewd, but never subtle and never tentative. Her mind was incapable of entertaining a doubt or a half shade. Things were frivolous or serious, sad or cheerful, right or wrong. Particularly right or wrong: childish vision went along with a child's ruthless unsleeping moralism. And its ruthless candour, too: as a little girl, it was noticed that though rebellious and passionate, the Princess could always be trusted to be rigidly truthful. At eighteen she was just as incapable of simulating a feeling or telling a lie. As she spoke, so she acted. The most formidably extreme of all her extreme qualities was her strength of character. Here she was not childish, nor feminine—if indeed weakness be a feminine characteristic. No one was ever less the creature of whim or vacillating impulse. Once she had made up her mind what she ought to do, she adhered inflexibly to it, however hard it might be for her and whether other people liked it or not. It was not in her to compromise. If other people were wrong, it would be wrong of her to give in to them.

The peculiarities of her nature had been sharpened by the circumstances of her upbringing. Her mother, the Duchess of Kent, suspicious and jealous of her royal in-laws, was determined that her daughter should not fall under their influence. The result was that the Princess spent her childhood in a strange, conventual seclusion, almost entirely in the company of women—notably her mother and her governess, Baroness Lehzen, who regulated and supervised every hour of her day. She was never allowed to be alone; she slept in her mother's room: never did she see anyone by herself except her mother and governess: if she kept a diary it had always to be shown to Lehzen. Very few grown-up visitors came to the house; and except for the daughter of her mother's secretary, or on the rare occasions when her German cousins came to stay, she did not have the chance of playing with other children. No window on the ordinary humdrum world was ever opened to let a whiff of fresh air into the soft, stifling atmosphere of meticulous feminine triviality and gushing feminine emotion which pervaded Kensington Palace.

But if her childhood was secluded, it was not obscure. As the future Queen of England, the Princess realized she was a personage of unequalled importance; and, as such, treated differently from other children. People did not bow and curtsey to other children: other children were not taught singing and dancing, as she was, by the most famous public performers in the world: other children were not prepared for Confirmation by the Archbishop of Canterbury himself. And with the glory of great position she was early introduced to its troubles. Uneasy lies the head that wears a crown, says the poet; and the head destined for a crown is hardly more comfortable. The four years before her accession, the Princess was the centre of a continuous turmoil of intrigue and conflict. There was the conflict between the King and her mother. The Duchess of Kent, a short, stout, foolish woman, rustling self-importantly about in velvet and ostrich plumes, was intoxicated by the idea of herself as mother to a future monarch; all the more because she considered she had never been treated by the English Royal Family with the respect due to her. Accordingly, at the same time that she strove to keep her daughter from them, she was always making efforts to bring her into prominence on her own; demanded that the Fleet should fire a salute in her daughter's honour when she was at the seaside, and paraded her round the country on official visits without getting the King's permission. She also intrigued with disaffected politicians, notably Durham, with the vague idea of creating a sort of Princess's Party in Parliament. The irascible William IV reacted violently against these proceedings of his sister-in-law. He forbade the Navy to fire a salute and incessantly abused the Duchess to his Ministers. On one of the rare occasions when she paid him a visit, he suddenly rose at the end of dinner and denounced her to the company in unmeasured and naval terms for deliberately keeping his beloved niece from him. The poor little Princess burst into tears of embarrassment. Thus early was she aware of herself as a bone of contention.

The King was not the only person trying to get control over her. Her uncle, Leopold, King of the Belgians, was a far-sighted statesman well aware of the political advantages of having a niece on the throne of powerful England. At his visits, therefore, and in a series of letters in which political advice, pious aspirations and demonstrations of highflown affection were artfully blended, he sought to get her under his influence. The Princess did not resent this, for Uncle Leopold was always tactful; but she realized that his views were not always the same as her mother's or her Uncle William's, and that she must be careful how far she committed herself to them. This added another complication to the already complex situation in which she found herself.

There was a more disturbing complication to face nearer home. Life at Kensington Palace, to outward appearance so tranquil, was in reality a scene of strife. On the one side stood the Duchess and her confidential secretary, Sir John Conroy, an intriguing vulgarian who saw in his position the means to advancement. He had found the friendless Duchess an easy prey and she soon became completely dominated by him. It was he who instigated her progresses and political *démarches*. Opposed to him was Baroness Lehzen, who rightly thought that his activities were not in the best interest of her royal charge. Her hostility was sharpened by the fact that Conroy together with the Duchess's maid of honour, Lady Flora Hastings, made fun of her German passion for caraway seeds. Friction between the two factions cooped up together in the segregated Palace was continuous and, though the occasions of dispute were trifling enough, they were the symptoms of a bitter animosity which poisoned the whole atmosphere which the young Princess breathed.

Such an upbringing, at once so strictly regulated and emotionally so disturbed, would have crushed an ordinary girl. It served to reveal that the Princess was very far from ordinary: for her character only gained strength from the ordeal. All the same, it profoundly affected her. On the one hand, the fact that she was so cut off from the world increased her *naïveté*. On the other, consciousness of her royal position increased her innate self-confidence. She took for granted that it was her natural right to be obeyed. So far, education had served to intensify the qualities with which she was born. But it also curiously modified them. The quarrels and hidden plots of which she found herself the centre undermined her sense of security; so that the spontaneous candour of her nature was checked and she became cautious and distrustful. Distrustful, too, of the person with whom a child should feel safest—of her own mother! For the Princess did not take the Duchess of Kent's side in her endless quarrels. William IV had been kind to her; now and again she complained violently that she was not allowed to see more of her uncle. About Conroy she felt even more strongly. Indeed, she actually hated him: and her hatred chilled any affection which she may have had for her mother. What made her feel so strongly on the subject is mysterious. Scandal had it that Conroy and the Duchess were lovers, and that the Princess had discovered them in each other's arms.

There is no reliable evidence for this sensational story. What is more sure is that the Duchess and Conroy did plot to have the Princess's time for coming of age delayed so that, should William IV die while she was still in her 'teens, the Duchess might become Regent with Conroy as the power behind the throne. If the Princess found this out, it was quite enough to put her into a passion of righteous wrath. Anyway, whatever the cause, for two or three years she had been forced to live on outwardly submissive and affectionate terms with people she distrusted and disliked. The consequence was that, continually on her guard and unable to give voice to the angry emotions that boiled within her, she had employed all her extraordinary power of will in teaching herself to be precociously self-controlled, precociously prudent and precociously secretive. Since she was incapable of saying what she did not think, she learned to say nothing at all; and to bide her time. Altogether, nature and circumstances had combined to make the eighteen-year-old girl who ascended to the Throne of England in June, 1837, an extraordinary and paradoxical mixture: blending a child's simplicity and a child's uninhibited violence of feeling with the self-command of a mature woman and the unhesitating authority of a born monarch.

This last quality showed itself at once, and alarmingly. "Since it has pleased providence to place me in this situation," runs the entry in her diary on the day of her accession, "I shall do my utmost to fulfil my duty towards my country; I am very young and perhaps in many, though not all things, inexperienced. But I am sure that very few have more real good will and more real desire to do what is fit and right than I have." There was no doubt in her mind that one particular course of action was fit and right. It was all over for the Duchess of Kent and her schemes. Already, when William IV lay dying, the Princess had taken the opportunity to have a blazing row about Conroy with her mother; with the result that the Duchess, so rumour ran, asserted her parental rights and locked her daughter up in her room. It was foolish of her, she always was foolish. On her accession the Queen took action. Conroy was given an annuity but banished from her presence, and the Duchess put firmly in her place. She asked, so the story runs, if there was anything she could do for her daughter. "I should like

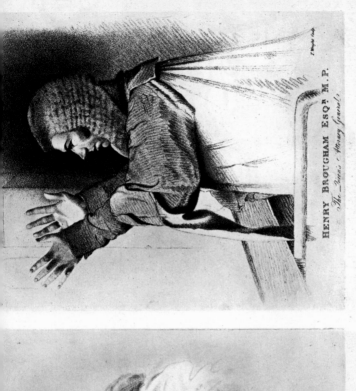

HENRY BROUGHAM ESQᴿ M.P.
The _Queen's Attorney General!

HENRY, 1st BARON BROUGHAM AND VAUX

THE HON. MRS. NORTON

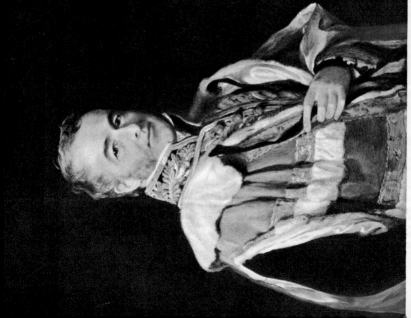

to be left alone," replied the Queen. Not only did she order that her bed should be removed out of the Duchess's room at once, but she also had dinner by herself. However, she did not attempt to rely completely on her own resources. Instinctively she looked about for someone to guide her steps through the unknown world in which she found herself. This came partly from consciousness of her own inexperience, but still more from her extreme femininity, a femininity which made her, for all her strength of will, the reverse of independent-minded in coming to a judgment on general and impersonal matters. The fact that she was a woman also meant she sought for her guide among the male sex. For the time being indeed, sex in its extreme manifestations was latent in her. She was emotionally at the schoolgirl stage, looking less for a lover than for a hero, for some wise, benignant, fatherly figure on whom she could pour out all her youthful capacity for admiration. Other girls find such a man in some sympathetic schoolmaster or kindly clergyman: Queen Victoria found it in her Prime Minister.

Indeed, no one could have filled the role better. For in addition to being wise and benignant, he was also extremely handsome, an accomplished master in the art of pleasing women, and one of the most fascinating talkers in Europe. As a matter of fact the Queen does not seem to have wholly realized how much of his attraction for her was due to these less serious qualities. In her diary she harps on his moral virtues; "a most truly honest, straightforward and noble-minded man," she notes, "there are not many like him in this world of deceit." Above all, not Sir John Conroy, she implies! And certainly, after Conroy it must have been pleasant to deal with someone who was a gentleman in the highest sense of that old-fashioned word. But all Melbourne's virtues could not have made the impression on her that they did, had they not been enhanced by his dark, charming eyes, his virile elegance, and his light ironic sweetness. After all, it was soon to appear that she much preferred him to the praiseworthy Sir Robert Peel, as in later years she was to prefer Disraeli to Gladstone. These are not the sentiments of one who, whatever her avowed principles, does in fact set solemn conscientious virtue above the charms and the graces. Perhaps, like many of the professionally respectable, Queen Victoria felt unexpectedly exhilarated by the company of

K

those who looked on the moral law in a more light-hearted spirit than she was able to do herself. Whatever the reason, Melbourne did exactly satisfy the Queen's emotional needs at this phase in her development. He became the object of her schoolgirl hero-worship; and this, like everything else about her, was more single-mindedly extreme than an ordinary schoolgirl could feel. People noticed that her eyes followed him wherever he went and that, if he left the room, an involuntary sigh escaped her lips.

He was equally drawn to her. Now that he was cut off from Mrs. Norton there was no woman in his life: and he could not do without one. No longer, however, did he wish to take on the role of lover, even in the most platonic sense of the word: he was too old. On the other hand, with age, his frustrated paternal instinct more and more felt the need of an outlet. He had reached the stage in life when a man of his type tends to turn for emotional satisfaction to a daughter; to someone to whom he can be a mentor— Melbourne had always liked being a mentor—and on whom he can lavish a tenderness that involves none of the ardours and tempests inseparable from most love affairs. The Queen supplied his requirements. Artless youth had always appealed to him; and in this instance its attraction was enhanced by worldly position. A young Queen is in herself a romantic personage, especially to a man with Melbourne's imaginative sense of the poetry of history. Exquisitely he appreciated the incongruous contrast provided by the childish figure and the august, venerable role it was called upon to play. Moreover, apart from her age and her situation, the Queen's character was one in itself to attract him. In most ways, no doubt, she was wonderfully unlike Caroline Lamb and Caroline Norton. But she did share with them the distinctive temperamental quality which had always appealed to him in women; the vitality, the positiveness, the high-hearted unhesitating response to life which were at once an entertainment to his own subtle melancholy scepticism and also its needed antidote. She added to them also an innocent straightforwardness which the other women in his life had not provided and which was infinitely refreshing to a spirit wearied and disillusioned by over fifty years' experience of the great world. "She is the honestest person I have ever known," he once said. "The only difficulty is to make her see that you cannot always go straight forward, that you must go round about some-times." Finally, he responded to her charm. For the Queen had charm; especially at eighteen years old before the soft contours of her immature character had been hardened by care and power; the charm of her ingenuousness and her dignity, her literalness and her enthusiasm, her composure and her unselfconsciousness, her childish gravity and her childlike sense of fun, all mingling to-gether in a comical, delicious Alice in Wonderland-like blend. Melbourne had the trained taste to savour its quality to the full. The Queen amused him and touched him and stirred his admira-tion and won his heart. For though his feeling for her was not so rapturous and unbridled as was hers for him, yet it went far deeper. He had been born with an intense gift for affection, but it had been starved of its proper fulfilment during a life-time; so that now, with a reckless completeness, he poured it all out on her. At once his sovereign, his daughter and the last love of his life, Queen Vic-toria inspired Melbourne with a sentiment tenderer if not more vehement than he had ever felt before.

As he felt, so he appeared. "I have seen the Queen with her Prime Minister," reported the sharp-eyed Princess Lieven in July. "When he is with her he looks loving, contented, a little pleased with himself; respectful, at his ease, as if accustomed to take first place in the circle, and dreamy and gay—all mixed up together." Other people made similar observations. So intimate an association between monarch and first Minister was too un-usual not to stir comment. But the comments were kindly. The relationship was too obviously and too charmingly innocent for people to want to be malicious about it. They made jokes, but they were good-natured jokes. "I hope you are amused at the re-port of Lord Melbourne being likely to marry the Queen," writes Lady Grey laughingly to Creevey. "For my part I have no objec-tion."

It was the climax of Melbourne's career. Never had he been so eminent; and never had he been so admired. It was right this should be so. For it was the first and only time that the public and private strains in him were working to harmony at one end. As we have seen, he was not primarily a public character. In spite of the fact that he became Prime Minister of England, he remained to the end of his day, a detached spectator, a little outside the political scene. His nature fulfilled itself more significantly and most profoundly in personal relationships; and especially with women. Now fate had willed that his duty as Prime Minister should involve him in a close personal relationship with a woman: so that at last he was able to put his whole self into his professional and official work.

It also happened to be the phase of his life in which we know most about him. The Queen kept a diary. With typical self-command she managed, in spite of all the distractions of her new life, to spend time every evening meticulously recording the happenings of the day. The most important happening was always her hours with Melbourne: with the consequence that we find in her pages an intimate day-to-day account of him, such as we get nowhere else. It is a wonderfully vivid account too. For the Queen was a born reporter. Her untiring interest in life and her taste for detail made her notice so much; while her literalness, her candour and her careful accuracy stopped her from colouring or altering what she noticed, in any way. When she came to describe Lord M.—so she always referred to him—the intensity of her feeling increased her natural powers. She observed him with the closeness of a Boswell. Indeed, there are moments when the Queen does oddly remind us of Boswell; an innocent schoolgirl Boswell, but with the same surprising mixture of *naïveté* and perceptiveness, unselfconscious enthusiasm and native shrewdness. Inevitably her picture has its limitations. She does not give us the whole Melbourne; but, rather, the bowdlerized version of him, which was all he was able, with propriety, to present to her view. Melbourne could not swear or lounge about, or put his feet up on the sofa at Buckingham Palace as he could at Brooks's Club. Instead, seated upright on a stiff little chair, he listened and replied to her quietly and in terms which he took care to keep strictly decorous. The matter of his talk was similarly modified. His "dashing opinions", his paradoxes and audacities appear in softened form. Nor could he exhibit to her either the depths of his scepticism, or the full freedom of his moral views. "He is so truly excellent and moral," exclaims the Queen in lyrical approval, "he has such a strong feeling against immorality and wickedness!"

All this meant his imposing such a change on his habits and manners that people both then and since have wondered that he did not feel himself intolerably irked and cramped. How could he, they ask, after the sophisticated ease of social life at Holland and Devonshire House, put up with the mixture of nursery simplicity and Court stiffness which surrounded the Queen? In point of fact, he does not seem to have minded it a bit. He had had enough of Holland and Devonshire Houses to last him a life-time. He was glad of a change. The nursery atmosphere soothed and refreshed his spirit inexpressibly. As for the Court stiffness, Melbourne was so practised a man of the world, so supple to respond to an alteration in social atmosphere, that he adapted himself to it without difficulty or effort.

Nor, in fact, did he have to suppress any essential characteristics of his personality. Shakespeare is unmistakably Shakespeare, even in Bowdler's version: Melbourne is unmistakably Melbourne even when seen through the eyes of the eighteen-year-old Queen Victoria. Some important aspects of his nature, indeed, found scope to show themselves in her company as they did not find it at Holland House. Mankind relaxes in the nursery: Melbourne could give rein there to his sensitive tenderness, his taste for gay, whimsical nonsense and his playful interest in little things in a way that is not revealed in any other descriptions of him. These things were just as characteristic of him, as his oaths and his paradoxes. Moreover, the basic attitude to life that came out in his talks with the Queen is the same as that in his letters to his colleagues, though it is less trenchantly expressed. Even the moralism she noticed in him was not an inconsistency. No doubt he thought it right to impress orthodox moral views upon her: for experience under George IV and William IV had taught him that it was much better for the monarchy that it should be respectable. Besides he appreciated the charm of her innocence so affectionately that he shrank from the idea of its being tarnished. Yet when it came to advising her as to what she ought to think or do in particular and practical issues, he did not take an uncomfortably moral line. She disliked Lord Lyndhurst, she once said to him, because he was a bad man. "Do you dislike all bad men?" said Melbourne, amused, "for that comprises a large number!" He was always for tolerance: always he warned her against expecting too much from anyone or anything. While, over the whole texture of his talk sparkled, though with a tempered gleam, the light of his irrepressible irony.

The Queen did not always perceive its presence. But that only adds to the reader's fun. It is impossible not to smile at the contrast between the joyous ambiguity of some of Melbourne's remarks and the artless gravity with which they are recorded. The subject of the new railroads comes up. "People who talk much of railroads and bridges are generally Liberals," says Melbourne: conscientiously the Queen notes down this valuable item of political information. Or the conversation turned on the Irvingite sect who proclaimed that they had been vouchsafed a divine revelation; "People should be quite sure," said Melbourne, "when they have any of these revelations from *what* quarter they come!" Once again the Queen wrote his words down as an important point to be remembered. Or, "I observed to Lord Melbourne," she writes, "that there were not many good preachers. He replied in the affirmative and added, 'But there are not many good anything', which is *very true*!" One day she asked him if she ought to go to church twice on Sunday, and he answered that it was unnecessary. "George III, Lord M. says, never went twice though a strict man, and was not at all for these puritanical notions; and he is the man, Lord M. says, to look to in all these matters."

More often, however, the Queen realizes when Melbourne is saying something amusing and laughs delightedly in response. But she is not always clear as to what exactly she is laughing at. All she knows for certain is that Lord M. is being "funny". "Spoke of my having got a letter from Feodore"—her cousin who had just returned home after paying the Queen a visit—"Lord M. said funnily, 'When these people get back among their children they do not dress, and there is nothing so bad for a woman'"; or, discussing young Lord Douro's engagement, "They said Lord Douro had been out shopping with the young lady; Lord M. said, 'Shopping is very demonstrative', which made us all laugh": or, "He examined my bouquet and talked of forcing flowers, and said in his funny way, 'Forcing flowers is questionable.'"

One is tempted to go on quoting for ever. Indeed, the story of

Melbourne's relation with the Queen confronts his biographer with a peculiar difficulty. Up till then he has had to construct his image of his subject's personality from scraps of information scattered few and far between, over political diaries, reports of public speeches and the records of ministerial negotiations. Now, suddenly, he is presented with a document, every paragraph of which contains something to enrich and amplify his portrait. He longs to put everything in. But to do so would mean including so much that the proportion of his general design would be fatally distorted. All he can do is, as it were, to let the reader look over his shoulder while, pausing now and again, he turns the pages of the Queen's diary.

There the idyllic tale of their first years together unfolds itself. For idyllic it is. There is something tranquil and garden-like about its atmosphere; and fresh too. Melbourne at this stage of his history has been aptly and beautifully described as an "Autumn rose". But he is an autumn rose blooming miraculously in springtime, the green, budding springtime of the new Victorian epoch, all ribbons and muslin frills and girlish smiles and tears and blushes and propriety. Vernal sunshine softly irradiates the stately background of Court ceremonial, against which move the two figures entrancedly absorbed in each other; the distinguished elderly gentleman bending forward in respectful devotion and the child Queen gazing rapt and eager up at him; and now her brows are knit with the effort of concentration as she tries to grasp some point in the British Constitution which he is explaining to her, and now she breaks into a peal of laughter, showing her little rosy gums, as he makes one of his unexpected comical remarks, and he, responding, throws back his head in one of his own rollicking laughs. Sometimes the scene is Buckingham Palace, sometimes battlemented Windsor: for a week or two in October, 1837, it is the incongruously exotic flamboyance of George IV's pavilion at Brighton. We see the pair in the morning alone in her little sitting-room—she in a chair, he in another "or on a sofa close to me"; we see them cantering together through the turfy glades of Richmond or Windsor Parks; we see them in the evening bent over the chess-board or seated at a lamp-lit table beneath the shadows of the high palace ceiling, looking at albums of prints representing historical figures, or after paintings by Old Masters. There were the great public occasions too; the Military Review at Windsor Park where from a carriage he watched her riding in flowing habit and with bright, proud glance down the red-coated lines of troops; and the Eton festival of Montem when they drove down together to be welcomed by the boys gallantly tricked out in military uniform and Cavalier fancy dress; and the opening of Parliament when she read her Speech from the Throne and he stood at its steps listening; and, above all, the Coronation. Melbourne carried the Sword of State in the procession. "He looked awkward and uncouth," said the young Disraeli, satirically observing the scene, "with his coronet cocked over his nose and his robes under his feet, holding the Sword of State like a butcher." But not thus did the Queen see him. "My excellent Lord Melbourne who stood very close to me during the whole ceremony was completely overcome . . . he gave me *such* a kind, and I may say, *fatherly* look."

For however crowded and official the scene she is describing, he is always in the picture, and more often than not in its centre. She noticed every fleeting nuance of his moods, every typical detail of his appearance, habits and manner; the odd, comical grimaces he made expressive of disgust or amusement; the size of his appetite, "He has eaten three chops and a grouse for breakfast," she relates on one occasion; his description of his room, "all wax and ink, where I sit up to my neck in books"; the fact that he is wearing a new olive-green velvet waistcoat; how absent-minded he became when tired and overworked—suddenly going off to sleep in company, or talking to himself in an unintelligible murmur so that at first she finds herself looking round, thinking that he is addressing her; his old-fashioned way of pronouncing his words, "goold" and "Room" for gold and Rome. Above all, she notices what he says. Nine-tenths of the diary is a record of Melbourne's conversation.

It was of a very varied kind. Much of it was necessarily about business. Every day he brought her the news of what was happening in Cabinet and Parliament; how John Russell was making difficulties about the ballot question, or Brougham trying to trip up the Government in debate in the House of Lords. There was the foreign news too: a hitch was occurring in our relations with Portugal, or there was trouble arising in our Jamaican and Canadian

Colonies. To make these things clear, generally entailed some account of previous events, and explanation of the wider issues involved. Melbourne found himself giving informal instruction to the Queen about the working of the English political system, or the recent history of the Continent. He also put her in the know about the characters of the public men, English and foreign, she might have to deal with. "John Russell," he said, "has feeling but he don't show it, his manner is rather short"; Lord Grey had not a bad temper but flew into a passion when you first told him anything; "The Duke of Wellington is amazingly sensible to attention. Nothing pleases him so much as when one asks his opinion about anything"; "Lord Stanley is a man of great abilities but says things out of place and just what he ought not to say"; "Lord Howick has a fretful, uneasy temper, but is better than he used to be"; M. Sebastiani, the French Ambassador, "slow and pompous, but clear and clever"; Don Migual di Alava, the Spanish General, had "that very open, honest manner which is never to be trusted".

Melbourne was, in fact, giving her a thorough political education. He did it very well, explaining things in a brief, colloquial, simple way which was easy for her to understand and not at all boring; and often illuminating his point by some lively anecdote which helped her to remember it. He was also careful not to appear to condescend to her ignorance. Alike in his talk and his letters, he addresses her on terms of equality and with an implied respect for her judgment. The substance of what he said was also adapted to suit her special requirements. He did not try to give her a political philosophy; there is nothing in the diaries about the theory of constitutional monarchy, or the trend and deeper significance of world events. The Queen's mind, Melbourne realized, was too concrete to grasp such things and besides, though he much enjoyed speculating about them himself, he had long ago given up thinking it served any useful purpose. What the Queen needed, in his view, was practical guidance as to what line she ought to pursue in the conduct of day-to-day business. This mainly meant for Melbourne any line which kept things running smoothly. To help her achieve this end he sought all the time to cultivate two qualities in her. The first was good will. If the Queen could be persuaded to like a man or, at any rate, to see his point of view, she would find him easier to get on with. In consequence, though Melbourne always told her frankly what he thought about people, his tone in speaking of them, except in a few instances like that of Don Migual di Alava, was friendly. He says what he can in their favour. And the few general maxims that do fall from his lips are on the side of sympathetic tolerance. "If people are made to do what they dislike, you must allow for a little ill-humour"; and "everything works for the best, even the worst intentions"; and "it is idle to talk to people of their faults, for, if they knew them, they wouldn't commit them"; and "if you want to influence a person you must not begin by reprimanding him". This last also illustrates the second quality he sought to instil into her, which was tact—this all the more perhaps because he realized that it is rarely found in young and truthful people. Clumsiness, he thought, was often as fatal as ill will. Emphatically he quotes to her the French saying, "*C'est les maladroits qui sont malheureux*".

He does allow his tone to grow sharper when he talks about doctrinaires and doctrinaire schemes, especially radical ones. Wilberforce, he told her, was actuated by good opinions, "but they were very uncomfortable opinions for those he acted with," and he could not bear the proposal to establish Normal schools for educating schoolmasters. "You will see, they will breed the most conceited set of blockheads ever known," he exclaimed, "and will be of no use whatever. . . . Walter Scott was quite right when he said 'Why bother the poor? Leave them alone'." Even these caustic remarks, however, went along with his wish to impress upon her the necessity to make things easier for other people. The type of schoolmaster likely to be produced by the Normal schools would only create quarrelling and discontent; the poor should not be bothered because it was of the first importance that nobody should be bothered: it was mistaken of Wilberforce to insist on his principles, if this involved disregarding the difficulty in which they might involve his colleagues. For, as he told the Queen, "Nobody should be troublesome: they should be made to realize that it is the worst thing there is."

He was her social as well as her political tutor. The Queen felt herself in need of one. Both in conversation and in letters she asked his advice about every detail of her social life. Who should she ask to meet Sir Robert Peel? Was the Duke of Sussex likely to get on with Lord and Lady Cowley? Was she to grant Lord Amelius Beauclerk's request that the aides-de-camps be permitted to wear sashes with their Court uniforms? She could not have found anyone who could help her better than Melbourne in solving these thorny problems. Natural talent assisted by a life-time of experience had made him an expert authority on English aristocratic and fashionable life; its traditions and factions and cliques and customs. Moreover, he was prepared to put the whole of his knowledge at her disposal. In the midst of all his other activities he always found time to give full answers to her queries. Lord and Lady Lansdowne, he said, would be very suitable people to meet Sir Robert Peel, but not Lord and Lady Cowley to meet the Duke of Sussex—he disliked Tories too much. As for Lord Amelius and his sash, Melbourne swept the request aside. "It was always refused by the old King as absurd and ridiculous; as it is—particularly considering Lord Amelius' figure," he remarked tartly. Sometimes Melbourne proffered advice on his own initiative. The Russian Ambassador, he writes, will be offended if he is not asked to dinner soon, and an official called Skinner may be hurt if his wife does not receive an invitation—"she is, Lord Melbourne understands, a vulgar woman, but it may be as well to keep him in good humour".

The Queen was more seriously concerned about her duties as guardian of social morality. Anxiously she asked Melbourne what plays were suitable for her to see, and whether she should allow Mrs. Gore, the fashionable novelist, to dedicate a book to her; and, more generally, should she receive people with bad moral characters at Court. Melbourne was equally fitted to advise her on these subjects. For though easygoing by nature, he had learned by bitter personal experience how foolish it was to disregard the opinion of the world and how important to keep up the right kind of appearance. His advice shows that he had always kept two objects in mind. On the one hand, the Queen should not appear so censorious as to get herself disliked. On the other, she must do nothing that might compromise the dignity of the Crown or tarnish her reputation for virtue. As a matter of fact, there was not much danger of this. Instinctively she leaned to the strict side.

On several occasions we are presented with the unusual spectacle of an old gentleman recommending a young lady not to be quite so nervous of doing something improper. The Queen need not fear, Melbourne said, that Sheridan Knowles' plays were too shocking for her to see, not even one called *The Love Chase*. On the more general question, he thought anyone should be permitted to go to Court who had not been proved guilty of immorality in a law court; "It is better to go according to what has been determined by a Court of Justice and, if there was nothing against them there, to receive and not enquire what their early lives have been." On the whole, however, he clearly thought her strictness was a fault on the right side. He will have a look at Mrs. Gore's book, he tells her, for "Your Majesty is always right to be cautious in such matters". And he was extremely pleased when she told him she thought that it would be improper for her to dance the waltz. "I think you are quite right," he said eagerly, "it is quite right!" Indeed, he took some steps of his own to stiffen Court etiquette. The maids of honour complained that Lord Melbourne would not allow them to walk unchaperoned on the terrace of Windsor for fear of making a bad impression on the populace watching them from below, and though Lady Holland was one of his oldest friends, he desired her not to come to Court, as he feared that the presence there of a divorcée, however distinguished and elderly, might be bad for the Queen's good name.

As the Queen and he got to know each other better, her reserve began gradually to thaw, and she found herself consulting him about intimate and private difficulties. She found the complexities of religious dogma very bewildering. Did Lord Melbourne think this mattered? For herself she felt that one could get oneself inextricably puzzled about such questions and thought it wrong to let this happen. Melbourne agreed: "It is best to believe what is in the Scriptures without considering *what* Christ's nature was. For that is not comprehensible; the Trinity is not comprehensible." The Queen was relieved. "This is all just as *I* feel. . . . Lord M's feeling is so *right*, *just* and *enlightened*." She felt all the more wholeheartedly comforted because Melbourne, whatever his own doubts, never showed any sign of wishing to weaken her faith. On the contrary he told her that a good Christian did not allow himself to brood on insoluble problems, such, for instance, as how was the existence of evil to be reconciled with the idea of a good and omnipotent God. Melbourne had grown into a very different man from the clever and iconoclastic youth who had taken an impish pleasure in undermining Caroline's beliefs during the first years of his marriage. It was not only that he would now have felt it cruel to disillusion the Queen, but also that his love for her stirred the depths of his heart and imagination in such a way as to set vibrating within him that mystical strain that no doubt could ever completely eradicate. We find him reminding her to remember to make her private devotions before her Coronation: and, at one of their early interviews, he read earnestly aloud to her a passage of scripture about the young Solomon, which he thought might bring home to her mind the spiritual significance of her royal position:

"And now, O Lord my God, thou hast made thy servant king instead of David my father; and I am but a little child: I know not how to go out or come in. And thy servant is in the midst of thy people which thou hast chosen, a great people, that cannot be numbered nor counted for multitude. Give therefore thy servant an understanding heart to judge thy people, that I may discern between good and bad: for who is able to judge this thy so great people?"

The ancient solemn words roused an echo in the Queen's heart. Strong character though she was, there were moments when her confidence failed her at the thought of the magnitude of her responsibilities. Sometimes she felt utterly unfit for her station, she told Melbourne. "Never think that," he answered reassuringly. "Try to do your best and leave the rest to fate . . . it never does when people think of what they ought to do and of what they do do."

She consulted him about other personal problems too. Her shyness for instance: she felt so nervous in company, she confided to him, and did not know what to say to people. Melbourne said that the longer one stood thinking, the worse it was. Better to say something commonplace and foolish than nothing at all! He was equally understanding about her difficulties with her mother.

These had not ceased with her accession. The Duchess of Kent, indeed, soon lost any hope she may ever have entertained of exercising political influence over her daughter. The Queen's treatment of her made it too painfully clear that such hopes were vain. The Duchess still remained at Court for appearances sake: but she was assigned apartments far away from the Queen's; mother and daughter met, as a rule, only in public, at dinner or in the drawing-room; if the Duchess wanted to see her alone she had first to send a message requesting an interview. All these arrangements showed the Queen's prudence. But the Duchess not unnaturally felt herself deeply injured by them. Her ample bosom seethed with wounded pride, disappointed ambition and furious jealousy of the two people, Melbourne and Lehzen, whom she considered responsible for her exclusion. And since, unlike her daughter, she was not self-controlled, these emotions found vent in word and action. To have the prestige of her position, if not its power, might be some consolation. She therefore wrote a letter, addressed for some confused reason of her own to the Speaker of the House of Commons, demanding to be given the rank and precedence of the Queen Mother. In time this request reached the Queen who refused it point blank. "It would do my mother no good," she said coldly, "and offend my aunts." The Duchess also relieved her outraged feelings when she was in her daughter's company by saying offensive things to her, disguised as words of warning and advice. One evening she would tell her she thought she had got into the habit of drinking too much wine; on another that she was letting down her dignity by going so often to the theatre. "Mama is always plaguing me," exclaimed the Queen irritably. Meanwhile, the Duchess proclaimed her wrongs to anyone who would listen to her. "There is no future for me, I no longer count for anything," she lamented frantically to Princess Lieven. "For eighteen years this child has been the sole object of my life, and now she is taken from me." Her friends joined their voices to hers. Conroy, in particular, went round London announcing that the Queen had broken her mother's heart by her cruelty. These remarks were repeated to the Queen and added yet further to her annoyance. It was not made less by the news that the Duchess had, by irresponsibly overspending, got herself into financial diffi-

culties which might involve her in a lawsuit extremely discreditable to the reputation of the royal family. The Queen poured this,
and the rest of the long tale of her mother's misdoings, into Melbourne's ears, beseeching his advice and clamouring for his sympathy.

He found it was easy to give. He had already had a lot of trouble
with the Duchess himself. It had begun during William IV's
reign. Her political intrigues were a nuisance to him, so was her
extravagance. The Duchess never seemed to have enough money
for her needs and had no scruple in asking for more. She also demanded furniture for her house and jobs and honours for her
friends, especially, of course, for Conroy. When she was not
bothering Melbourne to do something for her, she was quarrelling
with him. William IV she looked on as her active enemy, and
Melbourne, as his Prime Minister, came in for a share of her hostility. If she was peculiarly annoyed with her brother-in-law she
would refuse to receive communications from Melbourne on the
ground that he, too, must be working against her. Melbourne did
not allow himself to be moved by her goings on. Rows between
members of the royal family in his view were as undesirable as
were every other sort of row. He pursued his usual policy of pacification and strove both to bring the Duchess on to better terms
with the King, and to keep on good terms with her himself. When
William IV proposed forcibly removing the Princess from the care
of her rebellious mother, Melbourne persuaded him to give up the
scheme. And he discouraged the King from proposing any suitor
for the Princess who was likely to be displeasing to the Duchess.
Himself, he presented a front of urbane courtesy to her attacks and
caprices and, though he generally found himself compelled to refuse her requests, tried to soften his refusals by presenting them
agreeably clothed in a cloud of respectful compliment. On one
occasion, for example, we find the Duchess asking that Conroy
should be given a job at the Treasury. Melbourne answered that
he feared Conroy had not sufficient experience, but added, "I
lament this. But from my knowledge of your Highness's exalted
character and patriotic feelings I cannot but anticipate with some
confidence that your Royal Highness will appreciate the motives
by which I have been actuated." It is unlikely that he felt quite so

confident as he professed himself. Finally, during the last months
of William IV's life, the Duchess increased his poor opinion of her
by her intrigues to get herself appointed Regent. Ineffectively she
tried to deceive him into thinking that it was the Princess's wish
that this should be done.

Such experience disposed him to listen sympathetically to the
Queen's complaints. He began to think that he had been mistaken, he told her, in persuading William IV not to remove her
from the Duchess's protection. Indeed he did not try to disguise
his opinion of her mother from the Queen. So far from objecting
to this, the Queen seems to have found it an exhilarating relief.
Together they discussed the Duchess's defects with zest and a
startling candour. "Talked of my dislike of Mama," runs one
entry. "Lord M. said that she was a liar and a hypocrite." "I
never saw so foolish a woman," said Melbourne on another occasion; "Which," comments the Queen, "is very true, and we both
laughed!" Melbourne also pointed out that the Duchess felt no
shame in changing her mind and contradicting one day what she
had said another. "This is, alas, too true, and a sad reality it is!"
noted the Queen in a tone of melancholy satisfaction. Melbourne
agreed that it would be a great mistake for the Duchess to be involved in a lawsuit; but he did not think that this would stop her
embarking on it or appearing in court to give evidence. For as he
remarked, "Ladies are very fond of law and of appearing in courts
of justice and before magistrates." As for her pretensions to
higher rank and precedence, he thought them, he said, a parcel of
nonsense. The Queen told him that her mother publicly signal-
ized the varying degrees of favour in which she held the Baroness
Lehzen by sometimes bowing to her and sometimes refusing to do
so. "As if her doing so or not were such a great thing!" observed
Melbourne with amusement. "It is too absurd!"

All the same, he always worked to improve relations between
mother and daughter. The Duchess, he used to say, was not
primarily to blame for her worst indiscretions. Always they could
be traced back to Conroy's influence. Moreover, he said that it
would make a very bad impression on the public if the Queen was
known to be openly at war with her mother. He urged her, however much she might be provoked, to behave to her with studious

civility. And if she did show signs of softening and made a friendly gesture to the Duchess—sent her a special invitation to a party or dinner—Melbourne hastened to tell her how much it pleased him.

These gestures occurred rarely. Even Melbourne could not persuade the Queen habitually to act so much against the grain of her feeling. But his talks with her about her mother, the sympathetic understanding he showed over this long-hidden and central trouble of her life, bound her to him with an added closeness. "As for the confidence of the Crown," she exclaims, "God knows! No *Minister*, no *friend* EVER possessed it so entirely as this truly excellent Lord Melbourne possesses mine!"

Melbourne's lessons in statesmanship and in personal and social behaviour took place mainly during his official morning visits. At other times the Queen and he talked for pleasure and about every sort of subject. Even then Melbourne was often educating her, though not deliberately. He discoursed to her about literature. The authors he singled out for special mention throw a revealing light on his own taste. As might have been expected, he admired Dr. Johnson's works. "They have deep feeling," he said, "and deep knowledge of human nature." Among poets he put Racine first for beauty of taste and sentiment. It was characteristic of the classic and cosmopolitan nature of Whig culture that Melbourne, unlike the Victorians who followed him, could appreciate Racine. This same Augustan purity of taste qualified his admiration of Shakespeare, though he enjoyed him so intensely. *Hamlet* was one of the finest of Shakespeare's plays, he told the Queen, but he thought its end awkward and horrid. As for *King Lear*, "I have always thought Lear a foolish old man," said Lord M.

They talked about the other arts as well. The Queen was fond of music, Melbourne not so much so. He had never cultivated a taste for it when he was young, he said regretfully. However, she noticed that he listened to her own singing with absorbed attention—this perhaps was evidence of his interest in her rather than his interest in music—and that he venerated Mozart. When the Queen said that she found the music of *Don Giovanni* old-fashioned, Melbourne clasped his hands and cast up his eyes in astonishment. Indeed he had far too much native aesthetic sensibility not to realize what music could mean to people, even if he

did not respond to it intensely himself. "She has not much feeling
for the beautiful," he remarked to the Queen about some lady of
their acquaintance, "she praises the opera without feeling." He
was more at home with pictures. In harmony with his liking for
Racine and Mozart, he preferred the classic and ideal nobility of
the High Renaissance Italian artists to the realism of Flanders. It
did not surprise him that the Italians should never tire of painting
the Holy Family. "After all," he said, "a woman and child is the
most beautiful subject one could have."

Foreign nations, their characters and habits, were another subject of their talks. The Queen picked up some curious information
from Melbourne about them. The fact that the Indians burned
their widows, for instance—"not a good custom," Melbourne
said: and he explained that the natives in New Zealand, though a
fine race, had one unfortunate fault. "They eat men; and they
say it is impossible to break them of it; they say it is the best
thing!" The Queen was a little worried because Melbourne
laughed so much at the Germans, to whom she felt bound by the
tie of kinship. She told him she thought he disliked them. Laughing more than ever, he denied it. "I have a great opinion of their
talents, but not of their beauty," he explained. Melbourne's
favourite theme of instruction, however, was history. Here it was
that he blended useful information and entertainment most bril-
liantly. He conveyed to her easily and tersely the essential facts
she ought to know about the Conquest of Canada or the Civil
War, or whatever other famous events came up in the conversation, and made them live for her by the vivid way he described the
characters involved. His view of these was characteristic. As always, he spoke up for Henry VIII; "those women bothered him
so," he remarked surprisingly when speaking of Henry VIII's
treatment of his wives. But he condemned the cruelty of Edward
III; and deplored religious bigotry, alike in Protestant Edward
VI, Popish Mary and the rationalist Spanish statesmen who had
lately suppressed the monasteries and turned the monks out to
earn their living on the land: "To those accustomed to pass their
lives in prayer, to be told to dig is hard," Melbourne observed
with an ironical commonsense. Among foreign statesmen he
praised the moderate Sully, but spoke disapprovingly of Richelieu

and Mazarin: "Shocking fellows!" said Melbourne. He also made the past alive by his knowledge of the manners of past periods. Conditions at the Court of Queen Elizabeth were so primitive, he related, that gentlemen and Maids of Honour slept in the same room only divided from each other by a partition that did not reach the ceiling. The Queen was much amused to hear that the Maids of Honour petitioned that it should be made higher in order to stop the gentlemen climbing up and looking over. "It was a very right feeling of the Maids of Honour!" said Melbourne with his usual laugh. One evening he looked through a volume of Lodge's portraits with her. These gave him an opportunity of telling her about Raleigh and Hobbes, and Leibniz, and Addison, and other eminent persons. The Queen was enthralled. "I wish I had time to write down all the clever observations about *all*. It is quite a *delight* for me to hear him speak about these things; he has such *stores* of knowledge; such a wonderful memory; he knows about everybody and everything; *who* they were, and *what* they did; and he imparts his knowledge in such a kind and agreeable manner; it does me a *world* of good; and his conversations always improve one greatly."

It was even more interesting and delightful when they got on to more recent times and he talked about what he remembered himself, the social and political history of the last fifty years; about George III and his sons, and Mrs. Fitzherbert and Pitt—"a tall, thin man with a red face who drank amazingly"—and Fox and the Hollands and Madame de Staël with her square countenance and "fine full arms which she was fond of showing", and Byron and the lovely Duchess of Rutland, and the rest of the statesmen and wits and beauties who had made brilliant the distant past of his youth. As the Queen listened, the florid ghosts of the dead world of the Regency rose for a brief hour before her mental eye, to haunt the decorous salons of early Victorian Buckingham Palace. Through the midst of them moved the ghost of the young Melbourne himself. His reminiscences of social life turned often into personal reminiscences; of his childhood and his schooldays at Eton, where he wore his hair long—"How handsome he must have looked!" thought the Queen—of Cambridge, Brocket and Melbourne House. The Queen was inquisitive about everything connected

with him, asked him endlessly about his home, his mother, his
brothers and sisters. Above all, she was extremely inquisitive about
the woman he had loved, his wife. She could not very well ask
him about her directly; but she picked up any information she
could from others; notably the Duchess of Sutherland, who told
her some such strange and shocking stories about Caroline Lamb,
as to arouse all her royal indignation on behalf of her hero. "What
a dreadful thing that his wife should have embittered his life,
which it should have been her pride to render a happy one," she
exclaimed, ". . . he has now the greatest horror of any woman who
is in any way eccentric or extraordinary, which shows how very
much he must have suffered from such a wife!"

Indeed he had. An incident which occurred about this time re-
calls to us how acute his suffering had been. Melbourne's cousin,
who was also Byron's widow, came to live in Windsor in the first
months of 1838, and he went to call on her. They had not met for
many years, not, so far as we know, since the anguished period of
his married life, with which Byron had been so intimately connected: so that the sight of her brought it all fresh back to his
mind. In spite of the fact that Caroline had been dead for years
and that Melbourne's own heart was now absorbed in another object, he was, so Lady Byron noted, throughout the interview, in an
uncontrollable state of emotion.

Melbourne's conversations with the Queen during their leisure
hours were only instructive intermittently and, as it were, by
chance. Much of the time, delighted for a blessed instant to forget
the cares and boredom of public life, he talked simply to please;
allowed his mind to saunter irresponsibly in whatever direction the
changing mood of the moment might suggest; modulating at every
turn from fact to fancy, the playful to the pensive, the serious to
the trivial, from cooking to history, from religion to feminine
fashions. Even on this last subject he amazed the Queen by the
unexpected extent of his knowledge. "Lord M. was very funny
about caps and bonnets, he looked round the table and said, 'There
is an amazing cargo of bonnets and things come from Paris I
fancy. . . .' He spoke of Mademoiselle Laure; we laughed very
much and asked him how he knew about her; 'They tell me of
her,' he added, 'and I fancy she has beautiful things'." Mel-

bourne's taste in clothes was fanciful, he told the Queen; he disliked dresses made of shot silk—"like chameleons, it looks so faithless". Fanciful or not, his opinions on dress inspired as much respect in the Queen as did all his other opinions. "He is so natural and funny and nice about toilette, and has very good taste I think," she writes. She notes his reaction to any change she might make in her appearance. "Lord M. observed my sleeves, which were very long, with astonishment and said, 'Amazing sleeves!'" She was also interested to hear what he thought of her pets. The grey parrot seems to have pleased him most. One day the Queen found him talking to it alone. "It is a sociable bird," he explained. About her dogs he was less appreciative: so little that for once she actually felt annoyed with him. "Lord M. said that Islay was a dull dog, which really makes me quite angry, for Islay is such a darling!" and she refused to agree that Dashy had crooked legs. Together they lifted Dashy on to the table and watched him lap up a saucer of tea. "I wonder if lapping is a pleasant sensation," mused Melbourne. "It is a thing we have never felt."

Thus whimsically and gaily their conversations wandered on. Now Melbourne would be telling her of his feelings towards children; how he liked their company if he could talk to them in his own way, but found it a bore when they were brought in to be made much of; now he was admitting that he had never finished Wordsworth's *Excursion*—"But I have bought the book," he said, "it is amazing when you leave a book on the table, how much you know what is in it without reading it"; now describing how he often interviewed people when he was in bed in the morning, because he got up late and thought that they would rather see him in bed than not at all; now he was explaining why he avoided having much to do with artists, "a waspish set of people"; now giving his reason for taking two apples at dessert, even if he did not think he was likely to eat more than one, "I like to have the power of doing so." Did not he have the power equally when the apples were in the dish, asked the Queen with characteristic and literal simplicity? "Not the full power," he replied humorously. Or they compared their views on Christian names—"Louisa is a fastidious name," said Melbourne; or on faces with large features—"I like large features," he told her—"People with small features and *squeeny* noses never do anything"; or on the song of birds, which Melbourne thought overrated; "I can never admire the singing of birds. There is no melody in it. It is so shrill. That is all humbug: it is mere poetry." Unexpectedly, however, he liked the noise of rooks. "The rooks are my delight," he observed gazing dreamily out of the windows at them as they swooped and hovered and multitudinously cawed amid the yellowing October trees. Was it some Proustian memory of childhood days in the Brocket fields that spoke to him in the sound? Or something romantically poignant and haunting in its wild harshness? For, as always, romantic sentiment mingled strangely in Melbourne with sceptical good sense and, even while he mocked at it, disturbed his heart. The Queen scolded him on one occasion for risking his life by standing under a tree during a thunderstorm. His answer to her sums up both this fundamental duality in his nature, and his ironical awareness of it. "It is a hundred to one that you are not struck," he said rationally, but then—his mind moving to contemplate the contingency in the light of imagination, "It's a sublime death!" he added.

He said the words with a smile; but it might have been with a tear. The heightened key of feeling in which he now lived kept his emotions always close to the surface, so that at the slightest touch they welled over. Easily and often the unbidden tears would fill his eyes; at an act of generosity, a word of gratitude, a tale of bereavement, at the pathos of old age, at the Duke of Wellington's chivalrous friendliness to an old opponent, at the sight of the Queen taking affectionate farewell of her uncle or her thoughtful kindness to the veterans of Waterloo. For, of course, he was most easily touched if she was involved. When she had a fall from her horse riding in the Park, Melbourne was thrown into an extraordinary agitation. He grew dead-white and "Are you sure you are not hurt?" he asked her again and again, as they rode home. "Are you really not the worse?" Most deeply and significantly was he moved during her Coronation when it came to his turn to go through the ceremony of paying homage. It was indeed, in a very special sense, a sacramental act for him; the eloquent symbol of that tender and sacred relationship which was now the centre of his existence. Beneath the immemorial arches of the Abbey the girl-Queen sat on her throne, her brows surmounted by the great gleaming Crown of State. Melbourne approached to kneel and kiss her hand. His fingers lingered on hers in an involuntary pressure. She returned it; he looked up; she saw his dark eyes shining with tears.

(2)

Tears of devotion; tears of joy too! For Melbourne's feeling for the Queen had released his emotional nature, so long frustrated of proper fulfilment, in such a way as to flood his spirit with a dreamlike happiness unknown to him since his far away youth; and which was all the more intoxicating because it came so unexpectedly and in the evening of his life, many years after he must have given up hoping for anything of the kind.

Alas! It did not remain long unclouded. It could not. For it depended on circumstances of their nature transitory. The Queen was growing more confident every month: as she gained confidence, she revealed herself more freely. With the result that Melbourne began to discover that she could be a source of anxiety as well as pleasure. She had the defects of her qualities. Feminine devotedness went along with feminine prejudice, regal dignity with regal imperiousness, moral strictness with intolerance, a child's simplicity with a child's unreasonableness. Further, force of character together with violence of feeling disposed her to be on occasion self-willed and headstrong. Her accession to the Throne strengthened these tendencies in her. It is hard not to grow a little headstrong and imperious if you are treated by everyone you meet as the most important person alive. Altogether by the summer of 1838 the Queen's character was beginning to display itself in a manner incompatible with an atmosphere of perfect ease and serenity.

Her change of temper was visible in her appearance: she was looking bolder and more discontented, people said. It was also apparent in her growing sense of what was due to her royal position. The etiquette of the Court, fairly slack at the start of her reign, was now tightened up by the Queen's especial desire. If anyone deviated from it, even in some detail, she noticed it at once and signified her displeasure by a sharp, irate glance. What did the Duchess of Cambridge mean, she asked angrily, by asking her to her ball and then not coming down to meet her at the door? She was indignant, too, with anyone who showed signs of trying to thwart or manage her. Her Uncle Leopold had gone on writing to her about politics. Now he was dismayed to find that his careful, tactful, considered advice met, as often as not, with a decided snub from the Queen. More sharply did she snub her mother. "I told Lord Melbourne," she writes, "that I had carried my point with Mama about coming up to my room without asking. She was angry at first. I had to remind her *who I was*!" Melbourne was a little alarmed by so formidable a display of royal character. "Quite right," he replied nervously. "But it is very disagreeable doing so." The triumphant tone in which the Queen relates the incident suggests that she had not found it so disagreeable. On another occasion Melbourne had difficulty in persuading her from formally rebuking the Duchess of Sutherland for asking Conroy to her house. He often found himself trying to curb her. "For God's sake don't do that, Ma'am!" people would hear him saying in agitated tones. Sometimes she obeyed him: often she did not. Indeed, he sometimes incurred her displeasure himself. Not that she liked him less. But her very affection for him made her more and more exacting in her demands on his time and attention. She hated him to be away from her. "He *ought* to be near me, it is his place," she wrote in her diary. She commanded him—he was indeed willing enough to obey her in this—to join her four or five minutes after she left the dinner table, instead of lingering for half-an-hour's relaxation over the port wine; she scolded him for being late in his visits; if he failed to come owing to the pressure of public work, she was seriously annoyed. One evening he excused himself for not having looked in at a party at Buckingham Palace because he had been working till eleven o'clock and thought it too late. The Queen did not accept this as a reasonable excuse. "He could have come perfectly well," she said. The harassed Melbourne tried to make up for such lapses by patient reasonable letters of apologetic explanation. "Lord Melbourne presents his humble duty to Your Majesty, and cannot express how deeply concerned he is to find himself restrained from obeying Your Majesty's commands, and repairing without delay to Brighton.

Both his duty and his inclination would prompt him to do this without a moment's delay, if he did not find it incumbent upon him to represent to Your Majesty the very important circumstances which require his presence for two or three days longer in London. The Session of Parliament approaches; the questions which are to be considered and prepared are of the most appalling magnitude, and of the greatest difficulty. Many of Your Majesty's servants, who fill the most important offices, are compelled by domestic calamity to be absent, and it is absolutely necessary that there should be some general superintendence of the measures to be proposed, and some consideration of the arrangements to be made. Lord Melbourne assures Your Majesty that he would not delay in London if he did not feel it to be absolutely necessary to Your Majesty's service. . . ."

Indeed, he could not find it in his heart to feel annoyed with her even for a moment. It was her stomach, he told her comfortingly, which made her feel out of temper—that and the strain of the life she was living, so unnatural for a young girl. She hoped he was right. Certainly she did feel nervous, as never before. It was this, she told him, that made her need him so much; this was why she was so unreasonably cross if he did not come. "I am so very sorry," he replied. "I will take care and come another time." Did she not worry him dreadfully, she would ask him? "Oh no, never!" he would hasten to assure her with earnest, affectionate kindness. As a matter of fact, she worried him a good deal: and, what mattered more, he was beginning to be a little frightened of her. Rightly; that extraordinary and tameless force of personality which was going to make her a great Queen of England was something Melbourne could not in the long run control. Already the ignorant eighteen-year-old girl was gaining the upper hand over the elderly statesman, in spite of all his charm and diplomatic skill and the prestige of his experience. She might listen to him and love him: but once she had made up her mind to do something, she did it—whether he wanted her to or not.

This became dramatically apparent in the early months of 1839. The Duchess of Kent had a Maid of Honour called Lady Flora Hastings. The Queen had never liked her, partly for the simple reason that she was her mother's Maid of Honour, and still more because she knew her to be an intimate friend of Conroy's. So intimate indeed that at this very time there were some scandalous and light-hearted jokes going round the Court, arising from the fact that the two had travelled down together from Scotland in the same carriage. Whether the Queen had heard these jokes is unknown. But it is likely that she had for, in February, she and Baroness Lehzen were interested to notice that Lady Flora's figure was changing shape: and immediately their minds leaped forward to suspect a very discreditable cause for this phenomenon. When the Queen discovered that these suspicions were shared both by two of the Court ladies and by the Court physician, Sir James Clarke, she was convinced they were justified. "We have no doubt that she is—to use the plain words—with child!" she wrote in her diary in a blaze of righteous wrath: "the horrid cause of all this is the monster and demon incarnate, whose name I forbear to mention." With the Queen, to feel was to act. Such goings on must not be condoned: something must be done. Melbourne was consulted as to what it should be. As might have been expected, he recommended doing nothing at all. Whether Lady Flora was guilty or not—and Melbourne had no special reason for believing her innocent—the situation was clearly an extremely awkward one: and it would be better to wait and see what happened. But the Queen and her ladies were in far too militant a mood to be checked in this manner. The sight of Lady Flora flaunting it shamelessly about the Court in a condition more interesting than reputable was more than they could bear. "Mama is here with her amiable and virtuous lady!" the Queen wrote in her diary with bitter sarcasm after an evening party at the Palace. Accounts are somewhat confused as to what happened next, but the upshot was that Lady Flora was reluctantly forced to submit to a medical examination by Clarke and another doctor. The examination proved that the alteration in her figure was due to other causes and her character was completely exonerated.

Events, however, did not end here. By this time the story had reached the ears of Lady Flora's brother, Lord Hastings, who, not unnaturally, was furious at the insulting way his sister had been treated. Supported by his mother, the Dowager Lady Hastings, he besieged Melbourne with a demand for redress. The scandal, he said, must be traced back to its source and its author exposed. Meanwhile, Clarke should be dismissed. Melbourne was in a very uncomfortable position. As a just and generous man he could not but understand Lord Hastings's anger on his injured sister's behalf. On the other hand, he knew that closer investigation might well disclose that a prime instigator of the whole proceedings had been the Queen herself. To save her from annoyance and to maintain the good reputation of the Crown, he was prepared to sacrifice Lady Flora or anyone else. He therefore wrote off to the Hastings family in a curt, snubbing tone, saying that the incident was closed and that there could be no question of opening it again. Beside himself with frustrated rage, Lord Hastings resolved to make the whole matter public and sent the correspondence to the news-paper. The fat was now in the fire. The more scurrilous journals made the most of the story; disaffected politicians did all they could to make the scandal resound more loudly; and a wave of public indignation surged up in favour of Lady Flora. It was not until the Duke of Wellington intervened to lend all the weight of his venerable reputation to the cause of pacification that the out-cry began to die down. But irretrievable harm had been done. Though the Queen's full responsibility in the matter was not known, yet she had been enough implicated to get a bad name. In the space of a week or two, her early popularity had vanished.

It is a very odd story: and one of the oddest things about it is the behaviour of Melbourne. Why, when he clearly realized that it was better to do nothing at all, did he not see to it from the start that nothing was done? Why, since he was an experienced man of the world peculiarly equipped, it would have seemed, to deal with delicate situations of this kind, did he defer to the judgment of an excited girl of eighteen and her almost equally excited Ger-man governess? The only plausible explanation is that he was powerless to do anything else. The Queen was shocked as only a youthful moralist can be shocked; and the violence of this shock combined with her age-old horror of Conroy to rouse her to a pitch of indignation into which she concentrated the full strength of her personality. Faced by it, Melbourne was too rattled to dare to make a decisive stand. Instead he temporized; while he tem-porized, the Queen acted. Afterwards he could only passively watch events rushing to their catastrophic end. He was at length forced by the conduct of the Hastings family into taking hasty action in order to conceal the Queen's responsibility in the affair. But even then, he was still so flustered that he acted with unwise violence and so made matters worse. The Queen's accounts of her talks with him during these weeks reveal him in a state of mind at once unsettled and fatalistic, typical of a man who knows that, through his own weakness, he has failed to assert himself when he should have done so. Sometimes he seems to be making light of the matter: jokingly he suggests that Lady Flora should be married off to one of his supporters as a way out of the difficulty. "I laughed excessively," commented the Queen, "for Lady Flora has neither riches nor beauty nor anything!" Most of the time, however, Melbourne appeared subdued and anxious. Well he might. He wanted the Queen to do well more than anything else in life. Now, for the first time, she was doing badly and, as he would have been the first to admit, it was largely through his own fault.

(3)

There was little in the political situation to cheer him up. At first the Queen's accession had proved slightly to the advantage of the Whigs. It was more comfortable to have an engaging young Queen on their side than a grumpy old King against them. Moreover, some of the general good will that was felt for the Queen extended itself to the Prime Minister with whom she was so closely identified. Otherwise, the position of the Government was unaltered. A weak Ministry of the middle way, threatened perpetually by the House of Lords on the one hand and on the other by the Radicals, it still maintained a precarious existence, partly by the favour of O'Connell and his Irish followers who thought they would do worse under the Tories, and partly through the connivance of Peel, who was biding his time till he thought he had the country sufficiently on his side for him to be able to come in at the head of a strong Tory administration. Melbourne, too, continued to pursue his policy of tacking and balancing, making concessions in turn to the right and to the left according as to which seemed likely to be the greater nuisance if thwarted. Himself, he disliked change as much as ever; and always opposed it as far as he could, in small things as much as in big. "Whenever you meddle with these ancient rights and jurisdictions it appears to me that for the sake of remedying comparatively insignificant abuses you create new ones and always produce considerable discontent," he observed to someone who proposed reforming the financial administration of the Duchy of Cornwall. "Delay" and "postpone" were still his favourite words, if any political project was under discussion. In one respect only was he changed from the year before. His determination to keep in office had grown stiffer than ever. For party loyalty and fear of revolution were now reinforced by a new and more powerful motive. He realized that going out would entail his own separation from the Queen, and in consequence the end of his chief satisfaction in life. He endeavoured to persuade his colleagues that they really had a respectable majority of the country behind them, so that it was positively their duty to go on in office as long as they could. And even if this was not so, he had made up his mind not to budge till he was forced. "I am for standing our ground, even with the majority of one," he told the Cabinet in the spring of 1838. All the same, he was in reality far too clear-sighted not to recognize that in fact the Government might fall at any time. A crisis on a major issue, and the Peers or the Radicals or the Irish could upset the whole apple-cart in the course of one debate. Besides, there was always the risk that the Government might come to pieces from within. His colleagues had not the same motive as himself for clinging to office: none of them had the luck to be an object of royal hero-worship. On the other hand, there were those among them who did not think that all reforms were nonsense; and so felt it ignominious and frustrating to be continually prevented from carrying them out. Further, this sense of frustration made them quarrelsome. A Government that feels itself ineffective loses its *esprit de corps*. Melbourne did all he could to keep his Ministry a friendly, manageable group. However awkward the Radicals made themselves, he absolutely refused to placate them by giving them office: still more firmly he rejected the proposals that Durham should be admitted to the Government again. "It is impossible to be with him," he declared, "without perceiving not only that he can do no business, but that no business can be done where he is."

As a matter of fact Melbourne found his existing Ministers troublesome enough. Nothing could make Glenelg competent, Palmerston prudent or John Russell flexible and tactful. As in William IV's days, it was John Russell who especially minded having to compromise with the Tories. Apart from the fact that he genuinely believed in a policy of moderate reform, his priggish, doctrinaire habit of mind made him morbidly sensitive to any accusation of inconsistency. He could hardly bear it if he heard that the Radicals were saying he was not true to liberal principles. The Secretary at War, Lord Howick, son of the famous Earl Grey, had also begun to be a cause of trouble. Angular, high-minded, energetic, and with a perverse propensity to look for faults in his own side, he was always interfering with his colleagues' business; scolding Melbourne for inertia, or protesting against the inefficiency of Glenelg. If his protests were unheeded, he threatened to resign. His natural intransigence was increased by the fact that he was religious in the new-fangled earnest, strenuous fashion, much deplored by Melbourne in his conversations with Queen Victoria. Many others of his generation were too. It was something to which Melbourne was so unaccustomed in young men that it bewildered him. "All young people are growing mad about religion," he lamented. What, he asked, was he to think of Hobhouse who distrusted a man's political opinions because he lived a loose life? The more the Victorian age got into its swing, the less comfortable did Melbourne feel in it.

However, in spite of these difficulties, political affairs jogged along for the next year or so without running into any fatal trouble. A certain amount of legislation was put forward, notably three Bills dealing with Ireland. Like similar Bills in the past, they all came in for some drastic modification in the House of Lords. But only one, the Irish Corporation Bill, had to be dropped. The Poor Law Act and the Tithe Bill passed, though the Government found itself forced at last to give up the idea of appropriating any of the Irish Church revenues for secular purposes. This did not bother Melbourne who, for some time past, had been against it. He was a little more worried by John Russell who, in the autumn of 1838, decided that the Reform Bill of 1832 represented the furthest final limit in the extension of the franchise which his principles permitted him to accept, and insisted on declaring this in public. The Radicals, who looked on the 1832 Bill as a mere first step on the golden road to full democracy, protested violently; and John Russell was nicknamed "Finality Jack".

The end of the year was troubled by the first rumblings of a more formidable threat to Melbourne's peace of mind. This time it was Radical not Finality Jack who was the cause of disturbance. For some time past trouble had been brewing in Canada. It was split into two provinces, Upper and Lower Canada. In neither did the Colonists consider that they had enough to say in governing their own country. In Lower Canada feeling was made worse by the fact that the majority of the inhabitants were agricultural French Catholics who violently resented being ruled as they thought in the interests of mercantile English Protestants. The only cure for these evils was a drastic change in the constitutional system. If the Canadians were to be prevented from leaving the Empire, as the United States had done, they must be given some sort of self-government. A far-sighted English Government should have realized this and begun to think out a scheme by which it might be achieved. The existing English Government had not thought out such a scheme. It was altogether too big a job for the ineffective Glenelg; nor was Melbourne the man to supply the deficiencies of his Colonial Secretary. Such energy as he possessed was fully occupied in keeping the Cabinet quiet and the Queen happy. Moreover, he was in these matters, as in so many others, a figure from the past; a survivor from the eighteenth century when people did not bother much about the Empire. When it came to the point, he did in fact boggle at the idea of losing Canada; but he had no vision of the glories of a future British Commonwealth to inspire him to devise plans for preventing it. It is likely, too, that the failure of Catholic Emancipation to pacify the Irish made him sceptical about the good which there was to be gained from making concessions to the Canadians. Anyway, for whatever reason, nothing was done and the situation in Canada steadily deteriorated, till early in 1838 both provinces rebelled. The rebellion in the Upper province was put down fairly easily by the Lieutenant-Governor, Sir Francis Head. His methods of do-ing so, however, were thought indefensibly unconventional, and when he came home, he went to see the Prime Minister in order to complain that he had not been thanked for his success as he thought he deserved to be. He found Melbourne shaving. "I saved the Colony!" cried Head. "And so you did," answered Melbourne placably; and went on shaving. After a minute or two he put down his razor and turned round. "But, you see, you're such a damned odd fellow!" he commented. Head's outraged feelings were not soothed by this reception. However, since Upper Canada was now quiet this was not, from Melbourne's point of view, of much consequence. The trouble in Lower Canada was more serious, and needed more drastic treatment. Accordingly the Government suspended its constitution and decided to send out a Minister armed with special and dictatorial powers to deal with it. Who should it be? After a vain attempt to persuade Spencer to come out of his retirement, Melbourne turned to Durham. This was a very different kind of choice. Not that it was a bad one. Autocratic and independent, Durham was far better suited to be a dictator than a Cabinet Minister. What was more important, he was, unlike Melbourne, a man of the new age with a vision, rare among his contemporaries, of England's possibilities as an imperial power. This, however, was not why Melbourne chose him. He had always had a low opinion of Durham. Now he told the Queen that he thought him a man of not even second-rate ability. The fact was that, as usual, Durham had been making trouble. Frustrated once more of a post in the Government, Radical Jack had begun to foment discontent among his Radical followers. Yet again, Melbourne thought the best way to deal with him was to get him out of the country. Another reason for sending him to Canada was that his mission there was certain to involve arbitrary and despotic actions of a kind likely to annoy the democratically-minded Radicals. They would be more ready, Melbourne considered, to swallow these if the despot in question was their hero Durham. The fact that he thought Durham third-rate does not seem to have worried him. Colonial affairs were not important enough in Melbourne's eyes to require a first-rate man.

Altogether the appointment was an ill-considered affair, and reveals where Melbourne was weak as a statesman. He was soon

QUEEN VICTORIA AND THE PRINCE CONSORT

QUEEN VICTORIA AND LORD MELBOURNE riding at Windsor

LORD  MELBOURNE in 1844

punished for his weakness. For, though Durham's appointment turned out to be to the advantage of Canada in the long run, it brought nothing but trouble to the Prime Minister. As might have been expected, Durham proved to be just as tiresome to him on the one side of the Atlantic as he had been on the other. From the moment he landed he behaved with a lordly disregard alike of the feelings of his party and the opinion of his countrymen. Every despatch that arrived from Canada after he had got there contained something to worry Melbourne. To begin with, in order to impress the Canadians and please himself Durham arranged that his first official appearance among them should be marked by an unexampled and spectacular magnificence. He took so much luggage that it took two days to get it on shore; then, attended by a huge retinue, he made his entry in an elaborate silver-laced uniform and riding on a superb white charger. All this, as Melbourne expected, shocked the English who thought that they would have to pay for it out of taxes. They were still more shocked when they learned that Durham appointed to important posts two men, Turton and Gibbon Wakefield, of notoriously bad private character. Wakefield had been in prison for three years for abducting a young girl, while Turton had been involved in a peculiarly sordid divorce case. Melbourne, who had specially asked Durham not to bring them into public prominence, was furious. "Considering feeling here, it is really inconceivable that Durham should think it necessary to compose his Council of two such men," he lamented to the Queen, clasping his hands and casting his eyes to heaven. He wrote, and in his most trenchant style, told Durham what he thought of him.

"It is incredible that a man of common sense should show such an ignorance or such a disregard of public feeling and opinion as you have done in the selection of these gentlemen. If their abilities and powers were superhuman they would not counter-balance the discredit of their characters. They will materially weaken us; they will cause every act of your Government to be viewed with a jealousy and suspicion to which they would not otherwise have been exposed. I rely, therefore, upon your assurance that you will not give Mr. Wakefield any public

L

appointment whatever, that his name will not appear in any public documents; and that you will not put forward Mr. Turton in any more prominent situation, or place him in any other post of trust or dignity. . . . Only consider how you injure your own private character by the association of such men with yourself and your family. Only consider how you injure the Queen, whose age and character demand some respect and reverence."

This last sentence reveals the true cause of Melbourne's agitation. For him the one dominating consideration in deciding any course of action was how it might affect the position of the Queen. Durham, in neglecting this, had committed the sin for which there was no forgiveness.

In spite of Melbourne's words he continued to neglect it. He kept on Wakefield and Turton and did not answer Melbourne's letters. Instead, without informing anyone in England of his purpose, he proceeded to break the law. The rebellion had now been suppressed; what then should be done with the ringleaders? To try them for treason in the ordinary way would be unwise, for no Canadian jury could be trusted to convict them. Durham, therefore, had them transported by his own arbitrary ordinance to the Bermudas, a region outside his jurisdiction. There was something to be said for his action, but it was technically illegal. As such, it gave an opportunity to the enemies of the Government for which they had been waiting. The Tory lawyers leapt to the attack. Their protests were reinforced by a formidable assistant. For the last two years Brougham had been bursting to avenge himself on the Whigs for having turned him out. During the last two sessions of Parliament he had quarrelled incessantly with Melbourne in debate. Now he came forward as champion of the age-old and lawful liberties of British subjects, and delivered a terrific philippic in his finest manner in the House of Lords demanding that Durham's ordinance should be disallowed. Melbourne listened to him with an expression of contemptuous calm on his countenance. "If I had said anything," he remarked later, "the fellow would have gone stark staring mad." Afterwards he rose to make the official reply for the Government. Durham, he said, was in an extremely difficult situation and the House should wait for more information before taking action. But he himself was too annoyed with Durham to put up a very strong fight; all the more because Durham had issued his ordinance without consulting him and had not condescended to answer his request for a full explanation after he had done it. The Duke of Wellington and the rest of the Tories rallied to Brougham's support. In face of their representations the Government gave in and disallowed the ordinance. When he got the news Durham resigned in a rage; but before he left he relieved his feelings by issuing a public declaration in which he denounced the Government for betraying him and pointed out to the Canadians how much they were losing in being deprived of the only British statesman, namely himself, who had their interests at heart. He must have secretly hoped, said Melbourne irritably, to create so much bad feeling that rebellion would break out again as soon as he left.

The Government awaited his return with trepidation. If this was the sort of thing he said in Canada, what was he not going to say when he got to England? Their fears turned out to be unjustified. The strain of idealism which was intermingled so strangely with Durham's egotism and ill temper rose for once to dominate his actions. His imagination had been fired by a new conception of the relations between England and her dependants; and with the help of the disreputable Turton and Wakefield he was evolving a bold and brilliant scheme for giving self-government to Canada. By the time he reached England his temper was sufficiently under control to realize that the success of this scheme depended on making up his quarrel with Melbourne. He did not behave in an actively friendly manner to him—this could hardly be expected— but neither did he start a campaign of vengeance. Melbourne was not the man to refuse an overture of peace, however guarded. Moreover, he had now begun to discover more about Durham's conduct in Canada: and he realized that intolerably though he had conducted himself to the Government at home, in Canada he had done pretty well. Melbourne, therefore, did all he could to persuade his infuriated colleagues not to exacerbate Durham's wrath by telling him what they thought of him. "Whether Durham's resignation was right or wrong is a question which may be viewed in different lights and upon which there may fairly be much difference of opinion," he said. "His provocation was great, and though I think he brought it upon himself by his rash and imprudent manner of doing things in themselves right, it required much patience and forbearance to submit to it." Melbourne had been the more able to recover his temper with Durham because, though he disliked him thoroughly, he was not afraid of him. "It is very odd to see the terror that Durham inspires," he said. Hysterical *prima donnas*, however gifted, were to the placid and worldly-wise Melbourne always a trifle ridiculous. When all was said and done, he could not bring himself to respect Durham. "What he did was often right, but always so done as to be totally indefensible"; thus he sums up his final judgment on the episode.

Later historians have not always agreed with him. Melbourne has come in for a good deal of scolding from them because he did not put up a stronger fight for Durham and his ordinance. These strictures are unjustified. Melbourne must indeed be blamed for sending out Durham in the first place. It is not right to appoint a man you distrust to an important public job abroad just because it will ease the political situation at home to get him out of the way. But once the appointment was made Melbourne could not be expected to behave otherwise than he did. After all he did not share Durham's grandiloquent imperial dreams: so far as we know, Durham had never deigned to expound them to him. On the other hand, he thought that to fight to the death for Durham would almost certainly mean the fall of the Government. Melbourne's devotion to the Queen and his fear of civil strife united to convince him that his first duty was to keep the Government in. Moreover, as he saw it, Durham had forfeited all claim to extraordinary support from his colleagues by sinning deliberately and repeatedly against what Melbourne had all his life considered the first obligation of a statesman; personal loyalty to his Party, his leader; and, in this instance, to his Sovereign as well. It was not from want of warning either. Melbourne had been writing to Durham for months telling him how mistakenly he thought he was behaving: and Durham had paid no attention whatever. Why then should Melbourne imperil the existence of the Government for

Durham's sake? Since he was responsible for his appointment he was prepared to make a speech in the House of Lords saying what he truthfully could in his defence, but after that he would act as seemed best for his Government as a whole. Privately he cursed himself for sending Durham. "The fact is," he said, "that his mission is the greatest scrape and the greatest blunder we have committed."

It certainly weakened the little confidence people still had in the Whigs. Up till the middle of 1838 Melbourne had been able to feel fairly cheerful about their position. He even began to wonder if the Government might not be able to totter along indefinitely, as it had under William IV. No doubt it was a bore if it had not a comfortable majority: but they must make the best of it. "Equality of Parties makes government doubtful and difficult," he said soothingly to John Russell in August, "but it cannot be helped. It is a contingency that may happen, and has happened." Two months later he was not feeling so sanguine. "I am sure that there are some times of trouble approaching for which Your Majesty must hold yourself prepared," he wrote to the Queen. "Your Majesty is too well acquainted with the nature of human affairs not to be aware that they cannot very long go on as quietly as they have gone for the last sixteen months." Indeed, with the coming of autumn things had begun to take a turn for the worse. All the forces making for the downfall of the Government were getting stronger. The Tories were growing more popular, the Radicals more recalcitrant, the Irish more uncertain-tempered, while the members of the Cabinet squabbled more than ever. Sometimes it was about personalities. Glenelg did something stupid, and then Howick and John Russell began saying they would resign if Melbourne did not get rid of him at once. Melbourne, unwilling to be bullied, refused, and the squabbles sputtered on till in February, 1839, Glenelg resigned of his own accord. More often the quarrels were about policy. In order to win back the confidence of the Radicals, somebody proposed a progressive sounding measure; a Bill for educational reform, for instance, or for introducing the secret ballot. Melbourne opposed both, partly because he was always inclined to oppose changes, and partly because he wanted to do nothing that would exacerbate the Tories. As a matter of fact he had always been against educational reform. About the ballot his record had not been so consistent. In principle he was against it. But it was not a matter which he cared much about, and a year or two before he had toyed with the idea of adopting it in order to please the Radicals: at any rate it might be made an open question, on which Ministers could vote as they pleased. This device, as a way of avoiding Cabinet quarrels, appealed to Melbourne. In 1839 he came out definitely against the ballot. Equally he resisted a movement inspired by the Evangelicals to enforce the suppression of the slave trade more rigorously. No doubt it was still carried on to some extent but he did not see how this could be helped. "It is impossible," he remarked in a spirit of chilling realism, "not to feel and to expect that religion, morality, law, eloquence, cruisers, will all be ineffectual when opposed to a profit of a cent per cent and more."

The end of 1838 was disturbed by the first mutterings of a more formidable agitation. The price of food had recently gone up with the result that the working class were restive and discontented as they had not been for several years. Liberal-minded people now seized on this discontent as a reason to demand a reform which they had long desired; the repeal, or at any rate the modification, of the laws which controlled the price of corn. The more advanced members of the Cabinet agreed with them. Not so Melbourne: he could hardly be expected to, for the repeal of the Corn Laws involved a change almost as revolutionary as the Reform Bill itself. Indeed, it was its economic counterpart. It meant that the landed gentry of England would lose that economic predominance on which their political influence ultimately rested. The country would be run rather in the interest of the new urban and manufacturing community which was drawn predominantly from the middle and lower classes. For this reason Melbourne, wholly a man of the old régime, was bound to dislike it. "I doubt whether property or the institutions of the country can stand it," he said. Still more was he against it just because it was a major issue and was, therefore, bound to involve a major conflict. Never, so long as he could help it, was the country to be disturbed by a row like the row over the Reform Bill. "Depend upon it," he said sharply to John Russell, "any advantage that can be gained is not worth the danger and evil of the struggle, by which alone it can be carried. . . . We shall only carry it by the same means as we carried the Reform Bill, and I am not for being the instrument or amongst the instruments of another similar performance!" He employed his usual stonewalling tactics; objected, temporized, procrastinated. His colleagues were not sufficiently united on the question to defeat him. For the moment it too was dropped. Meanwhile he sought to soothe the Corn Law reformers of the country in any way he could; scotched a movement from the Right to check the development of the Trades Union Movement, and instructed Ministers to use extreme tact in replying to anti-Corn Law propaganda. He says to one who showed him the speech he was going to make on the subject, "I should not consider it very conciliatory. It is reproval and condemnation, and there is in it a good deal of sarcasm. The middle and lower orders are very touchy and, above all things, hate to be sneered at." For all that his political ideas were old-fashioned, Melbourne's perception of his countrymen's characteristic weaknesses was as acute and as up to date as ever.

For the time being then, Melbourne had managed to get his way and keep going. But the effort of doing so made the early months of 1839 a dreadfully wearing and anxious time for him, especially as these political difficulties coincided with the trouble about Lady Flora Hastings. He was less able to stand the strain too, because for the last month he had not been at all well. Physically old before his time, his health had begun to deteriorate. "I am listless and ill and unable to do anything, or think—which does not suit the time," he said to Lady Holland. He could not sleep, he could not digest easily. His health reacted on his spirits. To his dismay he found that natural buoyancy which had carried him through so much trouble beginning to desert him. Melbourne, who for so long had been the most cheerful member of the Government, was now noticeably the most depressed. "I do not know what the deuce is the matter with me!" he sighed to the Queen.

## (4)

In the ordinary course of things all this should have made him want to go out of office. In fact he did consider it. He was always talking about Charles V and Diocletian and other eminent persons who had chosen to retire from places of power to enjoy the peaceful pleasures of private life. After all, he had never been very enthusiastic about being Prime Minister. He did not like work, and he did not believe in power. Indeed, he would have been thankful to go—had it not been for the Queen. He hated parting from her and he hated giving her pain by doing so. For the very idea of losing him filled her with a sort of panic. It was not just that she minded being deprived of his company. She was convinced that without him she would be plunged back into the dreadful situation in which she had lived before she came to the Throne; alone in a dangerous universe without a soul she could consult and surrounded by secret enemies. The political situation presented itself to her in simple terms. On the one side was a great and good man, Lord Melbourne, who was always right about everything; on the other, a loathsome mixture of sinister Tories, revolutionary Radicals and weak treacherous Whigs. In all the Government quarrels she was his passionate partizan. How could creatures like Howick and John Russell dare to question the will of their noble leader? Melbourne listened to her, soothed her, assured her that he would stay in while it was humanly possible. But he cannot have thought this would be for much longer. In fact his downfall did come in May, 1839. Trouble had arisen in Jamaica in consequence of the emancipation of the slaves there. Some Radicals thought the Government so feeble and illiberal in the matter that they refused to support it, with the result that the Government only avoided being beaten in the House of Commons by five votes. This was the smallest majority it had ever had: clearly its position had deteriorated to a point on which it could no longer deceive itself into thinking that it possessed the confidence of the country sufficiently to continue as its official leaders. Even Melbourne recognized it was time to go out of office.

He had reckoned without the Queen, however. On 7th May she got a letter from him announcing his resignation in terms whose restrained formality could not conceal the passionate regret that filled his heart.

"Lord Melbourne is certain that Your Majesty will not deem him too presuming if he expresses his fear that this decision will be both painful and embarrassing to Your Majesty, but Your Majesty will meet this crisis with that firmness which belongs to your character, and with that rectitude and sincerity which will carry Your Majesty through all difficulties. It will also be greatly painful for Lord Melbourne to quit the service of a Mistress who has treated him with such unvarying kindness and unlimited confidence, but in whatever station he may be placed he will always feel the deepest anxiety for Your Majesty's interests and happiness and will do the utmost in his power to promote and secure them."

A few hours later he came to say good-bye. The interview was extremely distressing. It was a moment before they could trust themselves to speak. Overcome with emotion the Queen kept his hand clasped in hers. Then, "You will not forsake me?" she sobbed out at last. Melbourne, his eyes brimming with tears, gave her a long, pitying, loving look. "Oh no," he replied. Within a few minutes she was in such floods of tears that for the time being all he could do was to speak any words of sympathy that occurred to him and leave her to collect herself, returning later in the day in order to discuss details of her future. In the interim he wrote recommending her to send for the Duke of Wellington and, if he refused office, to accept Sir Robert Peel instead. He added that he feared he must give up dining with her while negotiations were proceeding lest she should be suspected of intriguing against her new Ministers. "Lord Melbourne," he ended, "felt his attendance upon Your Majesty to be at once the greatest honour and pleasure of his life, and Your Majesty may believe that he will most severely and deeply feel the change." The Duke of Wellington arrived the next day and, as Melbourne expected, recommended that the Queen should send for Peel. Peel came the same afternoon. He made a bad impression. A stiff, male, professional person, ill at ease in the company alike of royalty and of young girls, he gazed awkwardly at the ground, and replied to the Queen's questions with cold formality. "Oh!" wrote the Queen, "how different, how dreadfully different to that frank, open, natural and most kind warm manner of Lord Melbourne!" Nor were his words more re-assuring than his manner. At the close of the interview he suggested that the Queen should change some of the appointments in the Royal Household in order to show her confidence in the new Government. This stirred her besetting fear. Was he meaning to set spies upon her? She demurred. Peel took his leave. The Queen wrote off to Melbourne describing what had happened and asking his advice. Melbourne read what she said about the Household appointments with anxious feelings. His sole aim was to make things easy for her: and indeed, for this very reason, he had already told her that a new Government should not mean a complete change in her Household; her Ladies at any rate would most likely be left alone. She need not be frightened lest she should be left without any old friends. But equally he did not want her to get on the wrong side of her new Ministers by making demands on them which they might think unreasonable. Accordingly, he wrote her a long letter saying that though he thought her in the right about her Household, it was not a matter of the first importance; she had better compromise over it rather than risk an open break with Peel. He was all the more anxious to avoid this because of his old fear of political impasse. If a hitch occurred which made it impossible for either of the great Parties to form a Government, then a situation might be created in which, for want of an alternative, a Radical revolutionary movement might sweep the country and gain control. Meanwhile, in the last part of his letter he did his best to bring round the Queen to a more favourable view of Peel. Though he did not care for him personally, he knew it was vital the Queen should learn to get on with him as, sometime or other, he was almost certain to become her First Minister. Melbourne had tried to bring them together before now. Once at a royal party he had vainly tried to persuade Peel to come up and talk to her. Now he told her:

"Lord Melbourne earnestly entreats Your Majesty not to suffer yourself to be affected by any faultiness of manner which you may observe. Depend upon it, there is no personal hostility

to Lord Melbourne nor any bitter feelings against him. Sir
Robert is the most cautious and reserved of mankind. Nobody
seems to Lord Melbourne to know him, but he is not therefore
deceitful or dishonest. Many a very false man has a very open
sincere manner, and vice versa. . . ."

The Queen wrote back thanking him warmly for his letter, saying that he was a father to her and that she would follow his advice
in every respect.

She may have meant to; but in fact she did nothing of the kind.
As over Lady Flora, she had got the bit between her teeth. When
Peel arrived the next morning, trouble broke out at once. It was
over the question of the Court Ladies. The Queen said that she
was willing that the male members of her Court should be changed,
but not the ladies. Peel was taken aback. The Court Ladies were
all married to Whigs. As the head of a minority Government, he
felt, not unnaturally, that he could not afford to take the risk of
having the Court against him. If the Queen stuck to her point, he
said, he was not at all sure he could take office; he must talk the
matter over with the Duke of Wellington. His words had an
electrifying affect upon the Queen. Who was he to think he could
bully the ruler of England in this fashion? The wrath of outraged
majesty rose to reinforce the will to resist already implanted in her
by her fear of spies. Nor was this all. As she listened to his chilly
protests an unexpected gleam of hope flashed through her mind.
If Sir Robert Peel refused to take office, why then, Lord Melbourne might come back! Afire with mingled fury and exultation,
she rushed to the writing table to pour forth to him an account of
her interview with Peel. So beside herself was she that, forgetful
alike of royal etiquette and of the rules of English composition, she
burst out suddenly after a line or two from the third into the first
person.

"The Queen writes one line to prepare Lord Melbourne for
what *may* happen in a very few hours. Sir Robert Peel has behaved very ill, and has insisted on my giving up my Ladies, to
which I replied that I never would consent, and I never saw a
man so frightened. He said he must go to the Duke of Wellington and consult with him, when both would return, and he said

this must suspend all further proceedings, and he asked whether I should be ready to receive a decision, which I said I should; he was quite perturbed—but this is *infamous*. I said, besides many other things, that if he or the Duke of Wellington had been at the head of the Government when I came to the Throne, perhaps there might have been a few more Tory Ladies, but that then if you had come into Office you would never have *dreamt* of changing them. I was calm but very decided, and I think you would have been pleased to see my composure and great firmness; the Queen of England will not submit to such trickery. Keep yourself in readiness, for you may soon be wanted."

He very soon was. In vain the Duke of Wellington pleaded with her. In vain Peel suggested that she should give up just a few ladies; only those whose husbands were actually in Parliament. The Queen was adamant. "The Queen maintains *all* her ladies," she wrote to Melbourne, "—and it is her Prime Minister who will cut a sorry figure if he resigns on this." Melbourne was so agitated by her communications that he came to see her. Passionately she adjured him to back her: she trusted him, she said, to return to her if Peel stood out.

Melbourne felt painfully divided. On the face of it, it seemed his duty alike to his Party and to the Queen herself that he should advise her to give in to Peel. There was no chance of any Whig Government lasting long now: it could not be in the best interests of the Party that it should be dragged back, as the result of a Court intrigue, only to submit to a second and more ignominious defeat, within a few months. Further, the Queen's reputation was likely to suffer if people thought she was taking an arbitrary and partizan political line. But if Melbourne's conscience told him to go, his heart ardently urged him to stay. It went against his every tender and chivalrous instinct to desert her when she said she needed him: besides, he yearned for her company. It is indeed the measure of his self-sacrificing devotion to her that he had been able to make himself plead for Peel so strongly. Now he hesitated and said he must consult the Cabinet. The result of his consultation was unexpected. Though most of the Ministers had wanted to resign more than Melbourne had, yet now they were out, they found they did not like it. Was not Melbourne, they said, going rather far in his efforts to help Peel? When they met, and Melbourne read aloud the Queen's letter to them, their doubts became certainties. As the assembly of hard-bitten, middle-aged politicians listened to her naïve, touching beseechings they were swept by a wave of sentimental loyalty. Never, never, they cried, would they abandon such a Queen and such a woman! All this was too much in tune with Melbourne's own secret feelings for him to stand out any longer. He told the Queen they would support her. She informed Peel that she would not give in about the ladies, he thereupon declined office.

Melbourne did not feel very happy; and still less so when he discovered from a memorandum of Peel's that the Queen, carried away by the frenzy of battle, had failed to give him a complete accurate account of the proceedings. Peel, it appeared, had only asked for the removal of some ladies, not all. Melbourne was sufficiently dismayed by this information to make an effort through a third party to persuade Peel to come back after all. "He must have it, he absolutely must have it," he exclaimed. However, Peel refused. In a mood mingling apprehension, fatalistic resignation and secret joy, Melbourne found himself in office again. Meanwhile he did what he could to ensure that any blame in the matter might fall on himself rather than on the Queen. He defended his conduct in the House of Lords with an airy flippancy which shocked its more earnest-minded members. He was callous, he said, to accusations that he clung to office from ambition or avarice, "For, my Lords," he remarked smiling and chuckling, "I don't altogether deny the truth of any one of them."

He could have done. The Queen alone had made him return. For the second time, and over a more important issue, it had been demonstrated that if she put forth the full force of her will, she could get her way with Melbourne, even though he knew it was a mistake. In this he was true to his character as it reveals itself throughout his history. Personal obligations had always meant more to him than general principles just because he believed in them more. Moreover, coolly sensible though his judgment usually was, yet when his romantic heart was fully engaged, it

ruled his head. The most powerful force in his life was his love
for two women, his wife and the Queen. And, as the young Melbourne had disregarded every other consideration in order to stand
by Caroline when she asked him to, so now the old Melbourne disregarded every other consideration in order to stand by Queen
Victoria.

## CHAPTER VI

# THE QUEEN: SECOND PHASE

## (1)

" As the negotiation with the Tories is quite at an end . . ." wrote Queen Victoria gaily to Melbourne on the evening of 10th May, 1839, "the Queen hopes Lord Melbourne will not object to dining with her on *Sunday*?" Lord Melbourne was very far from objecting. How much he had minded the idea of parting from the Queen can be measured by the extent of his joy when he discovered that after all he would not have to do so. Even though he felt in his heart that he had been wrong to take office again, his error had not been of so heinous a kind as unduly to disturb his robust and good-humoured conscience. He found it all the easier to disregard its voice because his fear lest the Queen should have made herself unpopular by her action had not been realized. On the contrary, the British public seemed to have been as much stirred as was the Cabinet by the spectacle of the young Queen alone and gallantly standing up for her rights against an army of experienced and middle-aged politicians. As she drove to church on Sunday she was greeted by a crowd shouting "Bravo" and "The Queen for ever". Melbourne arrived to dine at the Palace in an unbridled state of high spirits such as he had not known for months. He laughed louder than ever, twisted his curly locks through his fingers, knit his brows in comical, extravagant frowns and murmured delightedly to himself. "I like what is joyous and agreeable," he ejaculated, "I hate what is disagreeable and melancholy." Entranced, the Queen listened to his words and observed his every movement: admired his hair in its picturesque disarray and gazed with amused surprise at his frowns. Melbourne caught her eye fixed on him. He smiled and rubbed his forehead. "Never mind. I was only knitting my brows," he explained. "I know it looks tremendous! But you should not judge by expression; very susceptible people constantly change expression." His conversation that evening was at its most fascinating, ranging

absorbingly and whimsically from the ballet to medieval troubadours, from the troubadours to the art of cooking, from cooking to
the character of King Francis I of France. "He was the first who
introduced that gaiety; he was the first King who had that gay
liberty which has since been practised," he said snapping his fingers and laughing.

Melbourne would have been in even higher spirits had he been
able to foresee the future. For his reprieve was to last for pretty
well two years; and with it the old intimacy. Once more we open
the Queen's diary to watch the day-to-day close-up moving picture
of her relationship with him. All seems as before; the daily companionship and daily correspondence, the visits to Windsor, the
rides in the Park, the evenings spent looking at prints, the hours of
business and of relaxation, the mingling, shimmering, enchanted
flow of entertaining instruction and ironical wisdom and delicate
sentiment and carefree fanciful fun. Now we see him sitting for
his portrait on horseback—very comical he looked, the Queen
thought, in a white top hat astride a wooden block—now in the
Royal Box at the opera, whither she had inveigled him rather
against his will—"That is too bad, rather a bore," he exclaimed in
murmured protest when the audience insisted on an encore—now
taking a lesson from her in the game of Cup and Ball; "I do it with
perfect steadiness, patience, perseverance and tranquillity, which
is the only way to do anything," he remarked. As before, he is full
of information about history and geography; "Catherine of Ara-
gon was a sad, groaning, moaning woman," he remarked, and that
the Spanish were unpopular on account of their sobriety, "Somehow or other sober nations do not get on well with other nations."
As before, he is always startling her agreeably by his unexpected
idiosyncrasies and opinions. On smoking, for example, "If I smell
tobacco I swear, perhaps for half an hour," he told her; or on bad
habits, "If you have a bad habit the best way to get out of it is to
take your fill of it"; or on old people dancing, "I consider when
old people begin to dance at a party all propriety is over"; or on
early rising, "For recruiting the spirits there is nothing like lying
a good while in bed"; or on fires, "I always have a fire when I am
worried or annoyed; it's astonishing how it dissipates trouble!";
or on feminine beauty, "There's nothing men get so tired of as a

continued look of great beauty—very fine eyes, for instance, nothing tires men so much as two very fine eyes"; or on foreign travel,
"The first time you go to Paris, the Capital of Pleasures, you
should spend four thousand pounds, it is not social not to"; or on
gardens; it was natural that the Queen should be bored by the
garden of Buckingham Palace, "For," he said, "a garden is a dull
thing." His contempt for gardens did not extend to the flowers
that grew in them. Every week there arrived for the Queen from
Brocket a carefully chosen bouquet gathered from his own garden
there. Their fresh fragrance symbolized the quality of his un-
changing feeling for her; that feeling which so often brought the
tears to his eyes and compelled him every now and then in the
course of a conversation to bend forward and impulsively to kiss
her hand.

All seemed as before! But in fact it was only now and again that
he recaptured the unalloyed delight of two years earlier. Melbourne's second phase as Queen Victoria's Prime Minister was
not quite so happy as his first had been. This was largely due to
physical causes. The events of the spring had accelerated the decline of his health. Almost all the time he felt ill and tired: he
suffered from lumbago and acute attacks of indigestion; the slightest worry kept him awake at night. Moreover, every month that
passed he found he could do less. By the end of the year it had become too great an effort for him to give dinner parties or go out
riding. Not only in the morning, but also in the evening he did as
much of his work as he could in his dressing-room. The moment
he got back from the office he would take off his cravat and put on
his dressing-gown to ease his exhausted body. Philosophically he
found diplomatic advantages in this change of régime. Having to
go up so many stairs, he said, left his visitors breathless and thus
forced to leave the initiative to him.

People noticed the change in him. He seemed to have aged
years in a few months. "Lord Melbourne begins to look picturesquely old," remarked a Court lady. Nor was it only his appearance that showed a change. His growing weakness betrayed itself
in his behaviour. Too fatigued to concentrate, he grew vaguer and
more absent-minded than ever. Ladies sitting next to Lord Melbourne for the first time at dinner would be enchanted by the

charm of his talk; then it would stop and he would begin murmuring and swearing to himself, or relapse into silent brooding which found vent in a remark wholly unconnected with the conversation round him. "Do you not consider," he suddenly asked, leaning across to address a shy young man opposite during dinner at Holland House, "that it was a most damnable act of Henry IV to change his religion with a view to securing the Crown?" Members of Brooks's Club were disconcerted to find Lord Melbourne standing in the hall remarking loudly to himself, "I will be hanged if I will do it for you, my lord." More than ever he was liable to go to sleep any time, anywhere; in the middle of an important Cabinet meeting, or talking to the Queen. During one evening's conversation with her he went to sleep three times. Gently, she teased him about it. "It is the sign of a composed mind," he replied humorously. Alas, this was not true. His health affected his nerves so that occasionally he would be swept by a sudden inexplicable fit of melancholy, during which he could not exert himself to speak, even when he was with his beloved Sovereign.

In fact he was too apathetic to do much about his health. Though he did not feel up to giving dinners himself, he dined out a great deal with other people, tiring himself by sitting up till two or three in the morning at John Russell's or Holland House, where on occasion he could still enchant the company by the breadth of his learning and the paradoxical wisdom of his discourse. And he ate more injudiciously than ever. "The stomach is the seat of health, strength, thought and life," he once said to the Queen; but he did not behave as if he thought so. Coming back from the House of Lords at four in the morning, he would consume a four-course meal and drink a whole bottle of Madeira; and the way he stuffed himself with pie and truffles and ices was enough to strain a constitution less impaired than his own. He felt guilty about this. Pork made him ill, he once informed the Queen after a night of indigestion, but he never liked to own it. "What makes you own it now?" asked she. "A fit of conscience," sighed Melbourne. Conscience, however, was not powerful enough to make him change his habits. This was not primarily because he was too self-indulgent. At heart he did not believe any change of habits would make any difference. It was not illness but mortality, inescapable, omnipotent mortality, this was his enemy. He was like his mother. Magnificently youthful she had remained till late middle-age, he remembered, yet after sixty she had sunk rapidly. So was it happening to him. The Queen pressed him to take advice about his health. "That will not do any good," he said sadly. "It is age, and that constant care!"

(2)

He was right about the constant care. Here was another reason for low spirits. It was partly connected with his work. The political situation was more uncomfortable than it had been before the crisis of May. It looked much the same: the Whigs still pursued their trimming, balancing, middle-way policy, making concessions now to the Right, now to the Left according as to which seemed likely to threaten its position the most: hedged about the Corn Laws in order to pacify the Radicals, gave way to Peel and the Tories about Jamaica and Ireland. Especially did they seek to placate the Tories because the tide of opinion in the country was now flowing more strongly than ever to the Right. However, this middle-way policy now appeared ignominious, as it had not done before. Up till May of 1839 it could claim that it had the country behind it. Now the Government's position had been shown up as too weak for this to be possible. Furthermore, before May it was easier to justify concession on genuine political grounds. To Melbourne at any rate the Whigs had seemed the only alternative either to a dangerously Radical Government, or to a reactionary Government that might provoke revolutionary opposition. Now even Melbourne thought that there was not much danger of a revolution; most people feared it so little that they took for granted that the Whigs were just clinging to office for selfish reasons, surrendering to each side in turn merely in order to stay in, at whatever sacrifice of principle. As Melbourne wrote to John Russell, "By one set of people we are told that we are ruining ourselves and losing support by allying ourselves with the Radicals and the Roman Catholics: by another that we are producing the same effect by leaning too much to the Tories and Conservatives; probably both statements are true and we are losing credit on both sides." Himself, he did not much mind if they were. It mattered little to him that his Party's actions should ultimately be controlled by Peel, for at heart he agreed with Peel's policy. "I do not dislike the Tories," he told the Queen, "I think they are very much like the others: I do not care by whom I am supported; I consider them all as one; I do not care by whom I am helped as long as I am helped," he said laughing. Indeed, he had never been a Whig because he believed in Whig principles. His loyalty to his Party had been a personal loyalty. Now that it had come into conflict with the stronger personal loyalty he felt for the Queen, he threw it over without a tremor.

But, if he did not mind what people said about his Government, his colleagues did. The sense of their ignominious position was destroying what was left of the morale of his Government; with the result that they became increasingly irritable and unmanageable. More often than ever Howick objected, John Russell talked of resignation, Palmerston acted with ostentatious disregard of his colleagues. Nor did Melbourne feel up to managing them in the way he used to. He was too tired. He still went through the motions of being Prime Minister, read the State papers, wrote off innumerable little notes to his Ministers. But in fact he exerted his will less and less. He did not give his full mind to affairs, evaded issues, shunned decisions, left the initiative to John Russell. Better make the ballot an open question if this would help to keep the Cabinet together, he said; better give in to Peel about Jamaica if it would stop him raising the question of Canada! Better continue the old Poor Law Act for another year, rather than stir controversy by discussing a new one! Throughout his political life Melbourne had been accused of laziness—on the whole unjustly. But now he really was growing lazy. Fatigue made him yield to his instinctive desire to turn his back on disagreeable facts. But alas, it was seldom possible. Do what he would, the unending squabbles in his Cabinet worried him. It was not the attacks from outside but the internal dissensions that vexed him, he complained. All he could do was ineffectively to try and forget them and concentrate such energy and attention as remained to him on the Queen.

(3)

And even his hours with her were no longer the source of satisfaction they had been. He felt them too precarious for one thing; with the Government's position so weak, it seemed as if they might end any day. The sunshine of his happiness was fading to an evening glow over which stretched the ever lengthening shadow of his imminent parting from her. Further, the troubles that had a little clouded them in the early part of the year had not passed away. The Hastings affair was not over yet. Though the populace might cheer the Queen, there was still a good deal of hostility to her in high society. "Mrs. Melbourne," shouted a gentleman in coarse, mocking tones as the Queen and her Prime Minister stepped forth on to the balcony at Ascot, and as she drove down the Course the sound of hissing made itself heard; two fashionable ladies, the Duchess of Montrose and Lady Sarah Ingestre, were protesting their disapproval. The Queen was furious. "Those two abominable women ought to be flogged!" she burst out to Melbourne. He strove to imbue her with some of his own ironical indifference to public opinion. Popularity is a capricious thing, he was always telling her: he urged her to try and ease the situation by making herself particularly pleasant to Lady Flora. The Queen was reluctant; how could she, she asked, be pleasant to someone she did not like? Worse was to come. In the beginning of June Lady Flora became dangerously ill. The tumour, which had given rise to such unfortunate interpretations, proved to be malignant: within a few weeks it was clear that she was dying. Melbourne was extremely concerned. It is a sign of his obsessed devotion to the Queen that even now he, usually the justest and most sympathetic of men, could not find it in his heart to be fair to those who threatened her peace of mind. Surely too much fuss had been made about the wrong done to Lady Flora, he said; no doubt inchastity was a shocking thing, but such things did happen in families. He was acutely anxious, however, lest the Queen should damage her reputation still further by incurring any accusation of heartlessness. At first she had refused to believe Lady Flora was really seriously ill: but he persuaded her all the same to stop all entertainments at the Palace, to send frequent messages asking how Lady Flora was, and to give orders that everything possible should be done for her comfort. Melbourne also pressed her herself to go and see Lady Flora. Not unnaturally the Queen shrank from this ordeal. But lack of courage was never one of her faults; once Melbourne had convinced her that it was her duty, she agreed—and, characteristically, decided to see her alone. The interview took place on 27th June. The dying woman, now a shadow of her former self, and with the mark of her approaching end written on every haggard feature, gazed at the childish figure of her Sovereign with a ghastly fixed stare and, clutching at her with a fevered hand, gasped out her thanks for the kindness that had been shown her during her illness. In the face of this, her first experience of death, the Queen's hard-heartedness melted away in a mingled flood of awe, pity and bewilderment. "Poor Lady Flora!" she kept on repeating as she described the scene to Melbourne. "Poor Lady Flora!" When, ten days later, Lady Flora died, the Queen burst into a torrent of tears. Her death was followed by a *détente*. Conroy left the Duchess of Kent's service soon afterwards: and, freed from his malignant influence, the Duchess became more friendly towards her daughter. Melbourne's continuous efforts to reconcile them were at last beginning to bear fruit. Also, thanks to him, the Hastings episode had not ended so badly for the Queen's good name as at one moment it seemed likely to do.

The Queen's political reputation was another worry to him. The events of May had given him a fright, for they revealed what an unbridled partizan she was. Since the Tories might come in at any time, it was vital that she should be ready to accept them in a spirit of goodwill. It would never do for her to be thought of as a Whig Queen. Rather late in the day, therefore, Melbourne set to work to implant in her the impartial and non-party point of view appropriate to a constitutional monarch. He also spent a good deal of time trying to make her like the Tories better, more especially Peel himself. Peel, he said, was reported to speak very highly of her; and his faults of manner were due to awkwardness and inexperience. "You must remember that he is a man not accustomed to talk to Kings . . . it is not like me; I have been brought up with Kings and Princes." The Queen was not placated. Peel, in her view, had been rude and presumptuous, and the Duke of Wellington not much better. She would rather have a Radical Government than the Tories, she told Melbourne. Horrified, he explained to her that, quite apart from their faults, the Radicals had not a chance of getting into power. They had little support in the country, and their Leader was the intolerable Durham. Besides, the Tories were not so bad. Personally, he had found them reasonable enough to do business with. Were not they always altering the Government Bills in the House of Lords? asked the Queen. "I do not know that those alterations did not do them good," answered Melbourne laughing. Moreover, he pointed out that it was not politic to quarrel with the Tories; how could she hope to exert any influence on them if she treated them as declared enemies? He strove to persuade her to be polite to the Tory ladies and now and again to ask important Tories to dinner. She did not want them, she replied, at least, not this year. "If you do that, you, as it were, cut them off," he said. "Flies are caught with honey, not with vinegar." These efforts to soften her were unsuccessful. Causes to her were indistinguishable from the people who supported them. Whiggism meant Melbourne, whom she liked, Toryism meant Peel, whom she disliked. Patiently, throughout 1839 Melbourne went on trying to weaken her hostility. In vain: nine months later we find her telling him that the Opposition was to blame for everything that went wrong.

It was not the only thing that she was obstinate about. Greville, meeting Melbourne, congratulated him on his skill in keeping the Queen straight. "By God, I am at it morning, noon and night!" he exclaimed with feeling. Indeed, the strain of the last months had affected the Queen's nerves as well as his, making her moody, on edge and more self-willed than ever. Her rumpus with Peel had left her extremely touchy about her royal position. At the slightest suspicion that she was not being consulted about a political appointment or a matter of State, she rushed to her writing table to indict a long, heavily underlined letter, indignantly proclaiming her royal rights and demanding an explanation.

"The Queen has been a good deal annoyed this evening," she wrote in August, "on Normanby's telling her that John Russell was coming to Town next Monday in order to change with him. Lord Melbourne never told the Queen that this was definitely settled; on the contrary, he said it would 'remain in our hands', to use Lord Melbourne's own words, and only to be settled during the Vacation; considering all that the Queen has said on the subject to Lord Melbourne, and considering the great confidence the Queen has in Lord Melbourne, she thinks and feels he ought to have told her that this was settled, and not let the Queen be the last person to hear what is settled and done in her own name; Lord Melbourne will excuse the Queen's being a little eager about this, but it has happened once before that she learned from other people what had been decided on."

Any criticism of herself, too, in Parliament or the Press roused her wrath. It ought to be stopped by law, she told Melbourne furiously.

At the same time that she grew more jealous of her privileges, she began to rebel against such obligations as bored her. Why must she have Ministers down to stay at Windsor when it was more agreeable to be there alone with Melbourne? Sometimes she said she could hardly bear the tedium of her official duties. Melbourne dealt with her moods with characteristic skill, apologized for any oversight and took care to keep her more closely informed than before about the details of affairs: more than ever he speaks to her as to an equal in these matters. He was extremely sympathetic, too, about her boredom. After all, he himself was often bored by politics; how much more a girl of her age! "You lead rather an unnatural life for a young person," he said, "it is the life of a man."

But if he was sympathetic, he was also firm. The Queen must get used to being criticized, he told her, and still more must she simply force herself not to show temper. "I cannot help it," objected the Queen mutinously. "But you must," he insisted kindly. "I am sorry to be so peremptory." Nor was boredom, however natural, a justification for neglecting her duties. No doubt being a constitutional monarch was a tricky, troublesome job but "you must bear it, it is the lot that has been cast upon you; you have drawn that ticket." Anyway, he said soothingly, her irritation was most likely due to the summer heat; he recommended her to drink more wine in order to calm her nerves.

Whether the Queen took his advice is unknown. If she did it failed to have the desired effect. Her temper remained uncertain even with Melbourne himself. Outwardly in fun, but with a glint of irritation showing through, she would scold him for his sleeping and snoring, his fits of apathetic silence, his tendency to over-eat. "I said to Lord Melbourne that I could not bear to hear that he thought so much of eating and drinking—that it is *low* to think of such things," she writes. And she made as much fuss as ever if she thought he was neglecting her; more often, too, because ill-health and pressure of work was making it harder for him to see as much of her as in the past. Why did he only spend two days a week at Windsor instead of five as he had in the previous year, she complained. Why did he leave her so early in the evening? What did he mean by writing to say that after all he would be unable to dine with her? "The Queen has received both Lord Melbourne's notes; she was a good deal vexed at his not coming as she had begged him herself to do so, and as he wrote to say he would, and also as she thinks it right and of importance that Lord Melbourne should be here at large dinners; the Queen *insists* upon his coming to dinner tomorrow." Could it be that he did not enjoy dining with her, that he preferred dining at Holland House? She had grown jealous of any woman who was reported to be his friend, and particularly so of Lady Holland who, from what she heard, sounded the sort of woman of whom she strongly disapproved. Melbourne teased her by telling her that Lady Holland had criticized her for trying to make her Ministers more religious. "A very good thing!" retorted the Queen; "she must be a bad person to think so." "She is a great enemy of religion, but one hopes she may be converted in her last hours," said Melbourne demurely. "That is too late!" asserted the Queen severely.

Nor was she altogether happy about Melbourne's own religious tone. Now that he knew her so well, he was not quite so careful as at first to keep up appearances in her presence; so that she began to wonder if he was, in fact, so pious as her first impressions had led her to suppose. Certainly he always seemed to find an excuse for not going to church; and why, she asked, when he did deign to come, did he fidget and sigh so much? Melbourne was amused. "It is right to sigh in church," he said. "He who despises not the sighing of a contrite heart. . . ." The Queen was a little shocked to hear the Liturgy quoted in this flippant fashion. "It is wrong to jest about such things," she protested. Melbourne denied that he jested about them. About other things he knew he did, perhaps too much—but never about religion. And he strenuously maintained that her first impressions of him were right, that there was nothing dubious about his view of religion. He admitted he did not like going to church, but this was for a highly creditable reason; "It is against my creed," he said with a twinkle. "I am a *quietist*; it is the creed which Fénelon embraced and which Madame Guyon taught. You are so perfect that you are exempt from all external ordinances." One wonders what the Queen can have made of this blissful account of Melbourne's spiritual state. But she was still too much under his spell to be anything but reassured.

All the same, their sparrings over religion were a symptom. As the Queen grew up she began to reveal herself as possessed of a point of view profoundly different from that of her Prime Minister: and now and again hints of this difference cast a fleeting shadow over the bright surface of their intercourse. The easygoing eighteenth century in the person of Melbourne found itself brought up with a bump against the stricter age of which the Queen was the representative. One day, for instance, he happened to say that people were not gay any more, they were too religious. "But that is quite right," said the Queen; "how can they be too much so?" "I think there will be a great deal of persecution in this country before long," explained Melbourne, "people interfering with one another about going to church, and so on." "The world is very bad," said the Queen sternly. "I do not see anything so very bad," Melbourne protested. Another time he told her that his nephew Spencer Cowper was rather a rake, "which is quite refreshing to see." "It is melancholy," answered the Queen; and she spoke with shocked horror of the hard-drinking days of the Regency, and the scandalous dissipations of her royal uncles. Wistfully recalling the days of his easygoing youth Melbourne sought to soften the harshness of her judgment. "But they were jolly fellows . . ." he pleaded; "times have changed, but I do not know if they have improved."

Such moments of dissonance between them were slight and they did not last long. The Queen was so devoted to her Prime Minister that she felt overcome with remorse the instant after she had been the least disagreeable to him. "I fear I was sadly cross with Lord Melbourne," she wrote the evening after one of these small moments of friction. "It is shameful, I fear he felt it, for he did not sit down for himself as he generally does, but waited until I had told him to do so. I cannot think what possessed me for I love the dear, excellent man . . . and he is so kind and never minds my peevishness, but is so amiable and forgiving." Indeed he was. When she apologized for plaguing him, "That's a good thing," he said; "it keeps people from being ill." His good humour bound her for the time being yet closer to him. Again and again in the Diary she reproaches herself for her ill temper, again and again protests her gratitude and love for him. To all appearances Melbourne possessed her heart as much as ever.

And yet . . . there are signs that his company was not quite the ecstatic unfailing delight to her that it had been. It could even disappoint her. One evening in June she was actually forced to admit that she had found an evening spent in Lord Melbourne's company had been dull! This was partly due to his infirmities. On the evening in question Melbourne had been feeling too ill to talk much. But there were deeper and more powerful forces working within the Queen to make her dissatisfied. She was very normal; and normal girls do not find all the pleasure they want in life can be provided by talks with elderly statesmen, however delightful. Now that the first excitement of being Queen had worn off, she longed instinctively for fun and gaiety in the society of her own contemporaries. Further—and this lay at the root of her restlessness and moodiness—she was growing up. The stage of schoolgirl hero-worship was passing; and there had begun to stir uneasily within her the desire for a more mature emotional fulfilment. She was hardly conscious of it but, in fact, when any attractive young man appeared her spirits rose. At the end of May the youthful Grand Duke of Russia paid a visit to the English Court and was entertained with appropriate celebrations. The Red

Drawing Room at Windsor shone with the light of a myriad candles as, to the seductive lilt of the violins, the Grand Duke and his retinue of dashing young nobles, their shapely figures resplendent in glittering uniforms, twirled and leapt and clicked their heels through the dance, with all the exuberance of their Slav temperaments. The Queen enjoyed herself wildly. How delightful it was to be whirled round in the Mazurka by the Grand Duke's strong arms, she noted. How they both laughed as he strove to guide her through the figures of a new German dance, the *Gross Vater*—and how dreadfully flat and dull it seemed the evening after he left! "I felt so sad to take leave of the dear amiable young man whom (talking jokingly) I was a little in love with . . ." she wrote in her diary. She confided her feeling of flatness to Melbourne. "A young person like me must *sometimes* have young people to laugh with," she said. "Nothing so natural," replied Melbourne with tears in his eyes.

The Grand Duke was only a forerunner. Early in October two other young foreign princes arrived in England; the Queen's cousins Ernest and Albert of Coburg. King Leopold of the Belgians had for some years past been working for a marriage between the Queen and his nephew Albert. Three years earlier, while William IV was still alive, Albert had been sent over for her inspection. She had found him attractive enough at any rate not to turn him down. Her accession to the Throne, however, had put her off marriage for the time being; and, with a comical assumption of maturity, she had sought to delay making up her mind on the question by telling her uncle that she did not think Albert was sufficiently experienced and grown up for her to be able to judge whether he was likely to be a fit mate for the Queen of England. Accordingly he had been sent on an educative tour of Europe under the tutelage of Leopold's confidential adviser, Baron Stockmar. Now in 1839 it was proposed he should return in order to give the Queen a chance of making a decision. She still felt reluctant. Dancing with the Grand Duke was one thing, surrendering her independence to her husband was another. Albert could come if he liked, she said, but he must realize that she did not regard herself as in any way committed. Certainly, she insisted, there could be no question of her marrying anyone for two or three years.

One sight of Albert, however, and these maidenly hesitations vanished. "It was with some emotion that I beheld Albert—who is *beautiful*!" she wrote in her diary on the evening of his arrival; and in subsequent entries she proceeded with growing enthusiasm to enumerate the catalogue of his perfections; "His beautiful blue eyes and exquisite nose and such a pretty mouth with delicate moustaches and slight, very slight, whiskers." Two days in the company of such an Adonis and she was head over ears in love! On 13th October she told Melbourne that she had made up her mind to marry Albert. "You have?" said he. "I am very glad of it . . . you will be much more comfortable; for a woman can't stand alone for long in whatever situation she is," and he proceeded to discuss what steps should be taken to make the engagement public.

Throughout the interview his tone, though tender, was calm. This was remarkable seeing how readily as a rule he showed emotion. For now, if ever, he had reason to do so. Her words meant the end of that close intimate relationship which had become the centre and sunshine of his whole existence. Even if he stayed in office, even if he remained her chief confidential adviser, he was no longer the first man in her heart. But Melbourne loved the Queen so selflessly that he did not want her newfound happiness to be shadowed, though but for an instant, by any regret he might himself be feeling. Indeed, to see her so happy did, in a sense, make him happy too.

Reason as well as affection strengthened him to resign himself to the situation. The disturbances of the last year had left him with no doubt at all that it was for the Queen's good that she should marry. She had to have a guide: and he himself was not going to be able to fulfil the role much longer. He was getting too old. Besides, his Government might fall any day. Melbourne had never been one to shut his eyes to painful facts: tender-hearted though he was, his heart did not rule his head to the extent of making him sentimentally self-deceived. He might, against his better judgment, give in to someone he loved, but he always realized that he was going against his better judgment, if he did so. Now he judged that the time had come when it was inevitable and right that he should lose the young Queen to a husband. Rigidly suppressing any indulgence in self-pity, he threw all his mind and energy into seeing that the transaction was effected as pleasantly and with as little fuss as possible.

The next few months were mainly occupied in settling the legal position of the Prince and making arrangements for the wedding. Both involved some ructions. The Opposition were in a cantankerous humour and sought to embarrass the Government by making every difficulty they could. There was a row because it was not categorically stated in any official document that the Prince was a Protestant: there was a row because the Government, following precedent, asked that he should have an income of £50,000 a year. There was also a row over the question of his precedence. The Queen wanted him to have first place in the kingdom after herself. But her royal uncles, notably the Duke of Sussex, objected to this; and they were supported in their objections by the more factious section of the Tory Party. Melbourne did not show his old skill in dealing with these difficulties. Here we notice that he was losing his grip. Considering the strength of anti-Papal feeling in England, he should have taken more care to do nothing that might stir it up; and rather than run the risk of letting the Queen's wishes become a Party issue, he ought to have tried to settle the questions of the Prince's income and precedence in private consultation with the Opposition leaders before bringing it up in Parliament. Instead he let things slide and inertly trusted that all would go right on the day. The result was that they got out of hand. After some public and distressing wrangling, the Prince's income was reduced to £30,000 and the Bill establishing his precedence looked so likely to be defeated that Melbourne had hurriedly to withdraw it and arrange that the matter should be settled later by an Order in Council.

The Queen did not make his task any easier. Her engagement, though it had raised her spirits, had not softened her temper. On the contrary, she felt more indignant than ever with the Tories for their impudence in opposing her will. "As long as I live," she burst out to Melbourne, "I never will forgive those infernal scoundrels with Peel—nasty wretch—at their head"; and she alluded to one of the venerable prelates who had voted for reducing the Prince's income as "that *fiend*, the Bishop of Exeter!" On

New Year's Day in her diary she solemnly recorded her thanks to God for delivering her from her enemies during the Government crisis of May. She added a petition; "From the Tories, good Lord deliver us."

The controversy over the Prince's precedence especially aroused her wrath. Originally she wanted to make him King Consort by Act of Parliament. "For God's sake, Ma'am," exclaimed Melbourne, "let's have no more of it. If you get the English people into the way of making Kings, you will get them into the way of unmaking them!" With such an idea of what her husband's position ought to be, she was not likely to be pleased by the proposal that he should yield first place to her uncles. She would rather he had no legal precedence at all, she said, than one so ignominious. "Oh no!" said Melbourne with robust good sense. "That's the foolishest thing. You should always get what you can." In spite of his fatigue, he had not lost his skill in dealing with her. Mingling firmness, sympathy and a sort of gay tact, he generally managed to keep her in check. When one Sunday he got a letter from the Duke of Sussex asserting his claim to precedence over the Prince, "I did not show the Duke of Sussex's letter to Your Majesty before you went to church," he told her with a smile; "I thought it would discompose you for devotion." The Queen still responded to Melbourne's arts. Once again she apologized deeply to him for losing her temper and promised with a touching artlessness not to do it again.

It was not easy for her though. Being engaged is notoriously trying to the nerves; and struggle as she might, the Queen remained irritable. She was annoyed by the Duchess of Kent who had again begun bouncing into her apartments uninvited; she was annoyed by King Leopold who continued to plague her with unasked-for political advice; at times she could even be a little irritated by the Prince himself. Her relations with him at this time show what an extraordinary mixture the Queen was. There was no doubt that she was violently in love with him. In her diary she rapturously records every detail of his caresses, his kisses, his tender words. Yet, even in the full flood of youthful passion, she never forgot that she was Queen and must maintain her position as such, even in relation to the object of her adoration. She disliked the idea of his taking any part in political business. So far as the official organization of his life was concerned, she required him to submit to her will without question. She chose all the officers of his Household without consulting him, including his confidential secretary, a Mr. George Anson, who had once been secretary to Melbourne. The Prince protested. Not only did he object to being ruled in this way, but Anson's appointment in particular conflicted with his views. He thought the Crown should be a neutral moderating power and that a Royal Household should therefore be composed of people with no marked political affiliations. The Queen reacted sharply and unfavourably to these signs of independence in her future husband. So far as English politics were concerned, she had no confidence in the Prince's judgment. For all she knew he might, if left to himself, fall, in his ignorance, under the sinister influence of the Tories. He must learn to trust her to know what was best for him in these matters. She spoke her mind to him. Anson was appointed.

The outside world put her insistence down to the influence of Melbourne who was suspected of wishing to get the Prince into his power. It was true that Melbourne did not sympathize with the Prince's political ideas. The conception of a neutral moderating monarchy was likely, in his view, to lead to the Crown taking an active line independent of the Government; whereas, according to the orthodox English doctrine, it was the King's duty to back whatever Party was in power. Moreover, Melbourne feared that whatever his intentions the Prince would, in practice, tend to choose Tories as his servants. Foreign princes in his experience had an instinctive bias against English Liberals. "They think our Liberal influence rough and disagreeable," he told the Queen. All the same, when he heard that the Prince objected strongly to have Anson as his secretary, Melbourne told the Queen she ought to give in to him. It was not a good thing that a wife should domineer over a reluctant husband in this fashion. Further, Melbourne himself did not want to appear responsible for any step that might alienate the Prince from him. From the moment of the Queen's engagement he made it an important part of his business to get on good terms with the Prince.

At first he had to feel his way, for he knew little about him. "He seems a very agreeable young man," he wrote to John Russell. "Certainly he is a very good looking one—and as to character, that we must always take our chance of." It was a safe enough chance had Melbourne known it. The Prince was eminently, even alarmingly, respectable. This did not mean that he would necessarily be easy for Melbourne to get on with. In fact, the two men made a comical contrast to each other; Melbourne a casual, ironical, pleasure-loving Englishman of the eighteenth-century world, the Prince a stiff, conscientious, serious-minded German, not above relaxing for an hour's innocent merriment in the bosom of his family, but with his spirit already shadowed by the anxious earnestness so typical of the nineteenth century. His affinity with the Queen lay precisely on that side of her nature which had least in common with Melbourne's. She was sufficiently aware of this to get a little feminine fun by playing off her fiancé against her Prime Minister. The Prince, she said, thought she should not receive anyone at Court whose reputation was doubtful. "The Prince is much severer than me," she announced to Melbourne. Melbourne could not suppress his surprise and vexation. Not only did the Prince's views strike him as intolerant, but, considering the free and easy morals of the English aristocracy, they seemed likely to get the Queen into disfavour with some of her most influential subjects. "That is a very bad thing," he said bluntly. "Albert thinks I should set an example of propriety," pursued the Queen. Melbourne was still sufficiently ruffled to disclose the worldly-wise nature of his approach to social morality in a manner more frank than prudent. "That is shown by your own conduct," he blurted out. "Character can be attended to when people are of no consequence. But it will not do when people are of a very high rank." A day or two later the Queen laughingly told Melbourne that she feared he did not like Albert so much as he would, if he were not so strict. By this time Melbourne had recovered his self-command. "Oh no! I highly respect him," he answered discreetly.

Sometimes it was his turn to tease the Queen. She said triumphantly that Albert did not care for fashionable beauties, indeed that in general he took no interest in women. From what he had seen of royal princes, Melbourne judged this to be improbable. "That

M

will come later," he mischievously remarked. The Queen was so outraged by the implication of these words that he hastily withdrew them and later took occasion to reassure her by telling her that from what he had observed of the Prince he seemed in these respects to be a glorious exception to the general run of young men.

When the Prince was actually present, Melbourne seems to have taken more pains to curb his tongue. Even so, now and again a remark slipped out which revealed the gulf between their points of view. One evening in Windsor, they were playing a letter game. Melbourne was given the word "pleasure" to guess. "It is not a *common* thing," explained the Prince in order to help him. "Is it truth or honesty?" enquired Melbourne.

"This made us all laugh," says the Queen relating the incident: and, in fact, whatever fundamental difference there might be between them, Melbourne and the Prince during these months contrived to get on pleasantly enough together. Melbourne's manner to the Prince was remarked on as perfect in its blending of respectful politeness with informal ease. The Prince responded to it: he speaks of Melbourne always as a kindly distinguished old gentleman devoted to the Queen's service. Melbourne reciprocated his goodwill. The difficulty of the Prince's position as a young foreigner suddenly pitchforked into the intricate hurly-burly of English public life stirred his sympathy: and he took pains to give him hints as how best to conduct himself in it. As he got to know him better, too, his opinion of him steadily improved. Melbourne meant what he said when he told the Queen that he respected the Prince. No doubt he was a bit of a prig like most Germans, but he was clearly a good young man who could be trusted to make the Queen happy. Since her happiness mattered to Melbourne more than anything else in the world, he felt growingly friendly towards the Prince.

This confidence in her future happiness may have helped him to keep up an appearance of good spirits. Certainly he managed wonderfully to do so. The accounts of him during the last weeks of her engagement are all sparkling and sunshiny. It was as though he was determined to extract every ounce of pleasure from his last days with her as an unmarried woman. Her diary is as full as ever of his conversation, and though once or twice he refers to his fatigue and depression, for the most part he is at his most delighted and delightful. He cajoled her into asking the Duke of Wellington to her wedding in spite of the shameful way she considered he had behaved over the Prince's precedence: he gave her his views on Scottish history—"There are too many Jameses and all murdered, the Scottish are a dreadful people"; he gaily gossiped to her about the appearance of her ladies. "Miss Montague," he observed, "has a peculiar way of carrying her nose"; he expatiated on the splendour of the new coat he was having made for the wedding. "I expect it will be the thing most observed," remarked Melbourne humorously.

One evening three days before the wedding he allowed his deeper feelings a little more play. The Queen noticed that his manner was unusually affectionate, even for him. She told him that she felt nervous. He comforted and encouraged her. "Depend upon it, it's right to marry," he said; "if ever there was a situation that formed an exception, it was yours; it's in human nature, it's natural to marry; the other is a very unnatural state of things; it's a great *change*—it has its inconveniences. . . . After all," he continued, "how anybody in your situation can have a moment's tranquillity!—a young person cast in this situation is very unnatural. There was a beautiful account in a Scotch paper of your first going to prorogue Parliament; 'I stood close to her, to see a young person surrounded by Ministers and Judges and rendered prematurely grave was almost melancholy'; 'a large searching eye, an open anxious nostril and a firm mouth' . . . a very true representation," he said, "can't be a finer physiognomy." The Queen smiled at his earnestness. "I am sure none of your friends are as fond of you as I am," she said. "I believe it," he answered. He spoke with deep emotion.

On 11th February the great day came. The Prime Minister was observed to be much affected, as he stood in his smart new coat watching the ceremony. Afterwards, at Buckingham Palace, when she had changed her dress, she sent for him for a final private interview. He kissed her hand. They remained a moment or two talking of how well everything had gone off. "You look very tired," said the Queen anxiously. Once more he gave her a long, loving look. His hand clasped in hers, "God bless you, Ma'am," he said. Then the Prince appeared. Together he and the Queen went downstairs and drove away.

(5)

Meanwhile the Government muddled its way ineffectively and uncomfortably along, frustrated by the Tories, sniped at by the Radicals and disturbed by the wranglings of its own members, notably Howick. At last in June he was so exasperated that he resigned. Melbourne accepted his resignation with easy indifference and made Macaulay minister in his stead. This made for a more peaceful atmosphere: for Macaulay was not temperamental. But neither was he restful. Brilliant, dogmatic, voluble and tireless, he at once dazed and dazzled his colleagues by the uninterrupted flow of his discourse. "I wish I was as cocksure about anything," said Melbourne, "as Macaulay is about everything!" However, he was not bored by Macaulay. On the contrary he sat listening to him "with an air of complacency and as if for instruction". Melbourne was unusually ready to tolerate monologists, so long as there was something original about them. This propensity got him into trouble about this time. In the summer, Robert Owen, celebrated in history as a pioneer of socialism, had persuaded him to present him officially at Court. It was surprising that Melbourne should have agreed because Owen, in addition to being universally recognized as one of the greatest bores alive, was a militant Left Wing atheist who had taken a leading part in attacking Melbourne for his treatment of the Dorset labourers. However, Melbourne never disliked anyone for attacking him, and had a strong objection to punishing a man, otherwise harmless, simply because he held unorthodox opinions. His respectable contemporaries did not share this view: presentation at Court, in their view, implied approval of a man's ideas. Melbourne was violently criticized for his action by important people at Court and by his opponents in the House of Lords. Though professing himself sorry if he had acted without due consideration, he took these attacks very lightly.

"I beg to assure you," he wrote to a correspondent, "that you may most safely and in the most decisive manner contradict the notion that there may be any approbation on my part of Mr. Owen's opinions. . . . I have more than once heard Mr. Owen's statements and I have always told him that his doctrines appeared to be the most absurd, and he himself one of the most foolish men I ever conversed with. I always considered that his principles were too ridiculous to be dangerous."

In Parliament, after a few perfunctory words of explanation and apology, he proceeded to air his views on the subject of free speech in general. It was no good advocating it, he said, on the ground that it led in the end to truth prevailing: mankind was far too foolish for that. But on the other hand he thought repression equally useless, for it was impossible to make it effective.

These characteristic and inconclusive reflections showed that Melbourne had not lost his taste for speculation. However, less than ever did this influence his practical activities as a statesman. These were solely directed to keeping the Government together until such time as he judged the Queen had learned to manage without his help. To achieve this end he employed his old tactics of combined obstruction and concession. Two important new measures were introduced during the latter part of 1839; one for an Education Bill and one for establishing the Penny Post. Melbourne did not believe in either. The Penny Post would do no good, he told the Queen: but he thought it sufficiently uncontroversial to be ready to back it in order to please his colleagues. There is an amusing account of Rowland Hill, the chief promoter of the measure, coming to coach him for his speech in the debate on the subject. He found Melbourne in his dressing room; and, running through the chief points, mentioned a Mr. Warburton who had views on the matter. "Warburton, Warburton," said Melbourne; "he is one of your moral force men, isn't he? I can understand your physical force man, but as to your moral force men I'll be damned if I know what they mean!" A few minutes later Hill was shown into another room while Melbourne interviewed Lord Lichfield, the Postmaster General who opposed the Bill because, oddly, he thought that the Post Office buildings would collapse under the weight of letters likely to be put in them, if postage became so cheap. Melbourne soothed him. "Lichfield has been here," he remarked to Hill after ushering the excited Postmaster General out of the room. "I cannot think why a man cannot talk of Penny Postage without going into a passion!"

Melbourne made more difficulties about the Education Bill. Not only did he disbelieve in educational schemes as such, but he rightly thought that they always raised trouble with the Church, who considered that no one else should have any control over them. Howick was still in the Government when the question was first discussed. "Thank God there are some things which even you cannot stop, and this is one of them!" he broke out furiously to Melbourne. Melbourne merely smiled and went on making objections. As he expected, the Church, supported by the Tory Party, did oppose the Government Bill violently. In the end a compromise was reached which left the control of education in Church hands.

The year 1839 also saw a slight revival of these civil disturbances which had marked the Reform period. That same economic distress that had led to the anti-Corn Law agitation also gave birth to the semi-revolutionary Chartist Movement. During May there was serious rioting in Birmingham, and at Newport in November. Melbourne dealt with the new disturbances as he had with the old: he advocated vigorous repression but only within the limits of the existing law. The ringleaders of the riots ought to be hanged, he said. On the other hand he was against John Russell's proposal that the Government should be given extraordinary powers to seize arms, etc. On the whole, however, he took the whole affair much more calmly than in 1831. When, on 10th August, the Cabinet was told that the Chartists were organizing a mass protest movement in support of their demands and that it was scheduled to start on 12th August, "God bless my soul," said Melbourne breezily, "that is the day after tomorrow! It is time for us to be looking about us." Clearly he had at last come to the conclusion that there was not much danger of bloody revolution breaking out in England. He was quite right. Lawlessness was easily stamped out. But the deterioration in the economic situation continued: and Melbourne did worry about this, especially as he thought it was likely to get worse and saw no way of stopping it. However, he still was determined to try and stay in office. Apart from anything else, the Queen was always asking him to: and he had told her he would. He preferred, however, that the outside world should not know this, for fear they might blame her for it. Let it be thought, rather, that he was doing it to please those members of his Party who were enjoying the sweets of office. "No one supposes I want to go on," he said, "but I must think of those poor fellows who would have to put down their broughams." By the spring of 1840 there did not seem any immediate danger that they would have to. The disturbances were over, the Radicals were losing heart. For the time being, at any rate, it looked as if things were settling down.

However, Melbourne was not fated to feel easy for long. In the summer a new crisis loomed up. This time it was over foreign affairs. These had never been one of Melbourne's major preoccupations up till now. Not that he neglected them. The subject interested him—he was the only member of the Cabinet except Palmerston who really understood it, said a foreign observer—and anyway he was not allowed to forget about it by his brother Fred Lamb, now British Representative in Vienna, and who distrusted Palmerston even more than he did himself. Both brothers were against his militant pro-Liberalism: they wanted to combine with Austria to create a middle force that might hold the balance between Russia and France. However, Melbourne was not prepared to try and enforce this view on his obstreperous Foreign Secretary. Once he had resigned himself to taking Palmerston back in 1835, he seems to have come to the conclusion that he had better let him run foreign policy as he wanted. For one thing, he knew he could not stop him, and for another it was a great saving of trouble. All he could do was to keep a vigilant eye on him and intervene from time to time to check his more perilous extravagances of word and action. Breezy and combative, Palmerston continued to pursue his liberalizing policy; backed the Constitutional Party in Spain and Portugal, encouraged Liberal Movements in Central Europe, hauled foreign monarchs and statesmen over the coals when he caught them doing anything that struck him as unusually tyrannical. None of this was much to Melbourne's liking. Palmerston did not seem to realize that "the worst thing in the world was to be troublesome". Besides, trouble abroad meant trouble at home, and trouble at home might easily lead to that downfall of the Government which it was Melbourne's chief aim to avoid. The situation at home always conditioned his view of the situation abroad. His first reaction to any proposal of Palmerston's is to ask him how it is to be defended in the House of Lords. His own advice to him was always on the side of caution. It is extraordinary how many sentences in his frequent letters began with the phrase, "For God's sake don't. . . ." He stopped Palmerston seizing the island of Goa from the Portuguese in 1839 because they had not kept their promise to put down the slave trade; in 1836 he warned him about getting entangled in grandiose schemes for moulding the future of Asia. "The Black Sea and the Caucasus and those great empires enflame the imagination wonderfully," he remarked ironically. He was also always suspicious of coming to any international agreement which committed England to some definite course of action in the future. "It may be necessary to defend Turkey," he says on one occasion, "but I should not like to be bound to defend her. Our policy is to have our hands free. . . ." And again when commenting on the French proposal for a comprehensive treaty of mutual defence, "Treaties of this comprehensive character are very dangerous transactions. They rarely answer the purpose for which they were formed and they often involve consequences which are in no respect foreseen." Melbourne realized, as Palmerston did not, that the English, however progressive and idealistic, liked their foreign policy to be cheap. They might cheer the spectacle of a foreign people rightly struggling to be free; the last thing they wanted was to spend money or soldiers in helping them to win the struggle. Melbourne, therefore, objected to Palmerston's tendency to speak strongly, because he knew he seldom had the power to enforce his words by strong action. What was the good of scolding the Czar for addressing his Polish subjects in offensive terms; much the Czar would care! And why promise to see that the Spanish gave generous terms to the Basques when there was no means of ensuring that they carried out these terms? Why encourage the Circassians and the Serbs to resist their oppressors when England had neither the intention nor the means actively to help them in their fight? The only consequence of such conduct was to irritate England's enemies without alarming them, and to leave her friends with the impression that she was either perfidious or ineffective.

All the same, in spite of these causes of disagreement, Palmerston and Melbourne did not get on so badly. For one thing, personal relations between them were easy. They had a family connection: Palmerston, who for many years it was suspected, had been Emily Cowper's lover, married her in 1839. Further, he and Melbourne were natives of the same fashionable Whig world, both talked the same blunt, flippant, male Whig language. Plainspoken though their letters to each other are, they are also goodhumoured. Neither was offended by the other's frankness. Further, each respected the other enough to make concessions. More often than not Palmerston listened to Melbourne's advice and modified his policy accordingly. On his side Melbourne, whatever he might say to Palmerston in private, loyally supported him in public. He always refused to hold any communication with foreign representatives who tried to negotiate with him behind Palmerston's back, and when Holland or John Russell grumbled to him about Palmerston, Melbourne replied that he thought he was doing well. He meant it, too. Melbourne had the open-mindedness of his scepticism. So long as Palmerston's risky-seeming policy did not get the Government into serious trouble, Melbourne was willing enough to give it his approval.

Altogether Melbourne had not found much to worry about in foreign affairs during the first five years of his Premiership. Alas, in the summer of 1840 he did. Trouble arose in the Middle East. It had been brewing some time. Early in the 'thirties Mehemet Ali, the powerful Pasha of Egypt, rebelled against his Suzerain, the corrupt and feeble Sultan of Turkey. The consequence was a long drawn out conflict between them which seemed likely to end in the victory of Mehemet Ali and the break up of the Turkish Empire. Palmerston was horrified at such a prospect. For he saw the Turkish Empire as a necessary bulwark against the rival ambitions of France and Russia to dominate the Eastern Mediterranean.

Accordingly, in the autumn of 1839, he set to work to persuade the great powers to agree to a treaty by which they pledged themselves to help the Sultan, by force if need be, to defeat Mehemet

Ali. This proposal produced a new alignment of powers in Europe. Russia, Austria and Prussia agreed to it, but the French, who saw a chance of getting Egypt on their side if Mehemet Ali won, hung back. Undismayed Palmerston set to work to bully them into acquiescence. Here he found himself at odds with some of his colleagues. Two in particular, Holland and Clarendon, the new Lord Privy Seal, shrank from any idea of quarrelling with progressive France, more especially as they feared that Palmerston's policy might lead to increasing the power of the arch-reactionary, Russia. They wanted Palmerston to drop his plan. Melbourne, as so often, felt divided on the question. Though he diplomatically denied it to Holland, on the whole he thought Palmerston right; for Egypt dominated by France would be a danger to England; and as for Russia, Melbourne had come to the conclusion that she was bound to get control of Turkey sooner or later. On the other hand, he wanted above all things to avoid a split in his own Government. He therefore took up his usual middle-way position and pleaded rather ineffectively with his colleagues for compromise. To the outside world he adopted his old tactics of agreeable evasiveness. In March, 1840, Guizot, the new French Ambassador, went to see him and expatiated with Gallic eloquence on the strength of his country's case. Melbourne, stretched out comfortably in an armchair, listened and laughed and seemed friendly and interested, and refused to commit himself in any way. In July, alarmed by Mehemet Ali's continued successes, Palmerston decided to force the issue. Since the French would not agree, he proposed making a treaty with the other powers, leaving them out. At once Holland and Clarendon said they would resign if such a proposal was accepted. Palmerston replied that he would resign if it was not accepted. "For God's sake," cried Melbourne, "let nobody resign or we'll have everybody resigning"; and he proceeded to try and persuade one side or the other to yield. In the end, Holland and Clarendon gave way and the Treaty was signed.

It was far from being the end of the trouble. The French were furious. Their excitable Prime Minister, Thiers—"he is a strange quicksilver man, this Thiers, he puts me in mind of Brougham," said Melbourne—fulminated threats of reprisal. It seemed possible that if the other powers went to the Sultan's help, France might go to the help of Mehemet Ali. For the first time for many years the shadow of a possible general war rose to brood darkly over the European scene. The result was an explosion in the English Cabinet. The pro-French party became frantic; and, what mattered much more, John Russell who had agreed to the Treaty was now so frightened by the idea of war that he changed his mind. He wrote clamouring for some compromise with France before it was too late. So also did those respected grand old men of the Whig Party, Lord Spencer and the Duke of Bedford. Melbourne communicated their agitated expostulations to Palmerston who paid no attention whatever. The French were merely bluffing, he said cheerfully; they were not such fools as to embark on a war in which they were bound to do badly. Melbourne was unable to feel so confident. Hitherto he had managed to stop himself worrying; now he became seriously disturbed. It was all very well for Palmerston to say that the French would be silly to go on standing out, but people often were silly. "You calculate a little too much upon nations and individuals feeling reason, right and a just view of their own interest," he said crisply. Even if Palmerston were right about the French, the defeat of Mehemet Ali was likely to be a long job; and meanwhile the English Government might fall. However, Melbourne reflected gloomily, it was too late for England to back out now without disastrous loss of face. Besides, to do so would mean Palmerston's resignation and that also would bring about the downfall of the Government. No—there was nothing to do but go on as they had begun; and his own particular task was to hold country and Government together in the hope that the situation might improve. The country in general added little to his difficulties for the public was not fully awake to the crisis; and Melbourne safeguarded himself against any attack from the official opposition by going to see the Duke of Wellington and persuading him to promise his support. It was his own colleagues who were the trouble; Holland, John Russell who had begun again to talk of resigning and, of course, Palmerston. In order to deal with them Melbourne pulled himself together to give such an exhibition of his diplomatic skill as had not been seen since the days of his prime. There was no longer any sign of his having lost his grip. Outwardly his old lazy, ironical self, he proceeded during two tense months to evade and temporize and pour oil, and now and again, genially but firmly, to read the riot act. Of course Palmerston was indiscreet, he told John Russell, but for John Russell to resign would only increase Palmerston's power. Of course John Russell and Holland were tiresome, he said to Palmerston— "Friends are generally more troublesome and often more hostile than adversaries," he remarked sardonically—but that was all the more reason for being cautious and circumspect. To both parties Melbourne insisted on the folly of doing anything that might break up the Government. If it fell, neither, he pointed out, would have a chance of getting their way in foreign affairs.

At first all his efforts appeared vain. Mehemet Ali did better and better, the French got angrier and angrier, John Russell went on threatening his resignation, Palmerston became more arrogantly intransigent than ever. Keeping him in order was the hardest part of Melbourne's task; and secretly he found himself turning more and more against him. Why, oh why had Palmerston ever embarked on so dangerous a policy? "Never," he wrote sharply to him, "was a great measure undertaken upon a basis of support so slender and uncertain." Not that Palmerston was much more of a nuisance than Lord and Lady Holland, who, it was reported, were now repeating every Cabinet secret at their parties in Holland House, even when the French Ambassador was present.

Certainly it was a wearing time, especially for a frail and ageing man like Melbourne. The strain began to tell on him. He suffered continually from indigestion and lumbago; he lost his appetite and could hardly sleep at all. He kept awake, it was noticed, even during Cabinet meetings! In mid-September, a new element insinuated itself into the situation, to disturb him still further. The Queen intervened. Prompted by the Prince, who in turn was prompted by King Leopold, she became extremely suspicious of Palmerston's policy and began to bombard Melbourne with excited letters complaining that she was not consulted and pressing for accommodation with France before things came to a crisis. "The Queen really could not go through that *now*," she protested, "and it might make her *seriously ill* if she were to be kept in a state

of agitation and excitement." Melbourne was extremely distressed. The Queen, as he knew to his cost, was likely to be just
as unmanageable as Palmerston. Besides, the last thing he wanted
to do was to upset her at the present moment, she was now several
months gone with child. However, he kept his head, soothed her
down with his usual skill and made use of her delicate condition as
an argument to impose his will on Palmerston and John Russell.
If they had an ounce of consideration for the Queen they simply
must try to be moderate. Meanwhile, with light tact he suggested
to the Hollands that they should cultivate discretion. "I know not
what can be done except to take care that as little of political affairs
transpires in conversation as possible," he wrote to Lord Holland;
"but this is inconsistent with a salon—which has many advantages and some disadvantages."

At last, his patience reaped its reward. The situation took a
turn for the better. Helped by the British Fleet, the Sultan began
to prevail over Mehemet Ali, and in France there were signs that
Thiers, the leader of resistance to England, was losing support.
Melbourne judged that the need for procrastinating was over.
Now was the moment for strong action. Without consulting anyone, he therefore wrote off to King Leopold, who had constituted
himself a sort of unofficial intermediary between England and the
French King, Louis Philippe, a letter written in his most trenchant style, in which he said that if Thiers called up the army he,
Melbourne, would summon Parliament and demand that England
should take effective counter-measures. He assumed that this letter would be shown to Louis Philippe. It was: and the effect produced was instantaneous. The terrified Louis Philippe dismissed
Thiers. Soon after news came that Acre, a principal fortress in
Mehemet Ali's defences, had fallen to the Sultan. The danger of
war was over. By the end of October the crisis was at an end.

(6)

A wave of relief swept over Melbourne. For a week or two he
was like a boy escaped from school, bubbling over with laughter
and high spirits. He had reason to be exhilarated as well as relieved, for England's success was partly due to him. The policy
had been Palmerston's: but unless Melbourne, in spite of his own

inner misgivings, had backed it so loyally and kept Queen and
Cabinet in check, Palmerston would never have been able to carry
it out. It had been a very trying time for Melbourne though, and
left him—once the first exhilaration had worn off—frailer and
older than ever: "Lord Melbourne is looking as old as the hills,"
said a Court lady. He felt it too. Clearly he would not be up to
going on with the work of a Prime Minister for much longer. In
fact he did not have to. The year 1841 saw the final collapse of the
Whig Government. The economic situation was its undoing.
This got no better: with the result that the agitation to get rid of
protective duties, more especially the Corn Laws, revived and intensified. More and more Government supporters went over to
the anti-Corn Law side: more and more did Ministers press that
the Corn Laws should be modified if not repealed. Melbourne
was still against this. He thought modification must lead ultimately to complete abolition: and he recognized—as some of his
colleagues did not—that abolition must fatally undermine the rule
of the English landed gentry. Melbourne continued to favour the
rule of the English landed gentry. Further, he realized that raising
the Corn Law issue also meant the end of the Whig Government.
It was bound to start a major political row: and the precarious
balance which kept the Whigs in power could only be maintained,
so long as it was not shaken by a major political row. Up till now
Melbourne had tried to stave things off by suggesting that the
Corn Laws, like the secret ballot, should be treated as an open
question on which Ministers could vote as they pleased. But this
was no longer a possible way out; the question had become so important that the Government must make up its mind to give the
country a definite united lead about it. Melbourne thought the
matter over, listened to his colleagues' arguments—and gave way
to the anti-Corn Law party. Airily he explained his position in the
matter to the Queen. "I do *not*," he said, "go the length of those
people who think the Corn Laws are against the Gospel and the
spirit of Jesus Christ! I am against the political principles of many
in this way. But I have always kept it open for me to change, if I
should think it necessary." Indeed, his change over about the
Corn Laws was not an inconsistency on his part. It had always
been one of his principles that a wise statesman compromised with

a movement once it had become too strong and too widespread to be checked without an explosion. He behaved over the Corn Laws as he had over the Reform Bill. All the same he could not bring himself to feel much interested in how they should be modified. It was the sort of practical subject that bored him to tears. Absent-minded and indifferent, he sat through one Cabinet meeting after another while his colleagues wrangled interminably about fixed duties and sliding scales. At last, in March, they came to an agreement and took their leave. As they went downstairs they heard the Prime Minister's voice calling to them: looking up they saw him leaning over the banisters: "Stop a bit," he said. "What did we decide? Is it to lower the price of bread, or isn't it? It doesn't matter which, but we must all say the same thing."

Indeed he seemed to take the whole crisis very lightly: and also the imminent eclipse of his Government which it portended. "Ten to one we shall not be in next year," he remarked cheerfully: and when Clarendon reported to him that Palmerston was said to be intriguing secretly with the Tories, he received the ominous news with detached ironical amusement. "It can't last—it's impossible this Government can go on!" he reflected aloud, chuckling and rubbing his hands. The fact was that he had at last resigned himself to the prospect of going out of office: and thought, characteristically, that it was best to make as little heavy weather over it as possible. After all, politics were not a subject that should be taken very seriously.

One serious task did however remain to him; to prepare the Queen for his exit. This was not so hard as it would have been once. For no longer was she going to be left alone. Indeed, one of the reasons that Melbourne gave way over the Corn Laws so easily was that his chief motive for staying in had been weakened by the Queen's marriage. During the last few months he had worked steadily to train the Prince for his future responsibilities as the Queen's personal adviser. It was not always easy; the Prince was so extremely unlike himself. "This damned morality will ruin everything!" Melbourne exclaimed after the Prince had expressed some view that struck him as peculiarly priggish. But his feelings about the Prince, like so many of his other feelings, were mixed. At the same time as he was irritated by him, he was

also impressed by him. And anyway he was careful to hide his
irritation. So successfully that the Prince told his uncle that
"Good Lord Melbourne" was the only one of his wife's ministers
that he really trusted. Melbourne arranged for him to see all the
foreign despatches; and the Prince would send them back to him
accompanied by long and detailed memoranda of his views about
them. Melbourne did not answer him in equal detail, in fact he
often did not answer him at all. But the Prince was flattered to
notice that he often acted as if he had modified his views in consequence of the memoranda. Meanwhile, Melbourne managed to
get his own opinions through to the Prince either in direct conversation or—more tactfully—by saying a word to Anson or the
Queen with the intention that it should be passed on. He took
pains, too, in the course of his talks with the Queen to tell her how
intelligent and judicious he thought the Prince was. With good
effect: the Queen, as we have seen, had started off with the idea of
not allowing the Prince to share in her political work. It was not
just that she wanted to keep power in her own hands; she also had
an uneasy feeling that political discussions might lead to political
disagreement; and that this would dissipate the atmosphere of
idyllic rapture which she desired to glow round every moment that
she spent in the loved one's company. The Prince, however, preferred interesting work to idyllic rapture, and complained to her
about his exclusion. The Queen rushed off to ask Melbourne's
advice. Was he tempted to back her up in her resolution to keep
the Prince out of politics? He might well have been, for politics
were the one subject concerning which he kept his old exclusive
position with her. But if he was tempted, he resisted. His love
was self-sacrificing and unpossessive. Earnestly he pressed her to
consult the Prince more: disagreements, he said, were less dangerous to married happiness than secretiveness, for secretiveness led
to distrust. At first the Queen demurred; but as time passed she
began to come round. It was inevitable she should. By nature she
tended always to look up to some man as her chief authority in all
matters; and who should it be but her husband? Already he was
modifying her outlook in other ways. Fancy the Queen talking
about botany and tree-planting! said the Ladies of the Household;
before the Prince came she did not know one plant from another!

And what about her new-found taste for sacred music? Clearly all these changes came from the Prince. About people, she was not so ready to follow his lead. The Prince wanted to invite learned men and scientists to the Palace in order that he might enjoy the benefit of improving talks with them. This prospect did not appeal to the Queen. She was too ignorant for such talk, she said. She consulted Melbourne, who, for once, found himself baffled. Even he did not know how to make the Queen enjoy the company of scientists. In general, however, she began to defer more and more to the Prince's opinions. These soon included his political opinions. His influence already showed itself powerful at the time of the Syrian crisis. By the spring of 1841 it had consolidated itself even further.

It was still not to be compared with Melbourne's, however. For the time being the Queen still turned to Melbourne before anyone else. This, he realized, was going to be a difficulty if the Government fell. For one thing, the Queen indicated that she wanted to go on keeping in touch with him afterwards. Though he must have longed for her to do so, yet he knew quite well that it was not the custom of the British Constitution for the Sovereign to be in habitual communication with the Leader of the Opposition behind the back of her Prime Minister. Some compromise must be found. Would it be possible for the Queen, if for once in a way she felt particular need of his advice, to tell the Prince who would tell Anson who would tell Melbourne? His advice would then be passed back through the same devious channel. The Prince thought this an excellent idea. Not so the Queen: she said categorically that she must be allowed to communicate with Lord Melbourne directly. Melbourne, who knew her in this mood, bowed to her words. Then there was the vexatious question of the Queen's ladies to be settled. By now, Melbourne was convinced that the original quarrel over it had been an error which would have ended disastrously had not Peel agreed to give in rather than to have a public row about it. The same mistake must not be made again, and the best thing would be to get the matter arranged beforehand. Once more with the help of the Prince, a secret negotiation was opened with Peel, by which it was tacitly agreed that he should not demand the dismissal of the ladies, but that the Queen should ask those few

who were most connected with the Whigs to send in their resigna-
tions when the Tories came in. Melbourne also asked Anson to
try and indicate to Peel the importance of being patient with the
Queen. Last time he had been too hasty. "He didn't give the
Queen time to come round," he said, "you should always give
people time to come round."

He had done what he could to smooth the way for the new
Government. Late in May the crash came. The Whigs were defeated over the Budget. They did not go out straight away because they could not make up their minds whether to resign or to
advise the Queen to dissolve Parliament. If she dissolved Parliament, there would be an election at once and they might have a
better chance of winning it: if they resigned, the Queen would
send for Peel who would then be in a position to have an election
when he thought it suited him best. All the same Melbourne was
for resignation. He judged that the Government would be defeated in any case, and he very much disliked the idea of an election fought, as it certainly would be, on the issue of the Corn
Laws; for it was likely to be a violent contest which roused popular passions in the way he most disliked. "No terms," he said,
"can express my horror, my detestation, my absolute loathing of
the attempt to enlist religious feelings against the Corn Laws."
More important, he thought that the Queen was for the time being
so identified with himself and the Whigs that she would be looked
on as a partizan in the election and that this would make her unpopular. Melbourne was not going to recommend any policy,
whatever its other advantages, that ran the slightest risk of making
the Queen unpopular. She did not agree, all she wanted was to
help the Whigs. John Russell and others took the same view. For
a week or two the question was undecided; people began to wonder if the Whigs were not intending to stick on, in spite of their
defeat. "Why is Lord Melbourne like a *very* serious young lady?"
said a wit of the time. "Because he won't go out *at all*." At last
after a lot of arguing and letter-writing, Melbourne bowed to
the will of his Sovereign and colleagues. Another Government
defeat was followed by the dissolution of Parliament; in August
an election took place. As Melbourne had prophesied, the
Whigs were soundly beaten. Parliament met again at the end of

August. The curtain rose on the concluding scene of Melbourne's premiership.

He played it in character. Never a parliamentarian, he had neither the will nor the energy to make much of his farewell to the House of Lords. The Tories moved a vote of no confidence in the Government; and the Duke of Wellington attacked Melbourne for changing his mind about the Corn Laws. Looking weary and dispirited, Melbourne rose to make a brief, negligent and flippant reply. Of course he had changed his mind, he said, but so did everybody when circumstances altered; "We are all very much in the habit of taunting one another with having changed our opinions, but the fact is we are always changing our opinions. . . . It is nonsense to proceed with measures which it is impossible can succeed." He was followed by Brougham who took the occasion to pay Melbourne back for turning him out of the Government by making a bitter, malicious and detailed personal onslaught on him. Melbourne seemed a little disturbed; leaning forward he asked one of his colleagues if he thought one particular accusation was in any way justified by the facts. But, whether from lack of heart or from a fundamental indifference, he did not bother to get up and answer Brougham. On 28th August, after they were defeated in the House of Commons, Melbourne, in a few short sentences, announced the Government's resignation.

Meanwhile, up to the very last minute he had gone on doing everything he could to make things easy for the Queen in the new situation she was about to enter. He suggested some final hints to Peel, through the medium of Anson, as how best to gain her confidence; and to the Prince as how best to increase and maintain it. Don't let him irritate her by talking solemnly *at* her about religion, "She particularly dislikes what Her Majesty terms a *Sunday Face*!" To the Queen herself Melbourne once more, and for the last time, earnestly urged the advantages of tact and discretion. The great thing was to avoid an open conflict with her Ministers. If she found she disagreed with them, she had better say that she needed time for further consideration, and not let herself be driven into a corner. For the rest, he made a final effort to remove her prejudice against Peel and the Tories. When the Queen complained that the Tory Ministers had looked cross at their first interview with her, Melbourne said that most likely they were only shy and embarrassed; "Strange faces," he explained, "are apt to give the idea of ill humour." He grew suddenly worried lest he had biased her unduly against some of them.

"In the course of this correspondence," he wrote off to her, "Lord Melbourne has thought it his duty to Your Majesty to express himself with great freedom upon the characters of many individuals . . . but Lord Melbourne thinks it right to say that he may have spoken upon insufficient grounds, that he may have been mistaken and that the persons in question may turn out to be far better than he has been induced to represent them."

The Queen listened to his words more calmly than in the previous year. She still said that losing him was the saddest event of her life, she still complained that she found Peel's manner disagreeably stiff. But when she and Melbourne met there were none of the passionate protests and emotional storms of May, 1839. She shed tears, but they were the gentle nostalgic tears of one who regrets the irretrievable past but is resigned to accept the inevitable future. Melbourne encouraged her spirit of resignation. This was for his own comfort as well as hers. He recognized the fact that even if the Tories fell, he himself was unlikely to be up to taking office again; and so was determined that for neither of them should his last hours with the Queen leave any needlessly painful memories behind them. He strove studiously to keep the tone of their intercourse as normal and even cheerful as possible. On the last evening he dined at the Palace as Prime Minister he actually managed to appear unusually merry. Not that he repressed sentiment altogether. Melbourne was the last man to cultivate an unnaturally stiff upper lip. He knew what she was going through, he told her, how the expectation of a dreaded event could cast its shadow over every pleasure, how hard it was to concentrate on work with a troubled mind. But, he said, work did dissipate trouble if one persevered with it; and he trusted that when the time came she would find she did not miss him as much as she had feared. He did not think she would because she now had the Prince to advise her. "The Prince understands everything so well," he said, "he has such a clear, able head. . . . When you married him," Melbourne added with a twinkle, "you said that he was perfection, which I thought a little overrated, but I really think now that it is in some degree realized."

For himself he admitted he was going to feel the separation deeply—"It is painful for me," he confessed to her on their last evening together, standing on the terrace in the starlight. "For four years I have seen you daily and liked it better every day." He noticed too, he told her, that he was beginning to wake earlier which, with him, was always a sign of depression and anxiety. All the same she must not worry about him, he slept well until he woke: indeed he was well altogether. The Queen tried to persuade him to accept the Garter as a token of the honour and love in which she held him. Melbourne refused it. This was not from any quixotic disinterestedness, he hastened to say; if he had been poor and she had offered him a pension, he would have taken it gratefully. But he had always refused honours, and—he hoped this showed no false pride—he would like to keep intact his reputation for refusing them. However, he was delighted to accept a present of some etchings which the Queen sent to him. "They will certainly," he wrote, "recall to recollection a melancholy day but Lord Melbourne hopes and trusts that with the divine blessing it still will hereafter be looked upon with less grief and bitterness of feeling than it must be regarded at present." In these words, while he professes to look forward to happier times, Melbourne does allow his grief to reveal itself a little more explicitly. And in a note on practical matters, written soon after his resignation, he took occasion to declare, though in plain and formal terms, his full sense of what his relation to her meant to him. "Lord Melbourne will ever consider the time during which Your Majesty is good enough to think that he has been of service to Her Majesty the proudest as well as the happiest part of his life."

Thus, quietly, gracefully, composedly, Melbourne took leave of Queen Victoria.

## CHAPTER VII

## LAST YEARS

(1)

C OMPOSEDLY, TOO, he settled down to the new phase of his life. Poor Lord Melbourne was going to feel the change dreadfully, said the gossips of the town to one another with gloomy relish. What was he going to do with himself? Melbourne seemed determined to show that he could do very well. On the 3rd September, the members of the Carlton Club looked out of the window to see him strolling idly and smiling down to the House of Lords for the first time since his resignation. As he passed them, he moderated his walk to a saunter as though purposely to exhibit his carefree demeanour to his Tory supplanters. He entered the House, too, with an air of easy composure which astonished his fellow peers. In private life he appeared equally cheerful. Indeed some people were shocked at his frivolity. "Lord Melbourne did not appear to advantage," complained the serious-minded Lady John Russell meeting him at Woburn a week or two after his resignation. "He showed little wish for conversation with anybody but seemed trying to banish the thought of his reverse by talking nonsense with some of the ladies."

So far as outward circumstances were concerned indeed, there were considerable compensations in his new form of life. No more State papers, no more Cabinet quarrels, no more speeches in Parliament, except when he felt inclined! Plenty of time for dining out, for lounging at Brooks's, for staying with his friends in their spacious country houses, for musing over French novels and patristic folios in the library at Brocket! Philosophically, Melbourne set to work to take advantage of these new-found opportunities for the life of pleasure. He dressed later than ever— people now found him shaving at half-past five in the evening— he pulled down his theological books from the shelves with the idea of writing a commentary on St. Chrysostom; he paid a special visit to the country in the spring, that he might savour at leisure for the first time for many years, the fresh beauty of bluebells and apple-blossom. He also went out a great deal in society. We hear of him staying with Lord Leicester and the Duke of Bedford and the Palmerstons, and dining often at Holland House and with Mrs. Norton.

For she had begun to come into his life again. She had never completely left it. He felt sufficiently responsible for her woes to keep in touch with her in order to see how she was getting on. It was a very discreet touch though: for the Queen was now on the throne, and not for Caroline Norton or anyone else was Melbourne going to risk compromising his good name in such a way as to harm the Queen. This consideration dominated his relations with Caroline. She wanted to be presented at Court by way of proving her respectability to the world. In principle Melbourne could not object to this, for she had been declared innocent in a court of law. But for him principle had never counted in the balance against hard facts; and he realized perfectly well that Mrs. Norton's reputation was too tarnished for strict persons to think her a proper person to be presented to a Queen who was also an unmarried girl. Melbourne therefore told her that she could not be presented till the Queen had a husband. She submitted, but she did not like it, and she said so. In a series of letters to Melbourne's young nephew, William Cowper, with whom she had made friends, she fulminated in a powerful vein of sarcasm against the injustice of the world and the hypocrisy of the great, in particular, of the Queen, whom she mistakenly considered responsible for her exclusion.

"Your uncle has walked over from Storey's Gate to Buckingham Palace and pursues the same course with her as with me. . . . No one talked of my inexperience and yet I did not forbid *my* mother to disturb our interviews, nor believe in *my* mother's misconduct. . . . I have waited because I have accustomed my mind and soul to walk about the world in chains, thinking what your uncle calls his good pleasure might be. If he thinks I can be brought to bear tamely what the Royal Girl considers a fit punishment for me for being her predecessor in the long conversations which take place at her palace, I can't help it."

The tone of these letters is not attractive. Alas, Caroline Norton was not the sort of woman who is ennobled by suffering; her character had deteriorated under the strain of her troubles. It may be said in her excuse that they were very real troubles. Through no fault of her own she was poor, cold-shouldered by good society and—what added an element of genuine tragedy to her situation—cut off from her children. Too spirited to let herself be crushed, she did her best to keep her flag flying; continued to cut a dash in pearls and black lace, to edit albums and write novels, to give lively dinner parties, to cultivate new friendships with interesting men. But misfortune brought out, in its most unpleasing form, that exhibitionist egotism which was the bane of her nature. For the rest of her life her own wrongs were an obsession with her; and she set up as a sort of professional injured person, theatrically lamenting the unexampled cruelty with which she had been treated, to every individual she met; and, if she got the opportunity, to the general public as well. She and George Norton wrangled endlessly about money. Provoked by some unusually offensive act on his part she would rush into print or the police court; and for a day or two the newspapers would resound with yet another recapitulation of the dreary sordid history of her marriage. It did her nothing but harm. People might have forgotten the scandal if only Caroline could have kept quiet about it. But keeping quiet was one of the things that Caroline simply could not do. Even Melbourne could not always control her. In 1840 she suddenly embarked on another vain attempt to get custody of her children, and sent a friend to Melbourne to ask him to help her. As usual he was shaving. "So you are going to revive that business," he said, "it's confoundedly disagreeable." "You know, my lord," pleaded the friend, "Mrs. Norton can't live without her children." "Well, well," sighed Melbourne, "it must be done effectively. You must have an affidavit from me. That story was all a damned lie, as you know. Put it into form and I'll swear it."

He had too much heart not to try to help her over her children. Indeed, if it involved no risk of harming the Queen, he was always ready to do what he could for Caroline; gave her money, paid her an occasional quiet visit of friendship, and, once the Queen was safely married, saw to it that she was presented at Court. His kindness had its effect on her. Misfortune, though it had made her tiresome and self-pitying, had not eradicated from her personality its streak of warm, crude, Irish good nature. She still found it natural to respond and to make things up. She did not revere Melbourne as she once had. He was weak and indolent, she told him with affectionate candour, and could be trusted to get out of doing anything unpleasant to himself, if it was possible. But she was fond of him, she knew he meant well, she would try not to worry him more than she thought right. And, in fact, as she was at pains to point out both to him and to others, she did more than once refrain from publicly proclaiming her unspeakable wrongs, in deference to his wishes.

Anyway, now he was out of office and the figure of the Queen no longer stood between them, there was every reason for her to let bygones be bygones. Melbourne was an ailing, ageing man. Remembering what he had been in the past, she felt a gush of affection and sympathy for him which showed itself in an energetic wish to help him. Besides, he was still a social lion who would be a distinguished ornament to her salon. Accordingly she asked him frequently to her house, wrote him letters full of rhapsody and vivacious scoldings and pleasantly daring jokes, took him to the play and once more began introducing him to coming young men. "What! Do these young fellows want to know me?" he remarked. "Bring them by all means." As always, they were charmed by his attention and entertained by his talk. Melbourne could not help feeling gratified.

All the same, to a penetrating eye it was apparent that his new form of life was not the success it might seem to a stranger. One day, soon after his resignation, Sir John Campbell, his late Attorney General, went to call on Melbourne in order to congratulate him on his release from the cares of office. "I hope you are happy," he said. "Oh, very happy!" replied Melbourne, and smiled. His smile, Campbell noticed, was not that of a happy man. It grew no happier in the succeeding months. There were several reasons for this. For one thing, Melbourne found he minded being out of office. This was natural. Pretty well every man minds losing a position of power and eminence, if he has held it for any length of time. We are happy in proportion as we believe

N

ourselves and our life to be of value; and few people are so disinterested or so conceited as to trust wholly to their own judgment
in this matter. A Prime Minister moves through life surrounded
by people who treat him as the most important man alive. Even
if he does not believe them, he feels better pleased with himself for
their admiration. When he loses power, this suddenly stops. Inevitably he feels flat, chilled, diminished. Melbourne, for all his
theoretical detachment, was far too human to be immune from
this common weakness of humanity. His sense of the value of his
existence dwindled in his own eyes because he perceived it dwind-
ling in the eyes of others; all the more since he could no longer
forget himself under the continuous pressure of hard and necessary work. Nor, so he discovered, could he force himself to take
up new work. Like an ageing horse he was only able to trot when
he was harnessed to the vehicle to which he was accustomed. The
projected commentary on St. Chrysostom remained unwritten.
He was too old and too tired for it. He was even too tired to read
in the way he used to do. Ironically enough, reading had been
easy for him when he had other things to do. During the last six
years he had astonished people by the way he had managed to keep
up with all the new books that came out, French and American as
well as English. Now he picked up a new book and turned its
leaves over and let it drop from his hand. Indeed, his zestful re-
sponsiveness to experience was leaving him, with the vitality of
which it was the expression. How could he respond to the beauty
of the spring? It only emphasized by contrast the November sadness which brooded over his own spirit. Social life was hardly
more heartening. He did enjoy it but nothing like so much as he
had. His gaiety had grown a little forced and febrile. That was
why some people now complained that he would never talk
seriously. He did not dare let himself be serious, he felt his depression would show too much if he did. Moreover, for him the
world of London society was a less entertaining place than it once
had been. Lord Holland had died at the end of 1840; and, bereft
of his genial presence, evenings at Holland House had lost more
than half their amenity. He had been Melbourne's oldest and
most congenial political friend, Melbourne felt his death as he had
never felt that of any other man. As for Mrs. Norton—well, she

was a good sort in her way, and he would always be fond of her. But her behaviour during the last years had rubbed off the bloom of her charm for him; he had learnt all too well what a nuisance she could be. She badgered him for money, her passion for self-advertisement embarrassed him, and she was intolerably indiscreet. "She's a passionate, giddy, dangerous, imprudent woman," he confided to Stockmar.

But even if she had been as fascinating as Cleopatra, Melbourne would have extracted little pleasure from her society. Irrevocably his heart was given to another woman; and she was the only one in England he could not see. Here lay the most powerful cause of his low spirits. Old age, fatigue, loss of friends, loss of power—he could have borne them all if life had still been irradiated by the light of the Queen's presence. Now this was withdrawn. The withdrawal had been a gradual process. His official parting with her had not turned out to be his final parting. The Queen would not allow it to be. Late in October she invited him to the Palace. He was so beside himself with joy at seeing her again that he wrote afterwards nervously apologizing, lest his exuberant spirits had betrayed him into talking too much and too heedlessly "which he is conscious they sometimes do." Meanwhile, defying previous warnings, the Queen had gone on writing him letters asking his advice, and Melbourne, forgetful of his former resolutions, had gone on giving it. He was too tired to resist her, and perhaps by now he felt her absence so much that he could not bring himself even to try to. As a matter of fact his advice was extremely circumspect. Now and again he gave his opinion as to the fitness of a candidate for some non-party post; but he avoided all controversial topics of policy and confined himself mainly to making good blood between her and her new Ministers. All the same people began to talk, and their talk got to the ears of Baron Stockmar who had hovered on in England as a sort of unofficial confidential adviser to the Prince. He rightly thought that for the Crown to be known as constantly communicating with the Leader of the Opposition was bound to do it great harm. Immediately he took steps to stop it. They were tactless, Teutonic steps. He wrote a long, solemn, scolding memorandum on the subject which he desired Anson to give Melbourne to read. Melbourne's reaction revealed how little his calm exterior corresponded with the grief and agitation which in reality filled his heart, and what a strain it must have been to him to maintain it all through these last months. With changing countenance and compressed lips he read the memorandum twice through. Then, "This is a most decided opinion indeed, quite an apple-pie opinion!" he said acidly. Anson went on to observe that Stockmar thought it a great pity, if Melbourne had meant to go on writing to the Queen, that he should, a day or two before, have publicly attacked the policy of the Government in the House of Lords. This was the last straw. To be lectured like a schoolboy by an officious foreigner, when two months ago he had been Prime Minister of England, was more than Melbourne could stand. For the first time his self-control deserted him. Leaping up from the sofa he began pacing wildly up and down the room, "God Eternal, damn it!" he exclaimed, "flesh and blood cannot stand this. I only spoke upon the defensive . . . I can't be expected to give up my position in the country, neither do I think it is to the Queen's interests that I should." Anson persisted. Did Melbourne honestly think that such correspondence was wise, he asked. With a supreme effort Melbourne pulled himself together. After a long pause, "I certainly cannot think it right," he muttered.

He did not find it so easy to give it up though. The Queen went on writing and he went on answering. A fortnight later, Stockmar returned to the attack. This time, more wisely, he went himself to see Melbourne and pointed out that by persisting in the correspondence, against what he must know to be his own sense of what was wise, he was encouraging the Queen in a course of action that must in the end get her into serious trouble. At his words Melbourne looked distressed, and agitated and guilty. What ought he to do, he asked. Stockmar replied that he should wait till after the Queen's confinement and then write and tell her that for the future he thought it best that all communications on politics between them should cease. Melbourne appeared convinced by his words: and in fact he soon afterwards did tell the Queen that he did not think for the time being he ought to dine at Buckingham Palace. Stockmar sat back in victorious calm. What was his horror two months later to learn that Mrs. Norton of all people was going

round London saying she had it on the best authority that the
Queen and Melbourne wrote to each other daily and that she consulted him about everything. Stockmar poured out his feelings in
another voluminous epistle to Melbourne in which he ended by
adjuring him in pained grave terms to be true to his better self,
and make the break. Melbourne was still too much upset to bring
himself to discuss the matter with Stockmar. He briefly acknowledged the letter without commenting on its contents. But it had
done its work. Henceforward his letters contained less and less
about politics. Nor did he ever lift a finger to keep his influence
over the Queen.

One wishes, for his sake, that he should have been able to carry
through the break to the end with the graceful calm with which he
had started on it. But the fact that he faltered makes us admire
him more; for it reveals what his self-sacrifice cost him. Nor had
he faltered for more than an instant: he had recovered himself
quickly and completely. So completely that he did not even let
himself feel annoyed with the man who had been responsible for
his momentary breakdown. He knew Stockmar was in the right.
Melbourne was too magnanimous to bear a grudge against an
opponent who had proved to be in the right. "He is an excellent
and most valuable man," he told the Queen, "one of the coolest
and soundest judgments I ever met."

Magnanimity did not save him from paying the full price for his
self-sacrifice. By refusing to advise her politically any longer,
Melbourne had broken the last link that kept the Queen in any
way dependent on him, stopped up the only remaining channel
through which flowed a stream that might keep their relationship
a living one. Henceforward their ways lay irretrievably apart.
Melbourne minded acutely: all the more because she was so painfully, so tantalizingly, close. It would have been more bearable if
she had died or left the country. But she was living within a few
streets of him, living the same life exactly as when he was with her.
He could visualize her every moment: now she must be riding,
now writing her letters, now going into dinner, now consulting
with her new Prime Minister.

Once or twice he actually caught a glimpse of her; but in circumstances so different from those of the past that it was almost

more unbearable than not seeing her at all. Once in May, 1842, he found himself at a ball where she was present. He missed, through some muddle, his chance of being presented to her. Pathetically afraid lest she should think he had been deliberately uncivil, he wrote off an agitated letter to her.

"Lord Melbourne is very sorry indeed and entreats Your Majesty's pardon for his great omission on Monday evening. He was never told that he was to pass before Your Majesty at the beginning; at the same time he admits that it was a piece of blundering stupidity not to find this out for himself. After this he never saw the glimmer of a chance of being able to get near Your Majesty."

On another evening in April, 1842, he drove by the Palace. Through the window of the Queen's sitting-room, open to the warm spring air, he caught sight of the familiar pictures and furniture, gleaming in the light of the newly-lit candles. Suddenly the great doors of the Palace were flung open and a small, stately, well-known figure was ushered out to step into a carriage waiting in the courtyard; the Queen was setting out for the opera. But Melbourne was not going with her. In the gathering dusk he drove on alone.

He missed her every hour of the day, missed her more even than he feared he was going to do, and more with every month that passed. The handsome, genial old gentleman, who swore and chuckled and sparklingly conversed at club and dinner table, bore within his breast a starved and aching heart. Gradually the disturbance of his mind began to make its impression on his enfeebled body. His infirmities rapidly grew worse throughout the year. In November he had a stroke. For a day or two people wondered if he was going to die.

(2)

Better if he had! For though Melbourne recovered sufficiently to linger on for six more years, yet the mainspring of his vitality was finally broken and the rest of his life is no more than a sad chronicle of decaying faculties and declining spirits. A brief chronicle too; the records of it are scanty. Already, before he died, the mists of oblivion gathered to hide his departing figure from our view. The outward form of his life did not change much, at least for two years. He divided his time between Brocket and London, with occasional visits to his friends' country homes and once or twice to the Queen at Windsor. When in London he dined out and attended the House of Lords; in the country he read and meditated. Sometimes he was alone; more often a relation was with him. It is lucky for the ageing to belong to a united family. The Lambs throughout their lively and varied careers had always contrived to remain intimate and devoted to each other as in the long ago days of Melbourne House. Now the only surviving members of the family rallied to look after their loved and distinguished elder brother. Fred Lamb, now Lord Beauvale, had returned to England from his long diplomatic sojourn abroad in 1842, handsome and debonair at sixty as at twenty-five, and newly married to an Austrian young lady nearly forty years younger than himself, sweet-natured and absorbedly in love with him. The Beauvales threw themselves into doing what they could for William. After his stroke they made their home at Brocket for much of the year. Fred took on the job of looking into his brother's financial affairs. It was high time that someone did. Melbourne, when he succeeded to his title, had been a very rich man. In 1835 he still had a gross income of twenty-one thousand a year. But he was generous, lavish and careless. He allowed his servants to cheat him—there were sixteen of them at South Street, all thievish and drunk, he said—and out of boredom he neglected to go into his estate accounts for years together. The result was that by 1842 his income had dwindled by more than a third, and what was left was so mismanaged that it looked as though it might diminish to a point where a man, who was living by the lavish standards demanded from the aristocracy of the day, would find himself actually embarrassed for money. Fred set to work to stop the rot and put things in order. Meanwhile, Melbourne's house as well as his estate needed attention. Since he did not keep his servants up to the mark, they did not run it well; and in the course of years Brocket had acquired that neglected, impersonal, unlived-in look so often seen in single men's residences. Here it was Lady Beauvale

who came to his assistance; taking over the domestic arrangements of the establishment and acting as hostess for Melbourne
when he had visitors. She also watched over his health. "I would
rather have a man about me when I am ill," he had asserted in the
days of his strength and of Caroline, "I think it requires strong
health to put up with a woman!" He did not think so now. To
Lady Beauvale's gentle ministrations he responded with a tender,
grateful affection. His sister Emily, too, helped to look after him.
She lived part of the year in her old home at Panshanger, only a
few miles from Brocket, and was always coming over to see him.
So did her youngest son, William Cowper, Mrs. Norton's friend,
an amiable youth who combined a fervent Victorian piety with a
propensity to fall frequently and romantically in love. He made
his uncle his confidant in these delicate matters. Melbourne,
touched and entertained by young William's enthusiastic *naïveté*,
gave him sympathetic and characteristic advice from the rich
stores of his own experience.

"My dear William," he writes on one occasion, "I think
you are quite right not to engage further in these affairs without the certainty of an adequate provision; and I am glad
that you find a consolation in St. Paul's epistle to the Corin-
thians. But you must not run about flirting with girls and persuading them that you intend to marry, unless you have the
intention. St. Paul would not approve of this. Indeed,
would he like to think his epistles made the instruments of
flirtation?"

And again, when William had at last actually got engaged.

"Remember that happiness is in a calm, settled and satisfied
state, and is totally inconsistent with a frequent change of objects . . . remember also what I said of happiness, that it lies in
the knowledge of causes of things and in rejection by yourself
of all vain and superstitious terrors."

In these words we hear the accents of the wise, amused Melbourne who had won the heart of the young Queen. Indeed, his
decline was gradual. Now and again the mists part to disclose a

glimpse of the old Melbourne; with Mrs. Norton at a performance of a play of Ben Jonson, for instance—"That it should be dull I had expected," he was heard exclaiming during the interval, "but that it should be so damned dull I had not conceived!" or talking to a Maid of Honour when dining with the Queen, "This dish is damned bad. On ordinary occasions I should try to leave out the adjuration; but on this occasion it is not worth while—it is *so* damned bad!"

These flashes, however, were few and far between. Old acquaintances who met him after 1842 were for the most part shocked at the change in him. White-headed, dim-eyed, with stiff gait and dragging leg, he showed no trace of that exuberant social vitality which had once been his distinguishing characteristic. Greville watched him at a house party at Broadlands sitting hour by hour grave, stern and silent, with an expression "as of a perpetual consciousness of his glory obscured" written on his face, then breaking for a moment into a feeble echo of his old style of conversation, then relapsing once more into silence: in the middle of a dinner at Lord Cottesmore's through which he had sat neither speaking nor, apparently, taking in what was said to him, he suddenly arose and hobbled out of the room. The effort needed for conversation was more than he could manage.

Politically the same process of decline showed itself. Up to the time of his stroke it was not noticeably apparent. Melbourne, though he cannot be said to have exerted himself once he had resigned, continued to play an influential part in the counsels of the Whig Party. He was against the Whigs going in for aggressive opposition, partly out of his own innate conservatism, and still more because he did not want to rouse the Queen's anti-Tory feeling against her new Government. Both at informal meetings of the party leaders and in letters to John Russell he preached the wisdom of doing nothing in particular, with his old incisive vigour. "As we haven't a majority," he said, "we may be allowed to think a little what is best for the country and the world." On the rare occasions, too, that he summoned up the energy to speak in the House of Lords, he could still be at his old independent-minded best. One speech in particular, during a Corn Law debate in February, 1842, was memorable. "Though I am ready to consider any measure for the alleviation of distress," he said, "I can never hold that the cause can be prevented by changes in the constitution or by changing the persons who administer public affairs. I am opposed to this, for if the existence of national distress is looked on as a reason for organic change in the constitution or in the individuals who compose the Government, there is an end of all stability in public affairs. In every state of the country, I fear it will not be difficult to make out such a case of poverty and suffering as may support an argument for great and immediate alterations. We have lived lately in a time of great change and many strong measures. It is supposed that these measures have produced disappointment, that Catholic emancipation has not ended in the tranquillity that was expected from it, that the Reform Bill has not improved the condition of people at large; and that those who recommended these measures do not enjoy with the country the same popularity that they formerly did. How this may be I know not. But I do know that, if there is disappointment, it does not arise from the vicious principle or the ill-working of those measures themselves, but from the wild, unfounded, exaggerated expectations of their effects which were indulged in and anticipated. A man does not know himself, nor is he a safe judge of his own conduct. But I believe myself never to have contributed to the raising of these wild and illusory hopes." In these words Melbourne states more fully and forcibly than anywhere else the reasons determining his ambiguous attitude to that great general reforming movement which had been the dominating feature of political history throughout his active career as a statesman. They may stand, indeed, for his political apologia.

For his political swan-song too. He made no important speech during the following months; and after his stroke he could not. He rose from his bed changed politically as much as socially. He still wrote to his colleagues about affairs and occasionally attended their meetings. But the letters, traced painfully out by his semi-paralysed hand, were illegible and rambling. And he sat through the meetings, for the most part, slumped in his chair in a dazed apathy, unable it seemed to take in what was going on round him.

Growingly he lost grip, lived in the past, seemed incapable of grasping what was happening in the world.

The change in him could not fail to make its impression on his colleagues. They were too fond of him not to listen deferentially and courteously whenever he spoke; but naturally they paid less and less attention to his opinions. The world in general noticed this; and followed their lead. Gone were the days of Melbourne's dressing-room levées with queues of people following one another up the stairs to ask him favours and regale him with gossip while he shaved. Whole afternoons passed now without a knock resounding on the front door of South Street. Melbourne minded. Well acquainted with Vanity Fair though he was, he was too incurably sensitive not to be hurt when he was brought thus face to face with the selfish fickleness of its natives. Besides, he needed company to keep up his flagging spirits. An old friend found him one afternoon alone and gloomy in his library. "I am glad," he exclaimed, "you have come. I have sat here watching that time-piece and heard it strike four times without seeing the face of a human being; and, had it struck the fifth, I feel I could not have borne it!" More unreasonably, he felt wounded and surprised that his colleagues consulted him less than they had. For it was one of the most distressing symptoms of his decline that he failed to realize it. At the time of his resignation he was well aware that he was not likely to be up to taking office again. Not so after his stroke. Early in 1844 it looked as if the Tories might be about to fall. One evening Melbourne was dining at the Palmerstons': "I was kept up half the night," he announced to the embarrassment of the company, "thinking, suppose that I was sent for to Windsor, what advice should I give the Queen: and it kept me long awake!"

As a matter of fact, by this time there was no question of his being fit for active work of any kind. Living in London at all was getting too much for him: during the next two years he spent more and more time down at Brocket. There, day after day, he would sit, an unopened book on his knee, gazing out of the window or at the fire, sunk in an apathetic melancholy. No wonder! In the quiet of the country he was forced inescapably to contemplate his true situation, to face the fact that he was now old and

infirm and on the shelf, with nothing to look forward to except
death. He would be heard mournfully murmuring over to himself some lines from *Samson Agonistes*:

> "So much I feel my genial spirits droop,
> My hopes all flat. Nature within me seems
> In all her functions weary of herself.
> My race of glory run, and race of shame,
> And I shall shortly be with them that rest."

His friends and relations did what they could to cheer him up.
Lord and Lady Beauvale hovered round; Lady Palmerston drove
over from Panshanger; Mrs. Norton wrote regularly; now and
again a visitor from the outside world—an old friend like Lady
Holland or one of Mrs. Norton's clever young men—came down
to spend a night. Melbourne could still respond to these efforts to
entertain him. He sat up till well after his ordinary bedtime talking and listening to the visitors; and he dismayed innocent, Victorian Lady Beauvale by the way he chuckled over the spicier passages in Mrs. Norton's letters. But these wafts of a brighter mood
evaporated with the occasion that stirred them; all too soon he was
plunged back into melancholy once more.

For in him the sadness ordinarily attendant on old age was reinforced by peculiar reasons for suffering. Amid much that was
dimming and fading one memory remained painfully fresh; the
memory of the Queen. People noticed that his eyes filled with
tears every time her name was mentioned: if he was unwell, it
could even produce a sort of hysterical outburst. He missed her
more than ever, when there was so little to distract his mind from
his sense of her loss. For he had lost her finally and completely
now. After 1841 the relationship was a dead one. Melbourne
made pathetic efforts to keep it going. He was always writing to
her; gentle, gossipy letters, lit up from time to time by a faint glint
of his old characteristic self. Let her not buy objects merely for
their historical interest, he urges—"What is the value of Cardinal
Wolsey's cap? A Cardinal's cap is no great wonder!"—or he
counsels her about the education of the child Prince—"Be not
over-solicitous about education . . . it may mould and direct the
character but it rarely alters it." Alas, his letters did not evoke the

response he yearned for. He would wait for the arrival of the post trembling with hope. More often than not it brought him nothing. The Queen did not write as frequently as he did. In his weakened state he could not restrain himself from gently upbraiding her for her neglect; he had begun to think Her Majesty's silence rather long, he told her wistfully. The Queen apologized. But she wrote no more often than before. Melbourne had to accustom himself to hearing from her only occasionally; and though these occasions were now easily the happiest moments of his life, yet the letters themselves were not what they once had been. No longer did she write to pour out her feelings, but filled up the page as best she might with mild family news and conventional words of sympathy and encouragement. "The change from progress to decadence is a very hard and disagreeable trial," he replies to her apologetically, "Lord Melbourne has been reading Cicero on old age, a very pretty treatise, but he does not find much consolation in it. It is certainly, as Your Majesty says, wrong to repine at everything, still it is difficult not to do so." Once or twice his longing for her betrays itself in a brief, understated, poignant phrase. "Lord Melbourne cannot say otherwise but that he continually misses and regrets the time when he had daily confidential communication with Your Majesty."

Their rare meetings did nothing to soothe him; short, stiff interchanges in company, utterly unlike the leisurely intercourse of the past. There is a distressing account of a visit to Chatsworth in the winter of 1843. Melbourne had arrived as excited as a child at the prospect of seeing the Queen again. And then she never saw him alone or talked to him for more than a few minutes; even at dinner she soon turned to the other side. Oblivious of the people round him, the old man sat, his face working with the unconcealed anguish of his disappointment. The Queen's conduct on this occasion seems to have been due to gaucherie, not lack of heart. She was flustered to see how he had changed and frightened of tiring him. Indeed, considering the limitations of her character and situation, she treated Melbourne after his fall as well as anyone could reasonably expect. She never forgot that she owed him a great deal, and sought conscientiously to discharge her debt: wrote to him when she had time, sent him presents, invited him for an occasional visit; and when she heard he was embarrassed for money, she lent him a considerable sum to tide him over his difficulties. All the same, it must be admitted that she was not the sort of woman who knew best how to soften the hard pang of parting. Her egotism and her honesty alike forbade it. She could not put herself in his place nor enter imaginatively into his feelings; and it had never been possible for her to pretend to a sentiment she did not feel. For Melbourne she now felt very little. Though the Queen could love intensely, she was only capable of loving one person at a time. The Prince had now completely replaced Melbourne in her affections; so much so that she somehow felt she had been disloyal in ever having been so fond of Melbourne at all.

"Reading this again," she notes in 1842, after looking back at some entry of two years before in her diary, "I cannot forbear remarking what an artificial sort of happiness *mine* was *then*, and what a blessing it is I have now in my beloved Husband *real* and solid happiness, which no Politics, no worldly reverses *can* change; it could not have lasted long, as it was then, for after all, kind and excellent as Lord M. is, and kind as he was to (me), it was but in Society that I had amusement, and I was only living on that superficial resource, which I *then fancied* was happiness! Thank God! for *me* and others, this is changed, and I *know what* REAL happiness is."

She never stopped to think what was real happiness to Melbourne. But, as a matter of fact, even if she had, it would have made little difference to him. Not the Queen, but the nature of human existence, was responsible for his sorrow. For what he minded was the fact of separation, and this was inevitable. An old man at the end of his life's journey, and a young girl just setting out on hers, what bond could hold them together?—especially when the girl happened to be Queen of England and newly married to a man of her own age whom she passionately loved. For a short time their ways had crossed. Now, with hopeless, regretful eyes, he watched her figure grow small and disappear over the horizon.

The trouble was that she had grown to be the only thing that made life worth living to him. Here we come to the crucial, cen-

tral, incurable cause of his melancholy, a cause that finds its origin
far back in the dim beginnings of his history. For all that it had
been so packed and brilliant, Melbourne's had been an unfulfilled
life. He was born with a strong, subtle intelligence, always restlessly searching to discover some ultimate truth and significance
in human existence. But his search had been frustrated by the
congenital, fundamental division in his nature. Never had he been
able to reconcile the sceptical realism of his judgment with those
ideal aspirations, which alone commanded the enthusiasm of his
heart. Indeed he had long ago given up trying to do so; and, resigning himself to accept the fact that he would never be sure of
the ultimate value of anything, he had surrendered himself in a
spirit of cheerful ironical detachment, to such immediate satisfactions as life offered to him; to the pleasures of society and the
interest and excitement of great affairs. So long as he was vigorous
and zestful, this policy had worked well enough. Now it did not
do so any more. He had neither the spirit to enjoy society nor the
strength to take part in public affairs. This would not have mattered so much if he had not been solitary, for, along with his intellect, nature had endowed him with an intensely affectionate
heart that might have enabled him to forget his own troubles in
the interests and happiness of others whom he loved. But, once
youth is past, such a heart can only find complete and continuing
fulfilment in family life, in the close stable relationship that a man
has with wife and children. Here Melbourne had been cruelly
treated by fate. Born to be a husband and father, he found himself, through no fault of his own, when near on seventy, a childless
widower; well liked by many, but needed by none.

In face of this situation, all his age-old, carefully constructed
defences crumbled. What good was a hedonistic philosophy,
however intelligently conceived, when the power to enjoy was
failing? What strength could he find in his detachment? Detachment can only strengthen the spirit if it is a positive detachment
founded on a sense of some timeless and absolute reality, immune
from the accident of mortal existence; whereas Melbourne's was
negative, sustained by nothing firmer than an instinctive response
to the call of the passing hour. Against the injurious onset of time,
age and death, the human soul is fortified by two things only, faith

and love. Melbourne had no one who depended on his love, nor had he ever been able to find ground on which to build a sure faith. During these last years he met the Archbishop of Canterbury who spoke to him of the help given by prayer. "Yes?" queried Melbourne, "but who is one to pray for and what is one to pray for?" After many changes of fortune the life-long battle between his sanguine temperament and his questioning destructive intellect had ended in his temperament's decisive defeat. At last he was forced to feel, as well as to think, that life was a vain and empty dream. A grey sense of the insubstantiality and fleetingness of things human possessed his spirit. "The fire is out," he muttered to himself as he sat gazing before him at vacancy. "The fire is out."

In a bitter-sweet mood of recollection, he mused on the time when it was still alight. His mind tended, as the eventless rural days succeeded one another, more and more to dwell in the past. It was natural that it should at Brocket. The chintz-curtained bedrooms, the gilded, elegant saloon, the leather-scented quiet of the library, the park with its grassy vistas and the swans sweeping down on thunderous wing to settle in the river reeds—all these were heavy with memories for him, memories stretching back as far as he could remember at all. Not a phase of his earlier life but was connected with Brocket. There on his holidays from school, he had romped and ridden with Pen and Fred and "that little devil Emily"; there he had argued and laughed with Lady Melbourne; there he had learnt to study and to meditate; within these walls had been enacted much of the long drawn-out ironical tragedy of his marriage, from its rapturous, troubled honeymoon, to the muted pathos of Caroline's last days. He spoke of her sometimes, and also of his mother. The most important figures in his life had always been women, these two pre-eminently. As he brooded on the past, it was their ghosts who stole forth most often to stand beside his chair. With them came another's, whom he had loved perhaps more tenderly than either. She was not dead, though as irrecoverably lost to him as if she were. At the thought of her, visions of youth and childhood vanished; Brocket faded as Windsor rose before his mental eye; and once more the tears gathered to prick his eyelids and trickle down his withered cheeks.

In 1846 an event took place which roused him from his reveries once again to make an active appearance on the contemporary political scene. Peel changed the declared opinions of a lifetime and came out against the Corn Laws. By so doing he split his Party. If the Whigs chose to ally themselves with the infuriated right wing of the Tories, they had a chance of turning the Government out. It would be an unscrupulous act on their part to do so, for up till then they had been in favour of modifying the Corn Laws themselves. Oppositions, however, like turning Governments out, and the Whig leaders were tempted. They held a meeting to discuss the subject. Melbourne struggled up to London to attend it. The arguments veered this way and that; suddenly, and for the first time that day, his voice, now slow and halting, made itself heard. "My Lords," he said, "it's a damn thing that Peel should have repealed the duty on foreign corn. But he has done it and the consequences are that you will all have to vote for it." He had gone to the heart of the matter. Whatever the immediate political advantage, there was no doubt that the Whigs would be disastrously discredited if they voted for the Ultra-Tories. After Melbourne had spoken, no one had the effrontery to suggest that they should do so. For the last time the flame of his energies had flickered up to exhibit a flash of his old penetrating shrewdness. It was not bright enough, however, to persuade his colleagues into thinking him once again fit for office. Alas, Melbourne still did not realize this. The Tory Government fell: and buoyed up by his passionate desire to return to the Queen, he hoped that he might be offered, if not the premiership, at least some less onerous office like that of Lord Privy Seal. Hopefully he waited. Then came a letter from the Queen tactfully explaining that she had not called upon his services because she thought his health would not stand the strain. Melbourne wrote back assuring her that of course and as always she was right. But for a short time at any rate he was acutely disappointed.

His friends noticed it. For it was another effect of his disintegration that he found it harder and harder to hide his feelings. The old characteristic urbanity of demeanour would be suddenly broken by outbursts of nervous agitation. In the same year he was dining one evening at Windsor: the conversation turned on Peel's *volte-face.* This had shocked Melbourne very much: to throw over party and loyal colleagues for the sake of a doctrine, and an economic doctrine at that, was the last sort of thing with which he could sympathize. "Ma'am, it's a damn dishonest act," he burst out. At once amused and embarrassed by his violence, the Queen laughed and tried to change the subject. But Melbourne was by now too upset to be diverted from his course even by the Queen herself. The company sat awkward and silent as, confusedly and frantically, he continued to rail against Peel and his anti-Corn Law activities.

Back at Brocket he at last resigned himself to accept the fact that his day was done. But resignation did not mean tranquillity of spirit. Melbourne never attained the famed serenity of old age. Few people do. Serenity implies an ability to rise above trouble, whereas age and weakness generally make people more susceptible to it. Certainly Melbourne was. He had been born with a high-strung, sensitive, vulnerable temperament, but he had early learnt to control it by the exercise of a cool, sensible judgment. Now his power of judgment was decaying along with his other faculties. He, once so conspicuous for his robust indifference to petty causes of annoyance, became an easy prey to fits of worry about ills, trifling or imaginary. Sometimes he fancied for no reason that a friend had turned against him; sometimes he was seized with a sudden fear that he was ruined; sometimes—and this was the strangest of all in him—he worried about his reputation. A newspaper would quote, slightly inaccurately, some public utterance of his. With trembling, laborious hand he wrote off asking that it might be immediately corrected. In 1848 it somehow came out that in 1832 Tom Young had written a letter from the Home Office to the leader of the Birmingham League encouraging them to raise an insurrection if Reform broke down. This revelation should not have distressed Melbourne much. Young had written the letter without his knowledge; and, anyway, who cared about 1832 now? But Melbourne was so upset, lest in some way he should be held responsible, that for a day or two he was actually ill.

It would be a mistake, however, to think of this final phase of Melbourne's earthly existence as all trouble and gloom. There was more of twilight than black darkness about it. If old age led him to worry easily, it also made him forget his worries soon; and much of the time he did not worry at all. His attacks of acute depression, too, seem to have grown rarer as his vital forces weakened. Strangers who came to Brocket found Lord Melbourne a genial, tranquil old gentleman. And a very agreeable one as well. He spent most of the day in his bedroom, but if a visitor came to stay, he would bestir himself to come down to dinner; and afterwards for an hour or two the company would be treated to a display—faint and fatigued, no doubt, in comparison with those that had dazzled society in his heyday, but still delightful—of his racy, whimsical, accomplished conversational art.

So two years slipped by. Then in November, 1848, he was suddenly taken dangerously ill. After two days racked by convulsive fits, he gradually became unconscious. Lady Palmerston, coming into his room on 24th November to see how he was, found him sleeping. In the pale light of the autumn day, his countenance, still beautiful in spite of the ravages that time and suffering had wrought upon it, wore an extraordinary look of contentment and resignation and peace. He lay for thirty-six hours more, with the life silently ebbing away within him. Then, at six o'clock on the following evening, he gave a long, soft sigh, and died. A few days later his body was borne through the leafless Hertfordshire lanes to be buried quietly near Caroline's in the neighbouring country churchyard of Hatfield.

The proper formalities were observed. Palmerston wrote announcing the sad news to the Queen; the Queen sent her condolences to Lady Palmerston; and a lengthy, if unenthusiastic, estimate of Melbourne's character and achievements appeared in *The Times*. But, in fact, his death made little stir. The world was changing fast in the nineteenth century. And, though he was only sixty-nine when he died, he had outlived his time.

# INDEX